LAWS OF EARLY ICELAND
Grágás I

University of Manitoba Icelandic Studies
General Editors: Haraldur Bessason
Robert J. Glendinning
Vol. III

Þingvöllr looking northeast from point A on Map II.
Photograph courtesy of Hjálmar R. Bárðarson

Laws of Early Iceland

GRÁGÁS

THE CODEX REGIUS OF GRÁGÁS

WITH MATERIAL FROM

OTHER MANUSCRIPTS

Translated by
Andrew Dennis
Peter Foote
Richard Perkins

I

UNIVERSITY OF MANITOBA PRESS

WINNIPEG CANADA

University of Manitoba Press
Winnipeg, Manitoba
Canada R3T 2M5
uofmpress.ca

© University of Manitoba Press 1980

Reprinted 2012

All rights reserved. No part of this publication may be reproduced or transmitted in any form or by any means, or stored in a database and retrieval system, without the prior written permission of the University of Manitoba Press, or, in the case of photocopying or any other reprographic copying, a licence from Access Copyright (Canadian Copyright Licensing Agency). For an Access Copyright licence, visit www.accesscopyright.ca, or call 1-800-893-5777.

Library and Archives Canada Cataloguing in Publication

Grágás.
Laws of early Iceland, Grágás
(University of Manitoba Icelandic studies;
v. 3 ISSN 0-88755-111-4)

Includes index.
ISBN 978-0-88755-695-1 (pbk.)

1. Laws—Iceland. I. Dennis, Andrew. II. Foote, Peter G., 1924–
2. III. Perkins, Richard. IV. Title. V. Series: University of
Manitoba Icelandic studies; v. 3

KLP 348'.4912'023 5   C79-091110-8   K348.491203 G73 1979

The University of Manitoba Press gratefully acknowledges the financial support for its publication program provided by the Government of Canada through the Canada Book Fund, the Canada Council for the Arts, the Manitoba Department of Culture, Heritage, Tourism, the Manitoba Arts Council, and the Manitoba Book Publishing Tax Credit.

Publication of this book has been made possible through the financial support of the Icelandic Language and Literature Fund, Icelandic Department at the University of Manitoba. Support was also provided by the Social Sciences and Humanities Research Council of Canada, the Páll Gudmundsson Memorial Fund, the Icelandic-Canadian Frón, E. Grettir Eggertson, and Dr. Thorvaldur Johnson.

Contents

Acknowledgments	iv
Foreword	vi
Introduction	1
The Codex Regius of *Grágás* in Translation I	21
Christian Laws Section	23
Assembly Procedures Section	53
Treatment of Homicide	139
The Wergild Ring List	175
The Lawspeaker's Section	187
The Law Council Section	189
Additions	195
Guide to Technical Vocabulary	239
Sources, Editions, Translations, Work in Progress	277
Abbreviated Titles	279
Plate: View of Þingvöllr	frontispiece
Maps	
I Iceland	280
II Þingvöllr	281

Foreword

Since making its appearance with translations of the *Book of Settlements* and Jón Jóhannesson's *A History of the Old Icelandic Commonwealth*, the series University of Manitoba Icelandic Studies has been followed with interest in many quarters. It is a pleasure to welcome, as a continuation befitting an impressive beginning, the present translation of the ancient laws of Iceland.

In the oldest account of the Icelanders as a separate nation, dating from about 1074, Adam of Bremen observes that this is a people governed not by a king but only by its laws. This much-quoted remark might be said to receive tangible corroboration in this great legal corpus of Commonwealth times traditionally entitled *Grágás*. Originally committed to writing in 1117-18 and preserved in two revised and enlarged versions dating from the late thirteenth century, this body of laws is significantly larger than comparable collections found elsewhere in the Nordic countries. *Grágás* is truly one of the great monuments of the Icelandic national heritage, at once testifying to the mature social outlook of the ancient self-governing community of farmers and providing an inexhaustible fund of information about great things and small in the day-to-day affairs of individuals and classes in the times that produced the great classical literature of medieval Iceland.

Grágás has never been considered easy reading; the ancient legal language is crabbed and abstruse. Perhaps that is the reason why it is a late arrival in the library of Icelandic works available to readers of English. The more credit must be given to the worthy scholars who have now accomplished this difficult task and to the University of Manitoba for making the result of their labors available to the public. Icelandic studies are now being pursued by an ever-increasing number of scholars at universities in every part of the globe. An English translation of so fundamental a work as *Grágás* therefore fills an urgent need. We Icelanders rejoice to see this noble document made available to such a wide reading public beyond our own shores.

We are happy to take this opportunity to express our gratitude to all those who have had a hand in the preparation and publication of this volume as well as our hope that University of Manitoba Icelandic Studies may enjoy the good reception the series so richly deserves.

Kristján Eldjárn

Introduction

Constitution and Law in the Icelandic Commonwealth

Iceland was settled, chiefly by people of Norwegian stock, in the decades around A.D. 900. The country had no indigenous population but it was not quite empty of humanity when the first Norsemen arrived. Celtic anchorites had come there in search of the isolation they so ardently desired. What happened to them, we do not know. If any stayed, they left no detectable mark on the development of the Icelandic community.

By the 920's the settlers must have been fully self-conscious as a community. We are told that at that time a Norwegian called Úlfljótr brought laws from Norway to Iceland.[1] They were modeled on the laws of the Norwegian west-coast law-province called Gulathing, variously modified and augmented. Then a general assembly was convened and we presume that Ulfljótr's proposals were approved more or less entire. Central to them was the establishment of the annual General Assembly with national legislative and judicial functions, meeting at the same place each summer, the famous Þingvöllr (see Maps I and II), under the presidency of an elected lawspeaker. Úlfljótr must have acted as the first Lawspeaker, but our earliest list begins with the man who took office in A.D. 930. We have a reliable record of the names and time in office of all the Icelandic Lawspeakers after Úlfljótr until the post disappeared with the introduction of law codes prepared under the supervision of a Norwegian king nearly 350 years later.

We have no direct knowledge of the laws of western Norway in the early tenth century, so we are little the wiser for the tale of Úlfljótr as the man who brought them in adapted form to Iceland. But if no story about Úlfljótr existed, we should have to invent a comparable legislator, for, as might be expected in the circumstances, the constitution on which the Icelandic legal system is based is much more the creation of theorists than an organic growth from immemorial custom. Once the settlers had decided among themselves that they would not have a single centralized power, no kingship as the ultimate arbiter, then acceptance of some such

---

1. Ari Þorgilsson. *Íslendingabók*, Ch. 2 (in Jakob Benediktsson, *Íslendingabók. Landnámabók*, Íslenzk Fornrit I, 1968, 6-7; this edition is referred to as *ÍF* I hereafter).

especially designed system doubtless provided the only alternative to anarchy and separatism.

It is possible to deduce a number of constitutional, procedural, and penal elements that must have existed in the earliest laws. The creation of the annual General Assembly at which a Law Council functioned with power vested in it to take decisions binding on the nation as a whole meant in effect the foundation of an Icelandic state. This Council, which made laws and could answer for Iceland in any exchange with foreign countries, was composed of the men recognized as chieftains, and the laws must have contained some definition of their rights and responsibilities, as well as the duties and prerogatives of the Lawspeaker, their president. The Law Council decided arguments about what was law, and a court could be established at the Assembly to decide rights and wrongs. The laws must also have listed a number of misdemeanors and stipulated how they should be prosecuted and penalized. We know very little about local assemblies until a complete regulation of them and of the number and distribution of chieftains was made about A.D. 960.[2] It was then decided that the country should be divided into Quarters. Each Quarter should have three springtime assemblies held in it, each at a named site, except the North which should have four assemblies (cf. Map I). Each assembly was attended by three chieftains, and there were thus twelve such leaders in the North and nine in each of the other Quarters, thirty-nine in all. The relations between the leaders and the men belonging to their assembly groups must also have been fully regulated at the same time. From then on there were four Quarter assemblies, which seem to have been little used, and four Quarter Courts at the General Assembly; these could act as courts of first instance or as courts of second instance in cases left unsettled at local spring assemblies. The discrepancy between the number of chieftains in the North and in other Quarters was made good in various ways in the legislative and judicial procedures of the General Assembly.

We have little reliable information about further laws made in Iceland in the tenth century. A most momentous piece of legislation was introduced in the summer of A.D. 999 (or traditionally 1000), when it was laid down that everyone in the country should be baptized and be Christian.[3] This must have affected existing laws in a number of ways. Pagan elements were doubtless most evident in the ceremonies that established a special sanctity at assemblies and in the oaths sworn as part of legal procedures. Some of these elements were perhaps simply

---

2. *Íslendingabók,* Ch. 5 (*ÍF* I 12).

3. *Íslendingabók,* Ch. 7 (*ÍF* I 14-18). Cf. Dag Strömbäck. *The Conversion of Iceland* (Viking Society for Northern Research, Text Series VI, 1975), pp. 27-30.

abolished, but others were reframed in Christian terms. Then, a few years after the acceptance of Christianity, the Law Council abolished dueling as a means of legal decision and established the so-called Fifth Court to complement the four Quarter Courts that could be constituted while the General Assembly was in being.[4] It acted as a court of first instance in certain matters but its most important function seems to have been as a court of further and final instance in case of deadlock in a Quarter Court, something which the system allowed but only with much procedural complexity (cf. "Divided judgment," p. 244). Decisions in the Fifth Court were by straightforward majority, but since it was composed of an even number of judges, provisions were made in case of a tie (cf. pp. 87-88).

In little more than seventy years a combination of social compromise, political ingenuity, and legal inventiveness had produced a constitutional and judicial system that was extraordinarily comprehensive. Icelandic society comprised chieftains; householders of standing with political rights and legal duties; householders of lesser means with the same rights but fewer duties; free members of households, men and women, who were legally independent but politically represented by their householders; minors and various incapable people who could not act at law on their own; and slaves, who were virtually the chattels of their owners. In theory every individual was attached to a household; every householder was attached to a chieftain. Through householder and chieftain everyone was attached to an assembly. The chieftain and the members of his assembly-third gave each other mutual support. They combined with the other two local chieftains and their followers at the spring assembly, and with their counterparts from all over the country at the General Assembly. Every spring assembly acted in the knowledge that within a few weeks there would be a meeting of the General Assembly, where the Fifth Court provided a judicial apex and the Law Council sat as the fount of legislation and the ultimate interpreter of law. Legislation was only possible with the agreement of the chieftains sitting in the Law Council, but it was hardly possible either without widespread approval from the free householders. They were the men who finally provided a chieftain with the means of enforcing his authority. The laws made no special provision for an executive arm. Acknowledgment of law, institution of proceedings, and exaction of penalties were in the last resort matters of individual responsibility and choice: but a man would expect the support of his chieftain, and a chieftain would expect the aid of his assembly men. Thus, for example, the chieftains were by law the superintendents of the confis-

---

4. *Íslendingabók*, Ch. 8 (*ÍF* I 19).

cation courts which were held after men had been outlawed, but the prosecution of those outlaws had normally been undertaken by individuals acting in an entirely private capacity. The chieftain then received a fixed fee for his work, while the confiscated property itself was shared between the prosecutor and the public purse of the local assembly or Quarter. Force might be used at an assembly to prevent a court passing judgment (cf. p. 81). That leaders would go to such risky lengths in preference to flouting a judgment once passed (which of course was not unknown either) suggests, among other things, that away from the assemblies chieftains did not always have assured means of protecting followers, and that respect for legal judgment and fear of legal reprisal for assisting sentenced men were factors to be reckoned with. Public sympathy would often be a decisive factor in gaining a successful outcome at law, but achievement of rehabilitation, recompense, and punishment was materially eased by working through legal procedures.

In the 1020's the Icelanders made a pact with the king of Norway which legally regulated their status and privileges when in that country, and at about the same time certain indulgences allowed the anti-Christian party at the time of the Conversion were abolished.[5] The next important legislation that we know is from the time of Gizurr Ísleifsson, bishop of the Icelanders from 1081 to 1106 and then of the diocese of Skálaholt until his death in 1118. He made his family property a permanent apanage of the episcopacy, he introduced a tithe law in 1096, and he established a second diocese, Hólar, for the Northern Quarter, to which Jón Ögmundarson was consecrated in 1106.[6] We are told that at the General Assembly of 1117, which Bishop Gizurr was not well enough to attend, a new law was made which prescribed "that our laws should be written in a book at Hafliði Másson's in the coming winter, according to what Bergþórr and he and other wise men who were selected for it said was law and after consultation between them. They were to introduce all such new laws as seemed to them better than the old laws. They were to announce them next summer in the Law Council and keep all those which the majority did not oppose. And the outcome was that the Treatment of Homicide and much else in the laws were written and read out by clergy in the Law Council the following summer. And everyone was well pleased with it and nobody spoke against it."[7] These words from Ari Þorgilsson's *Íslendingabók* were written some time between 1122 and 1133. We can infer from them that it was intended to make a complete

---

5. K (= *Konungsbók*, cf. p. 13), ‡ 248; *Íslendingabók*, Ch. 7 (*ÍF* I 17).
6. *Íslendingabók*, Ch. 10 (*ÍF* I 22-3).
7. *Íslendingabók*, Ch. 10 (*ÍF* I 23-4).

and unified codification of the Icelandic laws, but since Ari ends his short history with the death of Bishop Gizurr in 1118, we cannot expect him to tell us about any continuation of that first winter's work. In fact, as we shall see, there is good reason to suppose that the undertaking was never carried through completely and perhaps even stopped when that initial effort had been made. Bergþórr Hrafnsson was Lawspeaker between 1117 and 1122. He is not referred to in our texts of the laws, but his two immediate predecessors and his successor are (Markús Skeggjason 1084-1107, Úlfheðinn Gunnarsson 1108-16, Guðmundr Þorgeirsson 1123-34).[8] This last Lawspeaker, Guðmundr, is mentioned as the originator of an article in the Treatment of Homicide (p. 169), which must be regarded as an addition to the text established in 1117-18 — it shows that the codification was hardly looked on as any kind of complete and immutable authority and, indeed, it is probably safe to assume that legislative interest and energy continued unabated in this and the next generation of twelfth-century Icelanders. The Christian Laws Section was compiled and approved in the same Lawspeaker's time, within the outside dates of 1122 and 1133 (cf. p. 50 and n. 95).

A good number of clauses in our texts are marked in manuscripts as "new law."[9] This must mean that their first recording took place very soon after their enactment (cf. pp. 12, 51). Any that occur in the Treatment of Homicide may reasonably be thought to be subsequent to the revision of 1117, but very few "new laws" can be specifically dated and for the most part they do not appear to contain regulations of notable importance. From legal texts or external sources we learn the dates of a few laws from the end of the twelfth and the first half of the thirteenth centuries. They concern a standard ell measure (some time between 1195 and 1200), fast days and feasts (including those of the native saints, Bishop Þorlákr Þórhallsson of Skálaholt, instituted in 1199, and Bishop Jón Ögmundarson of Hólar, instituted in 1200), marriage in hitherto forbidden degrees and care of dependents (1217 or soon after), and a probably not wholly real acknowledgment of the supremacy of canon law over secular law (1253). Radical constitutional changes came after 1262-64, when the Icelanders agreed to accept the king of Norway as their overlord and to pay him taxes in return for certain guaranteed services. With the exception of the Christian Laws Section the laws were then soon replaced by new codes that derived only some of their material from older Icelandic sources: not much in *Járnsíða*, introduced in 1271 and un-

---

8. ‡‡ 73 (p. 120), 108 (p. 169), 143, 221.
9. In the present volume they are found as follows: p. 28, n. 13, 15; p. 42, n. 63; pp. 50-51; p. 133, n. 237; p. 143, n. 22; p. 150, n. 51; p. 166 and n. 137; Add. ‡‡ 29, 34 (ii), 38, 46, 55 (ii), 84 (ii), 87, 91, 98, 127.

popular, more in *Jónsbók,* introduced in 1281, long-lived and on the whole highly successful. In the diocese of Skálaholt the old Christian Laws Section remained in force until 1275, in the diocese of Hólar until 1354.

Procedures and Penalties

With the institution of the Fifth Court, soon after A.D. 1000, the judicial system was theoretically complete enough to ensure that, depending on its nature, a case properly pursued would almost certainly reach a conclusion either at the first spring assembly or at the first or, in rarer circumstances, the second General Assembly after it was prepared. The law texts we have were written at a much later date than the creation of the Fifth Court, but it seems certain that the major procedural elements and the penalties prescribed in them were already fully developed when that court of last instance came into being. These procedural and penal technicalities figure throughout the texts, whatever the main business of the legislation may be, and a brief account of them must make part of an introduction to the laws of early Iceland. In the following a case of personal injury is taken as a specimen but "civil" cases, which for the most part amounted to claims for payment or recompense or other fulfilment of obligations, were conducted in essentially the same way. The following outline is in broad strokes; more detailed information is given piecemeal in the Guide to Technical Vocabulary on pp. 239-62.

An injury should be published by formal announcement before suitably qualified people. The man who inflicted an injury published it as his act; the injured party published it as a charge against him. Men present at the time might also be named as witnesses to the offense and they could later be called to give testimony before a court. Witnesses figured more largely and were often obligatory in the stages of preparing and pleading cases: each step was usually taken in the presence of witnesses, formally named as such, whose subsequent testimony thus provided a record of the proceedings. Each case had a principal prosecutor and defendant but these could transfer the conduct of it to someone else; only free adult men could act at law in this way. In most cases of physical injury the offender was forbidden to attend the assembly, whether he had a defense to offer or not. Prosecution was undertaken either by formal publication of the case at the start of an assembly for judgment at a court set up at that assembly, or by a formal summons of the man charged to answer for the offense before a court — this was done at the man's home or as near to it as the summoner could safely get. In either event, the prosecution normally required the services of a panel of neighbors, five or nine of them according to the nature of the case, who had to be formally called to attend before the court that would judge it. These neighbors were normally householders who as well as living next to a specified place, usually the home of the man prosecuted or the scene of the offense, the "place of action," had to be qualified in various other respects. If the prosecutor proceeded by publishing at the assembly, he was expected to have called neighbors in the locality, those who actually lived closest to the place specified; but if he had summoned the offender locally, he then called neighbors at the assembly, taking those available there who were qualified and lived closest to the place in question. In some cases it was necessary to have a panel of twelve members, comprising a chieftain and eleven men selected by him. Courts probably had thirty-six judges; they were nominated by the chieftains and could be challenged by litigants and replaced if not suitably qualified. The prosecutor presented his case before them, with testimony of witnesses where appropriate and with verdicts from the panel of neighbors he had assembled on whatever relevant matters he put to them to substantiate his suit. A defense might turn on questions of fact but just as likely on questions of justification or on procedural defect. The defendant could ask for a clearing verdict from a group of five drawn from the panel of neighbors called by the prosecutor. It might be demonstrated, for example, that the injury inflicted was legally condoned retaliation or that publishing had not been properly done or that someone called to serve on a panel was disqualified for some reason. The judges could only find in accordance with the formal means of proof brought before them and had no discretion in imposing penalties. Many of the laws are "casuistical" in form, defining a conceivable offense, prescribing the punishment for it, stating the procedure for its prosecution and sometimes the grounds and procedure for a defense.

All free people enjoyed the same legal status but their immunity or right to legal redress might be diminished or lost by their own act. Their forfeit of immunity might be conditional (in relation to one or more specified persons or for a specified time and place) or absolute (i.e. anyone, anywhere and at any time, could do them hurt with legal impunity). In a sense this forfeit existed from the moment the act causing it was committed, but it received retrospective legal recognition when it was accepted as grounds for a clearing verdict in a lawsuit. Otherwise, forfeit of immunity was made an essential part of the public penalties of outlawry that were imposed for many offenses. Lesser outlawry meant confiscation of property, dealt with by a confiscation court held at the outlaw's home, and exile for three years but with temporary rights of residence and passage — reasonable arrangements in a remote island with unreliable sea traffic. Full outlawry meant loss of all goods through a confiscation court, loss of all status, and denial of all assistance — virtually a death penalty. An intermediate form allowed an outlaw passage abroad for life-long exile, but this mitigation of full outlawry was not decided by the judges of a court but depended on permission from the Law Council, as did other forms of mulct and banishment (often within Iceland itself) that might be imposed in cases privately settled by mutual agreement and arbitration. The standard penalty for minor offenses was a fine of three marks, and the Lawspeaker and chieftains faced loss of office as an additional penalty. In general, however, outlawry is the predominant feature of the penal system. We cannot tell what effect it had — it may have deterred both wrongdoing and litigation. It has often been pointed out that private settlement, though ultimately subject to public sanction by the Law Council, probably played a much larger part in ending disputes than the law texts reveal.

In certain cases a wronged person was entitled to personal compensation (a fixed sum, the same for all free people) from the offender, separate from the penalty enjoined by the laws. And in killing cases kindred payments were supposed to be made to members of the dead man's family by corresponding members of the killer's family: this atonement was legally due irrespective of the outcome of a lawsuit for the killing as long as a successful defense did not hang on a demonstration that the man killed had previously forfeited his immunity.

Although the Icelandic laws are generally far more elaborate than those in other early Scandinavian collections, the system in Iceland did not fundamentally differ from them in matters such as establishing notoriety by publishing an offense following prescribed rules, giving due notice of legal proceedings by local summoning or calling, maintaining a procedural record by constant reference to witnesses, and presenting cases before courts of lay judges, whose decision triggered specified penalties of fines and outlawry. The part played by panels of neighbors is a much more distinctive Icelandic feature, and panel verdicts appear to take the place of various forms of compurgation common to the other Scandinavian laws. On the strictest view it could be supposed that neighbors of standing, after the dismissal of those connected or involved with principals in a case, represented the best combination of local knowledge and impartiality that could be had, either because they lived closest to the place of action or to the man prosecuted. In the latter case, if there was room for doubt, it must have been assumed that general local satisfaction or dissatisfaction with the man in question would come out in his neighbors' verdicts. This innovation seems to have sprung from conditions of settlement in Iceland where, to begin with, people did not have any large circle of kin or acquaintance of accepted standing to appeal to, so that a compurgation system could hardly be introduced. The cooperative communes of neighboring householders (*hreppar*), which functioned under the national law but were largely self-regulatory, must have had their origins in the same conditions. Another distinctive feature of the Icelandic system is the detailed inclusion of everyone within the legal framework. Everyone had to be defined in terms of competence to perform legal duties and in terms of family, residence, householder, chieftain, assembly: if these were not known, or the right inquiries not made, the procedures of the law were delayed or blocked. Such complex emphasis on identification must have been consolidated with the legislation on local assemblies in the 960's, but it may have originated at a time when Icelandic society was largely composed of people who were strangers to one another and thinly scattered — as the Icelanders probably were when they began to foregather at the annual General Assembly around 930. It became essential to know a man's residence and all his attachments, as well as the defined place of action, to ensure that the right witnesses were named and the right neighbors called, the right chieftain approached for a panel of twelve, and the right court chosen to hear the pleading. Many of the procedural sections of the laws are concerned with exploring and solving problems caused by these rules.

Grágás and Lawmaking

The laws of the Icelandic Commonwealth that we know in sources originating before the 1262-64 contract of submission to the Norwegian crown are known collectively as *Grágás*, "wild goose" (literally "grey goose," a collective term for various species of wild geese). In a medieval source the name is used of a collection of Norwegian laws, and the application of it to Icelandic texts is thought to be the result of a sixteenth-century misunderstanding. No acceptable alternative name exists, however, and *Grágás* is in itself a pleasing, economical, and noncommittal term. Such a convenient single name may, however, mislead us into thinking of *Grágás* as a unified corpus of law, shaped and finite, like Mosaic tables or a code issued by Justinian or Napoleon, or even like *Jónsbók*. But that is not how we know *Grágás*, and in all probability the Commonwealth laws never quite existed like that either. What we know is a large number of laws from the early period preserved in manuscripts, whole or fragmentary, that differ a good deal in arrangement and content. We presume that all the provisions in them were law in Iceland at some time or other, but the existence of contradictory articles in them shows they could certainly not all have been in force at the same time. We can tell that some laws had long ceased to have practical application when they were recorded in our sources. Thus, it is probable that even when codification was begun in 1117, slavery was virtually non-existent in Iceland, but slaves still figure in a number of articles in the thirteenth-century texts we have.[10] Here and there articles seem to reflect a Norwegian rather than an Icelandic situation.[11]

In our text we find this statement:

> It is also prescribed that in this country what is found in books is to be law. And if books differ, then what is found in the books which the bishops own is to be accepted. If their books also differ, then that one is to prevail which says it at greater length in words that affect the case at issue. But if they say it at the same length but each in its own version, then the one which is in Skálaholt is to prevail. Everything in the book which Hafliði had made is to be accepted unless it has since been modified, but only those things in the accounts given by other legal experts which do not contradict it, though anything in them which supplies what is left out there or is clearer is to be accepted. If there is argument on an article of law and the books do not decide it, the Law Council must be cleared for a meeting on it.

(See pp. 190-91, where the text continues with a description of how the deliberation in the Law Council should proceed.)

Judging by Ari's words, given on p. 4 above, the intention of the revision and codification begun in the winter of 1117 was to produce an up-to-date and authoritative text of the laws of the country. But judging by the statement just quoted, it cannot have worked out that way in practice. One reason for this must be that Hafliði's book was not so comprehensive or systematized as to make it a universal code. Another reason was that law-making did not stop with its acceptance in 1118. A third reason is that nobody had a monopoly when it came to recording laws in writing. Private notation on some scale doubtless took place before 1117 and certainly did so thereafter. Written sources were in existence, some containing "accounts given by other legal experts," which could both add to Hafliði's book and contradict it. Such variance could result either from the survival of articles from the pre-1117 state of the laws which Bergþórr and his committee had changed or abolished, or from the introduction of erroneous statements and alternative opinions in writings

---

10. Cf. the references given under "Slave," p. 258, and Peter Foote, "Þrælahald á Íslandi," *Saga* xv (1977), 41-74.

11. Cf., e.g., p. 48, n. 86; p. 174, n. 169; ‡‡ 114, 115. It might be argued that at least some of the "Norwegian" references are there because they would be useful to Icelanders who traveled abroad.

made after 1117. Any text from before 1117 would contain valid law except where the committee had revised it, and a serious "legal expert" would doubtless wish to compare his reference book with Haflidi's and emend it accordingly. But if he had the opportunity and found the sense was similar, there is no reason to think he would care about the precise wording or arrangement.[12] (We may remember too that correction and revision in a manuscript book is a different matter from working with loose-leaf systems and transparent tape.) The existence of later texts derived from such early parallel sources, with variation in phrasing and order, would to some extent explain why the statement on the authority of written laws was necessary. Haflidi's book would, of course, also be copied in its entirety for use by others (it might be assumed that the first copy went with the office of Lawspeaker though we have no evidence that it did), and it would suffer the usual fate of works multiplied in handwritten copies. It is evident too that other "legal experts;" the sort of men the Lawspeaker in the pre-literate age was expected to confer with if he doubted his recollection of the laws (cf. p. 188), would insert new laws in the copies they owned or contribute them to texts owned by others. Probably they felt themselves free to vary and extend the wording in response to the casuistical queries that might occur to them or be put to them by other people. Haflidi's book and the bishops' books were looked on as a sort of public property, but we may expect that other men also brought their private books to the assembly with them. Nothing suggests that silence on the part of any of these written "authorities" was significant, not even silence in Haflidi's book: the absence of a clause from any book did not mean that the clause was not law.

It also seems likely that in addition to whole books of laws, which were perhaps relatively few in number, there were many scraps of law in written existence: oaths and formulas, specific prescripts consulted and saved for specific purposes (such as inheriting property, leasing land, holding a confiscation court, baptizing a child), perhaps notes of new laws to be made known by chieftains at their autumn assemblies. We must also recall that, although there was doubtless some diminution in the need and respect for capacious and accurate memory once men started to write the laws, people must have gone on learning them by heart all the same. Skill in law demanded quick recollection, and pleading was done in set form but not from notes. Again we may remind ourselves that swift reading and efficient indexing and rapid reference systems belong to our age, not to the twelfth century, and young men must have gone on learning law by rote and rehearsal in the old-

---

12. Cf. what is said on testimony on p. 68. Verbal variation did not matter as long as it did not affect the case at issue.

fashioned way. What was prescribed in a law would not always be remembered in precisely the same detail and order: one version noted down from such an oral source might easily be "at greater length in words that affect the case at issue" than another. Some provisions might be recorded in one book but not in another; there were doubtless some that have left no trace in our available sources.

The Lawspeaker had to recite the laws at the General Assembly over every three summers, repeating the regulations on assembly procedure each year. He could evidently act as an initiator of legislation: Ari says of Skapti Þóroddsson, for example, that "he established the Fifth Court laws."[13] It was also the Lawspeaker's duty "to tell everyone who asks him what the article of the law is" (p. 193). In the law texts three Lawspeakers are referred to by name and what they said was law is quoted (cf. n. 8 above). It is possible that a Lawspeaker's declaration of what he thought was law was tantamount to initiation of law, though always subject finally to the approval of the Law Council. But if in making such a statement the Lawspeaker was not merely recollecting what stood in the law (and if he were merely doing so, it is difficult to understand why a specific reference to what he said should then remain in our texts), he must rather have been articulating what was legal and undertaking, in advance as it were, one of the Law Council's main functions. Of the Council the text says: "Men are to frame their laws there and make new laws if they will" (p. 190). This seems to mean, first, that the Law Council should give clear expression to rights and obligations that were already held to exist but had hitherto been undefined or ill-defined and, second, that they should introduce such statutory novelties as seemed good to them. The result would be a prescript, quite possibly entailing alteration of older law, which would then be "declared among the laws," that is, first announced at the Assembly at which it was adopted and thereafter made part of the collection it was the Lawspeaker's duty to recite or read at the General Assembly during his three years of office. If it related to assembly procedure, the "new law" ought then to be in the recital every summer, and, if it was in some other section, it was bound to come up once before three years were out — if the Lawspeaker did not include it, presumably with general approbation, the new law was canceled. Presumably where laws are marked as "new laws" in our texts, this means that they were first noted while they were still in their trial period. How many of them survived that we cannot tell.

The formal phrase introducing a statement of law is *Þat er mælt í lögum (lögum várum) at* . . . which appears to have the general force of

---

13. *Íslendingabók*, Ch. 8 (*ÍF* I 19).

"It is prescribed in the laws (our laws) that . . .," as it is regularly rendered in the translation below. It is frequently reduced to *Þat er mælt at* . . . or even *Þat er at* . . ., for both of which the translation has "It is prescribed that . . .," but most often no introductory phrase is found at all. It is assumed that when a new law was announced the formal opening would have been used, but it is hardly safe to think that the appearance of this phrase in the texts is a remnant of the "new law" status of what follows. The prescripts themselves are usually framed with the use of the verbs *skulu* and *eiga*,[14] or else they are framed as a statement of what it is *rétt*, "lawful, right," to do, or of what one is *skyldr*, "required," to do.

It is generally agreed that the bulk of the material in our texts represents genuine laws approved by the Law Council, that by and large they reflect the state of Icelandic law in the twelfth century, and that their form is substantially the form they had in the Lawspeaker's recital. We are often reminded of the time and the place: we are told what we should do "here" at Þhingvöllr "today" and "tomorrow" and what "I" — the Lawspeaker — have just said or am about to enumerate. Such elements presumably go back to the dictation of Bergþórr at Breiðabólstaðr in the winter of 1117, but some may be from the words of others.

Grágás Manuscripts

Given the situation sketched above, with a variety of valid sources and no single *codex receptus* in existence, the state of our extant books of laws comes as no surprise.

The only large texts we possess containing *Grágás* laws (other than the Christian Laws Section, which needs separate discussion) are manuscript no. 1157 in folio in the Old Royal Collection, Copenhagen (*Codex Regius*, called *Konungsbók* by Icelandic scholars and referred to as K in the present volume), and manuscript no. 334 in folio in the Arnamagnæan Collection of the University of Copenhagen (called *Staðarhólsbók* and referred to here as St). The first is believed to have been written about 1260, the second about 1280,[15] give or take ten or fif-

---

14. *skal (gera eitthvat)* normally rendered in the present translation as "is to, shall, must (do something)"; *á (at gera eitthvat)* normally by "have to, must, ought to; have the right to, may (do something)."

15. Stefán Karlsson has recently suggested that the main part of K (from fol. 14, see p. 66 below) and of St were written by the same man but at about the dates commonly accepted for them; see *Árbók Landsbókasafns 1976* (1978), 19-21. Ole Widding has dated the first hand of K (on fols. 1-13, here pp. 23-66) to *ca.* 1300 or as late as *ca.* 1325, the main hand to 1270-80; see *Opuscula* II (Bibliotheca Arnamagnæana XXV 1, 1961), 65-75.

teen years either way in each case. Both are imposing volumes that were evidently prepared with lavish care, but we do not know for whom. In the generation in which they were produced there was active interest in law revision in Norway, but we have no specific evidence to connect these books with it, and it was certainly not these particular volumes that were used by the framers of the 1271 and 1281 codes prepared in Norway for the Icelanders.[16] On the other hand, they may well reflect Icelandic awareness of current and coming political and constitutional problems. From the 1220's the intervention of Norwegian royal authority in Icelandic affairs grew more pressing and from 1238 Norwegian bishops occupied the Icelandic sees. Both before and after the submission in 1262-64 some Icelanders may well have felt the need to fortify themselves with a record of what was law in their country, or of what might be regarded as law, on as comprehensive a scale as possible. The nature of our major texts, with their repetitions, their apparent reference to other accessible records,[17] their inconsistencies and disorganization might suggest some hasty and hungry effort to amass material. The major work of amassing may have been done by the editors of these particular volumes but possibly they are copies of large earlier collections. The latest item in K that can be dated is in the Christian Laws Section, laws introduced when Magnús Gizurarson became bishop (consecrated 1216; see p. 50 and n. 96); in St it is a reference in the same section to the second feast day of St Þorlákr, introduced in 1237 (see p. 45, n. 76).

The texts in K and St are very alike and very unlike, and they are not consistent in their variation. Sometimes one includes matter completely lacking in the other. Sometimes they are identical or virtually so; sometimes the substance is the same but sequence of matter, arrangement of phrase, and choice of expression may be different. The usual explanation is that any text they have in common must be ultimately derived from the same written source, which scholars are tempted to identify as Hafliði's book itself. The variations are then considered to be partly scribal and partly editorial, with expansion from other manuscripts, in some cases the same sources, in some cases not, and with individual arrangement of new incorporated matter. It is, of course, to

---

16. Ólafur Lárusson, *Grágás og lögbækurnar* (1923), pp. 69-73.

17. It is assumed that when the text is restricted to the opening words of an article (e.g., pp. 54, 140, 141, 143) this is because the whole was to hand elsewhere (in some cases we have the whole article at another point in the same codex). A similar indication that matter was available elsewhere is the phrase *usque ad finem* or *usque* followed by the last words of an article (cf. p. 109 and n. 150; there are more instances in Volume II). If, as seems likely, these references are inherited from earlier texts, their presence may suggest a certain uncritical avidity on the part of the compiler. Some of the texts owned elsewhere in this way may have been such "scraps of law" as are postulated on p. 11.

some extent an academic problem whether matter which is verbally identical in our two sources is so because it was derived by direct descent from Hafliði's book or because it was derived from some other recording of law which coincided with Hafliði's book not because it was copied from it but because both of them reflected the form in which the law existed in the memory of Lawspeakers or other men. Some of the additional manuscript sources available to the editors of the extant collections must have represented "accounts given by other legal experts." *Grágás* generally lacks the picturesque and proverbial utterance, vivid, forceful, often laconic and alliterative, found in some early laws from continental Scandinavia and normally taken as evidence of oral preservation and delivery. It has been suggested that this is because the committee of 1117 and the scribes who produced Hafliði's book gave the style a literary impress. It is to be hoped that new comparative work will show how much truth there is in this explanation, or whether we are to believe that, in the pre-literary age in Iceland, laws of extensive range and sophisticated casuistical nature were learnt and remembered in a style capable of comparatively elaborate sentence structure and with few obvious mnemotechnic devices.[18]

In general St has fuller phrasing, better organization, and a more "modern" content than K; for the most part it seems to represent the work of someone who was decidedly interested in having the laws "at greater length in words that affect the case at issue." But St does not contain some large and important sections found in K, whose contents may be listed as follows:

1. Christian Laws Section (‡‡ 1-19)
2. Assembly Procedures Section (‡‡ 20-85)
3. Treatment of Homicide (‡‡ 86-112)
4. Wergild Ring List (‡ 113)
5. Truce and peace speeches (‡‡ 114-15)
6. Lawspeaker's Section (‡ 116)
7. Law Council Section (‡ 117)
8. Inheritance Section (‡‡ 118-27)
9. Incapable Persons' Section (‡‡ 128-43)
10. Betrothal Section (‡‡ 144-71; general family law)

---

18. For further brief discussion of this problem see Peter Foote, "Some lines in *Lǫgréttuþáttr*," *Sjötíu ritgerðir helgaðar Jakobi Benediktssyni* (1977), 198-207; idem, "Oral and literary tradition in early Scandinavian law: aspects of a problem," *Oral Tradition. Literary Tradition. A Symposium* (ed. Hans Bekker-Nielsen et al., 1977), 47-55. Work on a computerised concordance of K in progress at the Universität des Saarlandes (see bibliography p. 278 below) will certainly help to answer many questions of vital importance to the legal and literary historian as well as to the linguistic and textual scholar.

11. Land Claims Section (‡‡ 172-220; general land law)
12. On investments (‡‡ 221-26; general commercial law)
13. Searches Section (‡‡ 227-33; on stolen goods and theft)
14. On duties of communes (‡‡ 234-36)
15. Miscellaneous provisions on verbal injury and poetry, finding other people's property, common land, dogs that bite, bulls and tame bears, settlements, the value of silver, prices agreed at the General Assembly, rights accorded to the king of Norway in Iceland and to Icelanders in Norway, inheritance of Norwegians who die in Iceland, claiming debts and prosecuting for claims, calling witnesses, betrothal, being principal in a case of wrongful sexual intercourse (‡‡ 237-54)
16. On tithe payment (‡‡ 255-60)
17. Miscellaneous provisions on baptism, burial services, carrying weapons in church, discovering paternity by ordeal, payment for priest's services, living on church land, burial, church inventories and contracts, forbidden work in holy seasons (‡‡ 261-68)

Some of this matter, notably most of the large section (2), all of (4), (6) and (7), most of (13), and a number of other individual chapters, is not in St. St's parallels to parts of (2) in K (chiefly ‡‡ 71, 76, 78-83) are in the section on investments, which is (12) in K. The overall arrangement in St is also different, with (16) joining (1) at the beginning and the order thereafter (8-10), (12), (3), (11).

A few other manuscript sources, from archaic twelfth-century fragments to modern paper copies, contain a certain amount of unparalleled or variant material in other sections than that of the Christian Laws. This section is in a special case because it did not originate with Hafliði's book or any continuation of it in the hands of laymen but was framed by the bishops and other clerics at some time in the years 1122-33 (see p. 50) and then accepted as the law of the land. It probably represented a unified regulation of existing custom and organization rather than any large-scale novelty. In *Járnsíða* (1271) and *Jónsbók* (1281), the codes presented to the Icelanders by the Norwegian king after their submission to him in 1262-64, there was nothing to replace the Christian Laws Section. In the Skálaholt diocese, however, it was superseded by a code issued by Bishop Árni Þorláksson in 1275, while it remained in force in the Hólar diocese until 1354. The demand for the old church laws thus continued well into the fourteenth century. They regulated all manner of daily activities, and church owners and priests needed to be well acquainted with them. A good many copies must have been in existence (a few figure in church inventories), and a number of independent medieval texts are known today, usually in volumes that contain *Jónsbók* and Bishop Árni's church laws as well.

The Present Work

The best way of presenting the *Grágás* laws to the English-reading world would be to publish a translation of both K and St, but this is forbidden by our present circumstances. Each text often throws light on the other but conflation is equally out of the question: apart from being a vast and imperfect labor, it would also imply a belief in a total codified corpus of early Icelandic law whose existence is dubious — and if it ever existed, it could not be reached merely by interlocking the texts we have. The only solution appears to be to adopt the principle of the early Icelandic legal experts who in their time agreed that the more comprehensive text should be favored as long as it remained relevant. Because K has important sections that are lacking in St, the overall preference must go to the former, and consequently the main text of the present translation follows the text of K as it stands, with only glaring scribal errors and omissions made good. The reader of the translation will thus get to know K as it is, with all its faults and puzzles, its unfinished articles and defects of arrangement. The choice for the main text was thus bound to fall on K, but obviously the same principle had also to be followed in cases where St improves on K, either by having fuller phrasing in shorter or longer passages ("at greater length in words that affect the case at issue") or by including articles altogether absent in K. The same applies to the other manuscript sources mentioned above. This material is translated in the Additions and is of three main kinds: smaller extra pieces that can be fitted into a parallel text in K (these are marked "+ K"), parallel texts with significant variation in wording (marked "cf. K"), and longer unparalleled passages (marked "÷ K"). Most of the additions are from St; a list of the few other sources that provide further material in this volume is given on p. 277. All the material in the early fragments belongs in sections that will appear in Volume II of the translation.

The texts of K, St, and other manuscripts are translated from the editions by Vilhjálmur Finsen, with recourse on occasion to the published facsimiles of K and St (see p. 277). The section titles and chapter numbers supplied by Finsen have been adopted (‡‡ 1-117 in this volume), and page references to his edition are included in parenthesis in the translated text. The paragraphing and the marginal synopses are our own. Square brackets mark (1) words which we may reasonably assume stood in K but have been lost because of damage;[19] (2) words which we

---

19. The top of fol. 1 is damaged and there is a lacuna, probably of two leaves, after fol. 37, cf. p. 169 and n. 146.

may reasonably assume the scribe of K inadvertently omitted; (3) explanatory matter introduced in the translation where footnote clarification is less appropriate (section titles, dates of saints' days, e.g., pp. 44-46, identification of parties, e.g., pp. 111, 211-12). The footnotes to the text are chiefly intended to supply cross-references and bare factual information. References to the main text from K are by page numbers only. The translations of passages from other sources, mostly short extracts, are referred to by their number in the Additions (Add. ‡‡ 1-134). Reference to matter in K that comes after ‡ 117 is by chapter number only (‡‡ 118-268) — this will of course become available in English in Volume II.

The aim of the translators has been to match the original Icelandic closely but still to write English. We have established a set of terms for the standard terminology and phraseology of the Icelandic and tried to use them consistently. We have generally avoided ready-made legal terms in English, because they would often mislead the reader; but we are well aware that many of the English equivalents we have adopted will seem painfully cumbersome beside the originals. Sometimes, of course, two or more English terms are needed for a single Icelandic word according to context. Obvious instances are *dómr,* which means both "judgment" and "the body of men who pass judgment, a court," and *kviðr,* "verdict" (literally "utterance") and "the body of men who utter a verdict, a panel." In some cases we have doubtless made needless attempts to match the Icelandic in using separate terms for varied expressions in the original, whose legal content in fact seems undifferentiated (cf., e.g., the entries on "Legal domicile," "Legal home" in the Annotated Glossary, p. 239 ff. below).

The prose of the laws is generally dense and business-like, seldom gaudy, fanciful, or dramatic — leaving aside the rhapsodic formulas for truce and peace guarantees (pp. 183-85). We have allowed the sentence structure and the constant repetition of words and phrases (a habit cultivated for the sake of precision and as much distinctive of the style as it is of modern statute language) to exert a steady influence on the English expression. We have chiefly interfered by leveling out the sudden changes that occur in tense and number, where slavish translation would produce intolerable confusion in English, by elaborating the sense of adverbs for the sake of clarity, and by identifying a person or party to whom the Icelandic refers only by a pronoun[20] — occasionally going so far as to add [A] [B] [C] to keep the thread plain. It may be noted that in formulas requiring proper names and patronymics we have kept the con-

20. "Pronouns are the devil, aren't they? You start saying 'he' and 'his' and are breezing gaily along, and you suddenly find you've got everything all mixed up. That's Life, too, if you look at it in the right way." (P. G. Wodehouse)

ventional *nescio nomen* abbreviation, N.N., wherever this (or N̊) appears in the manuscripts.

At the end of the book is a Guide to the Technical Vocabulary of the law texts, containing an annotated glossary, where numerous recurrent terms and procedures are explained, and lists of the English and Icelandic terms normally used as equivalents in the translation. These lists, which of course are not glossaries in the ordinary sense, may provide a handy first filter for the student and help to establish a received English terminology for reference to early Icelandic law by people without confident knowledge of the original language. A similar Guide will be provided in Volume II.

Although the glossary and a few of the footnotes offer relatively full explanation of various points, many of the textual and legal interpretations implied (or glossed over) by the translation need further discussion. This is expected to come in Volume III which, it is hoped, will contain a wide survey of the state of Icelandic law in the Commonwealth period and a commentary on all the texts translated in Volumes I and II. That volume will also contain a full bibliography.

The present volume has been made in the following way. After initial experiment and discussion, Perkins took the Christian Laws Section, Dennis the Assembly Procedures Section (on which he was already working for a Cambridge doctorate), and Foote the Treatment of Homicide, and each produced a translation and commentary. These were circulated among the three and variously emended and modified in the light of the criticisms made. A revision of the whole was then undertaken by Foote in order to make the translation more consistent and to harmonize the notes; he also selected and translated the Additions and drafted the Introduction and the Guide to Technical Vocabulary. The whole was subsequently checked by the other translators and improved on their advice. Many valuable suggestions for further improvement have been made by Dr. R. J. Glendinning and the whole work has benefited from the advice of Professor Haraldur Bessason. We are most grateful to them, as we are also to Mrs. Katja Tims, of the Department of Scandinavian Studies, University College London, who did much of our typing, to Mrs. Margaret Dennis, who read a proof of the whole book, and to the staff of University of Manitoba Press, who have accomplished the publication of the volume in the face of many difficulties.

THE CODEX REGIUS OF GRÁGÁS

IN TRANSLATION

I

[Christian Laws Section]

K ‡ 1; p. 3

It is the first precept of our laws that all people in this country must be Christian and put their trust in one God, Father, Son, and Holy Ghost.

Every child that is born is to be brought for baptism at the first opportunity, however deformed it may be. If the child's natural heir is present, he is to bring the child for baptism, and a second man must go with him if he asks him to. If the child's natural heir is not present, then the householder who is lodging the woman who has given birth is to bring the child for baptism and a second man must go with him if he asks him to. If neither of them is present, then the men who are legally resident in the house are to bring the child for baptism. If such men are not available, or if there are not enough of them, then those who live closest must take the child for baptism or give help. If someone whose duty it is does not bring a child for baptism or if a man who is asked to go refuses, the penalty is lesser outlawry and the case lies with anyone who wishes to prosecute. That is the penalty for both of them and the summons in the case (p. 4) is to be made locally and nine neighbors of the man prosecuted are to be called at the assembly.

A child must be taken to baptism; assistance is obligatory

A householder is required to board men who are taking a child for baptism, three men of age, the child making four, along with a horse or draught animal if they have one with them. If a householder has less property than requires him to pay assembly attendance dues, then he must give them house-room and sell them food and hay at a price to be assessed by neighbors. The price of the food and hay is to be paid within a fortnight. If a householder refuses them lodging or the help they ask for, then he is fined three marks and the case lies with the man who is refused lodging. The summons in such a case is to be made locally and five neighbors of the man prosecuted are to be called at the assembly.

The men who take a child for baptism are to go to the legal home of a priest — unless they meet him beforehand — and ask him to baptize the child. If he refuses, the penalty is lesser outlawry and the case lies with the men who brought the child for baptism. The summons is to be made locally and [nine of his neighbors are to be called at the assembly.

Priest's baptismal duties

If they meet the priest on the way, then he] lawfully administers baptism if he administers it at his [legal home], provided he has only been away from home within the day. If a priest has been away from home for a night or more and he is met on the way and asked to baptize a child, then he lawfully administers baptism if he administers it at the nearest church-farm, provided the child is not sick . If the child is sick, it is to be baptized at the first place where water is to be had. A priest is not to leave home for a night or more without having with him all the things needful to baptize a child.[1] If he does not have them, the penalty is three marks if there is no call for them. But if there is call (p. 5) for them and the fact that he is without them prevents a baptism, then the penalty is lesser outlawry and the case lies with those who brought the child for baptism.[2] The summons is to be made locally and nine of his neighbors are to be called at the assembly.

Children born on islands or on the highroad

It is prescribed that if a child is born on an offshore island and the child's heir is present, then he is required to take the child for baptism, and so are his hut-mates and everyone who would be required to bring the child for baptism if they were on the mainland. Anyone who is asked is required to lend a boat and anyone who is called upon must go as soon as weather permits. A householder is required to board five men who come to the mainland, the child making six. Those who brought men carrying a child for baptism to the mainland must also ferry them back again.

If a woman gives birth when she is on the road, her companions on the journey are required to bring the child for baptism or those men who are first asked to do so.

If a man whose duty it is to take a child to be baptized does not do so, or if someone refuses him passage or the use of a boat or draught animal without legitimate excuse, the penalty is lesser outlawry and the summons in such suits is to be made locally and nine neighbors of the man prosecuted are to be called at the assembly.

Baptism by layman in case of need

If a child is so ill that its life is in danger and a priest cannot be reached, then [a layman should baptize the child if it is at] a householder's home, and [water] is to be fetched [in a vessel]. If a child becomes ill as men journey with it, [it is to be baptized] wherever fresh water is nearest obtainable, or sea water if fresh water is not obtainable. The layman is to speak thus: "I consecrate you, water, in the name of the Father" — and make the sign of the Cross on the water with his right hand — "and the Son" — and make another sign of the Cross on the water — "and the Holy Ghost" — and make another sign of the Cross on the water. He is to use his thumb to make the cross (p. 6) as he utters each of these three phrases. He shall give the child the name by which it is to be called and speak thus: "I baptize you," he shall say, and name the child by name, "in the name of the Father" — and dip the child in the water — "and the Son" — and dip the child in a second time — "and the

---

1. Water, salt, holy oil, and chrism (oil mixed with balsam).
2. Add. ‡ 1.

Holy Ghost" — and dip it in a third time so that it gets wet all over.³ But it is also lawful to dip the child in only once or to pour or sprinkle water over it if there is not time enough to do otherwise.

Now if fresh water or sea water is not obtainable but snow is to be had, he is to make signs of the Cross on the snow and utter the same words over it as he should over water. He is to dip the child in the snow and accompany this with all the words he would use if he were dipping it in water. He is to melt the snow in his hands and rub it on so that the child gets wet all over. He is not to dip the child in the snow in such a way that it becomes chilled and in danger of death but rather rub snow over the child with his hands.⁴

A man must baptize a child. But if he does not know the words or actions, it is lawful for a woman to teach him. The father of a child is to baptize it only if no other men are at hand. But if a father baptizes his sick child himself, then he is to give up sharing one bed with his wife. If he does not give up sharing her bed, the penalty is lesser outlawry. His subsequent marriage is at the bishop's dispensation.⁵ *Baptism by a man, the father if necessary*

A man who has baptized a child is to go to see a priest and recite the words to him which he used when baptizing the child and tell him what his accompanying actions were. If the priest thinks that baptism was not correctly administered, whether it was words or actions that were deficient, then the penalty is lesser outlawry for anyone, man or woman, of twelve winters or more. If the priest thinks that baptism was correctly administered and the child dies, then it is to be buried at church and the burial service sung for it. But if the child survives, (p. 7) the priest is to administer the whole rite from the moment of immersion in water. A child is not to be baptized a second time if baptism was correctly administered the first time. If it has been baptized in the name of the Father and the Son and the Holy Ghost, it is not to be baptized a second time even though the water was not consecrated or the child was immersed only once. *Report to priest*

If the priest thinks that baptism was not perfectly administered, whether it was words or actions that were deficient, and the child dies, then it is not to be buried at church. But if the child survives, the priest shall administer complete baptism, as if no rite had been performed over it before.

---

3. Add. ‡ 2.
4. Add. ‡ 3.
5. Such obligatory divorce is prescribed only here. It was canceled by later legislation, see ‡ 261, St ‡ 5 (II 5/10-11), Staðarfellsbók ‡ 1 (III 58/18-20). (It should be noted that line references to [*Grágás*] I-III ignore in their counting those lines that contain only chapter numbers, cf. p. 279.)

Burial of prime-signed but un-baptized child

If a child dies who has received the *primum signum*[6] but not been baptized, it is to be buried out by the churchyard wall, where hallowed and unhallowed ground meet, and no burial service is to be sung over it.

Baptism delayed till Easter or Whitsun

If a child is born so close to Easter or Whitsun that it is wished to postpone its baptism until the Saturday before Easter Day or before Whitsunday, it is lawful to do that if the child is not sick. If it is sick, he must have it baptized at once. If a man wants to wait until the Saturday for the baptism, he is to go to see the priest, and the priest is to decide whether he will baptize the child sooner or wait till the Saturday.

All men must know baptismal words, and everyone must know Our Father and the Creed

Every male of age is required to know the words for baptizing a child and the accompanying actions. If he does not know them because of negligence, the penalty is lesser outlawry and it is for the bishop to take charge of that suit. Every one who has the capacity, man or woman, is required to know *Pater noster* and *Credo in Deum*. If he will not get them by heart but has sense enough to do so, the penalty is lesser outlawry and it is for the bishop to take charge of that suit and decide who shall prosecute.[7]

K ‡ 2
On Conveying the Dead

A corpse must be taken for burial

Every corpse with the right to church burial is to be taken to church as soon as men can get ready to do so. If an heir (p. 8) of the dead person is present, he is to bring the corpse to church, and the man he asks to go with him. If no heir is present or if he is not of age, then the householder who last gave lodging to the dead person is to take the body to church. If neither heir nor householder is present, then the nearest legally resident men are to take the body to church and take linen or homespun from the property owned by the dead and prepare the body for burial.[8] If he did not have the property to provide it, then the man who takes the body [to] church is required to supply what is needful to prepare the body.

---

6. As a preliminary to baptism people of any age were marked with the sign of the Cross (*primum signum, prima signatio*), exorcised, and given salt to taste. Before the Icelanders accepted Christianity in A.D. 999 (1000?) some of them became catechumens abroad by being prime-signed, in order to facilitate commerce with Christian traders and employers. Their baptism would have followed with the general Conversion. When Christianity was established, in Iceland as elsewhere, the *primum signum* (at the church door) and baptism (at the font) would ordinarily make part of the same ceremony, but it looks as though prime-signing was often undertaken as a cautious preliminary, while baptism might be delayed until the favored Easter or Whitsun festival, for example, as envisaged in the following. The laws regularly distinguish between a prime-signing sponsor and a baptismal sponsor.

7. Add. ‡ 4.

8. Eyes and mouth were closed, nostrils pinched; the body was washed, dressed in a winding-sheet of linen or homespun, and placed in a coffin.

It is lawful to prepare a body for burial, to make a coffin for it, and to take it and bury it on all established holy days in the year except two, Easter Day and Christmas Day. One may take a body to church on Good Friday but the earth is not to be opened for the committal of corpses.

But not on Easter Day or Christmas Day

A body is [to be taken] to a church at which the bishop permits burials.

A householder is required to board a man who is taking a body to be buried, with four others and a horse or draught animal if they have one with them. If he refuses them, he is fined three marks and the case lies with the man who is refused lodging. The summons is to be made locally and five neighbors called at the assembly.

[9]The man who has charge of a church must allow burial there and the body is to be buried where he and the priest who serves the church decide. A body naked or bloody is not to be taken into church. The body of a man who had no right to enter a church while he was alive is not to be taken into church. If a man takes into church the body of someone thus excluded, he is to atone to the church for that desecration with twelve ounce-units. If [he] will not pay that money, he is fined three marks for it and must still pay the church its money.[10]

Site of grave and state of body

No corpse is to be buried before it is cold. If (p. 9) a man buries a body before it is cold, he is fined three marks and the case lies with anyone who wishes to prosecute. If men hasten a burial so much that a panel gives a verdict that there was still breath in his body when he was buried, then it becomes a case of murder.

All graves are to cost the same whether nearer or farther from the church in the churchyard. Twelve ells is to be paid for a grave for anyone except a toothless infant when half as much is to be paid. A priest is to have six ells for the burial service. The man who brings the body to church is to pay the grave fee and the funeral fee. He is to pay it there at the church-farm where the body was buried, on the Thursday when four weeks of summer have passed,[11] there in the homefield in front of the main doorway. The man who has charge of the church and the priest may each of them name witnesses to their own fees if they are not forthcoming, and it is lawful to summon the man there on the spot and claim he is under penalty for three marks for withholding payment. That man has a valid answer if, when he brought the body to church, he offered to guarantee formally to pay the money — given that they share the same payment days — and to fix a settling day. The others must accept such formal guarantees.

Burial expenses and recovery

---

9. Cf. Add. ‡ 5.
10. Add. ‡ 24; cf. ‡ 88 (p. 146).
11. May 7–13.

Whoever brought a body to church has the right to draw his outlay from the property of the dead person or, if there was nothing in that quarter, to claim it from the heirs. If neither the dead nor the heir have the property to provide it, then one does not take money where it does not exist — grave and burial service are to be given free. If there is enough to cover some but not all expenses, it shall first be used to prepare the body for burial and then to pay for the burial service; the grave fee is to be paid last.

Death of vagrant   If a vagrant[12] dies in someone's house, the householder is to take his body to church. If the man had property on him, then what is needed for him is to be taken from this. If he had more property with him or owned it elsewhere, the householder (p. 10) who lodged him when he died has the right to take that property unless at the legal moving days lodging had been arranged for him at a place he could reasonably have stayed in and he had left it of his own accord and without kinsmen's consent — then the householder has the right to take what property the man who died in his house had with him but not more. The dead man's kin own the property which he had owned elsewhere.

Priest's duty to accompany corpse   [13]If a body is taken out to a priest's district, he is required to accompany it to burial provided he is sent word of this in advance and it is within the commune.[14] He is then to have the funeral fee, and he is also to have the funeral fee if no word is sent to him and even though he then does not go at all. A priest is not required to accompany a body out of the commune if there is a burial church anywhere in it. But if he will not accompany the body, as is now rehearsed, then the priest who sings the service has the funeral fee. If a priest leaves his district without procuring another in his place, he is not to have funeral fees if people die there.

Death on islands, at assemblies, in traders' huts, on the highroad and elsewhere   If a man[15] dies on an offshore island, then those men are required to take his body to church who would have to do so if he died on the mainland, or his hut-mates if he dies in a fisherman's hut. A man asked to lend a boat must lend it if he has one. If a man refuses boat or passage when asked, he is fined three marks.

If a man dies at an assembly or autumn meeting, his booth-mates are to take his body to church.[16] If a man dies at a spring assembly place or

---

12. Defined in ‡ 82 (p. 135).
13. A new law according to St ‡ 8 (II 11).
14. This local administrative unit (*hreppr*) was an association of at least twenty householders liable to pay assembly attendance dues (see p. 239). It had recognized geographical boundaries. The number of such divisions in the early period is uncertain; there were 165-67 of them at the beginning of the eighteenth century. See pp. 9, 243.
15. A new law according to St ‡ 8 (II 11).
16. Cf. Add. ‡ 5 (ii).

an autumn meeting place after people have left, then the man who lives nearest and who has at least two serving men over and above himself is to take his body to church. If a man dies at Þingvöllr after people attending the General Assembly have left, then the householder who lives here at Þingvöllr is to take the body to church.[17]

If a man dies in a traders' hut,[18] his hut-mates are to take his body to church. If a man dies (p. 11) on a journey, his companions on the journey are to take his body to church. If bodies are washed up from sea or fresh water, the landowner is to take such bodies to church. If any property is washed up with bodies, then what is needed for them is to be taken from it. If it amounts to more than that, the landowner is to keep the rest pending judgment. If a vagrant's body is found out in pasture land, the landowner is to take it to church and own any property he had on him. If the dead man owned other property, that is due to his kinsmen. If a body is found on a man's land or in an outlying building, the landowner must take it to church and look after any property he had on him for his kinsmen.

If a body is found on mountains where watercourses mark boundaries, it is to be taken to church by the man who lives in the inhabited district nearest the watercourse which has its source closest to the body on the mountain and who has at least two serving men over and above himself. The body is to be taken to the district towards which the water flows. If a body is found on communal pasture or on common land,[19] then whoever lives closest and has at least two serving men over and above himself must take the body to church. *Discovery of other corpses*

If a man whose duty it is in accordance with law to take a body to church does not take it, he is fined three marks and the case lies with anyone who wishes to prosecute. The summons is to be made locally and five neighbors of the man prosecuted are to be called at the assembly. If a man is prosecuted for not taking a body to church, he has a defense in the case if he gets a verdict that he thought that man had no right to church *Penalty for not taking corpse to church*

---

17. A farm probably existed at the assembly site from the Age of Settlement (*ca.* A.D. 870-930). The farmer there owned a church, built sometime after the Conversion. Its churchyard often figures as the legally prescribed place for payments, cf. e.g. ‡‡ 110 (p. 172), 116 (p. 188), Add. ‡ 29. For some time, probably *ca.* 1020-1118, a second church, apparently in public ownership, was also in use at the assembly; it can hardly have been a burial church.

18. Temporary dwellings where ships were berthed were used by seafarers from abroad and men waiting for passage (cf. ‡ 53, pp. 93-95). If foreigners wintered in Iceland they usually took lodgings in permanent households.

19. Communal pasture was owned by two or more men, sometimes by a whole commune; common land was owned by the Quarter as a whole, see ‡ 240.

burial, and then his fine lapses. But the court has to enjoin him by judgment to take the body to church within the fortnight following the end of the assembly. If a man takes a body to church which had no right to church burial, the penalty is lesser outlawry, unless he can get a verdict that he thought that man had the right to church burial, and he must have taken it away within a fortnight of the end of the assembly, and atone (p. 12) to the church for the desecration with twelve ounce-units.

Bodies not to be buried at church

There are four classes of corpse not to be buried at church.

The first is the corpse of someone who dies unbaptized.

The second is the corpse of a full outlaw who may not be sustained or given passage; it is not to be buried at church unless the bishop with jurisdiction in that Quarter permits.[20] But if the bishop permits it, the body may be taken to church.

The third corpse not to be buried at church is of someone who willfully inflicts on himself the injuries that cause his death, unless he afterwards repents and confesses to a priest, and then he is to be buried at church. Even if he is not able to reach a priest, but tells a layman that he repents, and even if he is not able to speak but makes such signs that men perceive that he repents at heart even though he cannot tell it with his tongue, then he is nevertheless to be buried at church.

The fourth corpse not to be buried at church is of anyone the bishop sees fit to ban from burial at church.[21]

Where such bodies are to be buried

A body with no right to church burial is to be buried at a place beyond bowshot of anyone's homefield wall, where there is neither arable land nor meadow land and from where no water flows to farms;[22] and no funeral service is to be sung for it.

K ‡ 3

Church moved from site or damaged

Every church shall remain on the site where it was consecrated if it may on account of landslips or snowslips or flooding or fire or tempest or unless there is desolation of districts in remote valleys or on ocean coasts. It is lawful to move a church if such things happen. It is lawful to move a church if the bishop permits it.

Removal of bodies and bones

If a church is moved a month before winter or is so damaged that it cannot be used, then bodies and bones are to be moved from it before the

---

20. The Skálaholt bishop was over the East, South, and West Quarters, the Hólar bishop over the North, cf. ‡ 5 (pp. 35-36).

21. Add. ‡ 21.

22. This constituted a no-man's-land which figures in other contexts, cf. ‡‡ 48 (p. 89), 62 (p. 112). A bowshot became fixed at 240 fathoms, at 3½ (longer) ells to the fathom, *ca.* 480 metres; see Add. ‡‡ 84 (ii), 134; p. 244.

30 LAWS OF EARLY ICELAND

next Winter Nights.²³ The bodies and bones are to be taken to a church (p. 13) at which the bishop permits burial. If a man wishes to move bones, the landowner is to call nine neighbors and their serving men to move the bones as if he were calling them for ship hauling.²⁴ They are to have spades and shovels with them; he himself is to provide hides in which to carry the bones and draught animals to move them. He is to call the neighbors who live nearest the place where the bones are to be dug up and is to have called them seven nights or more before they need to come. They are to be there at mid-morning. A householder is to go with his serving men who are in good health, all except the shepherd. They are to begin digging in the outer part of the churchyard and search for bones as they would for money if that was what they expected to find there. The priest who is asked to do so is required to go there to consecrate water and to sing over the bones. The bones are to be taken to a church at which the bishop permits burials; there it is lawful to do whichever one wishes, make one grave for the bones or several graves. All the wealth which belonged to the church where bones are dug up, whether it is in land or chattels or church equipment, is all to go to the church to which the bones are moved. If a landowner does not have bones moved as is prescribed, or if those men who are called do not go, each of them is fined three marks, and the case against those who are called lies with the landowner, and the case against him lies with anyone who wishes to prosecute. The summons in these cases is to be made locally and five neighbors of the man prosecuted are to be called at the assembly, and the court is to enjoin them by judgment to move the bones, and to bring them to church within the fortnight following the end of the assembly.

K ‡ 4

If a church is burnt down or is so damaged that it is necessary to build (p. 14) a new one, then [the church] is to be built where the bishop wishes and it shall be as large as he wishes and it shall be called what he wishes.²⁵ A landowner is required to have such a new church built on his farm, no matter who had had the previous one built. He is to begin building in such good time that, if he is able, the church is well enough finished within a twelvemonth of the damage for services to be held there. *New church to replace old*

The landowner is so to endow the church that on that account the bishop is willing to consecrate the church. Then the bishop is to go there *Feast of dedication*

---

23. Winter began on Saturday, October 11-17; probably the night of that Saturday and the preceding Thursday and Friday were counted the Winter Nights.
24. Cf. ‡ 166.
25. I.e., the bishop decides to whom the church is to be dedicated.

to consecrate that church. The householder who lives there is required to celebrate that dedication day on each anniversary, once every twelve months, with his household and any guests who have stayed there the previous night, and with all the people who pay their tithe there if it is the dedication day at that church which the bishop wishes these to celebrate. Everyone is to celebrate the dedication day at the church the bishop wishes. The dedication day is to be kept as holy as Easter Day and it is observed like other feast days.[26]

Payment of tithe   Everyone is to pay half his legal tithe to the church the bishop designates, and the bishop is to divide the district so that it is fixed from which farm everyone is to pay his tithe and to which church, whoever the householder is. Anyone who is to pay his tithe is to pay it there in the homefield in front of the main doorway of the church-farm on the Thursday when four weeks of summer have passed.[27] He is to pay that sum in homespun or trade cloaks[28] or in gold or refined silver. If he wants he can pay half the tithe he pays there — that is a quarter of his whole tithe — if he prefers, in wax or wood or tar. He may choose to pay it all in homespun if he wishes.

Recovery of unpaid tithe   If that sum is not forthcoming (p. 15) as prescribed, then it is lawful for the man who has charge of the church to name witnesses to witness that the sum is not forthcoming, and make the summons there in the homefield in front of his own main doorway for withholding tithe and claim that he is under penalty for payment of six marks and for payment of double the outstanding tithe as assessed by neighbors.[29] It is lawful for him to make a separate summons for each quarter of the tithe but it is also lawful to make a single summons for both the quarters, since the principal is the same in both suits, and claim it like other tithes.

Church deeds   If anyone endows a church with property, whether it is land or livestock or chattels or in tithes from farms where people of the district are directed to pay tithes to that church, then the man who has charge of the church is to have the whole agreement made in a deed listing what property he or other men of the district have given to the church. It is lawful for them to take that agreement to the assembly and to publish, at Lögberg or in the Law Council or at the spring assembly to which he belongs, what property that church is endowed with. He is to have the deed read out and the agreement published at home at the church once

---

26. Add. ‡ 6.
27. May 7-13.
28. Cloth and made-up cloaks of stipulated size and quality used as a medium of exchange, cf. ‡ 246. See further on tithes ‡‡ 255-60.
29. People normally made their own assessment for tithe, but on oath.

every twelve months when most people attend service there.[30]

If a man takes property which is church endowment and pays it out or gives it away or sells it to another man, the penalty for that is lesser outlawry both for the one who sells and the one who buys knowingly. The case lies with the man who has charge of the church if he wants to prosecute or with anyone who wishes if he does not want to prosecute. But if the man who has charge of a church or someone who has made a donation to it disposes of its property, the penalty for them is lesser outlawry, as it also is for anyone else who takes anything from a church, and the case against them lies with anyone who wishes to prosecute, and the summons in such a case is to be made locally and lesser outlawry made the penalty and nine neighbors of the man prosecuted are to be called at the assembly, and he is to be judged a lesser outlaw if the panel gives a verdict that he took property (p. 16) from the church; and if the object taken away has not been disposed of, it is to be adjudged back to the church, but if it has been disposed of, then such a sum is to be adjudged to the church as neighbors assess what was taken away was worth. Either the man who sold the church's property or the man who bought it, whichever seems the more likely to be able to pay, is to be summoned for repayment but both are liable to the same penalty.

Misappropriation of church property

The householder who lives at a church-farm or the man he calls on to do so may take fire[31] to the church and ring the bells. It is also lawful for the priest or the man he calls on to do so to carry fire to the church and light the candles and ring the bells. If a church suffers damage from fire through the actions of these men just enumerated or if a bell is damaged, they have no responsibility for it as long as they get a verdict that they treated them as if they were their own and had meant to treat them properly. If a man rushes off unasked to take fire to the church or to ring a bell, then he takes responsibility for church and bell.

Proper persons to handle fire in church and church bells

The man who lives on church land is required to feed a priest for a whole year if his legal home is there and if he sings mass there on all established holy days except for legitimate excuse. If the priest holds services at a place less often, then a householder who lives at a church-farm where burial is permitted is required to give the priest breakfast and supper on days when he sings mass there and also to feed his horse or a companion if he has one with him. If more than one householder lives at a church-farm, then each of them, whether landowners or tenants, is to

Householder of a church-farm: duty towards priests

30. The dedication day or other major festival.
31. Besides some general need for light, especially to use service books, churches needed candles for liturgical use. Fire was obtained from flint and steel or from friction, but it could be conveniently carried as a brand or embers (peat was the commonest fuel) or in forms of cresset and lamp. Fish-oil and tallow were in native supply but wax had to be imported.

board the priest according to the size of their share in the land. (p. 17) A man who refuses is fined for it.

Responsibility for repair of churches

³²If a tenant lives on a church-farm and the church becomes so dilapidated that services may not be held there in all weathers, then he is to send word to the landowner to come and repair the church. The landowner has to come in such good time that the church is repaired and services may be held there within a fortnight of the time word was sent to him. If this is not done, he is fined three marks for it. If the tenant is not able to get a meeting with the landowner — he has left the country or the Quarter — he is required to repair the church and to claim the cost from the landowner. But if a panel gives a verdict that services could have been held at the church even if it had not been repaired, then the landowner is not required to pay money for it: the tenant has God's gratitude for his trouble. If a church-farm is owned by a man under sixteen winters or a woman under twenty, then the man who is the legal administrator³³ of the young person's property has to maintain the church. He is to draw such a sum from the young person's property as neighbors assess he has laid out for the needs of the church.³⁴

Training a young man to serve one's church

It is lawful for a man to have a priestling taught for his church. He is to make an agreement with the boy himself if he is sixteen winters old, but if he is younger, he is to make it with his legal administrator. The whole agreement they make between them is to be binding. If they make no special agreement and a man takes the priestling for his church in accordance with the article of the law,³⁵ then he is to provide him with instruction and (p. 18) fostering; and have him chastised only in such a way that it brings no shame on the boy or his kin; and treat him as if he were his own child. If the boy will not learn and finds Latin tedious, he is to be put to other work and chastised at that only in such a way that he suffers no illness or lasting injury, but kept at it in all other respects with the firmest discipline. Should he now wish to return to his studies, then he is to be kept at them until he takes orders and is a priest. The man who provides him with instruction is required to provide him with vestments and such books as appear to the bishop to supply him with full means of holding services the whole year round.³⁶

---

32. Cf. Add. ‡ 7.
33. Cf. ‡‡ 81 (p. 135), 144, 156, 259, for other contexts in which the term "legal administrator" is found.
34. Add. ‡ 7.
35. I.e., in accordance with the following provisions.
36. Vestments are chasuble, alb, amice, stole, maniple, and girdle. The chief liturgical texts are those making up the missal (sacramentary, lectionary, gradual) and the breviary

The priest is to go to the church for which he was ordained and unless prevented he is to sing mass and matins and evensong there on all established holy days as well as through Lent and Advent and on all the Ember Days.[37] He is to publish the agreement he has made with the priest at Lögberg or in the Law Council. If he wishes it is lawful for him at Lögberg to forbid by veto any harboring of his priest.[38] *Duties of such a priest*

If a priest absconds from the church for which he was taught or absents himself so that he does not hold services as prescribed, then the man who receives him into his home or hears services from him or shares living quarters with him is liable to full outlawry. The penalty for sharing living quarters with him is the same as sharing with a full outlaw once it has been forbidden by veto at Lögberg. It is a case for the Fifth Court and it is to be published at Lögberg and the priest is to be claimed in the same way as slaves.[39] *If he deserts his church*

A priest may free himself from a church by teaching another man to serve in his place who seems in every way satisfactory to the bishop who has jurisdiction there. If a priest falls ill, the man who has charge of the church is to decide how long he is willing to look after him. If it seems to him that his illness is going to continue, then the man who has charge of the church may choose to deliver him to his kinsmen, but if in time he recovers then he is free from his ties to that church. But if a church-priest dies in service of the church for which he was taught and leaves property, then (p. 19) the church and the man who has charge of it are to take 360 six-ell ounce-units. If he owned more property, his kinsmen are to have it. *He can only resign if he produces a successor*

If such a priest is sick or dies

K ‡ 5
On Bishops

We shall have two bishops in the country. One shall have his seat at Skálaholt, the other at Hólar in Hjaltadalr.[40] The one in Hjaltadalr is to make a visitation in the Quarter of the Norðlendingar once every twelve *Duties of bishops*

(psalms, antiphons and responses, collects, lections, necessary for all the daily services other than the mass). In western Europe the mass texts were commonly collected in a single volume from the eleventh century onwards, the breviary texts similarly from the twelfth century. Both books normally include a calendar.

37. Three days observed by fasting, Wednesday, Friday and Saturday in four weeks of the year. Cf. ‡ 15 (p. 47) and Add. ‡ 20.

38. Add. ‡ 25.

39. Cf. ‡ 44 (p. 84).

40. Skálaholt was the private home of the first Icelandic bishop Ísleifr Gizurarson (1056-80), and became the permanent episcopal residence in the time of his son and successor, Gizurr Ísleifsson (1081-1118). The second see, with its bishop's church and residence at Hólar, was established for the consecration of Jón Ögmundarson (1106-21). See Map I.

months, while the bishop in Skálaholt is to visit three Quarters, one each summer, the Quarter of the Austfirðingar, the Quarter of the Rangæingar, and the Quarter of the Vestfirðingar. When he travels through the Quarters the bishop is required to visit every established commune so that people may meet him, and to consecrate churches and chapels and oratories, and to confirm children and to hear confessions.

Consecration of churches

When a bishop consecrates a church a fee of twelve ounce-units is due to him but he gives that money to the church he has consecrated. Wherever he consecrates a chapel or oratory, whichever of the two he consecrates, he is to take six ounce-units.[41]

Horses for the bishop

The householder who gives the bishop lodging is to provide him with horses on the day he leaves. His serving men and neighbors are required to lend the bishop horses if the householder asks them to do so. The man who refuses is fined three marks if he has a horse to lend.

Payment of the bishop's tithes

The bishop is to have it announced in every commune, when people attend church, to whom the money people have to pay the bishop is to be delivered. Every one is required to have a quarter of his tithe delivered to the householder whom the bishop appoints. The payment day for that sum is the Thursday when four weeks of summer have passed.[42] If the sum is not forthcoming as prescribed, then it is lawful for the man whom the bishop has made his agent to name witnesses to witness that payment is not forthcoming. It is lawful for him to summon (p. 20) for that and to claim it like other tithes; it is also lawful for him to publish his claim for the money at the assembly and the penalties are the same in either case. When a man is to pay a tithe to the bishop, he is to pay in gold or refined silver or homespun or trade cloaks.

Bishop's agents

If a man accepts property belonging to the bishop on his direction and that property disappears or is lost in some other way, then the man who accepted it bears no responsibility if he can get a panel verdict that he had treated it as if it were his own. If property belonging to the bishop is stolen, the principal in the case is the man who had the property in his charge, although it is also lawful for anyone the bishop wishes to prosecute the case. It is lawful for anyone to claim the bishop's property if he makes him his agent without any formal transfer of the case to him. There is no need to have testimony of this unless desired.

Property is nowhere to be taken from a church even though services are no longer held there, unless the bishop, the landowner, and the donor or his heir permit it to be taken away and they all agree; but otherwise in no circumstances.

41. Add. ‡ 8.
42. May 7-13. Cf. ‡ 4 (p. 32).

K ‡ 6
Priests' Section

Priests are to move into legal homes in the moving days but it is also lawful for them to move at any time up to the established autumn meeting held on the Sunday next following the Saturday when eight weeks of summer are left.[43] A priest who serves a district is to report his legal home at the autumn meeting. If he does not report his legal home at the autumn meeting, he is required to report it to five of his neighbors.[44] If when eight weeks of summer are left he has not reported or moved into a legal home, he is fined three marks for that and it is lawful for the man who prosecutes the case to summon him at the home of any householder he pleases among those in the district whose church the priest has served in that year. The case lies with anyone who wishes to prosecute.

Priests' residences

Priests (p. 21) have the right to sell their services and price them at not more than twelve marks from one General Assembly to the next. A priest is to take six of his twelve marks in six-ell ounce-units, but the other six according to the current scale used in debt-settling by the local men among whom the priest has come to lodge. That money is to be paid to the priest in trade goods or livestock or in any form of legal tender. If a priest prices or sells his services dearer than in accordance with law, he is fined three marks for it; furthermore no one is required to pay him more than the legal fee even though he contracted to pay him more.

Priests' fees

If a district is especially difficult to travel through or to reach, then the bishop has the right if he wishes to increase a priest's takings, even beyond the legal fee.

A priest does not have to sing more than two masses. A priest does not have to sing mass by night except on Christmas Eve — if he does not then, he is fined, and for that mass moreover no payment is ever to be made to him.[45]

Priests' duties and dress

Priests must be obedient to their bishop and show him their books and vestments.[46] Only a priest whom the bishop permits is to sing mass and no priest at all whom the bishop forbids that office. A priest must not wear fashions forbidden by the bishop, and must have his moustache and beard cut off and be tonsured once a month,[47] and obey the bishop in all things. If a priest will not do as the bishop orders, he is fined three marks for it, and the case lies with the bishop. He is to prosecute the case before

---

43. Sunday, August 17-23.
44. Cf. ‡ 80 (pp. 128-29), Add. ‡ 32.
45. Add. ‡ 9.
46. See p. 34, n. 36.
47. In the Roman form of tonsure the crown is shaved and only a small fringe of hair left around the head.

Priests' court at General Assembly

a court of priests at the General Assembly,[48] and nominate twelve priests as judges in the court, and there present his case against him. The bishop himself, along with two priests, is to give panel verdicts in the case and that case is to be prosecuted without oaths. If a priest is found guilty of the charge, the court must enjoin him by judgment to pay three marks to the bishop at the Assembly in the householder's churchyard[49] the following summer on the Wednesday in the middle of the Assembly.[50] If that money is not forthcoming, it is to be prosecuted like any other judgment-breaking.[51]

Foreign priests

If priests come to Iceland who have been here before and were then allowed by the bishop to hold services, it is lawful for people (p. 22) to pay them for services once they have shown their books and vestments to the bishop or to the priest the bishop makes his agent. If foreign priests come here who have not been here before, they are not to be paid for services, and they are not to baptize children unless a child is so sick that otherwise a layman would have to baptize it; rather than laymen do it, they are to baptize the child if no other priest can be reached. It is lawful to pay them for services if they have the writ and seal of the bishop, and the testimony of two men who were present at their ordination and who repeat the bishop's words saying that it is lawful for people to receive all priestly offices from them.[52]

Foreign clerics not versed in Latin

If bishops or priests come to this country who are not versed in the Latin language, whether they are "Armenian" or Russian, it is lawful for people to hear their services if they wish.[53] But they are not to be paid for services and no priestly office is to be accepted from them. If anyone allows a bishop who is not versed in Latin to consecrate a church or to confirm children, he must pay a fine of three marks to the resident bishop and the latter is also to take the consecration fee. Churches are to be consecrated and children confirmed as if nothing of the kind had previously been done when the rites were performed by men not versed in the Latin language.

K ‡ 7

Men are to put their trust in one God and His saints and are not to worship heathen beings. A man worships heathen beings when he assigns

People must not

48. Add. ‡ 9 (ii).
49. See p. 29, n. 17.
50. June 24-30.
51. Add. ‡ 9 (iii).
52. The reference is to the bishop who ordained such men abroad. Cf. Add. ‡ 10.
53. "Armenian" (*ermskr*) may mean either from Armenia or more probably from Ermland (on the south-east Baltic coast); churchmen from the former would have used Armenian as their liturgical language, from the latter Slavonic.

his property to anyone but God and His saints. If a man worships heathen beings, the penalty is lesser outlawry.

worship heathen beings

If someone uses spells or witchcraft or magic — he uses magic if he utters or teaches someone else or gets someone else to utter words of magic over himself or his property — the penalty is lesser outlawry (p. 23), and he is to be summoned locally and prosecuted with a panel of twelve. If a man practises black sorcery, the penalty for that is full outlawry. It is black sorcery if through his words or his magic a man brings about the sickness or death of livestock or people. That is to be prosecuted with a panel of twelve.

or practise witchcraft

People are not to do things with stones or fill them with magic power with the idea of tying them on people or livestock. If a man puts trust in stones for his own health or that of his livestock, the penalty is lesser outlawry. A man is not to keep "unborn" livestock.[54] If a man has "unborn" livestock and lets it stay unmarked with the idea of putting more trust in it than in other livestock or if he uses superstition of any sort, the penalty for that is lesser outlawry.

or put faith in special stones or animals

If a man falls into a berserk's frenzy,[55] the penalty is lesser outlawry, and the same penalty applies to the men who are present unless they restrain him — then they are liable to no penalty if they succeed in restraining him. But if it happens again, the penalty is lesser outlawry.

or fall into berserk rages

K ‡ 8
On Observance of Sunday

We shall observe Sunday every seventh day by doing no work save what I shall now enumerate. Men may drive livestock out and in again, women may do milking and may carry the milk wherever it is to be carried or take it by boat or by horse if there is water between the farm and the milking place, and women may begin to see to the milk. It is prescribed that if a man's buildings or his stores, whatever kind they are, catch fire or if flood water approaches or landslips or snowslips or tempest, howsoever such things threaten to damage a man's property, then he may employ every means to save it from damage as if it were an ordinary day.

Permissible work on Sundays

If a man's livestock becomes sick out in the pasture, it is lawful to bring it in if that gives it a better chance of surviving. And (p. 24) it is also lawful to slaughter the animal and deal with the carcass as if it were an ordinary day.

---

54. The term "unborn" implied Caesarean delivery but also seems to have been used (by extension perhaps) of an animal whose ownership was not attributed to a human being and so not indicated by marking.

55. Berserks were people capable of running amuck, voluntarily or involuntarily.

Sunday traveling

People may travel on a Sunday and each person may have with him forty pounds of baggage; but if one person has more and another less, the latter may not help the former. It is lawful for men to carry their baggage themselves or to go by boat or carry it on horseback. A man may also move with a vagrant's baggage[56] on a Sunday even if it weighs more than forty pounds. A man may also travel with his assembly baggage and with food for use at the General Assembly even though it weighs more than forty pounds. It is lawful for him to have forty pounds of trade goods in addition if he wishes. If a man has heavier packs and arrives at a farm on a Saturday, the householder is required to board him and his party over the Sunday. They shall arrange it so that one man looks after one pack horse or two men three if that is more convenient.[57]

A householder is required to board as many assembly men as he has people in his household, taking those who arrive first, if they are traveling to the Assembly for its opening or from the Assembly after its close. A householder who refuses is fined three marks and the case lies with the man who is refused lodging, and it is lawful to summon there and then and call five neighbors at the assembly.

Other movement

It is lawful for a man to go to a shieling on a Sunday and to take with him, even though the weight is over forty pounds, pails or a sleigh or whatever implements he needs for moving the things he intends to take from the shieling after the Sunday. It is lawful for a man to go on a Sunday to beaches where driftwood is to be found or to any woodland he may own with whatever implements he needs for moving the timber or charcoal he intends to take home after the Sunday. They shall arrange it so that no one has more than a single horse in lead. No penalty is incurred if more horses run free with them.

Drying clothes and picking berries

It is lawful to dry clothes outside, even though it is Sunday, or trade goods[58] if men are hard pressed. It is also lawful to pick berries and take them home, but no more than can be carried in one's hands.

Moving house

When a man moves house on the Sunday in the moving days, it is lawful for him (p. 25) to drive his dairy stock to the farm where he is going to live in the coming year, but he is not to ferry it over water or carry it by other means. If a man finds his sheep in the common fold in the autumn, it is lawful for him to take it home, whether he prefers to carry it or take it by other means. If a man buys stock not in milk in the autumn, it is lawful for him to drive it home and see to it on a Sunday, but he is not to ferry it over water or carry it by other means.

---

56. Presumably because vagrants were expected to carry all their belongings with them.
57. Add. ‡ 11.
58. Trade goods normally consisted of homespun cloth.

If men put in from the open sea and are in such straits that their lives or property are in danger, or if men ferry cargoes here offshore along the coast, then it is lawful for them, even though it is a Sunday, to unload the vessel and carry its cargo ashore if goods or vessel seem to them in any danger. Every man who was there must have given, within seven nights of such unloading, either an ell of homespun or raw wool amounting to one-sixth of a hank[59] to men who have so little property that they do not pay assembly attendance dues. If a man does not make this gift, he is fined three marks for it, and the case lies with anyone who wishes to prosecute.

Seafaring men in danger; obligatory thank-offering

A man may also fish on a Sunday or feast day or hunt if he wishes. But he is to attend mass in the morning before he sets out and not allow his fishing or hunting to prevent his attending services. If he does otherwise, he is fined three marks for it.

Fishing after mass

If a man in a boat finds driftwood, it is lawful for him to take it on board. If the piece is too large for him to take on board, he must not cut it up. It is lawful for him to bring it ashore and he is to make a gift of one-fifth of it.

If a man finds driftwood on his foreshore, he may, even though it is Sunday, roll it up above high-water mark. If he cannot get it up, he may put his mark of ownership on the wood. He is not to cut it in pieces. It becomes his wherever it comes ashore if he puts his lawful mark on it.

Securing driftwood

It is prescribed that a [fifth] part of all catches made on a Sunday or feast day is to be given away and this must be done within seven nights (p. 26) of making the catch. It is to be given to those men of the commune who do not pay assembly attendance dues. If a man does not make a gift in this way, he is fined three marks. The case lies with anyone who wishes to prosecute.[60]

Obligatory thank-offerings

If a man travels on a Sunday and comes to a place where an established right of way has been closed,[61] he has the right to break through, even though it is a holy day. The man who closed the right of way is fined.

Opening right of way

K ‡ 9
On Observance of Saturday

We shall keep Saturday every seventh day as a holy day from nones onwards. That is the day before Sunday. Then no work is to be done from *eykt* onwards save what I shall now enumerate.[62] Everything one may do on a Sunday may be done then.

Saturday after eykt like Sunday

---

59. In modern times in Iceland a hank (*hespa*) was over 800 metres of spun yarn.
60. Fishing at holy seasons is forbidden according to ‡ 268; cf. St ‡ 52 (II 60/12-13).
61. Cf. ‡‡ 181, 188.
62. Latin *nonae* (originally 1500 hours) and native *eykt* seem to have come to define about the same time, 1500 to 1530 hours.

Definition of eykt

Eykt is the time when, if the southwest eighth of the sky is divided into three, the sun has passed through two parts and has one part still to pass.

Slaughtering on Saturdays

If men slaughter beasts on a Saturday, the flaying must be completed before *eykt*; the carcass may be chopped up during the evening, and the suet cut, and what is needed as food for Sunday may be seen to even though it may be intended that some should be left over, and for this no legal penalty is incurred.

Diminished responsibility of workers and slaves if they work after eykt

[63]If men work after *eykt* on a Saturday, then they are fined three marks and the householder is to be first prosecuted if he took part in the work. If household men have taken part in the work and bounden debtors or slaves, then it is the free men who are to be first prosecuted. [64]If they have worked after *eykt* and are prosecuted for this, they have a defense in the case if they can get a panel verdict that the sun was not visible and they would have stopped work sooner if the sun had been visible.[65] It is also a clearing verdict if the panel decides that they had accomplished so little that they did not dare go home on account of the iron rule of the householder; and in that case the householder is fined and not they.

Travelers' rights to lodging on Saturdays

If a man is traveling with pack horses on a Saturday and wants to get home, then he may go on until the sun is shaft-high.[66] If he cannot (p. 27) get home, he must have taken lodging for the night before the sun is in the west and have taken his packs off by then. A householder who refuses him lodging is fined. The man shall then go on with his pack horses to the next farm on his way and ask for lodging. The householder is fined if he refuses. The man shall go to the third farm and there take off his packs and ask for lodging and somewhere to put his baggage. If the householder refuses him lodging, he is fined for it, and he also bears responsibility for the packs should the owner leave them lying there in the homefield.

A man may come down from a mountain with pack horses if his journey has gone slower than he meant it to, even though it is in a part of the day established as holy.

K ‡ 10
Further Observance of Saturday

[67]People may travel to or from a wedding with pack horses on a Satur-

---

63. A new law according to St ‡ 24 (II 34).
64. Add. ‡ 14.
65. Add. ‡ 14 (ii).
66. Cf. the definition on p. 43. The time indicated will obviously vary from place to place and season to season. About mid-May in south Iceland it would probably work out at *ca.* 1500 hours (cf. nones and *eykt*, p. 41, n. 62).
67. Cf. Add. ‡‡ 12-13.

day until the sun is shaft-high. A householder is required to board up to five of them if the bride or bridegroom is among them but up to three otherwise. A householder who refuses them lodging is fined. Traders may travel with pack horses on a Saturday until the sun is shaft-high. A householder is required to board up to five of them if the ship's master is among them, otherwise up to three. A householder who refuses them lodging is fined three marks, and the case lies with those who were refused lodging; the summons is to be made locally and five neighbors are to be called at the assembly.   *Wedding and other travelers, their rights to lodging*

Householders who pay assembly attendance dues are required to board people but not those who have less property.

It is lawful for a man who attends a spring assembly acting in a chieftaincy to travel with pack horses or to go by boat even after *eykt* on a Saturday; and likewise assembly participants who are traveling to the assembly for its opening; they may have with them their clothes, tents, and food; a man may have forty pounds of trade goods in addition if he wishes. A householder is required to board overnight men who are going to a spring assembly and board half as many as he has people in his household when it is assembly participants who come.[68]   *Travelers to spring assembly*

A chieftain is to come to a spring assembly in time to roof his booth[69] on a Saturday before the sun is shaft-high and to be ready then to go to the formal inauguration of the assembly (p. 28). If he works longer he is fined.   *Time of chieftain's arrival at spring assembly*

The sun is shaft-high when a man standing on the shore where land and sea meet, with the tide half out, can look out to sea — assuming it is clear weather — as the sun is sinking and visualize a spear, of such a length that one could reach up to the socket [and viewed, as it were, at a distance of nine paces[70]], with its point touching the bottom of the sun and the butt of the shaft touching the sea.   *Definition of shaft-high sun*

If anyone works on a Sunday or on a Saturday after *eykt* or on an established holy day at tasks other than those now enumerated, he is fined three marks for it, and the case lies with anyone who wishes to prosecute. The summons is to be made locally and five neighbors of the man prosecuted are to be called at the assembly. The night before an established holy day is to be kept sacred in the same way as the following day. When the day after a feast day is an ordinary day, it is lawful for a man to go about his work before dawn.[71]   *Penalty and procedure*

---

68. Add. ‡ 15.
69. Walls of these temporary buildings, made of turf and stones, were left standing; they were tented with cloth when in use; cf. ‡ 61 (p. 112), Add. ‡ 31.
70. From St ‡ 25 (II 36/11-12).
71. Add. ‡ 13 (ii).

K ‡ 11
On Observance of Christmas

Permissible work in the Christmas season

We in this country must keep Christmastide holy. It lasts thirteen days. The first day of Christmas [25/12] and the eighth [1/1] and the thirteenth [6/1] are to be kept like Easter Day. The second day of Christmas and the third and the fourth [26–28/12] are to be kept like Sundays in all respects save that it is then lawful for a man to clear out dung from his animals on the third or fourth day, whichever of the two days he likes. But on all the in-between days of Christmas [29-31/12, 2-5/1], it is lawful for a man to muck out and carry dung onto his land, to that part of it nearest the byre, if draught animals are available and if it is tipped there. If a man clears out dung but has no draught animal available, he is to make a heap of it. Men also have the right to do these tasks on the in-between days of Christmas: slaughter livestock and dress their carcasses for food needed over Christmas; brew beer; and given that they did not get draught animals for it before Christmas, they may bring in such outlying stores of hay as are required, if it seems better to use that for fodder than what is already at home; (p. 29) but one may not bring in more hay than what will reasonably last over Christmas.

K ‡ 12
On Observance of Easter

Observance of Eastertide, Rogation Week, Ascension, and Whitsun

We must keep Eastertide holy. It lasts four days. We are to keep Easter Day like the first day of Christmas, but we are to keep Easter Monday, Tuesday, and Wednesday like Sundays.

From the first day of Easter there are to be five weeks to the Sunday introducing Rogation Week. We are to keep the Monday of Rogation Week and the Tuesday and Wednesday like Saturdays, and people on the list of those who should fast are to eat only one meal each day. It is lawful to eat foods made from milk[72] during the night if desired. If the Monday or Tuesday of Rogation Week coincides with the feast of Philip and James [1/5] or the Invention of the Cross [3/5] or a dedication day, then it is lawful to eat two meals but not meat. But if the Wednesday in Rogation Week coincides with one of these feast days, people are to continue to fast as before.[73] The Thursday in Rogation Week is Ascension Day and we are to keep it like Easter Day.

From Easter Day there are to be seven weeks to Whitsunday. There is a whole week between Rogation Week and Whitsun. On the Saturday

---

72. Icelandic *hvítr matr*, "white food;" Latin *lacticinia*.
73. A night and day fast before Ascension Day and Whitsunday is prescribed by ‡ 18 (p. 51) and St ‡ 27 (II 38/2, 6-7).

before Whitsun people are required to fast the whole day. [74]Whitsunday is to be kept like Easter Day and we are to keep the Monday and Tuesday like Sundays. On the Wednesday it is lawful for men to travel with pack horses if they are moving house, and to ferry cargoes and trade goods to a ship, to drive livestock to communal pasture, and to shear sheep.

K ‡ 13; p. 30

Established feast days, with and without preceding fast

We have to keep as established feast days these days I shall now enumerate. From the thirteenth day of Christmas [6/1] there are seven nights to the octave of the thirteenth [13/1]. Then there are eight nights to Agnes's day [21/1]. Then there are four nights to Paul's day [25/1] and there is no fast before it. From then it is seven nights to Brigid's day [1/2]. There is no fast before it. Then there is one night to the Purification [2/2]. Then there are twenty nights to Peter's day [22/2] and no fast before it. Then there are two nights to Mathias's day [24/2] and a day and night fast before it. Then there are sixteen nights to Gregory's day [12/3], seventeen if it is leap year; nine nights to Benedict's day [21/3], four to the Annunciation [25/3]. Then there is one night less than thirty to Jón's day [23/4].[75] Then there are two nights to the major Rogation day [25/4]. We are to keep that day like a Saturday and fast unless it falls in Easter week or on a dedication day. In the latter case it is lawful to eat two meals but no meat. But if it falls in Easter week it is lawful to eat meat if desired. From then it is six nights to Philip and James's day [1/5]. There is no fast before it. Then it is two nights to the Invention of the Cross [3/5] and no fast before it. Thirty-seven nights to Columba's day [9/6] and no fast before it. Fifteen nights to John the Baptist's day [24/6] and a twenty-four-hour fast before it. Five nights to Peter's day [29/6] and a twenty-four-hour fast before it. Nine nights to the day of the Saints of Selja [8/7][76] and no fast before it. Seventeen nights to James's day [25/7] and a day and night fast before it. Four nights to Óláfr's day [29/7][77] and a day and night fast before it. Twelve nights to Lawrence's day [10/8] and a day and night fast before it. Five nights to Mary's day [15/8][78] and a day and night fast before it. Nine nights to Bartholomew's

---

74. Cf. Add. ‡ 22. St ‡ 27 (II 38/9-10) allows the activities specified in what follows on both Tuesday and Wednesday.

75. St Jón Ögmundarson, bishop of Hólar 1106-21, feast day instituted 1200.

76. St Sunniva and her companions; her shrine was moved from Selja to Bergen in 1170. St ‡ (II 39/13) adds: "From then there are twelve nights to Þorlákr's day and no fast before it." This feast of St Þorlákr's translation, celebrated July 20, was introduced in 1237.

77. St Óláfr Haraldsson, king of Norway 1016-30, relics enshrined 1031.

78. The Assumption; also called the "first Mary's day" to distinguish it from the "second," the Feast of the Nativity, September 8.

day [24/8] and a day and night fast before it. Fifteen nights to the Nativity of Mary [8/9] and no fast before it. Six nights to the Exaltation of the Cross [14/9] and no fast before it. Seven nights to Matthew's day [21/9] and a day and night fast before it. Eight nights to Michaelmas [29/9] and (p. 31) a day and night fast before it. One night less than thirty to Simon and Jude's day [28/10] and a day and night fast before it. Four nights to All Saints' day [1/11] and a day and night fast before it unless it falls on a Monday — in that case the fast is to be observed on the previous Friday night. A householder is to give the food which those of his household legally required to fast would then have eaten for supper, together with the supper food before two Ember days,[79] to the men of the commune who do not pay assembly attendance dues. Every householder is required to give three of his household's evening meals, but not meals of fish, and the men of the commune are to divide up gifts of food at their meetings in the autumn.

Gifts of food to needy at All Saints and on two Ember Days

From All Saints' day there are ten nights to Martinmas [11/11] and no fast before it. Eleven nights to Cecilia's day [22/11] and if it falls on a Friday there is a fast by day before it. One night to Clement's day [23/11] and no fast before it. Seven nights to Andrew's day [30/11] and a day and night fast before it. Six nights to Nicholas's day [6/12] and a day and night fast before it. One night to Ambrose's day [7/12]. Six nights to Magnús's day [13/12].[80] Eight nights to Thomas's day [21/12] and a day and night fast before it. From then there are two nights to Þorlákr's day [23/12][81] and a fast on bread and water before it. That day is one night before Christmas.

K ‡ 14
On Observance of Festivals

Permissible hunting on certain feast days

There are fifteen days each year when men are not to hunt and fish more than I shall now enumerate. Men may catch a polar bear and leave house for this purpose, and the bear is the property of whoever gives it a death wound, no matter who owns the land, unless slaves catch it or bounden debtors — then it is the property of the man who has money owed him by such men.[82] Men may hunt walruses and the man who catches one has

---

79. See p. 35, n. 37; Add. ‡ 23. On food gifts see also ‡‡ 234, 255.

80. Reading *vi nætr* for *iii nætr*; cf. St ‡ 28 (II 40/10). St Magnús Erlendsson, earl of Orkney was killed in 1115; his relics were enshrined in Christchurch, Birsay *ca.* 1135, and later moved to the new cathedral in Kirkwall.

81. St Þorlákr Þórhallsson, bishop of Skálaholt 1178-93, feast day instituted 1199; cf. p. 45, n. 76.

82. Polar bears are not indigenous to Iceland but occasional visitors on drift ice from Greenland.

half (p. 32) and the landowner has half. A drifting or stranded whale may be moved and secured or cut up if it cannot be secured. If fish "come ashore," then men may catch them. Fish "come ashore" when they can be gaffed or caught by hand. Nets and hooks are not to be used. Men may take birds with damaged feathers if they can be caught by hand. A fifth part of such catches is to be given away, like the fifth part of Sunday catches. Men may hunt and fish as now enumerated and no more than that on the first, eighth, and thirteenth day of Christmas, Easter Day, Ascension Day, Whitsunday, the four Mary days, All Saints' day, John the Baptist's day, Peter and Paul's day in the summer, on dedication days, and on Þorlákr's day. But all other Sundays and feast days have a common form of observance.[83]

Obligatory gifts of portion of catch

K ‡ 15
Observance of Lent

We must keep Lent. It lasts seven weeks. We shall start Lent on the Sunday announced at the assemblies and autumn meetings. When a man starts Lent, he may eat meat up to midnight but after that he is not to eat meat in those seven weeks until the sun shines on the mountains on Easter Day. On the Monday and Tuesday of the first week of Lent, it is lawful to eat two meals a day, but not meat, but on all other days except Sundays people are to fast from then until Easter. There are eleven nights when people are legally required to fast in Lent: the seven Friday nights, the first and last Wednesday night, and the Wednesday and Saturday nights in the Ember Days.[84]

Beginning Lent

We must observe a Christmas fast. We shall start abstaining from meat on the Monday (p. 33) when there are three Sundays to go to the first day of Christmas. Meat is not to be eaten during that time except on Sundays and established feast days. We must fast on Fridays and the nights before them during the Christmas fast; and fast by day on the day before Christmas and before the thirteenth day of Christmas.

Advent, Christmas, and Epiphany fasts

We must keep twelve Ember Days by fasting every year and also the nights before them. We are to keep Ember Days in the second week of Lent and during Whit week. On the night before the Saturday of the Ember Days in Whit week it is lawful to eat foods made from milk.[85] We shall similarly keep Ember Days before Christmas and Michaelmas as announced at the assembly and the autumn meetings.

Ember Days

---

83. Add. ‡ 17.
84. Cf. ‡ 18 (p. 51).
85. Cf. Add. ‡ 20.

K ‡ 16
On Times of Fasting

Failure to fast: penalties and procedures

If a man eats meat in Lent or the Ember Days or on any Friday or on the Saturday before Whitsun, the penalty is lesser outlawry. But if he eats meat at any other time of fasting, he is fined three marks, and these cases lie with anyone who wishes to prosecute. Anyone who is on the list of those who should fast is always fined not only if he eats meat but if he eats foods made from milk during an established fast. The summons is to be made locally and neighbors of the man prosecuted are to be called at the assembly, nine for lesser outlawry cases, five for fining cases.

Breaking fast to save life

If a man finds himself on an offshore island in Lent and has no food except meat, he is to eat it rather than let himself expire from hunger. He is not to eat meat on Ember Days or Fridays. He is to eat it to keep himself alive, not to put on weight. He must have gone to confession with a priest within seven nights of coming from the island.

Definition of meat

Meat (p. 34) is what comes from slaughtering cattle, sheep, goats, and pigs. If a pig gets into horse meat, it is to be kept for three months but starved to shed its flesh and then fattened for three months. If a pig gets into dead human flesh, it is to be kept for six months, and if it has put on weight, it is to be starved to shed its flesh and then fattened for six months. Then it is lawful to use the pig for food.

Walrus and seal give meat

Men may hunt bears and eat their meat, whether brown bears or polar bears, and deer, red deer, and reindeer.[86] They may be eaten when meat may be eaten. Walruses and seals are only to be eaten when meat may be eaten. Men may eat birds that swim. People are not to eat taloned birds, those with carrion claws, eagles, ravens, falcons, and hawks. It is lawful to eat poultry and ptarmigan. The eggs may be eaten of birds which may be eaten. Eggs may be eaten at times when people eat foods made from milk.

Birds and eggs that may be eaten

Gifts to needy from meat not slaughtered by oneself

Men may use for food the livestock they themselves slaughter, but it is also lawful to use livestock which they themselves have not slaughtered if they know what has happened to it, whether it perished in water or was killed by landslip or snowslip or storm or whatever happens to it so long as it is known, then it may be used for food, but not if the cause of death is unknown.[87] A fifth part of any animal which a man has not slaughtered himself is to be given away. The gift is to have been made within seven nights of its death to those men of the commune who do not have to pay assembly attendance dues. A man is fined three marks if he does not make such a gift.

---

86. No kinds of bear or deer are indigenous to Iceland.
87. Add. ‡ 16.

A calf is to be kept for three nights, but it is also lawful to use it for food if slaughtered sooner as long as it has been given nourishment, and a fifth part of it is to be given away.

An animal may not be eaten which is known to have killed someone. *Forbidden meat* People must not eat horses, dogs, foxes,[88] and cats; and no beasts with claws and not carrion birds. If a man eats these animals which are excluded, (p. 35) he is liable to a penalty of lesser outlawry.

Everyone is required to keep established fasts who has reached the age of twelve winters at the beginning of the previous summer. A winter is not to be counted in anyone's age if he was born when even a single night of winter had passed.[89] People must keep established fasts until they are seventy. A healthy person has to keep established fasts but not one who is sick. Anyone younger than twelve winters or older than seventy is not required to fast unless he wants to. A woman with a living child in her womb is not required to fast.[90] A woman who is breast-feeding a child is not on the list of those who should fast during the first Lent; she may have the child at her breast until the third Lent but save in that one Lent it is not to prevent her from keeping established fasts. All these people are required to abstain from meat during times of fasting in the same way as those who are[91] on the list of those who should fast.

Age for obligatory fasting

Calculation of age in winters

Pregnant women and nursing mothers

If a man has charge of someone under age or mentally deficient and allows him to eat meat during times of fasting or forbidden food outside times of fasting, then he is liable to legal penalty as if he himself had eaten it, but not the person who ate it if he lacked sense to refrain. If a man puts forbidden food in someone's ordinary food in order to disgrace him, then his penalty is lesser outlawry but there is no penalty for the one who eats it.

Responsibility for minors and simpletons

K ‡ 17
On Times of Fasting

People who stay at the farm are required to fast during outfield haymaking but not the workmen who go out to work at the outfield haymaking nor the man who brings in sheep for milking nor anyone who does laboring work for someone's farm. It is laboring work if a man does such work daily as the householder orders. No one at the farm is to rush off to such

Workers excused from fasting during haymaking

---

88. The only fox in Iceland (and the only native land mammal) is the Arctic fox (*Alopex lagopus*).

89. Someone born on or after October 10-16 did not reach the age of one winter until the first day of summer (Thursday, April 9-15) eighteen months later.

90. This probably means 40 days after conception.

91. Omitting *eigi*, "not;" cf. St ‡ 33 (II 44/9-11): "Those people who are not on the list of those who should fast are required to abstain from meat in times of fasting in the same way as those who have to fast."

Period of no exemption

work when he ought to fast in order to eat rather than go without. Established fasts are kept in the same way by (p. 36) everyone once the Ember Days in autumn start until Peter's day in the summer is past [29/6].

When someone has to fast, he is to finish eating his food by midnight if he is to fast next day and not eat again until after nones. When one is legally required to fast by night then one is to abstain from meat in the same way as when one fasts by day. Night in autumn and winter is to be counted as the time when there is no daylight to be seen by a man who, it is presumed, is standing in a place where he can look out to sea in cloudless weather. Night in summer is to be counted the time when the sun passes through the northern eighth: the northern eighth extends from the sun's arrival midway between northwest and north to its arrival midway between north and northeast.[92]

Definition of night in autumn and winter

and in summer

Permissible food includes whale but not walrus, seal, and other sea beasts

When a man fasts by night, he is to have dry food:[93] dry food is plants, fruit, and all that grows out of the earth. He may also eat this when he fasts: fish of all kinds and whales other than walrus and seal — these may only be eaten when meat may be eaten. Horse whale is not to be eaten, nor narwhal nor the red comb.[94]

Prosecution procedure for all offenses in Christian Laws Section

It is prescribed in all the cases now enumerated in the Christian Laws Section that the summons in each case is to be made locally and nine neighbors of the man prosecuted are to be called at the assembly in cases of outlawry and lesser outlawry except when a man has made a summons for magic — then the chieftain to whose following the man prosecuted belongs is to be called on to form a panel of twelve; and in cases involving fines of three marks and other fines five neighbors of the man prosecuted are to be called.

Laws established by Bishops Ketill and Þorlákr

Bishop Ketill and Bishop Þorlákr laid down the Christian Laws Section in consultation with Archbishop Özurr and Sæmundr and many other priests, as it has now been rehearsed and recited.[95]

K ‡ 18
New Laws. Marriage

New fast days

That new law was made when Magnús Gizurarson became bishop[96] that

---

92. Azimuth 337½ degrees through North to 22½ degrees.

93. Icelandic *þurr matr* "dry food"; Latin *siccus cibus*.

94. It is not certain what kind of whales "horse whale" (*hrosshvalr*) and "red comb" (*rauðkembingr*) were; the latter may have been *Otaria stelleri* or *Otaria ursina*.

95. Ketill Þorsteinsson, bishop of Hólar 1122-45; Þorlákr Rúnólfsson, bishop of Skálaholt 1118-33; Özurr (Asger, Asser) Svensson, bishop of Lund from 1089, archbishop of Lund and metropolitan of the Scandinavian countries 1104-37; Sæmundr Sigfússon, priest, called *inn fróði* "the learned," 1056-1133.

96. Elected 1215, consecrated 1216, died 1237.

people are now legally required to fast on eight nights for which (p. 37) there was no legal requirement previously. One is the night before Christmas, two is the night before Easter, three is the night before Ascension Day, four is the night before Whitsunday, and then the four Wednesday nights in Lent that were not previously included in the law.[97]

A second new law was that where marriages are arranged people may wed in the same degree of affinity and kindred, in each case in the fifth degree. Where kinship is in the fifth degree, a capital tithe is to be paid.[98] Where kinship is in the fifth degree on one side and in the sixth on the other, 120 ells are to be paid. When both are in the sixth degree, 10 ounce-units are to be paid. No fee is to be paid from that point onwards should a marriage be arranged.

Marriage within fifth and sixth degrees

It used to be law that a man should contribute 10 ounce-units towards the maintenance of a needy kinsman if they were related in the fifth degree but that is now abolished.[99]

Abolition of law to do with maintenance of kinsmen

K ‡ 19
Calendar

The first day of summer is to be a Thursday; from then three months of thirty nights and four nights in addition are to be counted to midsummer. From midsummer there are to be three months of thirty nights to winter.[100] The first day of winter is to be a Saturday and from then there shall be six months of thirty nights to summer; and ten weeks of summer are to have passed when men come to the General Assembly.[101] Throughout the calendar a day precedes a night.

Division of the year

All the laws are to be recited over three summers. Then the Lawspeaker is to relinquish the law-speaking.[102] No new law is to have effect for more than three summers and it is to be announced at Lögberg the first summer and at formally inaugurated spring assemblies or autumn meetings. All new laws become void if they are not included in the recital every third summer.[103]

*Recital of laws
New laws last three summers in first instance*

---

97. Cf. ‡ 15 (p. 47).
98. Cf. ‡ 144.
99. Cf. ‡ 143.
100. From Thursday, April 9-15 to Monday, July 13-19 (midsummer); then to Saturday, October 11-17.
101. Thursday, June 18-24.
102. Cf. ‡‡ 116-17 (pp. 187-93); cf. *Íslendingabók*, Ch. 7 (*ÍF* I 15).
103. AM 58 8vo, fol. 117r (III 443), written early in the seventeenth century has this note: "On new laws. All new laws are to be put to Lögberg [sic] for three summers, thereafter regarded as law." The phrase "put to Lögberg" presumably means "announced at Lögberg as part of the Lawspeaker's recital." The antiquity of this is doubtful.

Assembly Procedures Section

K ‡ 20; p. 38

It is prescribed in our laws that we shall have four Quarter Courts. Each chieftain who has an ancient and full chieftaincy shall nominate a man to join a court. And those are full and ancient chieftaincies which existed when there were three assemblies in each Quarter and three chieftains in each assembly. The assemblies were then not split up.[1] If chieftaincies are divided into shares, then those who have part of ancient chieftaincies are to arrange it so that nomination is made in the way now told. Then the Quarter Courts are complete. *Quarter courts* *Chieftaincies*

It is prescribed that the courts are to be nominated or decided today.[2] Each chieftain is to nominate a man from his assembly third to join a court unless he has leave from the Law Council to do otherwise. A male of twelve winters or more, capable of taking responsibility for what he says or swears, free, and with a settled home, is to be nominated. A man who is a principal in prosecution or defense or who has a transferred prosecution or defense in a case now prepared for the Assembly is not to be nominated to join a court. A man who has not learnt to speak the Norse language in his childhood is not to be nominated to join a court until he has been in Iceland three winters or more. *Nomination of judges* *Disqualifications*

If a man such as has now been excluded allows himself to be nominated to join a court or transfers a case to someone else because he wishes to have himself nominated to join a court, then he is fined three marks for that, and any cases he had are invalid, whether prosecutions or defenses, unless he gets a panel verdict (p. 39) that he did not know that cases were prepared against him.

If a chieftain nominates a man who has been excluded to join a court or nominates to a court other than the one allotted,[3] then for either he is fined three marks and forfeits his chieftaincy, unless he gets a panel verdict that he did not know that the man had a transferred prosecution or defense or was the principal in a prosecution or defense. The chief-

---

1. On this cf. Introduction, pp. 2-3.
2. Friday, June 19-25, the day after the Assembly gathered.
3. The precise meaning of this is not clear; it perhaps refers to contravention of a given order of nomination.

tain is to be summoned at Lögberg and neighbors of his are to be called and the case lies with anyone who wishes to prosecute.

Nomination formula

A chieftain is to go to Hamraskarð[4] and seat his judge there if he wishes to nominate him to join a court, and name two witnesses or more — "I name witnesses to witness that I nominate this good man and true to join the court" — and name him by name — "to judge all those suits that come here before this court and the law requires him to judge. And I invite prosecutor and defendant to challenge this court, and I am content that he should have a seat in the court unless rightful rejection at law arises. Then if he is dismissed in accordance with law, I shall nominate another qualified man in his place." And state which court he nominates him to join. "And I nominate a lawful court."

Judges available for challenge

The courts are to go out on Saturday and be out for challenging until the sun comes onto Þingvöllr on Sunday.[5]

If it is not then possible to go dryshod to Hólmrinn.[6]

K ‡ 21
On Publishings

Time of publishing at the Assembly

Men must publish today and tomorrow all the suits which are to go before a Quarter Court. But it is equally right to publish on Monday if men[7] wish to include that in the assembly procedure. And similarly if men wish to publish in tithe suits — men who are (p. 40) selected for that prosecution or who are principals or who have taken over cases from principals — these must have published their suits no later than has now been told. But other men have the right to publish in tithe suits up to the time the courts go out.[8]

Manner of publishing

If a man wishes to publish a suit against someone, he is to name three witnesses or more — "I name witnesses to witness that I publish a suit against him" — and name him by name, and state the suit, and the penalty he claims he is liable to. He is to publish it at Lögberg at a time when the majority of men and the Lawspeaker are present, and publish a legal publishing, and as a transferred case if it is one, and publish it for judgment in a Quarter Court. And he is to say if it is a suit which he published the previous summer.

---

4. The probable location of this is marked on Map II.
5. Sunday, June 21-27, sunrise approximately 0200. See ‡ 25 (pp. 59-63).
6. It is uncertain what this introduced, perhaps something on the procession described in ‡ 24 (p. 59). *Hólmrinn* "the island" is in the River Öxará, see Map II.
7. I.e., men of the Law Council, cf. ‡ 117 (pp. 189-93).
8. On tithes see ‡‡ 4-5, 255-60. Courts did not go out to hear cases before the first Monday of the Assembly, June 22-28. On what follows cf. Add. ‡ 94.

K ‡ 22
To Ask about People's Assembly Attachment

Men may ask about the assembly attachment of people they wish to prosecute here at the Assembly, and ask today; or if they wish to challenge a court, ask tomorrow, though it is also lawful to ask up to the time courts go out to hear prosecutions.[9] The man who wants to learn another man's assembly membership is to name witnesses — "I name witnesses to witness," he shall say, "that I ask all householders out loud at Lögberg who has formally guaranteed N.N. legal domicile. What concerns me in that query is that I wish to know which neighbors I am to call in the case I have begun against him. I ask a legal asking." He is to name witnesses to the answers he gets if someone admits the residence of the man he asked about, and similarly if no one admits it. He shall name witnesses again "to witness that I ask all chieftains, out loud at Lögberg, who recognises N.N. as a man of his assembly group or his assembly third. What concerns me in this query is that I wish to know in which Quarter Court I am to prosecute a case against him. I ask a legal asking." He is (p. 41) to name witnesses to the answers he gets. And if someone admits the assembly attachment of the man asked about, then he has to bring his case before the court for the Quarter to which the chieftain who admitted his assembly attachment belongs. He has to call on that chieftain to form a panel of twelve if it is a case in which a panel of twelve is appropriate. But it is also lawful to ask the man himself about his legal domicile and his assembly membership and that is as satisfactory as when a chieftain admits his assembly attachment. It is lawful for a chieftain to admit a man's assembly attachment as long as lots have not been cast for the order of presenting cases[10] and provided he has not already been called on to form a panel of twelve. Further it is equally lawful to admit a man's assembly attachment before witnesses elsewhere than at Lögberg should he meet the other party in person.

Asking legal domicile

Asking assembly attachment

If someone has asked a man elsewhere about his residence and assembly membership, he does not need to ask at the Assembly about the assembly membership of a man he asked about it without guile elsewhere.

If a man has summoned someone before the moving days in a case which involves a panel of twelve and he has not asked him elsewhere about his assembly membership, the summons having been made at his home, then at the Assembly he is to ask about his assembly membership within the Quarter in which he had his home when he summoned him;

---

9. Challenging of judges was to be done by early Sunday, cf. p. 54, n. 5; asking about assembly attachment for other purposes could be done up to the time courts went out, cf. p. 54, n. 8.

10. Cf. ‡ 29 (pp. 64-65).

and ask all the chieftains at Lögberg which of them recognized that man as one of his assembly group or assembly third before the moving days. "What concerns me in that query is that I wish to know which chieftain I am to call on to form a panel of twelve in the case I have summoned him to answer. I ask a legal asking."

Witnesses to every question and answer or failure to answer

Whenever a man asks another man a legal asking or if he asks several men, he is to name witnesses to the asking and to the answers and also if there is no answer.

In cases which a man published last summer for prosecution here or for which he made the summons before the moving days without knowing the home of the man summoned, he is to ask who recognized that man as his assembly man last summer, if he did not ask then.

If assembly attachment or residence is not admitted

When a man's assembly attachment is not admitted, the case is to be brought before the Quarter Court for the Quarter the principal is in (p. 42). If a man's residence is not admitted in a case involving a panel of neighbors, then neighbors of the principal of the original suit are to be called, and similarly if a man's assembly membership or his residence is not admitted, and similarly too if a man does not answer when asked in person or if he answers with a deception at law; and it is a deception at law if a man answers other than the truth or stays silent. If a man is asked about his assembly membership and answers other than the truth, the penalty is a fine. It is moreover lawful to call on the man to whose assembly group he says he belongs to form a panel of twelve, and it shall then be judged that the panel verdict goes against the defendant if that man maintains — whatever objections the other makes — that he does not belong to his assembly group or if he says he is not acting in a chieftaincy.

Deception at law

It is only needful to ask a second time about a man's assembly attachment if he asked him about it before the Assembly and then the man in whose assembly group he said he was, or the man who admitted it if he asked about it the previous summer, does not come to the Assembly — then he has to ask who is now acting in that chieftaincy. If men have not admitted the assembly attachment or residence of a man asked about before the courts go out, or similarly if a man answers nothing when asked in person or answers with a deception at law, and then tries to use it as a defense, that the prosecutor brings the case before a court other than the one it should come before, or that some chieftain other than the one whose assembly group he belongs to gives a panel-of-twelve verdict on him, or that it is not his own neighbors who give a verdict on him should that be appropriate, then the prosecutor is to bring before the court in which the case is prosecuted the testimony of his asking about the man's assembly attachment or residence, and the witnesses he named to witness that it was not admitted or those he named to witness the deception at law.

If a man (p. 43) is asked about the assembly group he belongs to and he does not know, he answers lawfully if he answers that "I am lodging with so-and-so" — and name the householder. If a man is asked about the assembly group he belongs to and more men than one own the chieftaincy he follows, he answers lawfully if he answers that "I am in the assembly group with [that one] of them who acts in the chieftaincy" — and name the men who own shares in that chieftaincy. *Right and wrong answers*

If a chieftain admits a man's assembly attachment when he is asked but the man does not belong to his assembly group, he is fined three marks for that and forfeits the chieftaincy, unless he gets a panel verdict that the man had been in that assembly group and had left without his knowledge: then he has a defense in the case. If a chieftain denies the assembly attachment of a man who belongs to his assembly group, he is fined three marks for that and forfeits his chieftaincy, unless the chieftain gets a panel verdict that the man had joined the assembly group without his knowledge.

Publishing concerning maintenance of dependents may be made while the courts are sitting.¹¹

K ‡ 23
How Chieftains Are to Come to the Assembly

All chieftains are to come to the Assembly before the sun leaves Þingvöllr¹² on the Thursday when ten weeks of summer have passed, and if they do not come in this way they pay fines and forfeit their chieftaincy unless some necessity occurs to prevent their coming. The chieftains of the same assembly group have to decide which of the men belonging to the assembly third of the chieftain who stays at home should act in that chieftaincy and take it up. *If a chieftain does not arrive at the proper time*

(p. 44) Assembly participants are to come to the Assembly on Thursday and go to the same booth¹³ as the chieftain to whose assembly group they belong, and each shall bring an awning to reach across the booth. Each of them shall then receive but not pay assembly attendance dues, and each of them is then an assembly participant for his own affairs and for those of others. The chieftain is then required to provide him with booth space. If he does not provide it, his assembly man is under no legal penalty if he goes to another booth, and he still has the right to claim assembly attendance dues. *Arrival of assembly participants; their dues and accommodation*

If a man does not come to the beginning of the Assembly but does

---
11. On dependents see ‡‡ 128-43.
12. At this time of year the sun sets at about 2300 but it leaves the assembly ground much sooner, at about 2030, because of the land-rise to the west.
13. See p. 43, n. 69.

come on the first Sunday of the Assembly, he is still an assembly participant for his own affairs and for those of others, and he is not to pay assembly attendance dues but he is not to receive them either; and he shall not leave the Assembly before the close of the Assembly unless it is permitted. If he leaves, the penalty is lesser outlawry. It is lawful for him to receive assembly attendance dues if he joins courts or gives panel verdicts. It is lawful to nominate men to join a court who come to the Assembly before courts are nominated.

Time of arrival for prosecutors, defendants, and men called to attend

All men who have to prosecute cases or defend them or men who are called to attend the Assembly and to be there on the first Sunday of the Assembly, if they do not come in this way, the cases and the defenses they bring forward are invalid and the witness they were called locally to bear is worthless.

If a man comes after the first Sunday of the Assembly then he is not an assembly participant, either for his own affairs or for those of others, and he may ride from the Assembly when he likes, and he is to pay assembly attendance dues but not receive them.

Agreement on what dues are to be paid

Men shall pay assembly attendance dues at the rate they agree on with the chieftain in each assembly third.

Temporary absence from the Assembly

Assembly participants are not to be away from the Assembly for a night or longer. They are away from the Assembly if they are outside the Assembly boundaries.[14] Men may go to look for their horses by day if that does not delay production of formal means of proof or court nominations by a chieftain, (p. 45) should he wish to nominate them to join a court or to have them join him in some legal duties. But if they go away, that is assembly-balking and the penalty is lesser outlawry.

What men are assembly participants

Householders are assembly participants and chieftains and those men who are called locally to attend the assembly and to provide formal means of proof.

An assembly participant who does not join his chieftain

If an assembly participant does not go to the same booth as the chieftain to whose assembly group he belongs and the chieftain wishes to prosecute him for it, he is to summon him at Lögberg and make a three-mark fine the penalty and summon him there to judgment. If the other takes it on himself to leave that chieftain's assembly third because he was prosecuted, his penalty is a fine of three marks at the suit of the chieftain, and that case is to be summoned locally and five neighbors of the man prosecuted called at the Assembly to decide whether it was for that reason that he left the assembly third or not.

---

14. The exact boundaries are not known.

K ‡ 24
On Going to Lögberg

We shall go to Lögberg tomorrow[15] and move the courts out for challenging at the latest when the sun is on the western ravine crag, seen from the Lawspeaker's seat at Lögberg.[16] The Lawspeaker is to go first if he is in good enough health; then the chieftains with their judges if not prevented — otherwise each of them is to procure someone in his place. Then the chieftains are to seat their judges and the authority of any man now selected to act in a chieftancy has the same validity. The Lawspeaker shall decide and state where each court is to sit, and the Lawspeaker shall have the bell rung for the courts to move out.[17] *Order of procession*

Places appointed for courts

It is lawful for those who have come here on the (p. 46) first Sunday of the Assembly to prosecute and defend cases but not for anyone who comes later, unless events occur to give rise to suits or such events become known so late that they could not get to the Assembly sooner than after the Sunday — then those men will be prosecutors of cases and assembly participants in all the cases they had to conduct, provided they come so early that they can go about the making of callings before the courts move out. They do not have the right to challenge courts in their suits. *Cases arising too late for principal to arrive at proper time*

K ‡ 25
Challenging a Court

The man who wants to challenge a court is to go to where the man he wants to remove sits in the court and speak so that he or the chieftain who nominated him to join the court can hear. If neither of them is there, it is nevertheless lawful for him to speak the words of challenge at the place where he thinks the man he wants to remove from the court was sitting; and it is moreover lawful for him to proceed in the matter even though he is quite uncertain where the other's place has been.

Prosecutors of cases and defenders of cases may challenge a court if they wish and shall swear oaths to it. If a man wishes to challenge a court he is to name witnesses. "I name witnesses to witness that I swear an oath on the Cross, a lawful oath, and declare before God that I shall reject a man from court in the way I think most true and right and most in accordance with law." If he does not [wish] to swear an oath again,[18] he is to add: "And that I shall prosecute cases in the same way," he shall *Challenging formula on oath*

Oath can be extended to

---

15. I.e. Saturday.
16. There was probably a specific mark on the western cliff of Almannagjá (see Map II) used as a day mark. The time referred to is thought to have been approximately 1330.
17. Most likely a church bell.
18. Cf. ‡ 35 (p. 75).

cover other business

Proving family connections

Men who may challenge without support of others

Challenge on grounds of relationship with principal

Anyone may call for clearing verdict for someone unrepresented; limited right of challenge

Who is disqualified

Formulas

say, "and defend them and give testimony and bear witness and perform all legal duties that fall to me while I am at this Assembly."

A man must (p. 47) begin an enumeration of kinship with brothers, or with a brother and sister, or with sisters, and enumerate the family branches until he reaches the man who sits in the court and the man who is principal in the prosecution or defense. If the man who enumerates the kinship is of remoter kin than second cousin to the prosecution principal or defense principal, he does not need other men to vouch on their word of honor for his enumeration of kinship. If in his enumeration he uses an either-or definition of the kinship in question, the judge is not required to withdraw from the court. If a man enumerates wrong or bears false witness at the General Assembly, the penalty is outlawry. Challenges are to be made on grounds of connection with those who are principals in a case.

It is lawful for anyone who wishes to call for panels to give clearing verdicts for a man against whom a prosecution is brought if the latter is not at the Assembly and has not transferred his defense to anyone. [A man] who has not taken over the defense of a man prosecuted [may] not challenge a court but he may challenge any panels he wants to. Both those who prosecute and those who defend have equal rights of challenge.

Second cousins have to withdraw from the court and closer kinsmen and those disqualified by legal involvement[19] and three close kinsmen by marriage: whether it is the man who sits in the court or the principal who is married to the daughter or sister or mother of the other. And men related by three kinds of spiritual kinship have to withdraw from the court: if either of them stood sponsor for the other at prime-signing or at baptism or at confirmation.[20] A man is not to challenge on grounds of his own spiritual kinship with a judge.

Men are to name witnesses "to witness that I give my word of honor that that enumeration of kinship between them is right and true," and name both the man to be removed from the court and the principal.

If he challenges on grounds of kinship by marriage: "that I give my word of honor that kinship by marriage exists between them in that he is married to such-and-such a woman (p. 48) or was married to her when I knew of it." His word of honor is rightly given even if the man is divorced from the woman but the man is not then required to withdraw from the court.

When a man wants to challenge on grounds of spiritual kinship he is to give his word of honor on the spiritual kinship between the principal and

---

19. This seems to refer to the claims to kindred payments that automatically arose after a killing, in accordance with the wergild ring list, see ‡ 113 (pp. 175-83).

20. Cf. p. 26, n. 6.

the judge and name each of them.

If he is to challenge a court on grounds of legal involvement, he is to enumerate the kinship between the man who sits in the court and the killer and the principal and the man killed, and give his word of honor that the [enumeration] of kinship between them now made is true and right, and that such-and-such cases are at issue between the principal and the man who sits in the court, and name each by name. Challenge on grounds of legal involvement is to be made with reference to the man chosen as the killer in accordance with law and not with reference to more men even though they were present at the killing.[21]

If the man who gave his word of honor is not qualified to enumerate kinship, he is to have two other men who give their word of honor that the enumeration of kinship made by him — and name him — is true and right. The men who vouch for this are to swear the oaths that should go with giving one's word of honor.[22] In selecting men to vouch for this, regard is to be had to their kinship with principals in that they must be remoter than second cousins.

Men to vouch for enumeration of kinship; qualifications

The challenger has to name witnesses to witness "that I dismiss you from the court" — and name him — "because a rightful rejection at law has now arisen" — and state whether he dismisses him with his own dismissal or someone else's.[23] If he will not withdraw from the court and means moreover to stay there, that is assembly-balking and the penalty is lesser outlawry. Then he is to forbid him his seat by veto.

If a judge refuses to leave

If the chieftain has not personally heard his challenge, nor the man who is removed, then the challenger is to go to the chieftain's booth and tell him that he has rejected from the court a man of his assembly third and state which court it is and name the man by name and name his father or mother. If the chieftain will not believe that he has lawfully rejected him, then (p. 49) the challenger is required to speak all the words in front of the chieftain which he spoke when he removed him from the court, except that he does not need to swear the oath. If he cannot get inside the booth, he is to speak at the booth doorway so that it carries in to them. If they cannot get to the booth, they are to speak the words of challenge as close to the booth as they can get. If they go into the booth and there are booth residents who have cases conferring rights of veto[24] at issue with them, then they are to go out again and the first who came in last.

Informing a chieftain that his judge is dismissed

21. Cf. Add. ‡ 57.
22. In this case it is presumably meant that the men who vouch for it swear an introductory general oath (pp. 59-60, 75) and then continue with the relevant "word of honor" formula (p. 60).
23. Whether he acts in his own or in a transferred case.
24. Cf. ‡‡ 80 (p. 132), 113 (pp. 175, 182-83).

A chieftain must nominate a new judge and not conceal the nomination

If the chieftain permits the challenger to leave unspoken the words of challenge a second time, the challenger is to name witnesses to the permission, and the chieftain is then required to nominate forthwith some other man to join the court, so that the challenger sees him doing so if he wishes to keep an eye on it. If the challenger did not see whom the chieftain nominated the second time to join the court, the chieftain is required to tell the challenger whom he nominated to join the court if he asks, and name the judge and also his father or mother if they were Icelandic. If the chieftain will not say, then the challenger is to name witnesses "to witness," he shall say, "that I ask you" — and name the chieftain — "to say whom you nominated to join the court. I ask a legal asking." If the chieftain does not say, he is fined and forfeits his chieftaincy. If he does not find the chieftain, he is to ask at his place and say which booth he belongs to.[25] If the chieftain avoids meeting him to the end that he should not find out whom he has nominated to join the court or delays court nominations to the end that fewer judges get[26] challenged, the penalty is a fine and forfeit of his chieftaincy.

Mistaken pledge of word of honor only invalidates when a marriage has ended in divorce

When men challenge courts, the man who is dismissed is required to withdraw from the court if the words of challenge are spoken in accordance with (p. 50) law even though words of honor were wrongly given, except in cases where men give their word of honor on kinship by marriage and the man who sits in the court is divorced from the woman in question.[27] Then the chieftain is to go out and nominate a man to join the court and have named him before the sun has come onto Þingvöllr[28] if there is time enough for that.

A chieftain procures a new judge, if necessary, from his fellow chieftains

If the chieftain has no man from his assembly third available to nominate to join the court, and the challenges go that way, then he is to ask the chieftains who have chieftaincies in the same assembly to provide him with a man from their assembly thirds and nominate him to join the court. They are required to provide him with a man if they have one available. If one of them has a man available and the other not, the one who has is required to provide him, and he is required to join the court as if the chieftain to whose assembly third he belongs had nominated him. But if he does not join it, his penalty is lesser outlawry, and if he does join it, he is to take there an assembly man belonging to the chieftain who nominated him to join the court.[29] But if the chieftains disagree as to

---

25. The "place" is probably the chieftain's seat in the Law Council, cf. ‡ 117 (p. 190); the "booth" is probably that of the challenger (but cf. ‡ 35, p. 71).

26. Omitting an apparently redundant *verða*, "to be; are."

27. Cf. p. 60.

28. See p. 54, n. 5.

29. I.e., as a court-guard, see ‡ 41 (p. 80).

which of them is to provide him with a man, they are to draw lots, and the one to whom it falls is to provide him if he has men available. If only one of them has a man available, then he is required to provide him, and if he will not, he is fined and forfeits his chieftaincy.

If a chieftain has not completed his nomination to a court before the sun comes onto Þingvöllr,[30] then he is fined and forfeits his chieftaincy, and similarly if he nominates some man other than he ought to join a court. A court then has to judge all suits as if the court were complete. Courts are not to be challenged after the sun comes onto Þingvöllr. A chieftain is to be prosecuted by the man among those bringing cases before that court who is willing to prosecute him to the limit of the law; and if they disagree, they are to draw lots and the one to whom it falls is to prosecute.

Time limit for nominating and challenging judges

Who prosecutes a chieftain who neglects his duties

K ‡ 26; p. 51
On Testimony

A man is to have called all the witnesses and panel members that are required for his conduct of the original suit, before the court goes out.

It is lawful to call on a chieftain to form a panel of twelve before the court goes out and also at the court. The calling is rightly made if the chieftain hears it himself or if it is made at his place or if his booth-mates hear it. When a man wants to call for a panel of twelve, he is to name witnesses "to witness," he shall say, "that I ask you" — and name the chieftain — "whether you act in a full chieftaincy which authorizes you to nominate complete courts and give panel-of-twelve verdicts. I ask a legal asking." If he says he does, then the man asking is to name witnesses to his answers, "and to witness," he shall say, "that I call on you to form a panel of twelve" — and name the chieftain and state what he calls on him for — "and to give a verdict with eleven men of your assembly third and you yourself are to be the twelfth. I call a legal calling."

Calling for a panel of twelve

K ‡ 27
Calling Neighbors

If a man wishes to call a man to join a panel of neighbors, he is to go to the booth where the man is whom he wishes to call, and it is lawful for him to call him there where the other hears it, but it is also lawful for him to make the calling at the place of the man he wishes to call so that his booth-mates hear it. If a man does not know whether the man he wants to call is a householder or a household man, he is to ask him before witnesses whether he is a householder or a household man and say what concerns him in the inquiry and ask a legal asking (p. 52) and name

Queries to identify status of man to be called

---

30. See p. 54, n. 5.

witnesses to the answers he gets. If he wants to call a man who is an assembly participant on behalf of someone else's household, he is to ask before witnesses — if he does not know already — whether he has his legal home there or not, or whether he is an assembly participant on behalf of the household of such-and-such a person, and name the householder.[31] Whether he calls him is to depend on the answers given by the man asked. But if the man asked will not say or lies about it, he is under penalty for three marks and the case lies with the man who asked him or with the neighbor who is called instead of him if the former will not bring the case. The summons in the case is to be made at Lögberg and five neighbors of the man prosecuted are to be called. If a man calls a household man and thought he was a householder or calls a household man on behalf of someone else's household when he did not have his legal home there, that calling is lawful — should men try to oppose him on those grounds — if he gets a panel verdict that he called the man he thought best qualified and had had no opportunity of asking. If a man calls a household man to join a panel of neighbors or calls a man who is not an assembly participant on behalf of someone else's household and calls them so that they themselves hear his calling and he has the opportunity of asking for legal information if he wants to, then he makes his own case void. He saves himself by a clearing verdict that, though he called them, he did not call them in their hearing.

False answer or none: penalty and procedure

Mistakes in calling may make a case void

K ‡ 28
Moving out Courts

Courts are to be moved out on the day men[32] appoint, and not later than the time when the sun comes onto the higher ravine side seen from Lögberg from the Lawspeaker's place.[33] Then the Lawspeaker and (p. 53) all the chieftains are required to go out with their judges and also the men who have the conduct of cases. A man who conducts a case is fined if he goes to court with more than ten men.

Neither party to bring more than ten men to court

K ‡ 29
On Drawing Lots

If six or more judges have come out, it is lawful for a man who has the conduct of a case to invite all the men who have cases to bring before that court to draw lots at the court and to appoint the place where they are to draw lots on presenting their cases. Each man who has a case to conduct before the court is to put one lot into the cloth, even though he has more

Order of cases arranged by lot

---

31. Cf. ‡ 89 (pp. 151-52).
32. I.e., men of the Law Council; not before the first Monday of the Assembly, June 22-28.
33. Cf. p. 59, n. 16.

than one case to bring before the court. Each man is to mark his own lot and all the lots are to be put into the cloth and someone is to draw out four at a time.

If a man who has a case to prosecute does not come out by the time the sun is on the western ravine slope, seen from the Lawspeaker's place,[34] he is under penalty for three marks for that and the case lies with the man he has a suit against. The summons in the case is to be made at Lögberg and five neighbors of the man prosecuted are to be called. If he gets a panel verdict that he would have come out sooner had the sun been visible, he has a defense in the case. *Case against prosecutor who does not come to court at proper time*

Those whose lots are drawn are to present their cases first and then one after another as their lots are drawn. If some do not come to the lot drawing, they are to present their cases last. It is also lawful for someone else to put a man's lot into the cloth for him, and the order in which the cases are presented shall then be in accordance with the lots they draw. Cases, not more than four in number and not less than four either, in which no judgment was reached last summer are not to be subject to lot. If there are more than four, they are to draw lots for them.[35] All these cases are to be presented first and then any cases (p. 54) that have arisen here at the Assembly. If the man whose lot is drawn first is not ready, then the man whose lot is drawn next is to ask his permission to present his case first, and he is to permit him to do so; and if he does not permit him, it is lawful for him to present his case if the judges permit and the other is not ready. *Cases left from previous summer*

Possible re-arrangement of order

K ‡ 30
Inviting Men to Hear Oath-Taking

The man who intends to present a case is to name witnesses — "I name them to witness that I invite the man I intend to prosecute here" — or the man who has the defense for him, and the chieftain who is to give a panel-of-twelve verdict on the man he has a case against — "to hear my oath-taking and my presentation of the case."

K ‡ 31
On Presenting a Case

He is to swear to it on oath that it is his case he is presenting and state whom he summoned and for what he summoned him and what he made his penalty and state to which assembly he summoned him, and that he summoned with a legal summons, and that he presents his case before the *Summoning*

---

34. Cf. p. 59, n. 16.

35. It is not clear what happened if fewer than four cases were held over from the preceding year; presumably they joined the lottery. Cf. ‡ 46 (p. 85).

Testimony of summoning

court, speaking especially to N.N.,[36] in the same form as he summoned him.

Then one of the witnesses is to utter the testimony and use all the words in testifying that the prosecutor used in summoning the defendant, and the other witnesses are to give their assent to his testifying, but it is lawful for them to be speedier in their testifying. They are to state whom the prosecutor summoned and what he claimed his penalty was, and that he had used all the same words as he used in presenting his case, and had summoned (p. 55) with a legal summons, "and that is the testimony of us all," they shall say, "and we bring testimony in such form before the court." But if they disagree, they are to draw lots to decide who is to bring forward the testimony, and the one whose lot is drawn is to utter it.

If the preliminary oath is omitted

If a man presents his case without swearing an oath to it, it is as if he had not presented the case and he is to swear an oath and present the case a second time and have testimony of the summoning brought, and if he goes about it in that way his case is not spoilt but it must not happen to him more than once. If testimony is brought without an oath sworn to it, it is as if it were not brought, and the witnesses are to swear oaths and[37] thereupon bring testimony of the summoning, and his case is not spoilt if it does not happen to them more than once. If he presents his case without inviting them to hear his oath-taking[38] or his presentation of the case, it is as if the case had not been presented. He is to present the case a second time and speak in every way as if he had not spoken on it previously, and on those terms he saves the suit as long as no other formal means of proof have been brought forward in the meantime. If a man presents a case in which a panel of twelve has to figure and does not invite the chieftain to hear it, he is required to present it a second time before the panel of twelve unless the chieftain permits otherwise.

If the preliminary invitation to listen to oath and presentation is omitted

If the preliminary invitation to chieftain is omitted where panel of twelve is needed

K ‡ 32
If Witnesses Stay at Home

Suit against witness who fails to attend

If the witnesses of a man's summoning do not come to the Assembly as prescribed in the laws, he is to summon them at Lögberg for staying at home and make lesser outlawry their penalty. It is lawful for him to summon them, as he prefers, either on the first Monday (p. 56) of the Assembly[39] or when he has to have recourse to them. He is to present his

---

36. The precise meaning of the Icelandic expression here, *yfir höfði N.N.*, literally "over N.N.'s head," is uncertain. In *Njáls saga*, Ch. 144, N.N. is identified as the judge appointed to do the summing up, cf. ‡ 40 (p. 79).

37. The second scribe of K begins here with the word *ok* "and".

38. Cf. ‡ 30 (p. 65).

39. Assembly participants were to arrive not later than the first Sunday of the Assembly. Cf. ‡ 23 (p. 58).

case against them before the same court as the original suit should come before. He shall have testimony brought of his calling the man locally to attend the Assembly.[40] He is to call five neighbors of the man he is prosecuting to give a verdict as to whether the latter had arrived here on the first Sunday of the Assembly or not, and if they give a verdict that he had not arrived here on the first Sunday of the Assembly, he becomes a lesser outlaw for that unless as a legal defense he can get a verdict that he is not assembly-fit on account of some ailment, and this verdict has to be given by five of his neighbors, and the man who has the defense for him has to call them to give this verdict, and he has a successful defense in the suit if he gets one of the clearing verdicts listed for this purpose.[41]

If only one summons witness is present

If only one summons witness is at the Assembly, he shall testify to the summoning, as long as the men who witnessed the calling of the summons witnesses are present, and five men are to support his testimony and give their word of honor that those who stay at home were also named as witnesses of what he has testified. Such men are to support his testimony as would qualify to be witnesses of the summoning made by a principal in the case.

If no summons witnesses are present

If all summons witnesses stay at home, or similarly if they withhold their testimony, having been called, their penalty is lesser outlawry. The prosecutor shall then call five of his neighbors to hear his presentation and to give a verdict as to whether he had named the same men as summons witnesses as he named when he presented his case, and whether he had made the summons in the case in the same form as he presented it before the court.

If calling witnesses are absent

If a man lacks witnesses of his calling of men to attend the Assembly, his case is not spoilt as long as he did not permit them to stay at home and a panel gives a verdict that he had had such calling witnesses as he thought would attend the Assembly, and they are known as "reliance witnesses."[42] He is to call five neighbors of his instead of the calling witnesses, if these have not come to the Assembly, to give a verdict as to whether he had, as he says, called locally (p. 57) this man who has stayed at home — and name him — or whether he had not. The same neighbors are to decide on that as gave the verdict on whether the man who was called was not at the Assembly on the Sunday.[43]

Procedural order

After every case is presented, testimony of the summoning is to come next, but then it does not affect the case how the formal means of proof are produced.[44]

40. A formula for calling a witness is in Add. ‡ 61.
41. On grounds of sickness or other necessity.
42. Named as witnesses but not themselves specifically called to attend the Assembly.
43. Cf. ll. 3-4 above; there is a discrepancy in the definition of the panel ("five neighbors of the man he is prosecuting," "five neighbors of his", the latter supported by ‡ 33, p. 70).
44. But testimony should always precede panel verdicts, cf. ‡‡ 33, 37 (pp. 70, 76).

Framing and delivering witness

If a man has to prosecute a case in which testimony figures, he has to ask the witnesses to frame the wording of it and deliver it. Witnesses are first to swear oaths and then give their testimony. They give their testimony rightly if they utter all the words they were named to witness. If they rightly utter the words they were named to witness but leave out some which affect the case, that is false witness. If a man rightly utters all the words he was named to witness but adds some words which affect the case and which he was not named to witness, that is false witness. If a man does not speak every word in the form in which he was named to witness it and it does not affect the case, the testimony is rightly given in spite of this.

Testimony rightly delivered, and false witness

Disagreement among witnesses

As soon as they are agreed, one of them is to utter the testimony and the others give their assent. If they do not all agree on the same thing, then those in the majority are to prevail, and a man from that group is to utter the testimony. The minority are to give their assent, because they do not have the numbers to do otherwise, but when that testimony is given, they are to say that they would have given different testimony if they had the numbers, and state what testimony they would give, and this is then not false witness on their part even if the majority are prosecuted for that. If they turn out to be equal in number, the two groups who each want to give their own version, then those are to prevail who give longer testimony, in words that affect the case between them, unless that proves to be false witness. If they each give testimony of the same length and are equal in number, then it shall be deemed that the testimony is given in favor of the man who called them to give testimony.

Resignation of witness called in error

If a man is called to bear witness when he thinks he should not be, he is (p. 58) nevertheless to go to the Assembly and resign at court and swear an oath first and name witnesses and speak in this way: "I resign from this witnessing" — and state what it is — "I resign from it because I was not named for it." And if he was named for it, his penalty is as if he bore false witness. The penalty for the man who called him when he had not been named as a witness is lesser outlawry, unless he called him because he thought he really had been named as a witness. A man called locally to give testimony in this way may choose to make the summons in the case at Lögberg and prosecute the same summer, but he may also choose to prosecute later.

At least twenty men must be present at summons or publishing at Lögberg except in maintenance suits

There are never to be fewer than twenty men present when men make a summons or publish suits at Lögberg, except in cases concerning dependents.[45]

When witnesses are called, it is not required of them that they should testify if the man calling them is vague in his approach or recollection,

---

45. See ‡ 39 (p. 78).

unless when they were named as witnesses they consented to testify even though there were only two of them — in that case they are to testify all the same.

It is required of witnesses that they testify to everything they were named to witness if they are called as prescribed in the laws.

A man must have called his witnesses or neighbors locally at the latest a fortnight before the Assembly. But if a man's witness falls ill or is wounded, the witness is to send word to the man who called him to attend the Assembly to come to see him at the place he appoints or to the sick man's home if he thinks himself incapable of moving. The man who called him is to send word to the other men he has called to attend the Assembly, and they are to go to see this man, and the sick man is to frame the wording of the testimony in their presence, and he is to swear an oath before they do this. He is to frame the wording of the testimony as they agree and speak all the words as if at court.[46] Two men are to take over his testimony, but if two witnesses fall ill, then it is lawful for three men to take over the testimony of the two of them, and it is then equally valid (p. 59) if they testify what the others who were the original witnesses would have testified.

If a man arrives at a ship with his goods and is called to be a witness and to attend the Assembly, and his goods are on board and afloat, then he is to proceed as if he were sick, but if he does not wish to go to the Assembly, it is for him to go to see the man who has called him and to invite him to come to a meeting with witnesses and frame the wording of the testimony.[47]

K ‡ 33
To Make a Claim for Aid in Response to a Calling

If a man who is not an assembly participant is called to give testimony when he had had no right to excuse himself from being named as a witness and, further, did not know that attendance at the Assembly would follow from it, it is lawful for him to claim horse and food from the man who called him and appoint where he is to bring them. It is lawful for him to make a claim for this at a place where the man calling him hears it himself or at that man's home. Attendance at the Assembly is not required of him unless a horse is brought to him fit for him to ride to the Assembly along with other men. He shall then accompany the man who called him to the Assembly, and to his booth if he will have it so, and when they come to the Assembly he is to ask him before witnesses for the food which he had claimed from him. But if the other does not allow him

---

46. Add. ‡ 62.
47. On the matter of ‡‡ 32-33 cf. ‡‡ 68, 251-52; St ‡‡ 291, 337 (II 328-29, 364).

that food, he is to summon him for that and make his penalty a fine, and he has to pay him the food as well.⁴⁸ But even if (p. 60) the other withholds food from him, he is to stay at the Assembly until he has spoken those words he was called locally to speak.

Majority of witnesses named are to be called; an exception to the rule

A man is to call locally the majority of his witnesses, those he remembers naming, unless when they were named as witnesses they consented to give testimony even though there were no more than two of them, and in that case it is sufficient for him to call only a minority of his witnesses. They are then required to give that testimony, even though it is only the two of them who are called.⁴⁹

Testimony precedes panel verdict in same suit

And where both testimony and a panel verdict are to figure in the same case, the testimony is to come before the panel verdict.⁵⁰

If all summons witnesses die or lose power of speech

If a man's summons witnesses all die or lose the power of speech, he is then to call five of his neighbors and they shall then vouch for the testimony of his summoning in the same way as when witnesses called to give testimony of summoning stay at home.⁵¹

K ‡ 34
If Neighbors Stay at Home

Suit against absent neighbor

If a neighbor called locally stays at home it is lawful to summon him at Lögberg after the first Sunday of the Assembly, and make his penalty the same as should be deemed to follow from the original suit in true and unspoilt form. It is equally lawful to summon him at the time when the panel is necessary and he discovers he is not there. He is to let the suit against him proceed straightway after the original case is presented and both before the same court, and call five neighbors of the man prosecuted to give a verdict as to whether he was at the Assembly on the first Sunday of the Assembly or not. He is to have the testimony of his calling him locally brought before the court, and it is lawful for him to call another man

Possible defense

instead of him to serve on the panel for the original case. Any man who wishes has the right to ask five neighbors of the man prosecuted for a clearing verdict as to whether he has stayed at home for such necessity (p. 61) as is prescribed as legitimate in the laws or not.⁵²

If a man is called locally to serve on a panel or give testimony when he is unable to travel full days' journeys — whatever the ailment which causes it that he is not required to attend the Assembly — that gives a legal defense. Or if a man is wrongly called, so that on that account he

---

48. Cf. Add. ‡ 61 (ii).
49. Cf. ‡ 32 (p. 69).
50. Cf. ‡ 37 (p. 76).
51. Cf. ‡ 32 (p. 67).
52. The laws prescribe recognition of necessity but do not define it except in the case of sickness.

need not go unless he wants to — whatever the deficiency in the calling which causes it that he is not required to attend the Assembly — then the case for which the calling was made is void, whether the man who was called attends or not. And when a panel has given a verdict against him for staying at home, the man conducting the case is to call another man instead of him, the neighbor who lives nearest the place for which he made his calling, drawn from those qualified to be on the panel and at the Assembly. *Replacement of absent neighbor*

If he does not get a clearing verdict that he stayed at home on account of such necessity as is prescribed as legitimate, his penalty is such as I told just now,[53] and that case is to be prosecuted once the original case is presented and testimony of the summoning given, and both cases are to come before the same court.[54] *Prosecution procedure*

K ‡ 35
To Challenge a Panel[55]

Where panels have to decide on men's affairs, then the man who has assembled a panel is to go to the court and before witnesses invite the man he has a case against — and name him — to come and challenge the panel he has assembled, and state where it is and name all the neighbors and speak so that the majority of the judges hear it if they are willing to listen, and the man who wants to challenge the panel is to go to the place. He is to swear an oath before he begins to challenge the panel. Afterwards he is to name (p. 62) witnesses "to witness that I give my word of honor that a man lives closer who has not been called" — and name him and say which booth he belongs to. But if he challenges a panel on grounds of kinship, second cousins and men of closer kin are to withdraw, and three close kinsmen by marriage, where one man is married to another's mother or daughter or sister. He is to challenge on grounds of kinship and of kinship by marriage with himself. He is to challenge on grounds of spiritual kinship those three for whom a man has stood sponsor at baptism or at prime-signing or at confirmation.[56] A man is not to challenge on grounds of his own spiritual kinship with a panel member. *Procedure for challenging on grounds of distance* *and on grounds of various kinds of kinship*

If a man is called who is so infirm that assembly attendance would not be required of him even if he were called, it is lawful to remove him. If a man is called who has less property than requires him to pay assembly attendance dues or who farms single-handed, it is lawful to remove him. *and on grounds of health and economic status*

---

53. In the first sentence of this chapter, p. 70.
54. Cf. Add. ‡ 38.
55. Cf. ‡ 25 (pp. 59-63) on challenging judges.
56. Cf. p. 26, n. 6.

Challenge on grounds of relationship with principal

Men who vouch for a challenge on grounds of kinship or distance

He is to challenge on grounds of connection with the prosecution or defense principal, no matter who conducts the case. When he challenges a panel on grounds of spiritual kinship or of kinship or of kinship by marriage, he is to have two men to vouch for it unless the man enumerating the kinship would in terms of attachment himself qualify to serve on the panel. The men who vouch for it are to be remoter than second cousins of the prosecution or defense principal. When he challenges a panel on grounds of distance,[57] he is to give his word of honor on that along with two other men, even though he is qualified to enumerate kinship.[58]

If most members of a panel are wrongly called

If challenges go in such a way that the majority of the neighbors called locally prove to be wrongly called the prosecutor's case is not spoilt if he swears to it on oath that he called those whom he thought best qualified but he is under penalty for three marks at the suit of the man he has the case against.

Dismissal from a panel

Words of challenge are to be spoken so that the majority of assembly participants hear them.[59] Afterwards he is to name witnesses to witness that he dismisses so-and-so from the panel, and state whether he dismisses him with his own dismissal or someone else's.

If all are wrongly called

If all the neighbors are wrongly called, the challenger may choose to dismiss them all at once, and have two men to vouch for it. They are to give (p. 63) their word of honor that there is a whole group of men living nearer the place for which neighbors ought to be called, and name them all and say what booths they belong to. The other is to call those instead whom the man challenging the panel names. And his case is not spoilt by a panel of neighbors he has called at the Assembly even though he has called them all wrongly in terms of proximity as long as he went about the calling in a lawful way.

A household man in place of a householder

If a household man who is a rightful assembly participant for someone's household is called, it is lawful to challenge him if he is not in settled lodging there.[60] If he will not challenge and tries to use it to spoil the other's case that a household man has given a verdict on a panel where he should not rightly be, and tries to make that spoil his opponent's case, then that case is[61] spoilt by it unless testimony comes forward that before the man was called he had answered that he had his

---

57. Because someone else qualified to join the panel lives closer to the place for which the calling is made (most often the place of action or the home of the man prosecuted).

58. Qualified to enumerate kinship without other men to vouch for his enumeration, cf. ‡ 25 (p. 60).

59. This can have been only the assembly participants involved in the particular case.

60. On this and the following cf. ‡ 89 (pp. 151-52).

61. Omitting -*at*, "not."

settled home in the household for which he was qualified to serve on panels, or unless five neighbors of the principal in question give a verdict that when he called him he thought he had his settled home in the household for which he was a rightful assembly participant and qualified to give verdicts, as long as he did not meet the man himself on the occasion when he called him and was unable to ask him about his status.

Whenever a man who is a rightful assembly participant on behalf of someone's household goes to the Assembly on behalf of a householder, the householder is required to provide him both with a horse and with food — a horse fit to ride to the Assembly — and the householder shall then not pay assembly attendance dues while the man who attends the Assembly is to receive them like other assembly participants. *Householder to supply food and horse to assembly participant on his behalf; payment and receipt of attendance dues*

The prosecutor is to name witnesses to witness that the other has finished challenging the panel or that he says he does not wish to challenge. Thereupon he shall ask the panel to deliver the verdict. It is prescribed that before a verdict is given they are first to swear oaths in the court. They are all to fit (p. 64) their words together so that they are all agreed on the same thing. They are to draw lots among themselves to decide which of them shall utter the verdict, and the man whose lot is drawn shall utter it, unless they agree on something else and then they do not need to draw lots. The others are to give their assent to the verdict. If they do not agree on what verdict they should give, those in the majority have the right to decide and they have to utter that verdict and all of them must give their assent, but the others are to say in the court that they would give a different verdict if they had the numbers to do so and state what verdict they would give. But if that proves to be a false verdict, those who wished to give a different verdict are under no legal penalty if they spoke those words in the court.[62] *End of challenging* *Oaths and delivery of verdict* *Disagreement on verdict*

If neighbors are prosecuted because a panel verdict was given later than prescribed in the laws,[63] and it is claimed in this that this amounted to withholding the verdict, they have the right to ask a panel for a clearing verdict as to whether such numbers obstructed their panel that they could not give a verdict because of it, or whether they were so involved in panels in other original suits that on that account they could not give a verdict as prescribed in the laws. They have a successful defense in the case if they get such a clearing verdict. *Defense if a panel is charged with delay*

If some of the neighbors are not involved in this way in other matters of law, they are to go to the court and name witnesses to witness that they are prepared to act on that panel as soon as they have their fellow-members.

62. Cf. ‡ 37 (pp. 76-77).
63. Cf. pp. 74 and 75.

Assembly-balking by delay

If it is so late when a panel is asked for or challenge of it invited that they cannot on that account give a verdict as early as prescribed in the laws, the panel members are under no penalty, but the man's case is void and his penalty is lesser outlawry and it is assembly-balking. If the man invited to challenge a panel dissembles, or is so slow in bringing forward his challenges or other matters he wishes to bring forward that because of (p. 65) this no verdict is rightfully given before the time prescribed, the penalty for such a man who balks the assembly thus is lesser outlawry, but the panel members are under no penalty and their verdict is moreover to be deemed as valid as if it had been given in time.

After the proper time only a favorable verdict is accepted, and it is not obligatory to prosecute for delay

If neighbors withhold a verdict in an original suit until the sun comes onto Þingvǫllr,[64] no value is to be attached to their verdict-giving when they give it later, unless they give it against the man in question; and prosecution of them for withholding a verdict is not required if they give the verdict against him, even if they have not given it before the sun comes onto Þingvǫllr. But when a verdict is withheld it is not required that more than one of the neighbors be prosecuted unless so wished.

If the wrong kind of panel is called

If a chieftain is called on to form a panel of twelve where a panel of neighbors is appropriate, or neighbors are called to give a panel verdict in a case where a panel-of-twelve verdict is appropriate, they are to go to the court and name witnesses to witness that they make it an obstruction to their verdict-giving that they are called to give a verdict in a matter on which they have no right to decide.

Panel of five for clearing verdict

Challenge of such a panel

Use of such a panel

If a man needs clearing verdicts when a panel of neighbors has already given a verdict against him, he is to call to act on that panel five neighbors who have already given the verdict against him, even when it was a panel of nine neighbors who gave the prosecution verdict against him. It is lawful for him to call them all as a company at one place. He is to invite the man who has the case against him to challenge the panel, and tell him where they are sitting, and the latter is to challenge them if there were men on the panel for the original suit who are closer neighbors and have not been called. And if he needs more clearing verdicts in the case he shall ask them to deliver all those verdicts in the court, and they are required to give all the verdicts they are asked to give in accordance with law and that affect the case between them. If defense verdicts are withheld that have been called for in accordance with law and affect the case, the penalty is lesser outlawry and it shall be deemed as if the verdicts are favorable.

If a verdict is asked on an irrelevant matter

If a man calls for a panel verdict, whether it goes with a prosecution or defense, which does not affect the case between them, his case becomes

---

64. Cf. p. 54, n. 5.

void, and people call that a "baiting verdict."⁶⁵ *Defense after an unfavorable verdict from a panel of twelve*

(p. 66) If a man needs a clearing verdict in a case where a panel of twelve has given a verdict against him, he is to call five of his neighbors.

Men are to invite challenge of all panels for original suits whether called for prosecution or defense, and they need not do that more than once. *Invitation to challenge all panels*

All men who have to speak in any legal matter before courts at the General Assembly, whether they are to prosecute cases or defend them or give testimony or act on panels, before they speak their words they shall first swear oaths so that the judges hear them. *Preliminary oaths to be sworn by everyone*

Whenever a man has sworn an oath to cover several points and doubt is raised about his oath when he comes to perform other legal acts in which oaths ought to figure, then he is to have the witnesses brought whom he named to witness it when he swore the oath or else he is to swear again. *If an oath is suspected*

Whenever men withhold formal means of proof at the General Assembly the penalty is lesser outlawry and it is to be prosecuted before the court in which the original suit is prosecuted. *Prosecution for withholding means of proof*

Men are to have brought cases forward before the sun is down,⁶⁶ all that were prepared before the courts go out to hear prosecutions; and if they are not so presented, that is a defense; and the formal means of proof in an original suit are to be brought before the sun comes onto Þingvöllr next morning.⁶⁷ *Time limits for presenting cases and means of proof*

If a man has cases before more courts than one, he is nonetheless not required to swear an oath more often than once, and if doubt is felt about his oath-swearing he is to have the witnesses brought in the other court whom he named to witness it when he swore his oath.⁶⁸ *One oath valid in more than one court*

K ‡ 36
On Giving Panel Verdicts

If a man has called for a panel of twelve, the chieftain is to nominate men of his assembly third to join him on this panel, and it is (p. 67) lawful for him to nominate either householders or household men. He is to nominate eleven men besides himself. The chieftain is to go to the court and invite the man who called on him to form a panel of twelve to challenge the panel, and name him and tell him where he has assembled the panel, and he has to challenge a panel of twelve in the same way as a court.⁶⁹ *A panel of twelve*

---

65. The name suggests that the man who called for such a verdict had unwarily misread the situation, perhaps enticed to do so.
66. Cf. p. 57, n. 12.
67. Cf. p. 54, n. 5.
68. Cf. ‡ 25 (p. 59).
69. See ‡ 25 (pp. 59-61).

Disagreement on verdict

If they do not agree on what verdict they are to give, then those in the majority are to prevail, and if they are in equal numbers they are to give the verdict the chieftain wishes.

If a chieftain has to form a panel to give a verdict on himself

If there is a case against a chieftain in which a panel of twelve is appropriate, he has to nominate a panel to give a verdict on himself, and the prosecutor is to ask a chieftain of the same assembly, which of the two he pleases if they are equally qualified in terms of connection but otherwise the one who is better qualified, to deliver the verdict, and they are to go to the court and swear an oath and this chieftain is to utter the verdict which the eleven agree upon.

Or to give a verdict on a man of his assembly third

If a chieftain has a case against a man of his assembly third in which a panel of twelve has to decide, he is to call eleven men of his assembly third to frame the wording of the verdict, and the eleven are to set about framing the verdict among themselves and those in the majority are to prevail if there is a split between them, and the chieftain is to utter the verdict which the others have agreed on without him.

If a chieftain withholds a verdict

If a chieftain withholds a panel-of-twelve verdict, the chieftain is fined for that and forfeits his chieftaincy, and the other may choose, as he prefers, to prosecute the chieftain or not. But if the chieftain withholds a verdict it is to be deemed as if given against the man in question, unless the latter gets a clearing verdict that the chieftain would not have given a verdict against him and that he withheld the verdict because he wished to do him a mischief, and five of his neighbors are to decide whether he withheld the verdict to his mischief and whether, if they had given a verdict, they would have given it in his favor.

K ‡ 37; p. 68
On Testimony Opposed to Panel Verdicts

Prosecution precedes defense

Prosecution of every case shall come before defense unless it is one and the same and one man's defense is another man's prosecution. Where

Testimony precedes panel verdict

panels are called for the prosecution and the man who is to defend has witnesses, testimony is to come before panel verdicts, even though it goes with the defense. He is not so to delay the testifying that the panel verdict is not given by the time the sun comes onto Dingvöllr.[70]

Veto on giving panel verdict

If the verdict the neighbors wish to give and the testimony of the witnesses are not one and the same, provided it is the same issue on which they have to decide, the defendant shall then say that he has testimony on the issue for which the panel is called, and he shall then forbid them by veto to give their verdict. If they give their verdict before the testimony comes forward, though forbidden to do so by veto, the verdict must be deemed worthless and the penalty is a fine for all of them, and he is then

---

70. Cf. ‡ 33 (p. 70); p. 54, n. 5.

to have the testimony brought nevertheless. If this does not prove to be false witness, it is possible to prosecute the others for giving a false verdict.[71]

Men are not to give contrary testimony here at the Assembly, and if they do, the penalty is a fine and the testimony must be deemed worthless. And contrary testimony is when men deliver in opposition to what has already been delivered, testimony against panel verdict or panel verdict against testimony, so that both cannot be right. But if contrary testimony turns out to be both contrary and false, then the penalty for the false witness is full outlawry and lesser outlawry for the contrary testimony.

Contrary testimony

K ‡ 38
On Defense

Before a man brings forward a defense he is to ask before witnesses the man who has a case against him whether he (p. 69) has brought forward the prosecution against him to the extent he thinks sufficient or whether he has not. Then the other has to answer that he has brought forward the prosecution to the extent he thinks sufficient unless something arises in the defense of such a kind that he would then wish to use it in the prosecution. When these words have been spoken, it is lawful to begin the defense, though it is also lawful for him to bring forward the defense, even if the other does not answer in these words, as long as the judges permit it and it appears to them that he is trying to balk the other's defense by it, and that is assembly-balking if the prosecutor delays the defense.

Defense procedure, preliminary

The other man is to begin the defense[72] as soon as he wishes and five neighbors are to decide on all clearing verdicts, all neighbors of the man prosecuted, but if he is prosecuted with a nine-neighbor panel, then he is to call five of the nine neighbors from that panel to give him a clearing verdict, those who live closest to the place of action for which the calling was made. If a neighbor on a panel falls sick, those who are on the panel with him are to fetch his verdict from his booth. He has to swear to it on oath which verdict he gives his assent to. They are to name witnesses to his words and utter the verdict in the court. If a man from a panel dies or loses his power of speech, another is to be called instead of him. The question of his power of speech has to be decided by whether it exists when they ask him.

Clearing verdicts

If a panel member falls ill, dies, or loses power of speech

---

71. False witness and false verdicts at the General Assembly were punished with full outlawry; they were prosecuted in the Fifth Court, cf. ‡‡ 25, 44 (pp. 60, 84); on procedure and penalty at spring assemblies see ‡ 58 (pp. 101-02). Counter-statements as to facts were in effect forbidden within the same case: they would have to form the grounds for a separate suit. Cf. ‡ 41 (p. 81).

72. Reading *taka til varnar* for *taka til sóknar*, "begin the prosecution."

Defense procedure; invitation to hear oath and defense

Presentation of defense

The man who wants to bring forward a defense is to go to the court and name witnesses to witness that [he] invites him, the man who has brought a case against him — and name him — to hear his oath-taking, if he has not sworn an oath already, and the defense he will there bring forward. And afterwards he is to bring forward his defense, whether he uses panel verdicts or testimony. When his formal means of proof for the defense have been produced, the prosecutor is to ask with witnesses whether he has brought forward a defense (p. 70) against the charge to the extent he thinks sufficient, and as soon as it is brought the other has to answer that he has now brought forward a defense to the exteht he thinks sufficient. But once he has brought forward some formal means of proof for the defense, the other need not wait for him to bring forward the whole defense to the extent he thinks sufficient. Each of them may then bring forward prosecution and defense as they are prepared to do so.

K ‡ 39

Suit for maintenance and care of dependent

One[73] is to begin with the heir of a dependent. The prosecutor is to publish the case at Lögberg as a claim on the heir for maintenance and care of the dependent, and he is to name both the dependent and the man against whom it is published and state to which court he publishes it and publish it as a legal publishing. The man who prosecutes is to call five neighbors of the man prosecuted to give a verdict whether this man has the right to inherit from that dependent or whether it is his dependent and name them both. If the panel gives a verdict that it is this man's dependent, the dependent is to be adjudged to him.

Defense in such a suit

A man who wishes to defend the case is to call the same five neighbors to give a verdict on whether he has the property or means to maintain that dependent or not. If a verdict of destitution is given, it is lawful to publish the case then as a claim for maintenance on whichever one he pleases of the dependent's next of kin with the property or means to maintain him. He is to enumerate the kinship between the dependent and the man against whom it is now published, and along with the two other men give his word of honor that that enumeration of kinship between them, N.N. and N.N., is right and true. Then the dependent is to be adjudged to that man unless a legal defense comes forward.

Enumeration of kinship supported by two other men

Nearest kinsman with means may be sued

A man who wishes to publish a case concerning a dependent may choose to publish it straightway as a claim on the man who is next of kin with the property or means available without previously publishing it as a claim on the heir.

---

73. Cf. ‡ 130; ‡ 39 is evidently misplaced.

K ‡ 40; p. 71
On Summing Up

As soon as men have brought forward prosecution or defense to the extent they wish before the court, then each of them with a prosecution or defense before the court is to have a man to sum up his case, whether he needs this for prosecution or defense. It is lawful for him to use the man among those nominated to join the court who is willing to do him that service. If none of them does him the service of summing up his case, he is to ask them with witnesses to sum up his case. They have to draw lots among themselves to decide who is to sum up his case, and the one who draws the lot is to sum it up. If they do not draw lots among themselves, the penalty for all in the court is lesser outlawry, and that is assembly-balking on their part if they do not take up his case. It is also prescribed that prosecution of the suit against them lies with the man who conducts the case which the judges do not take up. *One judge sums up the prosecution, one the defense* *Penalty if judges refuse to sum up*

If a case comes against a man nominated to join a court he may lawfully do whichever he pleases, either defend the suit or transfer his defense to someone else. If the case comes before that court, [he] is to keep his seat in the court nevertheless, and he is moreover to give his assent to the judgment they announce. It is also prescribed that if he has a case to prosecute which arose after he was nominated to join a court, he may lawfully do whichever he pleases, either prosecute it himself or transfer it to someone else. If that case comes before the court he is in, he is to keep his seat in the court nevertheless. His words on the case are not to count, neither is he to join in giving a divided judgment on the case. He is also to give his assent to the judgment the others announce. *If a judge becomes a defendant in the court to which he is nominated* *or a prosecutor*

K ‡ 41; p. 72
On Judges

It is also prescribed that before they begin their judging they are to swear an oath, unless they have already sworn.[74] They are to name witnesses. "I name them to witness that I swear an oath on the Cross, a lawful oath, and declare before God that I shall give such judgment as I think to be law." *Oath to be sworn by judges*

It is also prescribed that they shall sum up men's cases, those first which have come forward first. They are to sum up the prosecution in every case before the defense. The man who sums up a prosecution or defense shall in summing up rehearse the formal means of proof that have come forward and say to whose disadvantage they were, whether prosecution or defense. And the prosecution of every case is to be summed up before the defense of the same case. The man who is to sum *Manner of summing up*

---

74. Cf. ‡‡ 25, 35, 38 (pp. 59-60, 75, 78).

up a defense is to rehearse all the formal means of proof that have come forward for the defense.

Court-guards supplied by chieftains on request

If the judges think men crowd too close in the court, those who sit in the court are to ask three of the chieftains who belong to the Quarter by which the court is known — and ask them with witnesses — to provide them with three men for court-guarding, and the chieftains are fined and forfeit their chieftaincies if they do not do this, provide men for court-guarding, and the case against the chieftains lies with the judges. They are so to arrange it among themselves that they provide one man for each of the ancient chieftaincies.

Penalties for trespassing on court area

The men selected for court-guarding are to scratch two lines around the place where the judges sit, and if men step in over these, they are to name witnesses to witness that they have stepped in over them. If a man hurries out again, then he is not fined, but if he lingers, he is fined and the prosecution of that case lies with the court-guards. They are to go to Lögberg and make the summons in that suit and (p. 73) that case has to come before the court for the Quarter from which the guards come. They are to prosecute that suit with testimony and the court-guards have half the fine and the judges half.

If a judge must leave to attend another court

If a man who sits in a court is involved in matters of law that have to come before a different court, then before he leaves the court he has to say that he [declares] his agreement with the judgment they agree on while he is away.

Order of judging cases

They are first to judge cases in which no judgment was given last summer if there are any.[75] And next those cases which have arisen here at the Assembly, if they are prosecuted in that court. Then they are to judge those which are summed up first, unless there is a prospect of divided judgment in them.[76] If there is a prospect of divided judgment in them they are to judge them last.

Judgment to be given by a full court

They are to take a count to see the court is complete and they are to announce their judgments with a complete court if that is possible for them. If a man nominated to join a court falls ill or is wounded so that he cannot be out of doors, they are to go to the booth where the sick man is, and he is to swear an oath in their presence such as he would swear at the court. He is to give his assent to the judgment they agree on. Then it is lawful for them to judge all cases without him unless there is prospect of divided judgment. If a man nominated to join a court dies or loses his power of speech, it is as lawful for them to give judgment without him as if their court were complete. They have to judge in accordance with the formal means of proof that have come before the court for prosecution or

If a judge is sick or wounded

or dies or loses power of speech
Judgment to be given in accor-

75. Cf. ‡ 29 (p. 65).
76. Cf. ‡ 42 (pp. 82-83).

defense. They have to judge every case as either valid or invalid.

If a protest is made against any of the formal means of proof that have come before the court and affect the case at issue, they are first to judge other cases in accordance with the formal means of proof brought forward in them. If the man prosecuting thinks the defendant makes a protest against some formal means of proof, because he wishes to delay judgment and not because he wishes to test it in the Fifth Court, then he has to summon him (p. 74) at Lögberg for assembly-balking and make his penalty lesser outlawry and call nine neighbors and let the case come before the court in which the original suit is. If the panel gives a verdict of assembly-balking against him, he becomes a lesser outlaw. They shall then give judgment in the original suit as if no protest had been made against any of the formal means of proof.

dance with the means of proof

If protest against means of proof is regarded as a delaying tactic

If judges do not give judgment in men's cases, the men in question are to go to Lögberg and ask the judges to go out to give judgment in the cases which they have not brought to an end, and similarly ask any chieftain who nominated them to the court to move out his judges. If the judges then go out when asked to give judgment in the man's suit, they have a successful defense in any case brought against them. If some judges [are willing] to give judgment and some not, the penalty for those who are not willing is lesser outlawry, and it is lawful to summon such a judge for assembly-balking straightway at Lögberg and prosecute him the same summer and before the same court as soon as six judges or more have come out into their seats, and their court is then as complete as if they were all there to give judgment. If they do not give judgment in his case it is lawful for him to prosecute them with a nine-neighbor panel, either the same summer or the next summer, as he prefers.

Asking judges to give judgment, and if only some are willing

They are to give judgment in all the cases that are before that court in the place where they have been seated if they can in the face of force. If they cannot sit there because confronted by force, it is lawful for them to sit where they think themselves best able to finish their judging, and that judgment of theirs is then lawful. If they cannot sit there because confronted by force, the man who summed up the prosecution is to appoint where they are to meet in order best to finish their judging. They have to go to that place and finish their judging there if they can. If they are not all willing to go there, their court is complete even though no more than six of them give judgment there, and lesser outlawry is the penalty for the others who do not come (p. 75) to the place, and that is assembly-balking. Now, wherever some judges balk the assembly by being unwilling to give judgment in suits which they have to give judgment in, then the judgment of those who are willing to give judgment, as long as there are six of them or more, shall count as if the court were complete.

Change of site of court in face of force

If judges are guilty of assembly-balking, the judgment of six or more may stand

A man who summed up is to announce the judgment they have agreed

Announcement of judgments and assent of judges

on: the man who summed up the defense is to announce it if they mean to judge the suit invalid and the man who summed up the prosecution if they mean to give sentence against the defendant. And the man who announces judgment shall speak in this way: "I maintain that we give a legal judgment if we judge . . ." — and state what judgment he means to give — "and that is the judgment of us all," he shall say. All of them must also give their assent to the judgment they are agreed on and answer that that is the judgment of them all. If one of them stays silent and will not give his assent to the judgment on which they have agreed, that is assembly-balking and with his silence he condemns himself to lesser outlawry.

K ‡ 42
On Divided Judgments

If there are cases in which they do not agree on their judgment, they are to give divided judgments. Not fewer than six men are to join in giving a divided judgment. They are to exchange seats, however they were sitting previously, and those who join in giving a divided judgment are to sit all together. They are to sit so close that each group can catch the words of the other. Each group is to ask the other to come together with them, and name witnesses to witness that they offer them their company in giving the judgment they wish to give (p. 76) and state what judgment it is they wish to give. Each group is to speak these words.

Judges of different opinion to sit in different groups

If one of the men nominated to join the court is so ill that he may not be out of doors but is able to speak, both groups are to go to see him and tell him what they mean to give as a divided judgment. He is to swear the divided-judgment oath and state which group he will be with in giving a divided judgment.

The opinion of a judge absent through illness to be obtained

The judges are to go to their places. Then those who side with the prosecution are to invite the others to draw lots to decide which of them is to make the divided-judgment speech first. Those who draw the lot are to make the divided-judgment speech first. Each group is to invite the other with witnesses to listen while they swear the divided-judgment oath and to hear any other matters concerning the divided judgment which they are to bring forward, and offer to come together with them and ask them for their company in giving the judgment they wish to give, and say what that is. Each group is to speak in this way to the other. Afterwards those who join in giving a divided judgment are to swear the divided-judgment oath. They are to take a cross in their hand, or a book bigger than a prayer book,[77] and name witnesses "to witness that I swear an

Order of announcement of divided judgment decided by lot

Divided-judgment oath

---

77. Icelandic *hálsbók*; it might mean "neck-book" but the etymology is not certain. It is possibly a loan from Old English which has a word like it, *h(e)alsboc*, used to translate

oath on the Cross" — or the book — "a divided-judgment oath, and I declare before God that I shall give the divided judgment that I think to be law" — and state what divided judgment he gives and state why he gives that divided judgment. Men in both groups are to swear such an oath. Afterwards they are each to announce the judgment they wish to give. The man who summed up the prosecution is to speak thus: "We give this divided judgment and we give and announce it as our judgment that we give sentence against him" — and name him and state what sentence it is. Those who joined him in that divided judgment are to give their assent. The man who summed up the defense is to speak thus: "We give (p. 77) a divided judgment and we give and announce it as our judgment that we judge him[78] under no legal penalty because it seems to us a legal defense has come forward." Those who joined him in that divided judgment are to give their assent. The prosecutor in the case and the defendant in the case are to go to Lögberg and name witnesses "to witness that I publish a case against them because they have given an unlawful judgment" and state what it is they have judged. They are to publish it as a judgment to be revoked and make their penalty a fine and publish it for judgment in the Fifth Court. Each of them has to speak in this way against the judges who side with his opponent.

Announcement formulas

Publishing by prosecutor and defender of Fifth Court suit against judges who found against them

K ‡ 43
On the Fifth Court

We are to have a fifth court; and its name is the Fifth Court.[79]

A man is to be nominated to join that court for each of the ancient chieftaincies, nine men from each Quarter. The chieftains who have the new chieftaincies are to nominate one dozen men to join the court.[80] That makes four dozen and twelve men from each Quarter among them. Nomination to the Fifth Court is to be decided when the Quarter Courts are nominated,[81] and they shall all go out at the same time to hear prosecutions unless the men of the Law Council agree on something else, and the Fifth Court is to be seated where the Law Council sits.[82]

Nomination of judges in the Fifth Court

Fifth Court sits in the Law Council

phylacteria (Matthew xxiii. 5), where the first element has been associated with *hals* "health, salvation," *h(e)alsian* "beseech, adjure, exorcise." In Icelandic it must have covered small books with invocations used for private devotions or as amulets or both. They might sometimes have been worn rather than carried.

78. The text has N̊. *hann* "N.N. him."

79. The Fifth Court was instituted in the time of Skapti Þóroddsson, Lawspeaker 1004-30. The literal sense of the name is something like "the court that makes up (the number of courts to) five".

80. Apart from nomination of judges to the Fifth Court, the powers and functions of these new chieftaincies are obscure.

81. See ‡ 20 (p. 53).

82. See Map II.

K ‡ 44

Cases to be brought before the Fifth Court

These cases are to come before the Fifth Court: false verdicts given here at the Assembly, and false witness,[83] and (p. 78) if a man wrongly gives his word of honor, and divided judgments that occur here;[84] offers of bribes that occur here and acceptances of bribes that occur here, and if men make payment a condition here, and all false witness that is borne here at the General Assembly; and assistance to outlaws whose outlawry is reported here without guile and who are on the list of those who may not be assisted,[85] and cases concerning the harboring of bounden debtors whose debt bondage is reported here at the General Assembly and of slaves,[86] and also if men accept work from such men, and harboring church priests[87] and also for sharing living quarters with them as soon as they act otherwise than prescribed in the laws.

Time of publishing at the Assembly

All the cases I have[88] now told are to be published today or tomorrow, and it is also lawful on Monday and Tuesday if they are ordinary weekdays.[89]

Publishing in cases of assistance to outlaws

If a man publishes for judgment in the Fifth Court a case concerning assistance to outlaws, he is to state the charge and claim that thereby the defendant has given the outlaw assistance deemed such by law.[90] No doubtful case is to be brought.

K ‡ 45
On Court Nominations

Formula for nominating a Fifth Court judge

The chieftains are all to go to the Law Council and each of them shall seat his judge. A chieftain is to name witnesses "to witness," he shall say, "that I nominate a good man and true to join the Fifth Court" — and name him — "to judge all the cases that come before this Court and the law requires him to judge, and I am content that he should have a seat unless he is dismissed. I nominate a lawful court." He is to name wit-

Chieftain's oath

---

83. Cf. ‡ 37 (p. 77).
84. Cf. ‡ 42 (pp. 82-83).
85. Cf. ‡ 73 (pp. 120-21).
86. Bounden debtors were in much the same position as slaves until they had worked off their debt; when ready cash failed, it was the prescribed way of paying for obligatory maintenance of dependents and personal compensation in seduction cases, cf. ‡‡ 128, 158.
87. Cf. ‡ 4 (pp. 34-35).
88. Reading *hefi ek* for *hefi eru* "[I] have are."
89. Friday and Saturday, June 19/20-25/26; Monday and Tuesday, June 22/23-28/29. St John the Baptist's day (June 24) and St Peter and Paul's day (June 29) might fall on the first Monday or Tuesday of the Assembly; both those feast days were preceded by a twenty-four-hour fast; see ‡ 13 (p. 45).
90. Cf. ‡ 73 (pp. 120-21).

nesses "to witness," he shall say, "that I swear an oath on a book, a Fifth Court oath: so help me God in this world and the next as I think I have (p. 79) nominated a man to join the court" — and name him — "than whom no one is more able and willing to bear responsibility for our laws and common weal among those I have to choose from in my assembly third who are here at the Assembly." Every chieftain who nominates a man to join the Fifth Court is to swear such an oath.

K ‡ 46

Inviting to Draw Lots

Men who have cases before the Fifth Court are to go to the court and one of them is to name witnesses and invite all the men who have cases before the Fifth Court to draw lots and appoint where they shall go for the purpose and there put lots into the cloth and proceed with the lot drawing as at a Quarter Court.[91] Cases in which divided judgments are prosecuted are not to be subject to lot. They shall be presented first unless there are more than four of them. If there are more, lots are to be drawn. *Order of cases; other than up to four divided-judgment cases, decided by lot*

A prosecutor is to go to the court and invite the man he has a case against or the man who is bringing the defense for him to hear his oath-taking and bid him listen to the presentation of his case and name the case. He is to take a book in his hand, bigger than a prayer book, and name witnesses "to witness that I swear an oath on a book, a Fifth Court oath: so help me God in this world and the next," he shall say, "as I shall prosecute my case against him" — and name him — "in the way I think most true and right and most in accordance with law, and I think he is guilty of the charge I bring against him" — and state the charge — "and I have not offered money for support in this case of mine to anyone in this court and I shall not offer it; I have not paid money and I shall not pay it, neither for lawful nor for unlawful ends." He is to be accompanied by two men to vouch for him. He is to select them in the same way as (p. 80) summons witnesses.[92] They are to take a book in their hand, bigger than a prayer book, and name witnesses "to witness that I swear an oath on a book, a Fifth Court oath: so help me God," he shall say, "in this world and the next as I think that N.N. will prosecute his case against N.N. in the way he thinks most true and right and most in accordance with law, and he thinks he is guilty of that charge" — and state the charge he brings against him — "and [he] has not offered money for support in this case of his to anyone in this court and he will not offer it, and he has not paid it and he will not pay it, neither for lawful nor for unlawful ends." The men who vouch for him are to swear such an oath. *Prosecution preliminaries*

Fifth Court oath with two co-swearers

---

91. See ‡ 29 (pp. 64-65).
92. Cf. ‡ 77 (p. 124).

Case to be presented as published
Books used for oaths

Afterwards he is to present his case against him in the form he published it.

Men are to swear all oaths in the Fifth Court on a book in which sacred words are written and bigger than a prayer book.

K ‡ 47

Defense preliminaries

The man who has a case to defend is to name witnesses and invite the man who has a case against him to hear the oath he will swear to that defense and to hear the defense he will bring forward against the suit the prosecutor has against N.N. Afterwards he is to take a book in his hand and name witnesses "to witness," he shall say, "that I swear an oath on a book, a Fifth Court oath: so help me God in this world and the next as I shall defend myself from the charge" — and state the charge — "which (p. 81) he brings against me" — and name him by name — "in the way I know to be most right and true and most in accordance with law; and I am not guilty of the charge" — if there is substance for such a statement — and he is to state what he has for a defense — "and I think that is a legal defense. And I have not offered money for support in my case to anyone in this court and I shall not pay it, neither for lawful nor for unlawful ends." He is to be accompanied in his defense by two men to vouch for him, and he is to select them in just the same way as summons witnesses.[93] They are to take a book in their hand, bigger than a prayer book, and name witnesses "to witness that I swear an oath on a book, a Fifth Court oath: so help me God in this world and the next as I think that he will defend himself from the charge in the way he thinks most true and right and most in accordance with law" — and name both of them — "and I think he is not guilty of the charge he brings against him" — and state the charge — "and he has not brought[94] money into this court for support and he will not offer it, and he has not paid it and he will not pay it, neither for lawful nor for unlawful ends."

Fifth Court oath with two co-swearers

Formula for presenting defense

He is to name witnesses "to witness," he shall say, "that I bring forward before this court a defense of myself" — and state what his means of defense are and what his defense is[95] — "and I call that a legal defense."

Each of the men who vouch for him is to swear an oath such as I just rehearsed.

---

93. Cf. p. 85 and ‡ 77 (p. 124).
94. K has *borit* "brought," and *bera fé í dóm* "bring money into court" — i.e. offer a bribe — is found elsewhere; otherwise the verb used here in these formulas is *bjóða* "offer" — the variation is perhaps unintentional.
95. His "means of defense" are testimony and panel verdict; "what his defense is" must mean the general tenor of his case. This short passage seems a remnant of an alternative form of the preceding oath by the defender.

If a man has more cases than one before the Fifth Court, whether against one man or more, he is in each case to swear an oath like the one I rehearsed just now, and he is to be accompanied in each case by men who vouch for him, as just now rehearsed, and who are also to swear oaths. A man who has a case to defend in the Fifth Court, whether one or more, (p. 82) is to swear such an oath, a defense oath, in each case, as I rehearsed just now, and similarly the men who vouch for him. *Fifth Court oath must be repeated with two co-swearers in every case*

The man who has a case to prosecute before the Fifth Court is to dismiss six men from the court and name witnesses to it and name them all and say, "I dismiss you from the court and I am not content that you should have a seat in the court for this case" — and state what case it is. And they are to withdraw from the court, and if they will not withdraw from the court they are fined and what they say is invalid. The man who has a case to defend before the Fifth Court is also to dismiss six men from the court and name them all by name. "I am not content that you should have a seat in the court for this case which he has brought against me," and name the other man who brings the case against him by name and state what case it is. And they have to withdraw from the court and sit within the circle of judges while the case is judged. They are not to go away unless it is on a necessary errand. But if they will not withdraw from the court, the penalty is a fine and what they say is invalid. If he will not dismiss them from the court, the prosecutor is then to dismiss both groups, and if the prosecutor will not dismiss them from the court, his case is void. Those who are dismissed from court are, however, qualified to sum up their cases[96] but they do not have the right to give judgment in them. *Six judges to be dismissed by each party*

Dismissed judges remain present and may undertake summing up

Before they begin judging all judges are to swear an oath, a Fifth Court oath, that they will give that judgment which they think is law. A judge is to name witnesses "to witness that I swear an oath on a book, a Fifth Court oath: so help me God in this world and the next as I shall give that judgment which I think is law, and I have not made payment a condition in this court, and I shall not do so, and I have not taken money and I shall not take it, neither for lawful nor for unlawful ends." They are to sum up men's cases both for prosecution and for defense just as in a Quarter Court, and those who are dismissed from the court remain qualified to sum up men's cases. When judgment is given in one case, they then have to join the court again; but men (p. 83) must dismiss twelve judges from the court for every case and they may choose to dismiss the same men or others as they prefer. *Oath of Fifth Court judges*

Summing up as in a Quarter Court

Return of dismissed judges

They are to judge all the cases that come before the Fifth Court, those

---

96. Cf. ‡ 40 (p. 79).

Disagreement of Fifth Court judges

first which are presented first, and it is good if they can agree among themselves. If they do not agree, the majority of the judges are to prevail; but if they all divide in equal numbers, they must judge that sentence is given against the defendant, except in cases of divided judgment when they must draw lots — again if they all divide in equal numbers.

In every case where judges have given divided judgment and both groups have gone about it correctly, then the judgment of those must be revoked who have judged less in accordance with law. But if the one group has gone correctly about giving their divided judgment and the other group incorrectly, then the judgment of those who went correctly about giving their divided judgment must stand, even though the others' case was better in substance at the outset. But if neither group has correctly gone about giving divided judgment, the judgment of those must be revoked who in going about giving divided judgment strayed farther from the law; and that judgment must be revoked which seems remoter from the law.

Time limit for judging cases arising at the Assembly

In all cases that have arisen here at the Assembly, courts [may] be asked to go out as long as the calendar has not been announced.[97] And if judges will not judge cases, their penalty is lesser outlawry.

When a sentenced man may be killed

No man may be killed with impunity in accordance with the judgment a court has given on him until after the close of the Assembly.

K ‡ 48
On the Confiscation Court[98]

Time and place

There is to be a confiscation court for every man who is outlawed when a fortnight has passed from the Assembly at which he was outlawed.[99] That court is to be held at the place which was his home when the case was begun against him before he (p. 84) became outlawed. Now if the man who got him condemned does not know where that is, the court is to be at the home of the chieftain to whose assembly group the man who has been condemned belongs.[100] If locally in the district the man under penalty has formally guaranteed to accept the outlawry or if he becomes an outlaw as the result of a private settlement,[101] the confiscation court is to be called

---

97. At the close of the Assembly, cf. ‡ 116 (p. 188).
98. For this and ‡‡ 49-51 cf. also ‡‡ 62, 69 (pp. 112-16, 118-19).
99. The Assembly ended on Wednesday, July 1-7.
100. Cf. what follows and ‡ 66 (p. 117), and the parallel passage in ‡ 62 (p. 112).
101. See ‡ 60 (pp. 109-11).

for at the next General Assembly after he was outlawed. The man who got him condemned is to ask at Lögberg about his residence and his assembly attachment, if he does not know already. If no one admits his residence but a chieftain admits his assembly attachment, the confiscation court is to be held at this chieftain's home and he is to be asked to nominate the court. If neither is admitted, the confiscation court is to be held at the home of the chieftain to whose assembly group the man who got him condemned belongs, and he is to ask him to nominate the court. He is to ask at Lögberg after judgments have been given or where the chieftain hears it in person. If the chieftain was not at Lögberg, the man is to report it to him, but if he asks the chieftain somewhere else, he is to report it at Lögberg. The man who wishes to ask for a confiscation court is to name witnesses "to witness that I call on and ask N.N. to nominate a confiscation court for N.N. a fortnight after the close of the Assembly." He is to state the place for it and bid him come there so that the court is nominated before midday. *Asking for a confiscation court*

The court is to be nominated somewhere outside the wall where there is neither arable land nor meadow land and not beyond bowshot from the wall and on a line from the wall towards the place where the man who prosecuted him has his home, if it can conveniently be there.[102] *Where the court is to be held*

Men are required to accompany a chieftain to a confiscation court, all who live nearest, if he wishes to call them to do so, whether they are his assembly men or not. The penalty for those who refuse is a fine of three marks if he can nominate a complete court without them, otherwise lesser outlawry. *Men must attend if required*

The chieftain is to come there before midday and nominate the court, and those men who have to discharge legal duties there are also to come by that time.[103] It is to be (p. 85) a court of twelve good men and true. That court is to be challenged like a panel of twelve. *Time of arrival; nomination and challenge of court of twelve*

The man who asks for the court[104] is to have called five neighbors three nights earlier or with longer notice, those who live nearest to where the court is to be. They are required to give all the verdicts needed there, no matter who asks for them. He is also to have called witnesses of the announcement of the judgment and the witnesses named to the terms of settlement if the man was outlawed as the result of a private settlement. *Panel of five and witnesses to be called*

Those men who had money owed them by him when he was outlawed are to have called their witnesses or their neighbors if they have no *Proof of claims*

---

102. Cf. p. 30, n. 22. The wall is the homefield wall.
103. Cf. ‡‡ 62, 69 (pp. 115, 119); they should wait till nones (1500-1530) if they had reason to expect men with dependents or with parts to play in the procedure, ‡ 77 (p. 123).
104. Members of such a panel were challenged like judges, cf. ‡‡ 36, 25 (pp. 75, 59-63).

witnesses and are to have called all the men needed to provide formal means of proof there four[105] nights earlier or with longer notice.

K ‡ 49
On Prosecution

Presentation of case

The man who asked for a confiscation court is to name witnesses "to witness that I swear a lawful oath on a book and declare before God that I shall bring forward all matters against N.N. here at this confiscation court in the way I know to be most right and true and most in accordance with law." Testimony of the announcement of judgment or testimony of the settlement by which he was outlawed is to be brought before the court. When the court has been challenged, testimony is to be given of the terms laid down for his outlawry and of what he was outlawed for and of where he was outlawed. Men are then to draw lots to decide how claims are to be brought forward.

Distribution of property

Suits concerning money are to be prepared for this court just as for a debt court,[106] and similarly in the matter of land-valuing and in adjudging to the wife what property is hers, if she had any, and in redeeming pledges, if there were any, and to each his full amount if that may be, but otherwise equally reduced as at a debt court. Personal compensation is to be paid from the property if it is a case involving personal compensation, and theft payment if it is a thieving case.[107] If the property will stretch farther, the chieftain (p. 86) who nominated the court, is to be adjudged a cow or four-winter-old ox; and if there is still more property, half is to be adjudged to the man who got the outlaw condemned and half to the men of the Quarter, if he was outlawed at a General Assembly, but to the men of the same assembly if he was outlawed at a spring assembly, those of the assembly for the district where the confiscation court is held. Care of the property which men of the Quarter are to have is to be adjudged to the man who got the outlaw condemned and it is to be shared out at the next spring assembly. Care of it is also to be adjudged to him when it is due to the men of the same assembly, and he is then to bring it to the next autumn meeting in which he himself participates. If they belong to the same assembly, then all the property he has so far collected is to be shared among them there. But what he has not collected by then, either in payments received or formally guaranteed, is to be shared out at the spring assembly. And if the man who got him condemned belongs to a

Payment to chieftain

Residue shared between prosecutor and assembly men; care and use of the latter share

---

105. Reading *iiii* for *xiiii* "fourteen," cf. ‡ 62 (p. 113, l. 9).

106. See ‡ 223; it is described simply as a "debt court" (*skuldadómr*) but was only held when someone died leaving debts.

107. "Theft payment" (*fólagjald*) was apparently to the value of the goods stolen.

different assembly, it is to be shared out at the next General Assembly. As much as possible is to be shared out at the confiscation court and entrusted to the chieftain who nominated the court.[108]

The property due to men of the same assembly is to be used by them for the assistance of dependents of the man who is outlawed, as far as it stretches, if he had dependents, but otherwise it is to be used for the needs of other incapable people who are legally itinerant among the members of that assembly or those assemblies. *Public share to go on maintenance of dependents*

Lesser outlawry is the penalty for anyone who conceals property under penalty and a panel of nine neighbors of the man prosecuted is to be called at the assembly. *Penalty for concealing property*

K ‡ 50

If dependents come to a confiscation court, a panel of twelve is to be asked whether they are dependents of the outlawed man or not. People from whom he had the right to inherit are to be judged his dependents and others for whose maintenance it is the panel verdict of the neighbors that he took money under a fair agreement.[109] If other men are equally closely related to a dependent, then the five neighbors who have come to the confiscation court are to make the division, and all dependents are to be judged itinerant, in the proportion (p. 87) that was the outlawed man's due responsibility, within the Quarter the confiscation court is held in if he was outlawed at the General Assembly. If men of a Quarter have divided up the Quarter for the maintenance of incapable people, then everything they have agreed upon is to be kept. If there are two assemblies on the same assembly ground,[110] then the dependents of men outlawed at one of these assemblies are to be itinerant among the people of both assemblies, as long as the confiscation court was held among them. *Panel of twelve to decide on dependents*

Dependents to be judged itinerant

It is prescribed that it is not required to bring to a confiscation court a child for whose fathering the man is outlawed, nor to call men to provide formal means of proof, but it is to be judged itinerant.

If men who are required in accordance with law to bring dependents to the confiscation court do not do so, they make themselves responsible for the dependent, if they knew a confiscation court was to be held and were *Men who keep back dependents take responsibility for them*

---

108. The property entrusted to the chieftain was what was actually available at the confiscation court. The property adjudged to the care of the man who got the outlaw condemned (to be shared between him and the men of the Quarter or assembly group) was what belonged to the outlawed man elsewhere and needed collecting.

109. Probably the five neighbors called by the man asking for the court, see ‡ 48 (p. 89), and further ‡‡ 127, 135.

110. As seems to have been the case at the Múlaþing in Eastern Iceland, see Map I; cf. ‡ 59 (p. 108), Add. ‡ 35.

not prevented by reasons of necessity from getting to it. If men hide dependents, they make themselves responsible for them but the heirs of such men [are] not required to maintain them.

If men are prevented from bringing dependents to the court

If men do not learn that there is to be a confiscation court or they are unable to get to it with a dependent, they are to publish it next summer as a claim on the men of the Quarter or the men of the assembly to which the chieftain belongs who had the confiscation court nominated, and he is to be called on to form a panel of twelve to decide whether N.N. was a dependent of the outlawed man or not. Five neighbors of his are to decide whether he was or was not prevented by reasons of necessity from getting to the confiscation court. If those verdicts are in favor of the prosecutor and no legal defense comes forward, the court at the General Assembly is to judge the dependents itinerant, just as they should have been by the confiscation court if they had come to it.

K ‡ 51
On the Confiscation Court[111]

Confiscation court after sentence of lesser outlawry

A confiscation court is to be held for a lesser outlaw just as for a full outlaw and all the formal means of proof adduced, and (p. 88) men are to claim what property of theirs he owed them in similar fashion there, and the dependents that were his are to be judged itinerant in the same way.

Full outlawry if dues not paid

If a man was outlawed on account of judgment-breaking or on account of money, all that money is to be paid at the confiscation court to the amount demonstrated by formal means of proof. But if that money is not paid there he becomes a full outlaw, one who may not be given passage. If he is outlawed for malicious damage[112] and the compensation for damage is not paid at the confiscation court, then he also becomes a full outlaw who may not be sustained.

Payment to chieftain

A mark in legal tender is to be paid at the confiscation court to the chieftain who nominated the confiscation court. That is called a "life ring" and one ounce-unit of that money is called a "sustenance pledge." If that money is not paid, then he becomes a full outlaw who may not be sustained. If "life ring" and "sustenance pledge" are paid, then the property under penalty is to be adjudged in the same way as the property of a full outlaw. The chieftain also has the right to take a cow or a four-winter-old ox, and if he does, the "life ring" is to be included with the rest of the property under penalty — otherwise the chieftain takes that mark

Payment may be postponed for fourteen days

for himself. It is lawful to pay that mark there at the confiscation court but it is also lawful for a man to give a formal guarantee to pay it at the home of the chieftain after a fortnight's interval, and that shall be the

---

111. Cf. ‡ 67 (pp. 117-18).
112. Cf. ‡‡ 63-64 (p. 116).

settling day for that payment. It is possible to pay it in objects of value as priced in legal tender by lawful valuers.

K ‡ 52
The Homes of a Lesser Outlaw

When a confiscation court is held for a lesser outlaw, his homes are to be reported. He is to have three homes. It shall not be farther between them than may be traveled one way in one day. He shall be immune at those homes and within bowshot of them in all directions and on the road between them as long as he does not travel by it more than once a month and within bowshot of the road.[113] If men come (p. 89) towards him, he is to go so far off the road that they cannot reach him with spear points. A lesser outlaw forfeits his immunity if his homes are not reported at the confiscation court. *Immunity at homes announced at the court*

Witnesses are to be named to witness that the "life ring" was paid or the other money for which he would become a full outlaw if it were not forthcoming. If a confiscation court is held for a man who has become a full outlaw who may be given passage, then witnesses are to be named to all the terms of the outlawry which it was demonstrated by formal means of proof were laid down for him, and they must all be kept. But if he has the same safeguards as a lesser outlaw, then homes have to be chosen for him there at the confiscation court just as for a lesser outlaw. *Witnesses must be named to the payment of dues* *On full outlaws granted passage abroad*

If a lesser outlaw commits a lesser outlawry offense, his penalty is full outlawry. *If a lesser outlaw commits a lesser outlawry offense*

And no one is to ban the passage of a lesser outlaw or of a full outlaw who may be given passage even though he is owed money by the outlaw. *Outlaw's passage not to be stopped for debt*

K ‡ 53
Asking for Passage for a Lesser Outlaw[114]

The man who goes with a lesser outlaw to a ship is to ask for passage before witnesses and ask the shipmen to take him on and have the testimony brought of those men named at the confiscation court to witness the testimony produced there of the terms laid down for his outlawry, and the testimony that the "life ring" was paid, if he was a lesser outlaw, or the other money for which he would have become a full outlaw if it were not paid. If this testimony is forthcoming, both the ship's master and members of the crew are liable to a fine of three marks if they do not take him on. Otherwise there is no punishment for them. He has the same immunity on the road traveling to a ship as if he were traveling between his homes. He is to ask for passage for him at a second ship and *Penalty if shipmen refuse an outlaw passage* *Outlaw immune on his way to a ship*

---

113. Cf. p. 30, n. 22.
114. Cf. Add. ‡ 37.

Failure to get passage at three ships in one summer

have the witnesses brought who (p. 90) were named at the first. If he is refused there they are to ask at a third ship in the same manner, but if they refuse, it is not required that they ask at more ships that summer. The refusal carries the same penalty for all of them, but if they have taken on three lesser outlaws or full outlaws before they were asked, they are not fined if they refuse this one. He is then to go to his same lodgings. He also has the same immunity on that journey until he comes back to his homes and in night lodgings if he travels by full days' journeys.

Attempts to be repeated in two further summers; penalties for failure and refusal

He is to try to get away again the following summer and in the same manner, and again those who refuse are fined. But the third summer the penalty for all who refuse is lesser outlawry, and if he is still here at the onset of winter their refusal helps him not at all.

Immunity at or near ship, and in case of enforced return or wreck

If they take him on and he is at the ship while they are using their huts ashore, he has immunity a bowshot[115] from the hut in all landward directions; and even though the ship lies farther than that from the hut, he is still immune between the two. But as soon as they use shelters on the ship he is immune within bowshot in all landward directions from the point on the foreshore where the ship is closest to land, and it shall be like that wherever they lie off the coast of Iceland and the inhabited islands that summer. And always when they are moored on the coast of Iceland with a gangway out, he is immune within bowshot in all directions from the end of the gangway. If they are driven back or if winds keep them in the same harbor and they do not get away, he is not to leave the ship until the ship is so wrecked that it cannot be made ready for a voyage that summer or so emptied of men that they do not have the numbers to set sail. If they are driven back and come to a landing place where they wish to lay the ship up on shore, then the immunity prescribed for him at (p. 91) the ship is the same as when he came to the ship as long as they go on using huts by the ship and the ship's masters are still there — and indeed at the ship his immunity is always the same.

If no attempt is made to take passage

And he is to try to get away in the same fashion in each of the three summers, and the same immunity is prescribed for him from one summer to the next. But as soon as he does not try to get away one summer as prescribed, then that autumn at the onset of winter he is an outlawed man, one who may be killed with impunity and may not be sustained.

Permitted lodgings if ship is forced back

If he is driven back, he is to go to his same lodging if he lands in the same Quarter as it is in. If he does not land in that Quarter. [he] may take lodgings where he pleases during the half-month after they make land and he is as immune on that road and in night lodgings as when he went to the ship. If he wishes he may choose to go to his same lodging,

---

115. Cf. p. 30, n. 22.

and he has the same immunity as long as he conducts himself as prescribed. Whatever place he goes to by full days' journeys his immunity is the same. But in the third summer, if he does not get away then, he becomes a full outlaw with the onset of winter.

Failure to get away before the third winter, and willful return before end of imposed exile

If he comes back here before he has been away three winters, he becomes a full outlaw. If he gets a panel-of-twelve verdict that the sea carried him here and that he meant to go to a different country, then he is to try to get away as if it were that summer he had become a lesser outlaw.

If he comes back here when he has been away for three winters, he is as free from penalty as if that outlawry had never befallen him. He is then to take all inheritances that fall to him and he is also to take over the dependents who were judged itinerant on his account at the confiscation court and any who then fall to him, and he is to pay what debts of his (p. 92) were not fully paid before he left the country if he has the money for it.

Reinstatement after three years' exile

The penalty of a lesser outlaw is revoked if a confiscation court is not held for him in accordance with law; and those who should have held the confiscation court are to be prosecuted and their guilt demonstrated; and that case may be prosecuted by anyone who wishes, but the penalty of the lesser outlaw is revoked no matter who prosecutes them.

Penalty revoked if no confiscation court held; prosecution of those responsible

K ‡ 54
If a Confiscation Court Is Not Held

If men do not hold a confiscation court for the men they have got condemned or if they do not hold it in accordance with law, the penalty is lesser outlawry, however it is that the confiscation court he has on his hands falls short of being held in accordance with law, and the case lies with the men who stand to maintain the dependents who ought to have been judged itinerant if the confiscation court were held. If they will not prosecute, then the case lies with those who had money owed them by him when he was outlawed. And if they will not prosecute, then the case lies with anyone who will.

Penalty and procedure

If a chieftain does not nominate a confiscation court, having been asked in accordance with law, or whatever failure on the chieftain's part causes it that the confiscation court is not held in accordance with law, the penalty for the chieftain is lesser outlawry, and the case lies with the man who asked for the confiscation court.

If more than one man has asked him for a confiscation court, it is lawful for a chieftain to transfer nomination of such a court to another man, one of his assembly third; and the penalty is also lesser outlawry for the man to whom the chieftain transferred nomination of a confiscation court if through his actions the confiscation court is not held in accor-

Chieftain may transfer nomination of confiscation court

dance with law. If the chieftain does not get someone to nominate a confiscation court, he is under penalty (p. 93) and it is his responsibility, supposing more men than one have called on him to nominate a confiscation court.

Possible defense   If a man who got an outlaw condemned is prosecuted on the grounds that the confiscation court for the man he got condemned was not held in accordance with law, he may as a defense undertake prosecution of the chieftain on the same grounds and demonstrate that he was guilty of the actions which brought it about that the confiscation court was not held in accordance with law. If the chieftain is prosecuted for it but had transferred nomination of the confiscation court to another man in accordance with law, then he is also to prosecute that man on those grounds and so defend himself. That one of them is under penalty whose actions

Prosecution procedure   are held by panel verdict to have been the cause. They are summoning cases and nine neighbors of the man prosecuted are to be called at the assembly.

Men in charge of property belonging to an outlawed man   Concerning men who have charge of property owned by a man who has been outlawed: now, if they learn where the prosecutor has asked for the confiscation court to be held, they are required to come to that place and report that property, whether the confiscation court is successfully held there or not. If there is no meeting or he does not learn where the confiscation court is to be or he could not get there for reasons of necessity, then he is to report at the autumn meeting in which he participates what property of that kind he has in his charge, and also at the spring assembly and at the General Assembly later that summer. It is, however, also lawful for him to report it in the summer at the General Assembly, in such a way that a majority of the men[116] and assembly participants hear him, once he knows that the man has been outlawed.

Recovery of money owed by an outlawed man   For men who had money owed them by someone who has become a full outlaw and whose confiscation court has not been held, it is prescribed that they should summon the people who they know have the property owned by the outlawed man to the General Assembly, and all to the same Quarter Court as he was outlawed in. But for men from a different Quarter and for those who learn of it so late that they cannot summon, it is also lawful to publish it at Lögberg and prosecute the same summer. Everyone who had money owed them by him are to bring their formal means of proof there just as to (p. 94) a confiscation court, and the Quarter Court is to adjudge to them all the amounts which the confiscation court ought to have adjudged to them if held in accordance with law.

If a man who is outlawed hastens from the country with the property

---

116. I.e., probably men of the Law Council.

he owned or if when the outlawry befalls him he is in Scandinavia[117] with the property he owns and which ought to be put under penalty at a confiscation court here, and he then comes back with that property or with profit he has made from it, then if it is taken from him here, whether he is killed or not, the man who got him condemned rightly claims that property.

An outlawed man with property abroad

Men who are outlawed but whose property is not under penalty and who die without breaking the terms of mitigation laid down for them — their heirs have the right to take the inheritance. But the man who got him condemned rightly claims all the property as soon as he breaks the terms of mitigation laid down for him with the condition that if he broke them he would become a full outlaw, one not to be sustained and not to be given passage, and that property is then to be treated like other property under penalty.

Outlaws whose property is only conditionally under penalty

K ‡ 55

In the case of assistance to men who become full outlaws but the full extent of whose outlawry does not come from a General Assembly court,[118] it is prescribed that the prosecutor should make a summons and make lesser outlawry the penalty and summon to a Quarter Court and call on the chieftain to whose assembly group the man prosecuted belongs to form a panel of twelve. Then the testimony is to be brought before the court of the men named at the confiscation court to witness the testimony produced there of the terms laid down for his outlawry. If (p. 95) a confiscation court has not been held, he is to have the testimony given in the Quarter Court which should have been given in the confiscation court if it had been held. Now, as soon as anyone has been prosecuted for assisting this outlaw in the manner now told and that testimony has come before the Quarter Court,[119] the penalty is full outlawry for anyone who assists that outlaw thereafter, and such people are to be prosecuted before the Fifth Court; but prosecution of those who had assisted him prior to that remains as rehearsed earlier.

Assistance to full outlaws not sentenced at the General Assembly; the first case of such

Procedure and penalty in subsequent cases

---

117. The Icelandic has the adverb *austr* "east, in the east," which was commonly used to mean in Norway and Baltic Scandinavia east from there, but the provision doubtless extended to other foreign parts.

118. This must refer to men failing to keep terms of private or arbitration settlements (cf. ‡ 60, pp. 109-11) imposed with the subsequent approval of the Law Council. A court of confiscation can hardly have been a condition for the enforcement of the penalty as it was for lesser outlaws judged by courts (cf. ‡ 53, p. 95); it looks as though a long time might elapse between the settlement and the confiscation court, which had to be applied for at the General Assembly following (‡‡ 48, 66, pp. 88-89, 117).

119. In K the scribe wrote *f*. This has been expanded to *fjórðungs* "Quarter," by a later hand; Finsen prefers to read *feráns* "confiscation." Cf. Add. ‡ 36.

Immunity for outlaw granted passage abroad

For outlaws for whom passage from the country is laid down, and for whom a confiscation court has not been held, one home is to be chosen and the five neighbors who live nearest that home are to be told, and then he is as immune at that home as if it had been chosen at a confiscation court, and so he shall be on the road from that home to the ship. When passage is asked for him, he is to have the testimony brought forward which should be brought before a confiscation court if it were held. If a greater degree of immunity was laid down for him than for a lesser outlaw, then there is no need to choose the home for him.

Outlawry on mitigated terms

Those men for whom terms of mitigation are permitted by the Law Council and announced at Lögberg to the effect that they may be given passage — passage is to be asked for them as for a lesser outlaw or as for a full outlaw who becomes an outlaw as the result of a private settlement, and testimony is to be brought by the witnesses named to witness the announcement of what terms of mitigation were permitted him. If men break the terms of mitigation permitted them, prosecution for assisting them is to be as for assisting outlaws who are outlawed as the result of a private settlement and the penalty made the same.[120]

Leave from Law Council for mitigation

If permission is asked in the Law Council for terms of mitigation for anyone, a full outlaw or lesser (p. 96) outlaw, it only counts if all the men of the Law Council permit it and no one outside the Law Council forbids it by veto in such a way that those sitting in the Law Council hear it. But besides members of the Law Council no one else's words are to count in opposition to it unless they forbid it by veto.[121]

Immunity of outlaws abroad

Men who go abroad from here as outlaws who may be given passage are as immune in foreign countries as if they were under no penalty here for those causes. Men who are here made full outlaws, ones who may not be sustained and not given passage, may be killed with impunity and they forfeit their immunity in relation to our countrymen in foreign countries just as here.

K ‡ 56

Spring assemblies; duration and date

[122]We shall hold spring assemblies in our country. Three chieftains together are to hold an assembly. They are not to hold an assembly of more than a week nor an assembly of less than four nights unless permission is asked for it in the Law Council. They must hold spring assemblies so that when the prosecution assembly is ended not more than six weeks of summer have passed. A spring assembly is not to be earlier than when

---

120. Cf. p. 97 above; ‡ 73 (pp. 120-21), cf. Add. ‡ 36.
121. Cf. ‡ 117 (pp. 190-91).
122. Cf. Add. ‡ 90.

four weeks of the summer have passed when the chieftains arrive.[123]

A summons to a spring assembly is to be made not less than two weeks before the spring assembly to which the summons is made, and men to provide formal means of proof are to be called a week before the assembly or with longer notice unless the cause arises later — then a summons may be made as close to the spring assembly as one pleases, but not if local calling is involved — then the summons is to be made and men to provide formal means of proof called at the latest one week before the assembly. *Summoning and calling before spring assemblies*

Cases between men of the same assembly are to be summoned to the spring assembly. It is lawful for a man to summon to the assembly he himself belongs to, but it is also lawful to summon to the assembly to which the man against whom he has a case belongs. *To which assembly a man should summon*

All the chieftains (p. 97) who belong to the assembly are to come to the beginning of the assembly. The chieftain who has the duty of formal inauguration there is to inaugurate the assembly on the first evening they come to the assembly.[124] While a man is at the assembly, his personal compensation is doubled for insults and for all inflicted injuries. The chieftain is to state what the assembly boundaries are and he is to inaugurate the assembly in the same way as the General Assembly, and he is to state what the assembly is called. *Chieftains' arrival and inauguration of assembly Personal compensation doubled at assemblies Assembly boundaries*

If chieftains do not come to the beginning of the assembly their penalty is a fine and forfeit of their chieftaincy if lawsuits are not brought to the assembly, but their penalty is lesser outlawry if lawsuits are brought to the assembly and similarly if any arise at the assembly. The prosecution of such a case lies with the men who prepared lawsuits for that assembly. If they will not prosecute, the case lies with the chieftains of the same assembly, the one of them who is the more willing to prosecute, and the one of them who is at the assembly if they are not both there. If they will not, the case lies first with men of the same assembly and then with anyone who wishes. *If a chieftain does not attend at proper time*

A name is to be given to every spring assembly.

Assembly participants are to come to a spring assembly not later than when one night of the assembly is over, and similarly those men who conduct cases and those who have been called locally to provide formal *Spring assemblies to have names Assembly participants' arrival*

---

123. Four weeks of summer had passed with the arrival of Thursday, May 7-13, six weeks with the arrival of Thursday, May 21-27. But a spring assembly did not necessarily begin on that Thursday, and the debt assembly could continue after May 21-27.

124. We do not know which of the chieftains had this duty, nor how the inauguration was conducted. At the General Assembly it was done by the man who held the chieftaincy descended from the family of Þorsteinn, son of Ingólfr the first settler, and he was called "chieftain of the whole host" (*allsherjargoði*). For the assembly places and their names, see Map I.

means of proof are to come not later than I have now told. And if those men who bring cases to the assembly or who wish to defend cases come later, their cases and their defenses are void if they come later to a spring assembly than when one night of it is over.

No horse and food provided Length of assembly

It is lawful for a spring assembly to be shorter than a four-night assembly if all the men of the assembly agree and all the cases prepared for that assembly are finished.

Witnesses have no right to make a claim for aid in response to a calling to attend a spring assembly.[125]

Who may be nominated as judges

All men who come to the assembly before the court is to be nominated may be nominated to join the court.

If cases arise less than two weeks before an assembly

If a case arises later than two weeks before a spring assembly and local callings are involved (p. 98), then the summons is to be made and the men called to provide formal means of proof a week before the assembly. If the case arises later than one week before the assembly then neighbors are to be called at the assembly.[126]

Householder may send substitute

It is lawful for a householder to send a man belonging to the same assembly group to participate in an assembly on his behalf.

Chieftains' arrival

If lawsuits are prepared for a spring assembly, a chieftain's penalty is lesser outlawry if he does not come to the beginning of the assembly, and similarly if suits arise there.

Summons for contracted payments

In a case to do with payment on a fixed settling day a man may, if he wishes, make a summons to the General Assembly during Rogation Week if that week comes during the spring assembly.[127]

Consequences of late attendance

If men who are called locally to fulfil legal duties come to the assembly later than after one night of the assembly is over, their performance of legal duties, should they attempt it, is void. If assembly participants come to a spring assembly later than after one night of the assembly is over or if they do not come to a spring assembly, they pay a fine for that at the suit of their chieftain.

Householder may send household man as substitute

It is lawful for a householder to provide a household man of his in place of himself, and he is as rightful an assembly participant as the householder. He is to tell the chieftain that he will participate in the assembly on behalf of a man of his assembly third and name him.

---

125. Cf. ‡‡ 33, 68 (pp. 69-70, 118).
126. Cf. p. 99 above and ‡ 64 (p. 116); on chieftains' arrival (ll. 19-21 below) cf. p. 99.
127. Cf. ‡ 58 (p. 102). Rogation Week is the week in which Ascension Day falls, i.e. Thursday in the sixth week after Easter. It would coincide with the first day of the fifth week of summer when Easter Day fell from March 29 to April 4, and would be May 14-29 when Easter Day fell from April 5 to 20 (cf. p. 99, n. 123). It was a great festival, observed like Easter and Christmas Day, ‡ 12 (p. 44).

K ‡ 57

Chieftains are to nominate a court there and each of them is to nominate twelve men to join the court to judge all the cases that come before that court and the law requires them to judge. He is to invite the prosecutor of a case and the defender of a case to reject men from the court — "and I am ready to nominate another if these are rejected from it in accordance with law."

Each chieftain nominates twelve judges; challenging

It is also lawful for them to use whatever assembly procedure the assembly participants agree on as long as they do not abate the formalities of the General Assembly though they may choose to (p. 99) add to them as they please. The chieftains are to decide by majority when the court is to go out.

Local procedures in addition to General Assembly procedures

When the court goes out

In all cases which men of the same assembly have against each other, they may choose to treat them as they prefer and take the cases either to the General Assembly or to the spring assembly, unless they are only fining cases and these are to go to the spring assembly; and when there are only fining cases, they are not to remain unsettled beyond the spring assembly if they arose before the summoning days.

Fining cases must go to spring assembly

It is prescribed that one may treat cases concerning dependents as one prefers: either publish for the maintenance of the dependent at the spring assembly or else summon in the suit locally.[128] It is lawful to publish maintenance of a dependent as a claim on someone at a spring assembly only if the man against whom the claim is published is himself at the assembly, and if he does not hear the publishing he is to be told of it in person with witnesses.

Suits over dependents, procedures

But if men wish to prepare killing cases or intercourse cases for a spring assembly, it is lawful for them to do which they prefer, to summon locally or to publish on the assembly slope. If cases are to be published, then neighbors must be called locally half a month before the assembly or with longer notice. It is also prescribed that all panel members and men providing formal means of proof in original suits are to be called before the court goes out in the same way as at the General Assembly.

Killing cases and sex cases, procedures

K ‡ 58
On Moving Out Courts

Courts are to go out so that all cases come before them before the sun is down.[129] Men are to draw lots for the order of cases just as at the General Assembly, and similarly swear oaths and proceed in all suits and defenses

Court procedures as at General Assembly

---

128. Cf. ‡ 39 (p. 78).
129. About 2100 hours around May 1, 2200 around May 27.

	as at the General Assembly.¹³⁰ If men withhold any formal means of proof their penalty is the same as for withholding it at the General Assembly¹³¹ and they are to be summoned on the assembly slope for
If the wrong kind of panel is called	judgment at the assembly. If (p. 100) neighbors are called to give a panel verdict where a panel of twelve would be appropriate, they must make it an obstruction to their verdict-giving that they are called to give a verdict in a matter they are not qualified to decide. If a chieftain is called on to
If a man from a different assembly withholds means of proof	form a panel of twelve where a panel of neighbors has to decide, he is to make it an obstruction to his verdict-giving, if he is not qualified to decide. If a man from a different assembly withholds any formal means of proof, the other man in question may choose whichever he prefers, summon him before the court there or to the General Assembly.
Temporary absence of assembly participants	If an assembly participant goes out over the assembly boundary and stays away for a night or more, the penalty is lesser outlawry, and it is lawful to make the summons in that case on the assembly slope for judgment at the assembly. Nine neighbors of the man prosecuted are to be called at the assembly.¹³²
Assembly-balking, transfer of cases to General Assembly	The penalty for every kind of assembly-balking that men commit there is the same as if committed at the General Assembly, and balking a spring assembly is to be prosecuted in every way as if it were done at the General Assembly. If there is assembly-balking at a spring assembly so that cases cannot be finished on account of it, the man who had the prosecution of those cases is to summon the men responsible for the assembly-balking and make lesser outlawry the penalty.¹³³ If the panel gives a verdict against them, he can prosecute those cases at the General Assembly and before the Court for the Quarter that assembly is in. There the cases must be deemed in accordance with the way they were prepared, and all the men previously called to provide formal means of proof in the original cases who have not discharged their duties are automatically called to the General Assembly, as are also those named or called to attest that formal means of proof were produced.
No summoning to General Assembly in Rogation Week except for contracted payments	If the assembly comes in Rogation Week that is not to be made an obstruction to any matters needful there at the assembly, neither to oaths nor to summonings, except that no summons may then be made to the General Assembly unless it concerns payment on a fixed settling day.¹³⁴ If men who belong to that assembly give false verdicts (p. 101) or bear

---

130. See ‡‡ 29, 25 (pp. 65, 59-60) and ‡‡ 20-47 (pp. 53-88) generally.
131. See ‡‡ 32, 35, 36 (pp. 66-69, 74, 76).
132. Cf. ‡ 59 (p. 107).
133. Cf. ‡ 117 (pp. 189-90).
134. Cf. ‡ 56 (p. 100 and n. 127).

false witness, a prosecutor is to summon them before the court there and make lesser outlawry their penalty and call on the chieftain to whose assembly group the men prosecuted belong to form a panel of twelve. If a man who belongs to a different assembly gives a false verdict or bears false witness, it is lawful to do whichever one prefers, summon him before the court there or to the General Assembly, and the chieftain to whose assembly group the man prosecuting at the spring assembly belongs is to be called on to form a panel of twelve. *False verdicts and false witness*

Wherever a protest is made against some formal means of proof and summons is made to the General Assembly, the court at the spring assembly is to give judgment as if the formal means of proof have been correctly brought. If there is protest at a spring assembly against formal means of proof which are thought to affect the case at issue, the court is to give judgment as if the formal means of proof were correctly brought. Then the man who protests against the formal means of proof is to summon it as a judgment to be revoked, and the judgment must be revoked if it proves to be a case of false witness.[135] *Procedure in case of protest against means of proof*

The procedure for summing up and for everything else is then to be as at a General Assembly court.[136] They are to judge men's cases, and it is good if they come to the same judgment. But if they do not come to the same judgment, they are to give divided judgments, and not fewer than six are to join in giving a divided judgment, and proceed in giving divided judgments as in a General Assembly court.[137] After judgments have been given men are to summon the judges at the assembly for giving a divided judgment and make a fine their penalty and summon them to the Quarter Court for the Quarter in which the assembly is, and summon their judgment as one to be revoked; though for giving a divided judgment it is also lawful to summon judges locally in the district at the home of each one of them. Cases in which men have given divided judgments at a spring assembly should then be finished in the Quarter Court for the Quarter in which the assembly is, if they can be finished there. But if divided judgments are again[138] given, then they are to be finished in the Fifth Court.[139] All the men they named to witness how each group proceeded in giving their divided judgment are to be brought before the Quarter Court. *Divided judgments* *Summoned to General Assembly*

---

135. The Icelandic here adds the words *ef dómrinn rofnar*, which are unintelligible to us in their context.
136. See ‡ 40 (p. 79).
137. See ‡ 42 (pp. 82-83).
138. Omitting *eigi* "not."
139. See ‡‡ 46-47 (pp. 85-88).

During prosecution assembly summons to General Assembly forbidden

Mode of summoning

Summons of and by men from other assemblies

While the prosecution assembly is in being, men of the same assembly are not to be summoned in cases which are not going to be prosecuted there at (p. 102) the assembly, but it is lawful to summon men of the same assembly to the General Assembly as soon as the prosecution assembly is over, even though the debt assembly is in being. A man is to be summoned so that he hears it in person. It is also lawful to summon him at a booth if they find him to speak to there. It is also a lawful summons if he hears the beginning, when the witnesses are named, even though he runs off. It is also lawful at a spring assembly to summon men belonging to other assemblies even while the prosecution assembly is still in being; and it is similarly lawful for men belonging to other assemblies to summon a man belonging to this particular assembly, even while the prosecution assembly is still in being.

If a man is summoned to an assembly to which he does not belong

If a man from a different assembly is summoned to a spring assembly, the judges have to give judgment in that case unless the case is forbidden by veto.[140] It is lawful for him to have the case that is brought against him forbidden by veto or to summon the judgment as one to be revoked, as he prefers. It is lawful for him to summon one or more of the judges, as he prefers, and summon on the grounds that they have judged a man from a different assembly and summon it as a judgment to be revoked. He is then to call five of his neighbors for a clearing verdict, to give a verdict as to whether, when he was summoned, he was or was not in an assembly group along with the chieftain he states. And if he gets that verdict, that he did belong to that assembly group when he was summoned, the judgment is revoked and the case becomes void. If he learns of it so late that he cannot do the summoning in the summoning days, it is lawful for him to do as he prefers, either summon it as near the General Assembly as he pleases or publish it at Lögberg for (p. 103) prosecution the same summer. If he does not come to the assembly and if he has not previously heard of it, it is lawful for anyone who wishes to do so to take up the defense for him as if he were the rightful principal.

Forbidding a suit by chieftain's veto

It is lawful for a man to have the suit which is brought against him forbidden by veto. He is to go to see the chieftain to whose assembly group he belongs, though it is also lawful for some other man to take the power of veto from the chieftain. He is to name witnesses "to witness that I ask you" — and name the chieftain — "whether you are acting in your chieftaincy which authorizes you to nominate courts and give panel-of-twelve verdicts or whether you are not acting in it." And the chieftain is to answer him, and he is to name witnesses to the answers that come from the chieftain. And if the chieftain answers that he is acting in that chieftaincy, the other is to name witnesses to witness that he takes power of

---

140. Cf. Add. ‡ 90.

veto from the chieftain and the chieftain transfers to him a chieftain's veto, a full legal veto, to forbid the judges to judge that case, and name the case and name who summoned him, and similarly to forbid all formal means of proof that may be forbidden by veto.[141] If the man who takes the power of veto is not the man against whom the case is brought but does it for the defense of the man against whom the case is brought, he is to name the latter by name and thereafter proceed as earlier rehearsed.

If a chieftain will not transfer power of veto for a man of his assembly third, then the other must request him to do so with a legal request before witnesses, and his penalty is lesser outlawry and he is to be prosecuted with the testimony of those who witnessed it when he was asked. For a clearing verdict the chieftain has to ask five of his neighbors whether he knew or did not know that the man against whom the case was brought was a man of his assembly third. If the panel gives a verdict that he did not know and that he would have transferred power of veto if he had known for certain that the man belonged to his assembly third, then he has a defense in the case. *Procedure if transfer of veto is refused*

The man who has taken power of veto from the chieftain is to go to the assembly (p. 104), and he is to go to the place where the court is seated and there he must forbid by veto the case the judges are hearing. He is to bring it forward as he prefers, either before the case is presented against him or afterwards. Before he brings the veto forward he is to name witnesses "to witness that I forbid the judges by veto, a chieftain's veto, a full legal veto, to judge that case" — and state what case it is — "which he is bringing against" him, or me — and name the chieftain and also the man the case is against if he is defending for someone else. And if he wishes he may also forbid panel members by veto to give verdicts on him and any formal means of proof except testimony of summoning and any other formal means of proof that may already have come forward. *Forbidding by veto*

If others use force of numbers against these men and do not let them go to the court, then they have to name witnesses and ask their opponents to allow them to go to the court, but if they cannot get to the court, they are to forbid by veto as close to the court as they can get and speak all the words there as if at the court. *If men imposing a veto are met by force*

If a man took power of veto from a chieftain, he is to have the witnesses of it testify and they are to use all the same words in their testifying as they were named to witness when he took power of veto from the chieftain. Before testifying they are to swear oaths just as at the General Assembly. If a chieftain brings forward his own veto, whether for himself or for someone else belonging to his assembly third, no witnesses of its taking are to accompany it. He is to name witnesses "to *Witnesses of transfer of veto; neither witnesses nor oath needed if chieftain acts in person*

141. Cf. lines 26-29 below.

witness that I forbid the judges by my own veto, a legal veto, to judge that case." No witnesses of its taking and no oaths need accompany it.

K ‡ 59
On Judges

Procedure when a veto is imposed

The judges are to name witnesses and make it an obstruction to their judgment that the case has been forbidden by a chieftain's veto — and (p. 105) name the case or cases if more than one. If a panel has been called in the case and they were forbidden to give a verdict, they also have to name witnesses to witness that they make it an obstruction to their verdict-giving that the case has been forbidden by a chieftain's veto. If witnesses figure in the case they are to make it an obstruction to their testifying that the case has been forbidden by a chieftain's veto. The man who has brought forward the veto is to name witnesses to what formal means of proof have so far come forward for the defense and rehearse them and name the man against whom the case is brought. And the man who has the case for prosecution is to name witnesses to witness what formal means of proof have so far come forward for the prosecution. They are each to have this testimony brought in a General Assembly court. All

Vetoed cases go to General Assembly

cases forbidden by veto at a spring assembly are to go to the General Assembly and before the Quarter Court for the Quarter the assembly is in, and all the men to provide formal means of proof in the original suit who have not done so at the spring assembly are automatically called to the General Assembly, as are also those named or called to attest that formal means of proof were produced.

Penalties and procedures in case of errors in use of veto

If a chieftain transfers power of veto to a man from someone else's assembly third, he is fined for that and forfeits his chieftaincy. If a man brings forward a veto that is not a chieftain's veto, the penalty for both of them is lesser outlawry, and each is a summoning case and nine neighbors of the man prosecuted are to be called at the assembly to give a verdict whether he took power of veto from a chieftain or not. Then he may ask five of his neighbors[142] for a clearing verdict as to whether he thought the man who transferred power of veto to him was acting in a chieftaincy. But if the verdict is given against the chieftain, that he was not acting in a chieftaincy when he transferred power of veto, he is under penalty. If a chieftain is prosecuted for allowing his veto to be used for a man of another chieftain's assembly third, he may ask five of his neighbors for a clearing verdict, (p. 106) to give a verdict as to whether the man was in that assembly group or not when he was summoned. And if the panel gives a verdict that he was then in that assembly group, he has a defense in the case.

---

142. Called from the nine called by the prosecutor, cf. ‡ 35 (p. 74).

If a man is asked before [witnesses] what assembly or assembly third he belongs to and he answers that he belongs to the assembly to which he is summoned, and someone then forbids that case by veto, the veto does not count when the testimony of the occasion when the man prosecuted was asked about his assembly membership comes before the court.

Asking a man's assembly attachment

If a man with witnesses asks another man what assembly he belongs to but meets him alone out in pasture land, it is lawful for him to answer that they should go to a house and that he will answer him there where he has witnesses, if he is not willing to rely on the witnesses the others have with them.

If a man does not answer when he is asked before witnesses what assembly he belongs to, his penalty for that is a fine, and the man who conducts the case is to summon him to the assembly to which he himself belongs and that case may not be forbidden by veto. If the chieftaincy to whose assembly third he belongs is owned by more than one person, it is lawful for him to answer this: "I am with that one of them who acts in the chieftaincy," and name them.

If a man summons a man to an assembly to which neither of them belongs he is fined for that and his case is void.

If a man summons another to an assembly neither belongs to

It is lawful for a householder to send another man, one who belongs to the same assembly group, to participate in the assembly on his behalf, and on the first evening he comes to the assembly he is to go to find the chieftain and tell him that the householder has sent him there to participate in the assembly on his behalf;[143] and he is qualified for nomination to the court and to join the chieftain in giving panel-of-twelve verdicts. If a householder sends no one to participate in an assembly on his behalf, the chieftain may choose, as he prefers, to prosecute him for staying at home or to claim half an ounce-unit in assembly attendance dues from him (p. 107). If a householder leaves the chieftain's assembly third because he was prosecuted for staying at home, his penalty for that is a fine of three marks and the prosecution of that case lies with the chieftain.

Householder may send substitute

If a man does not attend and sends no substitute

If assembly participants are away from a spring assembly for a night or so as to obstruct provision of any formal means of proof, their penalty is lesser outlawry and nine neighbors are to be called at the assembly, as preferred, either neighbors of the man prosecuted or those who live closest to the assembly ground, and the case lies with anyone who wishes to prosecute.

If assembly participants are absent

If a man is called to testify at two assemblies, he is to go to the assembly he belongs to and frame the wording of the testimony that is to

If men are called to provide proof

---

143. Cf. ‡ 56 (p. 100).

at more than one assembly	go to the other. If he is called to serve on a panel of neighbors at one assembly and to testify at another, he is to frame the wording of his testimony and attend the assembly to which he is called to serve on a panel of neighbors. If he is called to serve on a panel of neighbors at two assemblies, he is to attend the assembly to which he is called first.
Chieftain may call on men of his third to go to the General Assembly	A chieftain may do this if he wishes: go onto the assembly slope at the spring assembly and name witnesses to witness that he means to ask all assembly participants who belong to his assembly third to go with him to the General Assembly, and they are to draw lots or arrange it among themselves by other means, but one in nine of his assembly men and assembly participants[144] are to go.
End of spring assembly	The assembly is to be declared over at midday on the day when men have been there four nights and not before unless all the men of the assembly agree and all the cases prepared for that assembly are settled or judged.
Change and amalgamation of assembly sites	All the assemblies are to remain the way the spring assemblies are now established.[145] But if men wish to shift a spring assembly, the chieftains belonging to the assembly are to come to formal agreement on it and report it to the men of their assembly thirds at autumn meetings. If they wish, they may also choose (p. 108) to terminate an assembly by putting two together that were previously separated, if the chieftains of those assemblies all agree on it. But they are to ask permission for it in the Law Council and announce it at Lögberg and they are to give the assembly a name and state its boundaries.
Asking for a confiscation court after sentence at a spring assembly	If men are outlawed at a spring assembly, then on the day the prosecution assembly is over, the chieftain to whose assembly group the man outlawed belongs is to be called on to hold a confiscation court after a fortnight's interval at the home of the man who has been outlawed, and to proceed at the confiscation court as if he had been outlawed at the General Assembly.[146]
Sustaining men outlawed at a spring assembly	If men are outlawed at a spring assembly and are sustained between the time the confiscation court is held for them and the time their outlawry is reported at Lögberg, the penalty is lesser outlawry and the summons in that suit is to be made locally and the chieftain to whose assembly group the man prosecuted belongs is to be called on to form a panel of twelve. But such sustaining of men who are outlawed at a spring assembly carries a penalty only for those who hear of his outlawry.

The penalty is lesser outlawry for falsehood in any formal means of

---

144. Those of his assembly men who qualified as assembly participants.
145. See Map I.
146. Cf. ‡‡ 48-52, 62, 67, 69 (pp. 88-93, 112-16, 117-18, 118-19).

proof at a spring assembly or locally at district courts,[147] in giving one's word of honor or a panel verdict or testimony. They are summoning cases and the chieftain to whose assembly group the man prosecuted belongs is to be called on to form a panel of twelve.

Falsehood in means of proof: penalty and procedure

K ‡ 60

If a man is outlawed as the result of a private settlement.[148] A man becomes an outlaw as the result of a private settlement if he formally guarantees to accept outlawry or formally agrees that the other man may impose outlawry on him if he wishes. It is prescribed that one man alone may not impose outlawry on another unless (p. 109) the terms of the outlawry are stated when the latter guarantees to accept the outlawry and they stipulate them at once. If he has formally agreed that the other should impose outlawry if he wishes, the only way that he can impose outlawry on him is by nominating eleven men with himself as the twelfth.[149] But if terms of his outlawry were stated when the outlawry was formally agreed, then they cannot impose outlawry on other terms than were then stipulated before witnesses. The testimony of the witnesses named when he formally agreed to the outlawry is to be given in such a way that the arbitrators hear it, before the settlement is announced.

Outlawry as part of a private settlement

If outlawry for him was formally agreed by someone other than himself, the witnesses who witnessed his transfer to the other of his formal guarantee to accept outlawry are to be brought to testify there before the settlement is announced. They are first to swear oaths; and they are to swear oaths and bear witness in such a way that the arbitrators hear them. If a man formally agrees to let another man make what settlement he wishes . . . and so on to the end . . . that is to be binding.[150]

Agreement on behalf of a man so outlawed

If a man formally guarantees to accept outlawry on terms clearly stated, there is no need for a judgment. The outlawry is then to be reported at Lögberg.

Report at Lögberg

Outlawry may not be imposed unless its terms are stated when the man to be outlawed formally agrees to a settlement; and in other circumstances the other man may not impose outlawry unless he does so

Summary repeat of first two paragraphs above

---

147. District courts (*heraðsdómar*), a term that covers courts that were not held at assemblies and were not confiscation courts; variant names and some specific purposes are mentioned in ‡‡ 167, 234, 176, 202, 223.

148. These words are not a title in K. Cf. Add. ‡ 36.

149. He forms a court of twelve and this court sentences the man to outlawry, the "judgment" mentioned in l. 27. Cf. Add ‡ 36.

150. K expresses "and so on to the end" with the Latin *Usque in finem*. The whole text is found in ‡ 71 (pp. 119-20). There is a similar introductory passage but a different continuation in ‡ 244.

with eleven companions. Testimony of his formal guarantee is to be given before another man accepts outlawry on his behalf. They are to swear oaths and bear witness [in such a way] that the arbitrators hear it.[151]

Degrees of outlawry legally recognized

There are three kinds of legal outlawry in our country: when a man is made a full outlaw, who may not be given passage, or a lesser outlaw, or, third, when lesser outlawry has the added condition that the man has no right to return to this country.[152]

If joint prosecuting principals disagree

If two men are principals in the same suit and one of them wants to prepare it for a spring assembly and the other for the General Assembly, the one who wants to prepare it for the General Assembly is to have his way. But if the other has (p. 110) prepared the case for a spring assembly, the other may choose, as he prefers, either to bring it to the General Assembly, having forbidden it by veto at the spring assembly, or to summon the judgment as one to be revoked.

If one man has two suits against him

If two lesser outlawry charges are against the same man and in the same court, he is to be judged a full outlaw if the principal is the same in both cases. If two charges are against a man in the same court, one a lesser outlawry charge and one a full outlawry charge, judgment is to be given according to the full outlawry suit, and the prosecutor of that has to see to the confiscation court. And if two full outlawry charges are against one man, and different men have the conduct of those cases, they are to draw lots to decide which of them is to see to the confiscation court, but both of them are to bring all their formal means of proof to the confiscation court and have testimony given of the terms laid down for his outlawry. And they both have equal rights to the property under penalty and to prosecute for assistance to him.

The confiscation court after such double prosecution

And if two men have cases against the same man, they are to draw lots to decide which of them is to see to the confiscation court. Now, whatever the failures were which put him under penalty to both, they are to share everything as if both have made him an outlaw. But if one of them comes off badly, then it is [as if] he alone had got him condemned, but in all other respects they are to share the property under penalty in the same way as before.[153]

Prosecution of a man outlawed on

Whether more or less is unpaid of the compensation to spare a man from becoming a full outlaw, one not to be given passage, if he then in-

---

151. This repeats the matter of p. 109, ll. 8-18 above.

152. In ‡ 55 (p. 98) this last penalty is regarded rather as one of full outlawry mitigated in such a way as to allow passage abroad to the sentenced man. Cf. also ‡ 73 (p. 120).

153. The man who has come off worse has the privilege of acting as the one who got him condemned (and doubtless the right to prosecute for assistance to him), but he still shares the outlaw's property with the other prosecutor (that half of the residue which the man who got an outlaw condemned would normally take, see ‡ 49, p. 90).

curs a full outlawry charge, he is to be prosecuted like a man who is under no penalty and prosecuted then for the fullest (p. 111) penalty.[154]

conditional terms

If a man becomes a lesser outlaw, men have no right to ban his journeys and his penalty is not to be added to unless he commits offenses for which he must become a full outlaw.[155]

Lawful journeys of a lesser outlaw not to be barred

If charges are outstanding against a man [A] who has been outlawed as the result of private settlement or at a spring assembly, a lesser outlawry charge or a full outlawry charge, the man [B] who has to prosecute such suits is to summon the man [C] who got him [A] condemned and make [the penalty] lesser outlawry on the grounds that he [C] condemned him [A] to a deceptive outlawry, and wanted to destroy his [B's] case thereby, and that if this charge of his [B's] had not been against him [A], he [C] would not have proceeded against him [A]; and he [B] is to call nine neighbors of the man prosecuted [C], to give a verdict whether he [C] would have prosecuted him [A] to full outlawry in that suit or not and whether he [C] thereby wanted to destroy the case he [B] is conducting. If the panel gives a verdict that he [C] wanted to destroy his [B's] case thereby, the penalty for the man [C] who got him [A] condemned, is lesser outlawry; and that is called "deceptive outlawry" and that judgment must be revoked.

So-called "deceptive outlawry"

K ‡ 61
Autumn Meeting Matters

We are to hold autumn meetings and the chieftains who hold assemblies together are to hold autumn meetings together, and their autumn meeting is to be where their assembly place is unless they get permission to have it elsewhere.[156] An autumn meeting is not to be later than on the Sunday following the Saturday when eight weeks of summer are left and it shall not be earlier than a fortnight after the General Assembly.[157] An autumn meeting is to be a meeting lasting not less than one day and not more than two nights.

Site, date, and duration

(p. 112) An autumn meeting is to be formally inaugurated just like an assembly and a man's personal compensation is doubled at a formally inaugurated autumn meeting in the same way as at an assembly.[158]

Inauguration; personal compensation doubled

At an autumn meeting all new laws are to be announced and the calendar and the observance of Ember Days and the beginning of Lent,[159] and

New laws and calendar announced

---

154. A full outlaw with no mitigation permitted.
155. See ‡‡ 52-53 (pp. 93-95).
156. I.e., from the Law Council.
157. July 16-22; the later limit was Sunday, August 17-23.
158. Cf. ‡ 56 (p. 99).
159. Cf. ‡‡ 19, 116 (pp. 51, 188); p. 35, n. 37.

similarly if it is leap year or if any addition is to be made to the summer season,[160] and also if men are to come to the General Assembly before ten weeks of summer have passed.[161] And the chieftain who has the duty of inaugurating the meeting is to rehearse all that unless they have arranged it differently among themselves.

Assembly men and their booths at assembly sites

All men have the right to build booths for themselves at the assembly they belong to if they wish. They have the right to have their horses there and to build booths while they are at autumn meetings or assemblies. If men who have left that assembly own booths there, they are not to build booths there again, but they have the right to keep those booths in repair if they wish. If they do build booths there, the booths are forfeit to the man who owns the land they stand on, whether it is a man of that assembly who owns it or someone else, and they are under penalty for building them.

If men's booths collapse either at the General Assembly or at a spring assembly and fall to the ground and lie like that for three summers, then anyone who wants has the right to build himself a booth there.

K ‡ 62
The Confiscation Court[162]

When and where confiscation courts are to be held

It is prescribed that a confiscation court is to be held for every man who has been outlawed, and the chieftain to whose assembly group the man who has been outlawed belongs is to be called on at the close of the assembly for a confiscation court to be held a fortnight after the close of the assembly[163] at the home of the man who has been outlawed, within bowshot of it at a place where there is neither arable land nor meadow land.[164] But if he does not know the home of the outlawed man, he is to hold the confiscation court (p. 113) at the home of the chieftain to whose assembly group the man who got him condemned belongs.[165] The procedure is the same if he does not know the outlawed man's assembly membership as when he does not know his home.

Calling witnesses or neighbors

The prosecutor is to call witnesses of the announcement of judgment

---

160. Originally the Icelandic year was credited with only 364 days. The necessary adjustment was made by a native addition of a week to the summer season every five or six years (an invention attributed to Þorsteinn surtr Hallsteinsson in the 940's) and gradual adoption of the Julian leap-year addition of one day every four years.

161. We do not know in what circumstances this might occur.

162. This repeats much of ‡‡ 48-55 (pp. 88-98); reference should be made to the notes on those pages.

163. The Assembly ended on Wednesday, July 1-7.

164. Cf. p. 30, n. 22.

165. Cf. p. 88, n. 100.

three nights before the confiscation court or with longer notice if the man has been outlawed in a court, but otherwise the witnesses named to witness it when he was made an outlaw as the result of a private settlement, and he is to have the testimony brought of the men named[166] to witness it that testimony was produced that the outlaw had formally guaranteed to accept his outlawry.

The men who have money owed them by the man who has been outlawed are to have called the witnesses of their claims, or neighbors — for those who have no witnesses — four nights before or with longer notice. The man who got him condemned is to call neighbors three nights before or with longer notice to attend and decide what property is there under penalty. Those neighbors are required in the same way to decide on the claims of all who had money owed them by the man who has been outlawed and who do not have witnesses available.

If dependents come to a confiscation court, a panel of twelve is to be asked to give a verdict on whether they are dependents of the outlawed man or not. The verdict must be that people from whom he had the right to inherit are his dependents and those others for whose maintenance as dependents it is the panel verdict of neighbors that he took money under a fair agreement. If other men are equally closely related to the dependents, the neighbors are to make the division among them. The dependents are to be judged itinerant according to whatever the outlaw's degree of responsibility for them proves to be.

Panel of twelve to decide on dependents

Dependents to be judged itinerant

It is not required to bring to a confiscation court a child for whose fathering the man is outlawed.

If men who are required to bring dependents to a confiscation court do not bring them, they make themselves, but not their heirs, responsible for those dependents.

Men who keep back dependents take responsibility for them

The penalty of a man who conceals property under penalty is lesser outlawry, and the summons in that case is to be made locally and nine neighbors of the man prosecuted are to be called at the assembly to decide whether he had or had not concealed the property (p. 114) for which the other has summoned him.

Penalty for concealing property

To each shall be adjudged his due amount, if the property stretches so far, and personal compensation shall be adjudged from the property if it is a case involving personal compensation and then theft payment if it is a thieving case. If the property will stretch farther, the chieftain who nominated the court is to be adjudged a cow or a four-winter-old ox. If the sums do not stretch so far, then all sums are to be equally reduced.

Distribution of property

Payment to chieftain

Suits as at a debt court

If the man who has been outlawed had a wife, judgment is to be given

---

166. I.e., at the final settlement meeting, cf. Add. ‡ 36.

on her property as at a debt court.[167] All suits concerning money are to be prepared for this court, just as for a debt court, and similarly in the matter of land-valuing and in redeeming pledges, if people have any, and the procedure is to be as at a debt court in all suits concerning money where men had money owed them by him before he became outlawed.

Treatment of wife's property

The wife's dowry[168] is not to be reduced nor the bride price[169] if it was his own cash that went into the bride price, but if it was not his own property that went into the bride price, then the bride price is to be reduced just like other sums. If man and wife have incurred debts by mutual consent then each is to pay those debts in shares proportional to the benefits each has had from that property.

Treatment of property in pledge

If there is any property there which has been pledged to people, then whichever one of them has proceeded in accordance with law is to take the pledged property. If two men have the same article pledged to them, the one who had it pledged to him first is to take that object unless his procedure was not in accordance with law. If the procedure of the one who had the pledge secured to him second was in accordance with law, he is to take that article and not the one whose procedure was not in accordance with law. The procedure is in accordance with law when the article pledged is specifically shown to witnesses, though it is also lawful if the property pledged is known to them by sight, and the pledge is to be published (p. 115) before five neighbors of the man who put his property in pledge. If other sums are reduced, he is not to have more than he was owed by the outlawed man in the first place, even though something worth more was pledged.[170]

Oaths sworn by all concerned in the procedure

Everyone who is to fulfill legal duties by speaking there is to swear oaths just as at an assembly court.

Care of confiscated property and of dependents

They must adjudge care of the property until the next General Assembly to the man who got him condemned, and they must adjudge half to the principal and half to the men of the Quarter.

They must judge the dependents of the man who has been outlawed who have come there to the confiscation court itinerant among the members of the assembly in whose district the confiscation court is held. If there are two assemblies on the same assembly ground, then they are

---

167. Cf. p. 90, n. 106.

168. Reading *heimanfylgju* for *honum fylgju dœma*, words which the scribe in K seems to have tried to erase.

169. The dowry (*heimanfylgja*) was a customary contribution from the bride's family; bride price (*mundr*) an obligatory payment from the bridegroom's side. These were the wife's property though normally administered by the husband. Cf. ‡‡ 152-54, 223.

170. Cf. ‡ 223.

to be itinerant among the members of both those assemblies.[171]

Further on care of confiscated property

If the property stretches farther than was now told, then half that property is to be adjudged to the men of the assembly in whose district the confiscation court is held and in which the dependents, if any, are legally itinerant, and half to the man who got him condemned. Care of the property which men of the assembly are to have is to be adjudged to the man who got him condemned. If he and they belong to the same assembly, he is to bring the property he has so far collected to the autumn meeting in which he participates, and share it with them there. But what he has not collected by then, either in payments received or formally guaranteed, he is to share with them at the spring assembly. And if the man who got him condemned belongs to a different assembly, he is to share it at the next General Assembly. As much as possible is to be shared out at the confiscation court and entrusted to the chieftain who nominated the court.[172]

Public share to go on maintenance of dependents

The property which men of the same assembly get as their share is to be used, as far as it stretches, to settle any dependents there may be in fixed homes. If there is more, it is to be used for the needs of other incapable people who are legally itinerant among members of that assembly.

If no confiscation court is held: penalty and procedure

If a man does not hold a confiscation court as prescribed in the laws, his penalty for that is lesser outlawry, and the prosecution of the case lies with the man who stands to take care of the dependents who should otherwise (p. 116) be judged itinerant at the court. But if the man who has been outlawed had no dependents, the case lies with someone to whom he owed money. And if he had no debts, then the case lies with anyone who wishes to prosecute, and the summons in that case is to be made locally and nine neighbors of the man prosecuted are to be called at the assembly.

Time of day for nomination of court

Men are to come so that the court is nominated before midday, and similarly all the men who are called to provide formal means of proof and all the men who have property to claim there and all the men who ought legally to bring dependents there along with the dependents themselves.[173]

If men are prevented from bringing dependents to the court

If a man does not learn of the confiscation court in circumstances enabling him to get to it with a dependent, he is to publish maintenance of that dependent next summer at Lögberg as a claim on the men of the assembly to which the chieftain belongs who had the confisca-

---

171. According to ‡ 50 (p. 91), dependents of men outlawed at the General Assembly were to be judged itinerant within the appropriate Quarter; those of men outlawed by other courts, itinerant among the local assembly groups. On the preceding cf. ‡ 49 (pp. 90-91).

172. Cf. p. 91, n. 108.

173. Cf. p. 89, n. 103.

tion court nominated, and call for a panel of twelve to decide whether that was a dependent of the man who was outlawed or not. Five neighbors of his are to give a verdict on whether he was or [was not] prevented by reasons of necessity from getting to the confiscation court. Such dependents are to be itinerant.

K ‡ 63
On Willful Damage[174]

If compensation for damage is not paid at a confiscation court

Where a man is judged a lesser outlaw for malicious damage, then at the confiscation court such compensation for damage is to be paid to the man who prosecuted him as five neighbors assess by oath on a book. If compensation for damage is not paid at the confiscation court as prescribed, then as soon as the confiscation court is finished, he falls under the same penalty as if he had been judged a full outlaw at a General Assembly court, one not to be sustained and not to be given passage.

K ‡ 64; p. 117
On Chieftains

If a chieftain does not attend at proper time

If a chieftain does not come to the beginning of a spring assembly, he is fined for that and forfeits his chieftaincy, and that case lies with men who have brought lawsuits to that assembly. If they will not prosecute, the case lies with the chieftains of the same assembly, with the one of them who is the more willing to prosecute and with the one of them who is at the assembly if they are not both there. If they will not, the case lies first with men of the same assembly and then with anyone who wishes.

Summoning and calling at least one week before spring assembly

If a case arises in which local calling figures, it may only be prepared for a spring assembly if neighbors are called and the summons also made a week before the assembly or with longer notice.[175]

Charge of false verdict against a man of a different assembly

If a man at a spring assembly prosecutes someone from a different assembly on the grounds that he has given a false verdict, the chieftain to whose assembly group he himself belongs is to be called on [to form a panel of twelve].

Malicious damage: procedure, penalty, and definition

If a man starts doing malicious damage and damages men's property and does damage equivalent to the price of a cow or more, the penalty for that is full outlawry. Nine neighbors of the place where the malicious damage was done are to be called at the assembly. Malicious damage is when a man tries to damage men's property on purpose and with malice. A case of malicious damage is to be published at Lögberg and prosecuted the same summer.[176]

---

174. Cf. ‡ 64 below; Add. ‡ 107; ‡ 204; St ‡ 431 (II 495).
175. On this and the preceding paragraph cf. ‡ 56 (p. 100) and ‡‡ 56, 84 (pp. 99, 137).
176. Cf. ‡ 63 above.

K ‡ 65
On Fines

If there are only fining cases, it is to be enjoined by judgment that the money be paid at that spot at the assembly on which members of the assembly agree, a fortnight after the prosecution assembly. Half of all the fines and (p. 118) property under penalty from cases judged at spring assemblies is due to the men of the assembly and half to the man who prosecutes.[177]

Payment of fines: place, time, and division

K ‡ 66

[178]If a man has formally guaranteed at home in the district to accept his outlawry or if he becomes an outlaw as the result of a private settlement, the confiscation court is to be called for at the next General Assembly after he was outlawed. The prosecutor is to ask at Lögberg about his residence and his assembly attachment, if he does not know already. If no one admits his residence but a chieftain admits his assembly attachment, the confiscation court is to be held at this chieftain's home and he is to be asked to nominate the court. If neither is admitted, he is to hold it at the home of the chieftain to whose assembly group he himself belongs and then ask him to nominate the court.

Confiscation court after sentence by private settlement

K ‡ 67
If Money Is Not Forthcoming[179]

If the money which is to be paid at a confiscation court is not forthcoming, then the outlaw is under penalty as a full outlaw who may not be sustained and not given passage. If "life ring" and "sustenance pledge" are paid, his property under penalty is to be adjudged in the same way as the property of a full outlaw. From his property under penalty, if it stretches so far, a cow or four-winter-old ox is also to be adjudged to the chieftain who nominated the court, and then the "life ring" — that is a mark — is to be included with the rest of the property under penalty, but otherwise the chieftain takes only that mark for himself. It is lawful to pay that mark there at the confiscation court, but it is also lawful for a man to give a formal guarantee to pay it after a fortnight's interval at the home of the chieftain, and that shall be the legal (p. 119) settling day for that payment. A man may pay it in objects of value if he wishes, and each of them is to select his own lawful valuer.

Full outlawry if dues are not paid

Payment to chieftain

Payment may be postponed for fourteen days

When a confiscation court is held for a lesser outlaw, his homes are to be reported. He is to have three homes. It shall not be farther between

Immunity at homes announced at the court

---

177. Cf. ‡ 117 (p. 193), on fines due to the Lawspeaker at the spring assembly he participates in.

178. Cf. ‡ 60 (pp. 109-11).

179. Cf. ‡‡ 51-52 (pp. 92-93), whose matter is here largely repeated.

them than may be traveled one way in one day. He shall be immune at those homes and within bowshot of them in all directions.[180] He is also immune on that road and within bowshot of that road as long as he does not travel by it more than once a month. If men come towards him, he is to go so far off the road that they cannot reach him with spear points. He does not become immune if his homes are not reported at the confiscation court, and he does not become immune if the money that should be paid there is not paid.

K ‡ 68

Horse and food for men who are not assembly participants

[181]In response to a calling household men have the right to make a claim for a horse and food and everything needful for them to have at the Assembly. All householders who are not so rich that they are required to pay assembly attendance dues are to have the same right. Such a man may also make a claim for the horse to be brought to his home. A horse well fit to ride to the Assembly is to be brought to the home of the man who is called. They have the right to make this claim if they were named as witnesses for something which, when they were named, they did not expect would require their attendance at the Assembly or from which they had no right to excuse themselves. Such a claim in response to calling is to be made as soon as possible at a place where the man on whom the claim is made hears it or at his home. It is equally valid to claim this aid from whichever he prefers, the man [A]who called him or the man [B] who transferred the calling to him [A].[182]

When panels of twelve and five are to be called in suits concerning dependents

A panel of twelve is only to be (p. 120) called for if the heir against whom a claim for a dependent's maintenance is published is abroad. If the man against whom the claim is published is in this country, five neighbors of the man against whom the claim is published are to be called to give a verdict on whether he is his heir or not or whether the other is his inherited dependent.

K ‡ 69
Asking for a Confiscation Court[183]

After judgments have been announced, a prosecutor is to ask the chieftain at Lögberg for a confiscation court, or tell him of it if he is not present, or ask him somewhere where he can hear it. In that case he [shall] report at Lögberg that he has asked the chieftain to nominate a confiscation court and say where it is to be. The man who wishes to ask for a con-

---

180. Cf. p. 30, n. 22.
181. Cf. ‡‡ 33 (pp. 69-70), 251.
182. Cf. St ‡ 337 (II 364); and on what follows ‡‡ 130, 136.
183. Cf. ‡‡ 48-49 (pp. 88-91), whose matter is here largely repeated.

fiscation court is to name witnesses "to witness that I call on you, N.N. — or ask — to nominate a confiscation court for N.N. after a fortnight's interval," and[184] bid him come there so that it is nominated before midday.[185] Twelve men are to be nominated to join that court and it is to be challenged [like] a panel of twelve.[186]

Formula for asking for a confiscation court

The man who asked for a confiscation court is to name witnesses "to witness that I swear an oath on a book, a lawful oath, and declare before God that I shall bring forward all matters against N.N. here at the confiscation court in the way I know to be most right and true and most in accordance with law." Testimony of the announcement of judgment is to be brought or testimony of the settlement [by which he was outlawed and of] what terms were laid down for his outlawry and of what he was outlawed for and of where he was outlawed. Men are then to draw lots to decide how cases are to be brought forward.

Oath at a confiscation court

Testimony to be brought before the court

Order of cases decided by lot

K ‡ 70; p. 121
On Full Outlaws

If men bring back here a man who was made a full outlaw that same summer, the penalty for it is full outlawry. If they did not know he was outlawed, they are not under penalty, unless they keep him for three nights after they learn of it and then the penalty is full outlawry. If men bring back here a man[187] who was made a full outlaw the previous summer, they are to do one thing or the other, either kill him or take him to the man who got him condemned within half a month of learning that he had been outlawed. If [they] will do neither, their penalty is full outlawry.

If men bring full outlaws back to Iceland

K ‡ 71
On Formal Agreements[188]

If a man formally agrees to let another man make what settlements he wishes and they do not stipulate the matter more precisely than that, then the latter cannot impose any outlawry and he has no right to state surrender of specific objects of value belonging to him among the terms if that was not stipulated in their formal agreement. He is to impose what money settlement he pleases and state how many ounce-units the other is to pay or at what rate they should be, and how many should be paid in objects of value and how many in livestock. If a man makes a settlement

What penalties cannot be imposed after agreement to abide by private settlement

---

184. Reading *ok* for *at* "to."
185. Thursday, July 16-22. Cf. also p. 89, n. 103.
186. Cf. p. 89, n. 104.
187. Omitting *þá menn* from *Nú ferja menn þá menn út hingat þann mann* ...
188. Cf. ‡ 60 (p. 109), ‡ 244.

on terms other than now rehearsed, whether he imposes outlawry or says that he is to pay with his land or chieftaincy or states surrender of some specific objects of value belonging to him among the terms, (p. 122) it shall be binding in no particular. If he wishes, he is to include everything which they stipulated before witnesses in the terms of settlement, that is all to be binding.

K ‡ 72
On Summonings[189]

Which neighbors are to be called if summoning is done before the moving days

If a man is summoned at his legal home before the moving days, neighbors of that legal home are to be called, even if called at the General Assembly, and are to be those then living nearest the place for which the calling is made.

If panel members come late

If a neighbor who comes to a spring assembly on the Monday gives a panel verdict, that spoils a man's case.

K ‡ 73
On Assistance to an Outlaw

Úlfheðinn's statement on procedure in case of assisting an outlaw granted passage abroad

Úlfheðinn[190] said this was law in the case of a man who wants to prosecute someone for assisting a full outlaw or lesser outlaw who has passage from the country laid down for him but who does not try to get away as prescribed in the laws.[191] He is to summon him locally to the General Assembly and a Quarter Court for giving assistance to such men, and claim that his penalty is lesser outlawry. The case is to be presented in the same form as in the summons, and testimony of summoning is to be brought. The next witnesses are to be those named at the confiscation court to witness [the testimony produced there of] the fact that the court had judged him a full outlaw who could be given passage and with the same safeguards as a lesser outlaw, and with no [right to] return to the country if that was laid down for him. If any man prosecutes for assistance to a lesser outlaw, testimony of summoning is to come in the case and next the witnesses who were named at the confiscation court to witness the testimony produced there of what his outlawry was judged to be in the court where he became a lesser outlaw. The third witnesses are to be those named to witness the fact that his outlawry, as imposed on him by judgment or (p. 123) as imposed on him by an arbitrator, was announced without guile and without deceit at Lögberg. Then the testimony is to be brought of the witnesses named to witness the fact that the confiscation court was held for him.

---

189. Cf. Add. ‡ 111; ‡ 89 (p. 154).
190. Úlfheðinn Gunnarsson, Lawspeaker 1108-16.
191. See ‡ 53 (pp. 93-95).

Úlfheðinn said it was law that the confiscation court should give judgment to the effect that the sentence of outlawry, judged or imposed, should now fall on him.

The chieftain to whose assembly group the man prosecuted belongs is to be called on to form [a panel] of twelve to give a verdict on whether that man had shared living quarters with the outlaw or not and thereby given him assistance. Testimony is to be given to match the number of times witnesses were named [in the original action].

He further stated that sentence of outlawry is given effect by the confiscation court's judgment

Panel of twelve to decide on sharing living quarters with an outlaw

K ‡ 74
On Verdicts[192]

It is to be deemed as if a panel verdict is favorable to the other side if the man who called the panel delays until the sun comes onto Þingvöllr.

If in giving verdicts or testimonies men leave out any word that affects the case, then it is as if verdicts or testimonies are withheld.

Delayed verdicts are deemed favorable

If important words are omitted

K ‡ 75

If a man conducts a transferred case concerning property and dies on the journey to an assembly or at an assembly, the principal may take up his own case and prosecute the same summer. If he is not at the assembly he may prosecute the following summer. If the other has presented the case before he died, the principal is to take it up where he left off and proceed in everything as before, except that he is to repeat the presentation of the case. If the other has had judgment given on the property before he died, his heir is to summon in case of judgment-breaking, but[193] receipt of the property is due to the principal of the case concerning it.

(p. 124) In outlawry cases the procedure is similarly to be that the man who got an outlaw condemned, or his heir if he has died, is to prosecute for assistance to the outlawed man. But receipt of money taken by him in return for terms of mitigation is due to the principal of the original suit or his heir.

A man shall be qualified to sit in the Fifth Court even though he has cases in a Quarter Court.[194]

If a General Assembly court gives a wrong judgment, a summons is to be made for the judgment to be revoked and it is to be prosecuted before the Fifth Court that same summer. But if the principal in question is not there, it may be prosecuted the following summer.

If a man with a transferred case dies; rights of principals

A man with suits in a Quarter Court may act as a Fifth Court judge

Wrong judgments go to the Fifth Court

---

192. Cf. ‡‡ 35, 32 (pp. 74-75, 67-68); p. 54, n. 5.
193. Reading *en* for *ef*, "if."
194. Men with cases were disqualified as judges in Quarter Courts, cf. ‡ 20 (p. 53).

K ‡ 76
Responsibility for Horses[195]

Care of horses at General Assembly Claims in case of death or disappearance

When men put their horses into someone's keeping at the General Assembly in accordance with the article of the law, the man who accepts a horse is not to use it for anything except for driving horses to where they are kept or from there to Þingvöllr and for keeping paid watch on them,[196] and he is not to ride any horse so much that it does not stay well filled out. At the close of the Assembly he is to show the owner his horse alive or dead, and the man who accepted it is not responsible for it unless it has died from his mishandling. If at the close of the Assembly he does not show the horse, neither alive nor dead, then at the close of the assembly the owner is to publish a suit, to be prosecuted the following summer, for payment for the horse against the man who accepted it.

K ‡ 77

Chieftain to guarantee payment on behalf of his assembly man; recovery of payment

A chieftain has the right to make a formal agreement on behalf of a man of his assembly third for dependents or charges for keep or any formal agreement that is needed, at the lowest figure he can contrive and in a suit he thinks just. He rightly claims the sum for which he has made a formal agreement from the man in question, and the settling day for that money will be on the Monday of the spring assembly[197] in which the chieftain participates and on the assembly slope there. (p. 125) There he may summon for payment and call five neighbors of the man prosecuted to give a verdict on whether he had formally agreed to pay money on his behalf or not, at the lowest figure he could contrive and in a suit in which he thought he was justly charged. But a settling day for that money only comes into being if [the man who] owes the money is told of it at the autumn meeting[198] in which the man to whom the money is due participates. But if he does not learn of it then, he is to know of it at the latest at the beginning of summer,[199] and if he does not hear of it then or sooner the settling day is off. Then it becomes lawful to publish the suit at the close of the assembly for prosecution next summer. Moreover I think it is lawful to summon the case for judgment there at a spring assembly, if the man prosecuted learns of the formal agreement and they both belong to the same assembly group.

Other men may guarantee payment if chieftain will not

Other men have to invite a chieftain to be the first to make a formal agreement on behalf of a man of his assembly third. If he will not, other men may make a formal agreement

---

195. See also Add. ‡ 29.
196. The translation is conjectural, the text probably corrupt, cf. Add. ‡ 29.
197. See ‡ 56 (pp. 98-99) for times of spring assemblies.
198. Cf. ‡ 61 (pp. 111-12).
199. Thursday, April 9-15.

for him if they wish, and each man has the same right of prosecution for his money as the chieftain has.

Where someone undertakes prosecution or defense for someone else, it is fully adequate even if he does not name men on the other side, if he does not know them.

Absence of names no bar to legal transfer of a case

Confiscation courts are to be on a Wednesday when they follow any spring assembly that was over on a Wednesday. A confiscation court is to sit till nones if men know it is likely that dependents or men called to provide formal means of proof have not arrived.²⁰⁰

Time of confiscation court following a spring assembly

In no circumstances is a case to fall to a third person unless a man becomes ill or is wounded on a journey to or at the General Assembly: then a man may transfer a transferred case but in no other circumstances.²⁰¹

Transfer of a case already transferred

If a man takes a case from someone and then will not prosecute and so tries to make the case void, he is liable to lesser outlawry at the suit of the principal.²⁰²

Willful neglect of a transferred case

If a man who has transferred or prepared a case in which he is principal then dies, that suit falls to his heir, but if he has in no way begun the suit (p. 126) when he dies, it is [as if] he had in no way become the principal in that suit.²⁰³

If a principal dies

Those men who are rightly called locally to serve on a panel on behalf of the household of an unfit man are rightly called at an assembly if they are present, even if the man who stays at home is healthy. But no one can do panel service for someone else when the latter is called locally except father for son or son for father. Those men whom it is lawful to call on behalf of the household of an unfit man may also be called on behalf of the household of a man who has resigned from performing legal duties.²⁰⁴

Substitutes for panel members

Neighbors called to serve on panels at assemblies and [at confiscation courts] in cases of outlawry are to be selected with regard to wealth in the same way as when called locally.²⁰⁵

Selection of neighbors

It is lawful to summon for prosecution at the General Assembly any case in which local calling does not figure right up to the end of the Thursday when seven weeks of summer have passed,²⁰⁶ but it is not lawful to summon after that unless cases arise later.

Summoning cases that do not require neighbors called locally

---

200. Cf. ‡ 48 (p. 89 and n. 103).
201. Cf. Add. ‡ 74.
202. Add. ‡ 98, cf. Add. ‡ 74 (ii).
203. Cf. Add. ‡ 101 (ii).
204. Cf. ‡ 89 (pp. 151-52).
205. Cf. ‡ 89 (p. 150) and p. 125.
206. Thursday, May 28 - June 3. On other times for summoning see ‡ 104 (pp. 165-66).

Calling neighbors on days holy from nones onward

On a day observed as holy from nones onward a man has the right to call neighbors up to night-time if he began the calling early and cannot finish it before nones, calling them one after another.[207]

If joint householders disagree on harboring an outlaw

If men share a household and one of them takes in an outlaw and the other is unwilling, then the one who is unwilling is to name witnesses to witness that he is unwilling and that it is with his disagreement and report it to five neighbors. Then he is liable to no legal penalty for sharing living quarters with an outlaw as long as he gives him assistance in no other way. The same in all respects is prescribed for household people. Their words stay valid for twelve months. Boarding an outlaw in ignorance for three nights, consecutive or separate, [carries no penalty].

Men disqualified as summons witnesses

No one who is himself a principal in a case is to use his father or brother or son as a summons witness (p. 127). In a transferred case the principal is not to be used as a summons witness, nor his son, nor his father or brother. Their testimony is invalid, but the case is not spoilt as long as there are two or more other witnesses and they bring forward the testimony.

Father and son, and brothers, make one witness

Father and son or two brothers count as one in any matter or testimony for which one and the same man names them. They are qualified to be witnesses in any matter for which two different men name them.

Challenge always on grounds of connection with principals

All challenges of neighbors or judges are to be on grounds of connection with the prosecution principal or defense principal and not with the man who prosecutes or defends if he is not the principal.[208]

If a man acts in error as a prosecution principal

[209]If a man other than the principal prosecutes a case involving personal compensation because he thinks he is the principal, and the proper principal pays no heed because he thinks someone other than himself is the principal, then he, the proper principal, is to have three-quarters of the settlement sum and the man who did the prosecuting one-quarter. If he needs to lay out money in bringing the prosecution or to give it for support, then this is first to be subtracted from the settlement sum and they are to divide the rest between them. Now if he who prosecutes knows that he is not the principal, then the other, the proper principal, rightly claims the whole settlement sum awarded.

Bringing outlaws to the country or assisting them in ignorance

Men who bring outlaws to the country and did not know of their outlawry are not liable to legal penalty until they have been together with them for more than three nights after making land.[210]

---

207. Night-time (Icelandic *náttmál*) is about 2100 hours. On days observed as holy from nones (1500-1530) see ‡‡ 9-10 (pp. 41-43), Add. ‡ 27.

208. Cf. ‡‡ 25, 35 (pp. 60, 72).

209. This section is repeated in ‡ 95 (p. 159).

210. Cf. ll. 10-11 above and ‡ 70 (p. 119).

If a man does not know of someone's outlawry and assists him because he is sick or wounded or infirm because of age or gives him assistance because he does it for his soul's good, he is not put under penalty for such boarding in ignorance even though lengthy. He is not to give him passage from the country.

A man is to be called to serve on a panel at the house where he was householder when eight weeks of summer have passed,[211] and he is to be the rightful assembly participant for that household through the coming year unless he gets another qualified man (p. 128) to take his place, and he is to be called on behalf of the household, if he keeps his health so that he may be called,[212] and this even if he is out of the country. The rightful assembly participant in his place shall be the man who takes over the household from him, or that home man of his who he has said — either at the place where announcements are made at an autumn meeting or to his five neighbors at some later date — is to see to legal duties for him. *At what households men are to be called; and on rightful assembly participants*

A man who farms single-handed is rightly called to serve on a panel if he has so much property that there is an allotment of the price of two cows for each household member who is a charge on him.[213] *Property qualification for single-handed householder*

If men are sent to oppose men who are to call neighbors, and they cannot make their calling because they are confronted by force, it is lawful to summon the case for which the calling is appropriate at the nearest point they reach where they can successfully make the summons, and publish the summoning if those who oppose them do not hear it, and call nine neighbors at the assembly; and if all the neighbors cannot be called locally, it shall be as if none of them has been called. *If men calling neighbors are met by force they may summon instead*

If a man wants to leave the country he may transfer power of prosecution and defense if he wishes and care of what property he still owns here. Such formal agreements are to stand for three winters, but after that his heirs have the right to look after it.[214] *Transfer of legal obligations if a man goes abroad*

K ‡ 78
On Residences

We shall have four moving days in the country. The first is the Thursday when six weeks of summer have passed.[215] A man may choose to move house early that day. Second is the Friday, third is Saturday, fourth is Sunday. On the evening of that day the law says that a man is released *Moving days*

---

211. The eighth week of summer ended June 3-9.
212. Cf. ‡ 89 (p. 151) on men who are "assembly-fit."
213. Cf. ‡ 89 (p. 150).
214. *Fé*, "the property," St ‡ 62 (II 76).
215. Thursday, May 21-27.

Household attachment

from the household attachment he (p. 129) previously had. If a man has no household attachment by the evening of that Sunday or early next day, the penalty for it is a fine.

If a man has a wife, he is to have found a household attachment for her and told her about it at the latest on the Thursday when seven weeks of summer have passed.[216] If to her knowledge a place has not been found for her by then, it is lawful for her to join a household where she pleases, and she is to keep that place for that twelvemonth. If a man has not found places for the people he has to provide for on the last moving day, his penalty is a fine for each one of them and the case lies with anyone who wishes to prosecute.

Entering a household

A man is to enter a household as he agrees with the householder, either in the moving days or at midsummer.[217] A male sixteen winters old or older [may] arrange his own residence. An unmarried woman of twenty or more may also arrange her own residence.

Wages and duties of household men

A man may choose to enter a household at midsummer and do other work up to then if he wishes. If he does farm work he is not to take more pay than half a mark in six-ell ounce-units before midsummer, and from midsummer he is to work for his householder right on to winter and do whatever he wants of him except shepherding. He is to make one mountain trip for sheep-gathering and take part in slaughtering and go on journeys with the master of the house and spread dung in spring and repair homefield walling. He shall do that to earn his food.

Wages for tending animals and other work

There is no punishment either if household men take two ounce-units as pay from the Winter Nights to All Saints' day.[218] Men with dependents who do not have the property to maintain their dependents may take more if they wish. If a man looks after cattle, one ell is to pay for tending a cow or a four-winter-old ox, and two younger cattle count the same as one cow; six ells for thirty full-grown sheep and one ounce-unit for forty lambs; six ells of homespun for catering for ten people — (p. 130) an ounce-unit in legal tender, that is, or else let it be made up to that in other forms of payment.

Payments over and above legal wages

A householder may choose to give a man something over and above this. If he is summoned for doing so, it is not counted a gift if a verdict is given that it was a private pre-arrangement. If a man contracts to pay more than is prescribed he clears himself if a panel gives a verdict that he would otherwise not have got him, and if he does not in fact pay him more than the legal pay. If he tries to withhold the whole amount from

---

216. Thursday, May 28 - June 3.
217. Midsummer month normally began Sunday, July 13-19.
218. From mid-October to November 1; on Winter Nights cf. p. 31, n. 23.

the household man, the latter rightly claims the whole amount from him.

A man who does not move into his lodging is under penalty for three marks.[219] He is to be summoned at that place to the General Assembly or to a spring assembly or to whichever of these makes the third in a sequence of three assemblies, and similarly for any work wages he has been paid. The man who takes him in knowing that he had agreed to take lodging elsewhere is also under penalty for three marks to the householder with whom he had agreed to take lodging. Lodgings are taken from the moment they agree on it as decided by the verdict of a panel of neighbors. If a man breaks an arrangement with several men, all have the same right to prosecute the one who breaks it. Household men have a similar right to prosecute householders who break arrangements with them. A man is turned away if food is not served for him at meal times, even though it is only a single meal that is withheld from him. *If a householder breaks an agreement; being turned away*

If men do not move into agreed lodgings

If a man prices himself dearer than told earlier and similarly if he hires himself out at a dearer rate, the penalty is a fine of three marks for each. If a householder contracts to pay more than has now been told, his penalty is also a fine of three marks.[220] *Attempts to raise rates of pay*

Builders who make buildings from Norwegian timber[221] or bridges over rivers or lakes where fish run that can be netted or who build booths at the General Assembly, may choose to take day wages for outfield haymaking.[222] They must, however, have found themselves legal domicile in the moving days, even if they disregard it. Either the man himself or the householder must have reported it to neighbors that the former was attached to the household there, even if he has left the country or works at such things as were just told, and he is then treated as being in settled lodging with that householder and (p. 131) in the assembly group with the same chieftain as this householder with whom he has his legal domicile. *Position of builders and men who go abroad*

If a man joins someone's household, that becomes his legal domicile while he is away from the country. If the householder dies or if the man comes back to the country the same summer, it is lawful for him to join another household if he wishes; and it is lawful to summon him either at that home or else at the mooring stakes of his ship. If he is summoned at the mooring stakes, panels are not to be challenged on grounds of distance from that [home] and not from the home he joined later unless the *Position of a man newly returned to the country, and where he is to be summoned*

---

219. Cf. ‡ 80 (p. 129).

220. Add. ‡ 30.

221. Building timber was largely imported; native supplies were of driftwood and brushwood.

222. Add. ‡ 31.

people there have said at an assembly or an autumn meeting or to neighbors that he has his legal home there.

Disregard of household attachment

If a man joins someone's household and goes fishing[223] or does some other work and does not maintain the attachment, and he and the householder knowingly make that an agreement between them, the penalty is a fine of three marks for each of them.

Summons at last-known legal home

If someone does not know a man's legal home or where he has been formally guaranteed legal domicile or if the man has left from a different Quarter or if, even though in the same Quarter, he does not know where the man's mooring stakes are, it is lawful for him to summon him at the place he last knew was his legal home.

K ‡ 79

Summoning a man returned from abroad; joining a household

If a man comes ashore after a voyage it is lawful to summon him at the ship as long as he is using huts there by the ship, and he is to have joined a household within a half-month of leaving the ship if he wants to stay in that Quarter. If he wants to find a home in another Quarter, he is to have found a household to join within a half-month of coming into that Quarter. If a man has a wife and does not agree with the householder the woman is already lodging with about their both being there, he may choose to take lodgings (p. 132) in another place both for himself and his wife, and her leaving incurs no legal penalty, and the worth of her work and her keep is to be assessed.

A wife is free to leave her lodging to join her husband

Where a fisherman is to be summoned; his assembly attachment

If a man fishes till midsummer and then joins a household, he is then attached to that householder's assembly if he has legal domicile there, and it is lawful to summon him at that home, but as long as he is at the fishing huts it is lawful to summon him there for what he does there or has done before. If a man fishes through the working season and enters a household at the onset of winter, it is lawful to summon him at that home for all offenses that he commits after entering the household. He is to be summoned at the fishing huts for all offenses he commits before entering the household, and his assembly attachment is to the assembly to which the man who owns the land he is fishing from belongs.

K ‡ 80
On Priests' Residences[224]

A priest must have a legal home and report it

Priests are to be in legal homes when eight weeks of summer are left or sooner and they are to report their homes.[225]

[If a priest does not report his home], it is lawful for a man to summon

---

223. Cf. Add. ‡ 31 (ii).
224. Cf. ‡ 6 (p. 37).
225. Add. ‡ 32.

him at the home of any householder he pleases at whose church the priest has held established services. If a priest comes ashore after the beginning of "double month"[226] he is to have found himself a home within half a month of leaving the ship if he wants to stay in the same Quarter or within half a month of coming into the Quarter where he wants to be.[227]

If a man takes lodging for a whole year and is in the household for two weeks before the General Assembly and during the Assembly and for two weeks after it, then even though he leaves that lodging his legal home (p. 133) and his assembly attachment are there at the householder's where he spent those six weeks, and it is lawful to summon him there. *Six midsummer weeks at a lodging decide legal home and assembly attachment*

If a man moves about working for day wages it is lawful to summon him at any place where he stays a half-month or more in the working season. If he does not stay at any one place for half a month in the working season, it is lawful to summon him at any place where he spent three nights or more in the working season. If he was nowhere so long, it is lawful for a man to summon him where he last knew he spent the night. *Summoning an itinerant day laborer*

Whenever a man does not know a man's legal home and he has no opportunity of asking him with a legal asking, it is lawful to summon him at the place he last knew was his legal home.[228] He is to call his five neighbors to give a verdict as to whether that was the place he last knew was his legal home, and whether he had had opportunity to ask him with a legal asking or not. A man is only required to ask another about his residence in order to use it as the place for summoning if, having learnt of the offense and meaning to summon him, he meets him to speak to and recognizes him and has witnesses available. *Summons at last-known legal home*

When residence must be inquired for summoning purposes

If a man will not move into the household he has joined or leaves his lodging without good cause, his penalty for it is a fine of three marks and the householder has the right to summon him there at his own home [and] for any wages he has been paid.[229] *Penalties for not joining a household and for a householder who breaks an agreement*

If a householder breaks with a household man his penalty is a fine of three marks.

If someone dies after formally agreeing on household attachment with a man before the moving days, and his heir keeps the same household, the household-joining of that man stays fixed. The heir may choose to give up householding if he wishes. If he continues as householder, the penalty is a fine of three marks for either of them who breaks with the *What happens to a household when the householder dies*

---

226. *Tvímánaðr*, the month that normally began Tuesday, August 12-18.
227. Like other people ‡‡ 79 (p. 128).
228. Cf. ‡ 22 (pp. 55-57).
229. Cf. ‡ 78 (p. 127).

other. If the householder dies in the seventh week of summer,[230] the heir may choose whether he will continue as householder there or will give up householding if he prefers that, and then find the same sort of places and agreements for the household (p. 134) men already taken on as they had arranged for themselves. If the heir will do neither of those things, his penalty is a fine of three marks at the suit of each one of them. If the householder dies when seven weeks of summer have passed or later, the heir must continue as householder.

If a household man is sick or lunatic

If a household man is laid up off work, the householder is to keep him for half a month if he does not need tending. If he does need tending but is not out of his mind, it is lawful to take him to the man whose duty it is to maintain him. If he is out of his mind, he is to be taken to the nearest of his kinsmen who is a householder and who does not need to add anyone to his household in order to tend him. The need to add to one's household in order to tend him does not exist if a man has the household helpers to tend him if he can get them to do it. If it is not the householder's duty in accordance with law to maintain him, then the man who has the right to inherit from him must go to tend him if the householder sees need for it. If he does not go, he is under penalty for three marks, and the man whose duty it is to maintain the madman is to pay the householder the cost of his keep as neighbors assess it and he must also take over the madman at the moving days.

If a household man is laid up off work, the householder may choose, once he has been laid up half a month, whether he will take him to the man whose duty it is to maintain him or will keep him to the moving days and claim for his keep. [231]The man whose duty it is to maintain him may choose rather to bring the sick man to his home if he prefers that rather than put him into care elsewhere.

Whether a man is laid up and off work for a long time or for a short time neighbors are to assess the cost of his keep and the work he has done and what has not been done. It is to be assessed in accordance with the terms of the agreement between them.

Death of a household man

If a man who was supposed to do a particular job dies while attached to a household, neighbors are to assess which is worth more, the work from the time he was laid up (p. 135) or his keep.

or a man put into care

If a man put into someone else's care dies, neighbors are to calculate what he had used up and what he had not used up of his board and lodging, and by how much he was worse to keep when he was sick than when he took lodging there.

230. Week beginning Thursday, May 21-27.
231. Add. ‡ 33.

If a household man is laid up during outfield haymaking for three days, whether he is laid up continuously or not, the householder is not to be recompensed for that, but if he is laid up longer, the householder may choose to have his wages assessed for the whole period.

If a household man is off for three days during haymaking

If a household man takes a wife and each of them lives in different places, each is to stay in the place where they have their home if they are tied to particular jobs.[232] If they are not tied to particular jobs, they are to spend two-thirds of the time at his lodging and one-third at her lodging.

If a household man marries

If a household man says something to another household man which requires full personal compensation or does something to him which requires half personal compensation,[233] he is to leave the lodging and get nothing of his winter board and lodging. For all offenses which he committed before leaving the household and for the offense for which he left, it is lawful to summon those suits at that home, and for those suits he is treated as attached to the assembly of that householder. He is to have found legal lodging for himself within half a month of leaving, and it then becomes lawful to summon him at this home for offenses he commits thereafter, and for those suits he is treated as attached to the assembly of this householder.

If one household man offends another; dismissal and summoning

If a married man leaves his lodging on account of his offenses and his wife leaves too, her leaving incurs no legal penalty, and he rightly claims her winter board and lodging. Similarly also if the wife leaves on account of her offenses and her husband goes with her, his winter board and lodging may be rightly claimed.

Married couple who leave because of the offense of one of them

If a householder lets or makes a man leave who has suffered at another's hands, the household man rightly claims winter board and lodging, and he is not to pay because the particular jobs he was supposed to do are not properly done.

If an offended man is sent away

If a household man does something to the householder which requires full personal compensation, the household man must leave and get (p. 136) nothing of his winter board and lodging, though the householder still has the right to prosecute him. If a household man says something to the householder which requires half personal compensation, the household man is to leave. If he does not go, the case becomes one for full personal compensation, and his penalty for it is lesser outlawry. This, the one just told, is the only case where it is possible to prosecute words that require half personal compensation.[234] Again, in cases where a household man

If household people offend the householder or his wife

The only circumstances in which a half personal compensation offense can be prosecuted

---

232. Add. ‡ 33 (ii).
233. Cf. Add. ‡ 130 (ii); ‡ 237.
234. Cf. Add. ‡ 130 (ii); ‡ 237.

does or says something requiring full personal compensation to the householder or the mistress of the house and does not leave, their personal compensation is doubled.

Unjustified dismissal

If a householder turns a household man out of his lodging without good cause, the householder's penalty is a fine of three marks, and if the household man has asked the householder before witnesses for his board and lodging and he has not allowed it to him, he may rightly claim for his board and lodging from the householder.

How a household is affected by cases conferring rights of veto

If killing cases occur that confer rights of veto against men in the same household, a kinsman of the killer is to leave and get as much of his winter board and lodging as neighbors assess. Cases conferring rights of veto are those for which, in the wergild ring list, atonement of one ounce-unit or more is appropriate. That applies to fourth cousins and men of closer kin.[235]

K ‡ 81

What constitutes a household

A man who starts householding in the spring shall say he is joining an assembly group, whichever one he pleases. A household exists when a man has milking stock, but if he is a landowner he is to say he is joining an assembly group even if he does not have milking stock. If he is not a landowner and has no milking stock, he then belongs to the assembly group of the householder into whose care he puts himself. If he is at fishing huts he belongs to the assembly of the man who owns the land on which he is living.

Assembly attachment

Announcement of assembly attachment in person or by proxy

A man is to say at the General Assembly, or at a spring assembly if he wishes, that he is joining the assembly group of a chieftain, whichever one he (p. 137) pleases. He may choose to transfer to another man the business of saying at the General Assembly or a spring assembly that he is joining an assembly group. He is to have spoken to the chieftain earlier in the spring about wishing to join his assembly group if he gets someone else to say it at the General Assembly. If he has not said he is joining an assembly group and he is asked what assembly group he belongs to, he is to name the chieftain whose assembly group he wants to join and he is then attached to that assembly if the chieftain is willing. If a man has not said at a spring assembly that he is joining an assembly group, he is to have said it at the General Assembly before men go to the courts.

Time limits

Form of announcement

A man may say he is joining the assembly group of what chieftain he pleases. Both he and the chieftain are to name witnesses to witness that he says he is joining his assembly group along with his household people and his household stock and that the other accepts him.

---

235. See ‡ 113 (pp. 175, 182-83).

If someone other than the man who owns it acts in the chieftaincy and the chieftain has consented to a man's assembly membership but the man who acts in the chieftaincy will not accept him, he is nevertheless [to say that he is] joining that assembly group, and he then becomes attached there. *Disagreement between owner of chieftaincy and a man acting in the chieftaincy*

If someone says a man is joining an assembly group with a different chieftain from the one he told him to say, he becomes attached to the assembly he is said to be joining if he is willing, but if he is not willing to have that assembly membership, he is to tell neighbors as soon as he learns of it that he wants to be in that other assembly group, the one which he told the man to say he was joining. The man who said he was joining a different assembly group from the one he wanted to be in is fined three marks at the suit of each of the three, the two chieftains and the man he said was going to join the assembly group. The chieftain whose assembly group he was said to be joining is under no penalty for admitting his assembly attachment, and the other chieftain is under no penalty for not admitting it.[236] *If a proxy attaches a man to a chieftain he did not intend to join*

[237]If a chieftain attaches himself to the household of a man of his assembly third, he remains in his own assembly group. If a chieftain attaches himself to the household of a man of someone else's assembly third,[238] then in the spring, at the spring assembly and at the place where men make their speeches, he is to say, so that (p. 138) the majority of assembly participants hear him, that he has capital in the household with that man, though he meets no obligations on its behalf — then he remains in his own assembly group. If he puts in no capital, he joins the assembly group of the man with whom he is lodging. *Household attachment of a chieftain*

If a chieftain lodges with a householder who is not in his assembly group he is fined three marks for it, and he forfeits his chieftaincy if he acts in it himself,[239] and the case lies with anyone who wishes to prosecute. *If a chieftain lodges with someone not a member of his assembly*

If a man starts householding after the General Assembly it is lawful for him to say at a formally inaugurated autumn meeting that he is joining an assembly group. *Announcement of assembly attachment at autumn assembly*

236. I.e., on inquiry as prescribed in ‡ 22 (pp. 55-57).

237. A new law according to St ‡ 243 (II 274).

238. From here the text in St ‡ 243 (II 274/7-13) makes better sense: ". . . he is to report at the spring assembly on the assembly slope that he has capital in the household of a man of his assembly third, though he meets no obligations on its behalf, and state who that man is and have witnesses to his connection with him, and then he remains in his own assembly group. But if he puts no such word in, he straightway joins the same assembly as his householder and his penalty is a fine of three marks, and moreover he forfeits his chieftaincy if he acts in it himself."

239. Cf. ‡ 84 (p. 136).

If a household man acquires a household

If a man, a household man,[240] takes over a household by purchase he becomes attached to the assembly to which that household previously belonged, and his home is there for cases that arise afterwards.

If households are amalgamated

If men combine two fully equipped households, each of them remains in the assembly group he was in before[241] unless they wish to have the same assembly membership, and then it is to be said that one of the households is leaving its assembly group. If a man joins a smaller household to a larger, he is to let it be said that he is leaving the assembly group he previously belonged to and is joining the assembly group of the man he is sharing a household with, and this before the courts are held.

If a man has two households in the same Quarter

If a man has two households in one Quarter, he is to fulfill legal duties from the larger household, and if both are the same size, he is to report at the spring assembly from which he wishes to fulfill legal duties. If he says nothing about it he is to fulfill them from both.

Amalgamation of households in different Quarters

If men who were previously in different Quarters combine households they are to report to neighbors which household men belong to which. If they do not report it, they count as the household men of the one who made formal agreement with them. If they have not made formal agreements, it is lawful for a man to prosecute their household people at whichever he prefers of the assemblies to which the householders belong.

If a man has two households in different Quarters

If a man is householding in two Quarters, he is (p. 139) to say his household is joining an assembly group in each Quarter, and the legal home of the two groups of household people is to be where they are taken on to join the household. If household people move between households, the householder is to have said in the spring which of them have their settled homes at which household. If no report is made, it is lawful to summon them to which assembly one prefers, both him and his household people.

If a householder takes a wife with a household

If a householder takes a wife who has a household, it is possible for him at the marriage to choose to move his assembly attachment and residence to where she has her household, or to move her home and assembly attachment to his household, along with those of the people for whose words and actions they have to answer. If a man makes no choice, the assembly attachment of each stays as it was before.

If a household man takes a wife with a household

If a household man takes a wife who has a household, it is possible for him to choose to move his residence and assembly attachment to her household.

Attachment of household man's wife

If a household man takes a wife who is attached to a household, each of them stays in the assembly group where he or she was before, but at

---

240. Taking *griðmann* to mean *griðmaðr*.
241. Add. ‡ 34 (ii).

the wedding it is possible for him to choose to move her assembly attachment to the assembly to which he belongs.

If a householder takes a wife without a household, her assembly attachment is then moved to his household. *Attachment of householder's wife*

If a man who is a householder dies, it is lawful for the woman he was married to, if she wishes, to choose before five neighbors, and within a fortnight from the time her husband died, to move her assembly attachment to that of her legal administrator,[242] along with that of the people for whose words and actions she has to answer. If a married man divorces his wife, the law says that her assembly attachment moves to that of her legal administrator. If there are more than one, it is possible for her to choose to join which of them she pleases.[243] *Attachment of widows or divorced wives*

K ‡ 82

If a man moves about on pointless journeys within a Quarter for half a month or more, the penalty for it is a fine, and similarly if (p. 140) he does it for a month in all and leaves the Quarter with no purpose except to relieve his own household or the one he is attached to. If a man moves about and accepts charity for half a month or more and takes night lodgings where he can get them, he is a vagrant. If a man turns into a tramp — a healthy man and so able-bodied that he could get lodging for a whole year if he would do the work he is capable of — his penalty is full outlawry, and it is lawful to summon him at the place where he is last known to have spent the night and call nine neighbors of the place of summoning at the assembly.[244] *Penalties for vagrancy*

If a man wants to move his assembly attachment he is to stay where he is for three established assemblies, spring assembly, General Assembly, and autumn meeting.[245] *Change of assembly attachment must wait passage of three assemblies*

K ‡ 83

If a man wishes to say he is leaving an assembly group, it is lawful for him to say he is leaving at a spring assembly if he is joining the group of a chieftain who belongs to the same assembly as the other one and also if he is joining the group of a chieftain whose assembly is held within the same assembly boundary. At the General Assembly after the courts have been held it is lawful for him to say at Lögberg that he is leaving a chieftain's assembly third, if the chieftain hears him. If the chieftain does not hear him, he is to report it to him. It is also lawful for him to tell him in person before witnesses that he is leaving. He must on the same day say *Change of assembly attachment*

242. Cf. p. 34, n. 33.
243. Add. ‡ 34.
244. On vagrants, cf. ‡‡ 121, 131, 235, 254.
245. This sentence must belong to ‡ 83.

ASSEMBLY PROCEDURES   135

If an unauthorized man announces a change

that he is joining an assembly group with some other chieftain.

If a man who has not been told to do so says that men are leaving a chieftain's assembly group, then if they are willing to leave, that is lawful. If they are not willing, they are to tell five neighbors that they wish to keep their assembly attachment in the same place, and the other man's penalty is a fine at the suit of each of them.²⁴⁶

Assembly attachment in other than home Quarter

If a man moves his household from one Quarter (p. 141) to another, the law says that he has left his assembly group, unless he crosses the fjord in Hrútafjörðr — there he can keep the same assembly attachment. It is only lawful for a man to have an assembly attachment in a different Quarter from the one he lives in if the chieftain in question is permitted at Lögberg to accept someone from outside the Quarter as a man of his assembly third.

If a chieftain wants to exclude a man from his assembly

If a chieftain wants to say that an assembly man of his no longer belongs to his assembly group, he is to tell him a fortnight before a spring assembly or with longer notice. It is also lawful if he tells him at a spring assembly.²⁴⁷

K ‡ 84
If a Chieftain Leaves the Country

Announcement of who takes charge of a chieftaincy

If a chieftain wishes to leave the country, it is lawful for him to say at a spring assembly who is to act in his chieftaincy. If he leaves the Quarter in the month after Easter, he is to say at a meeting beforehand who is to act in his chieftaincy meanwhile.

Joint ownership of a chieftaincy

If two men own a chieftaincy jointly, the same one of them is to act in it for three assemblies, spring assembly, General Assembly, and autumn meeting. They are then to change over after the autumn meeting has been held — an autumn meeting has been held when the announcements have been made.²⁴⁸ It is also lawful if men transfer a chieftancy from one to another at an assembly after the courts have been held. If the man who is acting in a chieftaincy will not transfer it, the other is to summon him to a reckoning and claim he forfeits his share of the chieftaincy and owes a three-mark fine, and after that they are to test it by court judgment.

Charge of chieftaincy only transferable to man of own assembly third

A chieftain is to transfer power to act in the chieftaincy to a man of his own assembly third and not of anyone else's.

If a chieftain lodges with a man not of his assembly third

If a chieftain attaches himself to the household of a man belonging to a different chieftain's assembly third, he is not to take over the chieftaincy until he has left there.²⁴⁹

---

246. The parallel text in St ‡ 245 (II 278/7) says "each of the two of them", presumably each misrepresented man and his chieftain.
247. Add. ‡ 35.
248. See ‡ 61 (pp. 111-12).
249. Cf. ‡ 81 (p. 133).

If neither chieftain wants to act in the chieftaincy, the one acting in it is to invite the other to act in the chieftaincy. If he does not then take it over he forfeits his share of the chieftaincy and is fined three marks (p. 142), and [if he does] he is then to act in it for three assemblies.

If neither of the joint owners of a chieftaincy is willing to act

When a chieftain is fined and forfeits his chieftaincy, it is always the men of his assembly third who have the ownership of it. They are to draw lots among themselves.

Ownership of forfeit chieftaincy

If a man has bought a chieftaincy or if it was given him, it is to pass on by inheritance.

Chieftaincy heritable

If a chieftain is outlawed, then the men of the assembly third have the ownership of the chieftaincy and it is to be valued at the confiscation court.[250]

Forfeit chieftaincy owned by men of the assembly third but valued at a confiscation court

If a chieftain becomes infirm, it is lawful for him to transfer power to act in the chieftaincy. If he dies and there is a son left, twelve winters old, it is lawful for him to act in the chieftancy if men permit it.[251] If a woman takes the inheritance she is to transfer the chieftaincy to someone in that assembly third. If a chieftain dies before "single month,"[252] they are to draw lots and have a meeting to decide who is to act in the chieftaincy, cut cross-tokens, and let them go in all directions.[253] If he dies after "single month," they are to come to the spring assembly one night before other men and draw lots to decide who is to act in it. If he dies near the General Assembly or dies on a journey to the Assembly, his nearest kinsman who is at the General Assembly is to act. If there is no such man there, then the chieftains who held assemblies with him are to decide who is to act, and are to have decided before the courts are nominated.

If a chieftain is infirm or dies, with or without heirs

If lawsuits are brought to a spring assembly, lesser outlawry is the penalty for a chieftain who does not come to the beginning of the assembly, and similarly if lawsuits arise at the assembly.[254]

If a chieftain does not attend a spring assembly at the proper time

K ‡ 85
What Neighbors Are Required to Give Verdicts on

Neighbors are not required to give verdicts on any and every matter. They have no right to decide on matters that have arisen abroad or eastward of mid-ocean even though prosecuted here. Again, neighbors have no right to give a verdict on what is law here in the country. If

Panel verdicts not to be given on cases arising abroad or on what is law in the country

---

250. Cf. ‡‡ 49 (p. 90), 223.
251. Perhaps specifically the men of the Law Council.
252. *Einmánaðr*, the month beginning Tuesday, March 10-16.
253. Cf. ‡ 234 on sending cross-tokens to summon a meeting.
254. Cf. ‡‡ 56, 64 (pp. 99-100, 116).

If panels are called on for verdicts they may not give

If the wrong kind of panel is called

neighbors are called for the matters now told and on which they have no right (p. 143) to decide, they are to go to the court and name witnesses to witness that they make that an obstruction to their verdict-giving that they have been called for a matter on which they have no right to decide. Similarly if nine neighbors are called where there ought to be five, or five neighbors where there ought to be nine, or if a panel of twelve has to decide on a matter for which neighbors are called: then the neighbors are to go to the court and name witnesses to witness that they make it an obstruction to their verdict-giving that there are nine of them called for something five should decide, or five where there ought to be nine, or they are called for a matter where a panel of twelve is appropriate. If a chieftain is called on to form a panel of twelve for a matter he has no right to decide, he is to go to the court and name witnesses to witness that he has been called on to form a chieftain's panel for a matter which ought

Errors in procedure make cases void

to be decided by a panel of neighbors or by testimony. Whenever a man makes so great a mistake in formal means of proof as now rehearsed, other men incur no penalty for withholding formal means of proof and, whether it is prosecution or defense, his case is void.

[Treatment of Homicide]

(p. 144) Here Begins the Treatment of Homicide.

K ‡ 86

It is prescribed that if men meet as they travel and one man makes what the law deems an assault on another, the penalty is lesser outlawry. These are five assaults deemed such by law: if a man cuts at a man, or thrusts at him, or shoots or throws at him, or strikes at him.[1] And it counts as an assault if a man swings a weapon and a panel gives a verdict that he meant the stroke to land, and he was moreover at such close range that for that matter it could have landed if it had not been stopped on its way, or that he could have hit him; or that, no matter what missile he shoots or throws, he could have reached him with it and for that matter touched him if it had not been stopped, or that he could have hit him. An assault is stopped on its way if someone intercepts it or if a stroke offered meets a weapon or the ground or clothing.[2] The sixth assault deemed such by law occurs when a man fells another, and the penalty for that is outlawry. It is a fall if a man goes down on knee or hand, and especially if he falls further than this. The seventh assault is when one man shakes another (p. 145) and the penalty is outlawry. The eighth is when a man wrests something from another's grasp; the penalty is outlawry. The ninth is if a man throttles someone; the penalty is outlawry.[3]

Five assaults with lesser outlawry as penalty

Four assaults with full outlawry as penalty

A man who makes one of these assaults on another does so to the forfeit of his immunity at that place of action and of theirs who knew his intention unless the man assaulted had forfeited his immunity by his own act.

Assailants forfeit immunity

It is prescribed that if a man from the other side responds by making an assault on a man on the side of the assailant who did not know his companion's intention, then there has been assault on both sides.

Assault on both sides

It is also prescribed that if a man wounds someone the penalty is outlawry.

It is prescribed that if a man makes what the law deems an assault on another man at a place of action where injuries are given and received,

Outlawry for wounding, assault, and killing

---

1. Add. ‡ 40.
2. Add. ‡ 41.
3. Add. ‡ 42.

the penalty is outlawry. If men on both sides are wounded and killed, and three or more are wounded in all at that place of action, a verdict of assault has to be given against the side from which the assault first came.⁴

If a man kills someone, the penalty is outlawry.⁵

Men who kill or wound not to be sustained
Wounds defined

The man who kills someone or inflicts an internal wound or a brain wound or a marrow wound is not to be sustained pending judgment. A brain wound is when the skull is opened, whether the skull was cut or cracked.⁶ An internal wound is when a wound can bleed internally. A marrow wound is when a bone, which has marrow in it when broken, is asunder as far as the marrow.⁷

Planners of an attack forfeit immunity

Wherever men set out with the intention of inflicting wilful injury, the penalty is outlawry if it comes about; further, those that set off first with that intention (p. 146) to an encounter where injuries are given and received forfeit their immunity in respect of all injuries, even though the first assault comes from the other side.

Penalty for shielding a man who has killed or wounded

It is prescribed that if a man shields or gives help to a man who at that same place of action has killed or wounded someone, the penalty is outlawry; and further, such a man forfeits his immunity in respect of injuries received from any men trying to help the other side unless it was his wish to separate them in a lawful way and that was why he gave help to the one side, and such helping carries no penalty. And he separates them in a lawful way if he can get a panel verdict that he would have separated them in the same way if the wounded man had inflicted such injuries on the other man as he had now received from him.

Lawful separation

If men save the life of assailants.⁸

Striking; kinds of blows

(p. 147) ⁹It is prescribed that if a man strikes a man so that bones break, it is assessed like major wounds.¹⁰ Whatever a man strikes another with, the penalty is outlawry. It is a blow if a man hits another with the back of an axhead or whatever he has that does duty for a weapon. It is a blow even if a man thrusts or throws it, once it lands. It is the same, even though clothing or coat of mail or helmet intervenes, given that it would have landed on him if that had not got in the way. It is a blow if a man kicks at another or throws a punch at him. It is a blow if a man pulls whatever may do duty as a weapon away from a man, know-

4. Add. ‡ 43.
5. Add. ‡ 81.
6. Add. ‡ 45.
7. Add. ‡ 45 (ii); cf. Add. ‡ 84.
8. See Add. ‡ 46.
9. Cf. Add. ‡ 105.
10. Internal, brain, or marrow wound, cf. above.

ing that it will fly back at the other of its own accord when he lets it go. Similarly if a man causes something to fall on a man and hit him.

If not more than two men, one from each side, are wounded or killed or beaten so as to be left with blue or red marks, both may be sustained[11] pending judgment, if they accuse each other of assault, no matter which way the verdict on assault may go. *Mutual charges of assault permit sustenance pending judgment*

It is prescribed that a man on whom injury is inflicted has the right to avenge himself if he wants to up to the time of the General Assembly at which he is required to bring a case for the injuries; and the same applies to everyone who has the right to avenge a killing. Those who have the right to avenge a killing are the principals in a killing case. The man who inflicted the injury falls with forfeit immunity at the hands of a principal and at the hands of any of his company, though it is also lawful for vengeance to be taken by other men within twenty-four hours. *Who may take vengeance and when*

These injuries are assessed like major wounds: cutting out a man's tongue, poking out a man's eyes, (p. 148) knocking out a man's teeth, cutting off a man's nose or ears (and by cutting is meant when gristle or bone is reached), castrating a man, striking a shame-stroke across someone's buttocks. *Injuries assessed as major wounds*

It is prescribed that a man may not be sustained pending judgment after inflicting no more than a flesh wound, if he is caught in a house with witnesses.[12] *A flesh wound is enough to make it illegal to sustain the inflictor*

It is lawful to prosecute for an assault to which a man has preferred to name witnesses rather than publish it. If that is the sole charge, there is no prosecution case to be made unless one or the other of these is done. *Witnesses or publishing obligatory in case of assault*

It is prescribed that if a man falsely says he has a wound, or wounds himself or gets another man to wound him, whatever his reason, the penalty is lesser outlawry. Neither may he be sustained pending judgment any more than before, and the case lies with the man he charges with wounding him or with anyone among those who had been against him who is willing to take it up.[13] *If a man wounds himself and accuses another*

Even if a man is struck between the shoulders.[14]

A man wounds another if it bleeds where the blow lands.[15] Whatever a man does to cause a wound, it is to be published as a wound of his causing and as a mortal wound if death is the outcome. *Bleeding makes a wound*

The place of action is as far as one can shoot an arrow in all directions

---

11. Reading *eru ... œlir* for *eru ... óœlir*, "may not be sustained."
12. Add. ‡‡ 72, 104.
13. Add. ‡‡ 49, 86.
14. Add. ‡ 44.
15. Add. ‡ 84.

Place of action defined; separation

from the spot where the first assault was made, whether that was out-of-doors or indoors. And that is to remain the place of action even though they move beyond it before they are separated. They are separated when one side has gone more than a bowshot from the place of their last encounter.[16]

If a man is hit, he may prosecute for assault only

(p. 149) If a man is struck a blow, he may choose to prosecute for assault with a penalty of lesser outlawry, even though he does not prosecute for the blow itself. But if the other boasts of having given him a blow, the fact that he has not prosecuted him for the blow is no defense in the case, but the penalty is lesser outlawry and it is to be prosecuted like other malicious speech.

Penalty and procedure in all cases of blows. Classes of blows

There are three classes of blows and the penalty for them all is outlawry, and they are to be prosecuted with a panel of twelve. One is the blow which touches so lightly that it leaves no visible mark. Such a blow may be avenged at the place of action and not afterwards.[17] Second is the blow which is called an injury — thus, when a man strikes another and leaves a blue or red mark or it swells under the skin or the flesh recedes or blood spurts from mouth or nostrils or from under the nails. A man has the right to avenge such a blow through the same length of time as after wounding,[18] and so have those men who accompany him to achieve it. This applies to a blow from the fist or a kick if it leaves a visible mark. It is also a blow classed among injuries if hearing or sight is damaged by it, and similarly if a man is knocked out by a blow under the ribcage or in the balls, even though no mark from the blow is visible, and likewise always when a man is knocked into a daze.[19] In such a case a man may choose to publish the assault and the blow separately, and there are then two cases, and it is to be stated which of the injuries just rehearsed followed from the blow. The third class of blow is when bones are broken, and the man who has given such a blow is not to be sustained pending judgment, and he has no right to attend an assembly. It is to be prosecuted as for major wounds if it is published,[20] and in that case it is to be stated what bone fractures followed from which blows.[21]

When assault may be published, and before which five neighbors

It is lawful to publish wounds and (p. 150) assaults by night as well as by day, and also in holy seasons and in Lent, and the publishing is to be done before five neighbors. Neighbors to hear the publishing are not to

16. Cf. p. 30, n. 22.
17. Add. ‡ 47.
18. Up to the General Assembly at which the case should be brought, cf. p. 141, ll. 7-10.
19. Add. ‡ 48.
20. Add. ‡ 48 (ii).
21. Add. ‡ 48 (iii).

be especially selected save only in terms of distance and as long as they have none of the injuries laid to their charge or any lawbreaking. [22]When men are to publish assault or injury, then it is lawful to do so on the same day as the action, during the following night, and during the two days and two nights thereafter. Then the publishing has been done before the third sunrise, as the law recital's phrase has it — if what it says there is rightly understood.[23]

Time limit for publishing — before the third sunrise

If the assault which led to a wound is not published.[24]

K ‡ 87

Publishing of all these lawbreakings here told, killings, wounds, and blows and all assaults, is to be done before five neighbors qualified in terms of distance from the place of action to serve on a panel of nine neighbors; and the publishing must be done before the third sunrise from the time the two sides separated.

Publishing: when and before whom

It is prescribed that in cases of forcible seizure from another's grasp, causing a man to fall, shaking, and throttling, publishing of any of these as assault is not required when it is the sole charge and (p. 151) nothing more followed from it at that place of action; but in such cases nine neighbors of the place of action are to be called locally. But if something more did follow from them, they are to be published like other assaults and then deemed to involve forfeit immunity. A man is to publish all other assaults if he intends to prosecute for them.

Publishing not essential in some cases of assault, obligatory in others

It is lawful for a man, if he wishes, to publish assault as a charge against all the men who were in the party opposed to those on whom the assault was made, if he thinks he does not know for sure which individual made the assault.

Assault may be published as a charge against all opponents, wounds against not more than three

If a man is wounded with a single wound, that wound is to be published as a charge against one man only, but if he is wounded with two wounds, it is lawful for him to publish them as charges against two men; and it is further lawful to publish them as charges against three men if he is wounded with three wounds, but not against more than three, even if he is wounded with more than three wounds — at least such additional charges do not prevent attendance at the assembly.

It is lawful for a man to transfer the publishing to another man if he does not himself wish to publish his wound,[25] or wounds if more than one.

Transfer of publishing

---

22. A new law according to St ‡ 283 (II 316).
23. This determined definition of *fyrir ena þriðju sól* ("before the third sun") perhaps results from argument over counting the day of the offense as the first of the three days specified.
24. Add. ‡ 51.
25. Add. ‡ 51 (ii).

Making good wrong publishing

It is prescribed that if a wounded man is not fit to undertake publishing and the man procured to do it does it wrong, then it is possible for the wounded man to publish it a second time, and he is to[26] set about that publishing in this way: he is to set off within a fortnight, once he is fit, and he is to have published it before the third sunrise after his arrival for the publishing. The same applies in fact even if he did not get someone else to publish it in the first place.[27]

Publishing if a man has lost power of speech

It is prescribed that if a man has lost his power of speech, publishing is to be undertaken by the man, if at hand, who would be the principal in the killing case if the man in question had been killed; and he is first to name witnesses to witness that the man in question cannot speak, or similarly if he does not speak sense. But if that man is not at hand, then it is lawful for anyone who wishes to undertake the publishing.

It is prescribed that if he (p. 152) recovers then he may choose whether he accepts that publishing or publishes it again himself, and he is to set about the publishing as was rehearsed previously in case he transferred the publishing.

Publishing if a man is killed

It is prescribed that if a man is killed and the principal in the case is at hand, then he is to publish the killing and must have done so before the third sunrise. He may choose to publish it as a charge against one man if he wishes, but it is also lawful to publish it against as many of the men at the killing as there were wounds classed as mortal on the dead man. He has to name men as witnesses to the wounds classed as mortal and show them the wounds.[28] They do not have to testify how many there were. Men selected as mortal-wound witnesses are to be such as are not disqualified from serving on a panel of neighbors on grounds of connection with the principals in the case. But if men are not named as witnesses to the wounds classed as mortal, then the neighbors have to decide both who are guilty of the mortal wounds and how many mortal wounds there are.[29]

Moral-wound witnesses, or panel verdict

Major wounds on a corpse to be published as mortal wounds

It is prescribed that if injuries are found on a dead man such as might be deemed major wounds, then these are to be published as mortal wounds.[30]

Rights of principal when first steps in pro-

It is prescribed that if the principal is not at hand, then it is lawful for other men to name men as witnesses to the mortal wounds and to publish them.

---

26. Reading *skal* for *svá* "so."
27. Add. ‡ 51 (iii).
28. Add. ‡ 52.
29. Add. ‡ 52 (ii).
30. Add. ‡ 53.

It is prescribed that a principal may choose to accept other men's naming of mortal-wound witnesses and publishing, if he wishes to, but he may also choose to set off within a fortnight of hearing the news. He may choose to publish the killing as a charge against different men if he wants to, and he may also name different men as inflictors of the mortal wounds. He must have done the publishing and named men as mortal-wound witnesses, if the body is unburied, before the third sunrise after his arrival for the publishing.[31] But[32] a panel of neighbors has to decide how many mortal wounds there are if the body is already buried. It is in fact lawful for him to use (p. 153) in full or in part anything he pleases from what other men have done towards preparing the case.[33] *cedure are taken by others*

It is prescribed that if a major wound has been lawfully published as a charge against a man and later death is the outcome, then even if the killing is not published as a charge against that same man, the same right to prosecute anyone for assisting him exists as before.[34] *Right to prosecute for assisting a man charged with wounding*

It is prescribed that if a man publishes a major wound where a minor wound exists, the minor wound is thereby lawfully published, but the matter of sustaining the man charged depends on what the wound proves to be.[35] *Publishing wounds in mistaken degree*

It is prescribed that if a man publishes a minor wound where a major wound exists, then prosecution for assistance is to proceed as if the wound were a minor one, but otherwise it is assessed in every way according to its actual size.[36]

It is prescribed that where men give and receive injuries at gatherings where nine or more householders are present, then it is lawful to publish before all those nine neighbors together, as long as none of the injuries is laid to their charge, even though they prove not to be neighbors of the place of action; but it is also lawful to publish before the five nearest neighbors of the place of action if they are present at the gathering, as long as none of the injuries is laid to their charge. *Publishing where men assemble in large numbers*

It is prescribed that if there is an encounter on mountains or fjords, then the publishing must be done before the third sunrise from the time the men return. It is to be published in the way just rehearsed whenever *Publishing after an encounter on mountain or fjord*

---

31. Cf. Add. ‡ 82.
32. Reading *en* for *ef* "if."
33. Add. ‡ 53 (ii).
34. Whoever helped someone published as responsible for a major wound had broken the law, irrespective of the identity of the man selected from those present at the killing to answer the charge of killing when death was the ultimate outcome, cf. ‡ 102 (p. 164).
35. Though a major wound is published, sustenance carries the penalty appropriate to a minor wound, if a minor wound it proves to be.
36. I.e., as a major wound.

lawful reporters or lawful eyewitnesses of the encounter go off in different directions; but lawful reporters and lawful eyewitnesses are men, capable of understanding an oath, twelve winters old or older.

Lawful reporters and eyewitnesses

Publishing when survivors are on one side only

It is prescribed that where men go only one way from a killing, then the killer is to publish the killing as his work within the next twelve hours; but if he is on mountain or fjord then he must do it within twelve hours of returning. He is to go to the first house where he thinks his life is in no danger on that account[37] and tell one or more men legally resident there and state it in this way: "There was an encounter between us," he is to state, and (p. 154) name the other man and say where it was. "I publish those wounds as my work and all the injury done to him; I publish wounds if wounds are the outcome and killing if killing is the outcome."[38]

Corpses must be covered

If he leaves a man dead, he is to cover his corpse so that neither birds nor beasts may eat it. He is to say where it is. It is prescribed that if he does not cover the corpse in this way, the penalty is lesser outlawry, and it is a summoning case and nine neighbors, those who live nearest to where the corpse lies, are to be called at the assembly.[39]

If a survivor leaves his opponent wounded but capable of moving

It is prescribed that if the wounded man afterwards walks a bowshot[40] or more and himself tells other men of their encounter, then the other man is not required to publish it. If the man wounded is not able to find legally resident men to speak to, even after walking a bowshot or more, then the man who wounded him is to publish within twelve hours of hearing of his death before those five householders who happen to be nearest to him at the time he hears of his death.

Consequences of not publishing as prescribed

It is prescribed that if he publishes it in some other way than now told, then it is deemed murder, with the result that it cannot be claimed that the other man, no matter what offense he may have given, died with forfeit immunity, and no grounds of defense are to be accepted.

K ‡ 88
On Murder

Penalty and definition

It is prescribed that if a man murders a man, the penalty is outlawry. And it is murder if a man hides it[41] or conceals the corpse or does not admit it.

[42]It is prescribed that if a man is struck and it is not published, or if he

---

37. Add. ‡ 54.
38. Add. ‡ 79.
39. Cf. Add. ‡‡ 80, 93.
40. Cf. p. 30, n. 22.
41. Add. ‡ 78.
42. Cf. Add. ‡ 105.

shares living quarters with the man who struck him and shares sleep and food or work (p. 155) with him when he was nevertheless fit and able to leave, then he has no right to personal compensation from that man's goods — that is forty-eight ounce-units in legal tender — but in other respects the same right to prosecute at law exists as before, and an exception is in the case of a man who does not have charge of his own affairs at law, for whatever reason.[43]

If a man shares living quarters with someone who has struck him

It is prescribed that if a man publishes his own wounds and afterwards death is the outcome, the principal in the case nevertheless has the right to publish the killing, should he wish to do so, and name men as witnesses to the wounds classed as mortal and, if he likes, publish them as charges against other men than those against whom they were previously published.

Rights of principal when a victim has published his own wounds before he died

If a man chases a horse with a rider so that he falls off, and similarly if he chases pack horses or startles sheep or however he goes about it so that a rider falls off, the penalty is lesser outlawry if the rider lands on his feet; the man charged with the offense is to be summoned locally and nine neighbors called at the assembly.[44]

Offenses against person through agency of animals. While riding

If a man strikes a horse with a rider, the penalty is lesser outlawry if a panel gives a verdict that he meant the blow for the rider, even though he may have kept his seat,[45] and neighbors are to be called locally and [it is deemed] an assault.

If horses in a man's charge, laden or not, bring another man off his horse or cause him to fall if he was standing or walking, the penalty is lesser outlawry for the man in charge of the horses, but full outlawry if blood is drawn or if he is disabled, and nine neighbors are to be called at the assembly. But if the man dies as the result of it, neighbors are to be called locally.

If a man startles a horse in the direction of someone, or an ox or other beast, with the aim of getting him trampled or gored or struck, the penalty is lesser outlawry if the man falls or if a blue or red mark is (p. 156) left or if it bleeds, and nine neighbors of the place of action are to be called locally.

While on foot

If a man sets a fierce dog or a bear reared in captivity on someone, the penalty is lesser outlawry if no harm is done, but full outlawry if there is any visible mark of it or if he falls, and in that case neighbors of the place of action are to be called, but when no harm is done, neighbors of the place where the man set the animal on. If a man gets major wounds or

If beasts are set on someone

---

43. The apparent condoning behavior of such a man could be attributed to his diminished responsibility.
44. Add. ‡ 100.
45. Add. ‡ 100 (ii).

death or lasting injury from beasts, wherever they are and whether horse or ox, dog or bear, the penalty for the man who set them on to do harm is the same as if he himself had done it, and the prosecution is to be conducted in every way as if he had; and as soon as it is published, he forfeits his immunity and may not be sustained pending judgment.

If there are no visible signs of the manner of death

It is prescribed that if a man is killed in such a way that there is no visible mark on him and there is no mortal wound on him, whether he is chased into water or over a cliff or throttled to death or beaten or whatever death they deal him so that he loses his life through their actions but still there is no visible mark on him, then such a killing is not to be published as a charge against more than three men, even though more were at the killing — at least any additional charges do not prevent attendance at the assembly.[46]

Formula for publishing assault and injury

It is prescribed that the man who publishes assault as a charge against someone, or wounding or striking or killing, has to name two witnesses or more to witness that "I publish an assault so deemed by law against N.N." and he is to name the man who was assaulted and the man before whom he publishes it; "and I publish a legal publishing." And if he wishes, he can choose to have in the same publishing both the assault and the injury that followed from the assault and state what [injury] did follow, whether it was a blow or a wound, and one suit shall be made of it if he wants to use that publishing; but he may also choose to publish the assault and the injury (p. 157) that occurred in the assault separately, and then there are to be two cases.

Formula for publishing wounds or blows

The man who publishes a wound or blow is to name two men or more as witnesses to witness that he publishes wound or blow, a legal publishing, and state what the injuries are, whether brain wound or internal wound or marrow wound; or that he wounded the other with a wound which proved mortal when he [got] his death.[47] He is to name both the man on whom injury was inflicted and the man before whom he publishes it, and publish it as a legal publishing. It is also lawful for him to publish it before all the neighbors he wishes to publish it before collectively, if he can meet them in one place, but it is also lawful for him to publish it before each of them separately.[48]

K ‡ 89
On Preparing Cases

In all the causes here told, woundings, killings, and all lawbreakings oc-

---

46. Cf. ‡ 87 (p. 143).
47. Add. ‡ 55.
48. Add. ‡ 55 (ii).

curring at a place of action where injuries are given and received — planning, moving to attack, being present, shielding — then nine neighbors of the place of action are to be called locally.

Call nine neighbors of the place of action

Wherever a man strikes another, that is a summoning case and the chieftain to whose assembly group the man prosecuted belongs is to be called on to form a panel of twelve, and this is to be done at the assembly unless both blow and wound happened at one place of action, in which case neighbors of the place of action are to decide on both.

Panel of twelve to decide on blows

If a man avenges a blow with a blow at the same place of action and they accuse each other of assault, then nine neighbors of the place of action are to decide which made the first assault, but panels of twelve have to decide about the blows.

Retaliation and counter-charges of assault

If a man avenges a blow with a blow at some other place of action, panels of twelve are to decide about the blows, but he is to call five of his neighbors to give him a clearing verdict as to which of the blows was first.

Panels of five for clearing verdicts

Where a man (p. 158) avenges a blow by killing or by wounds at some other place of action, neighbors of that place are to decide on the killing or on the wounds and a panel of twelve on the blow.

It is prescribed that a killer may call a panel of five from the nine neighbors of the place of action who have given a verdict of killing or wounds against him to give him a clearing verdict as to which came first — the blow he got or the injury he did to the man killed or wounded.

Nine neighbors of the place of action are to decide on all those injuries here rehearsed.

It is prescribed that neighbors are to be called who are not disqualified by connections with those who have injuries laid to their charge or with principals. Neighbors are wrongly called to serve on a panel if they are second cousins or closer kin of the principal prosecutor or of the man accused. Three close kinsmen by marriage are also wrong: anyone who is married to a man's mother or daughter or sister. Three kinds of spiritual kinship: anyone who stood sponsor for a man at prime-signing[49] or at baptism or at confirmation. Further, people on both sides are to be as well qualified by freedom from legal involvement as on grounds of kinship.

Qualifications of panel members in terms of kinship and legal involvement

Where killing cases are at issue.[50]

(p. 159/4) A man is not to challenge on grounds of his own spiritual kinship with a panel member.

Neighbors are rightly called to serve on a panel, even though they were at the place of action, as long as no lawbreaking at that place is laid to their charge.

---

49. See p. 26, n. 6.
50. Add. ‡ 57 (ii).

Trumped-up charge to keep man off a panel

If a man prepares a suit against someone because he wants to disqualify him from serving on panels but not because he believes him guilty of the charge, the penalty is lesser outlawry, and the case lies with the man who conducts the original suit out of which this case arises. It is a summoning case and nine neighbors of the man prosecuted are to be called at the assembly.

Economic qualifications for panel membership

It is prescribed that neighbors are to be called who have such property that they have to pay assembly attendance dues. And the men who have to pay assembly attendance dues are those who for each household member who is a charge on them own a debt-free cow or its price or a net or a boat and all the things which the household may [not] be without. Household members who are a charge on a man are all those he has to maintain and those workmen he needs to provide the labor to enable him to do so.

Property qualification for single-handed householder

[51] A householder who works single-handed is rightly called to serve on a panel if he has such property that for each household member who is a charge on him he owns twice the price of a cow. He is not single-handed if he takes on someone at the moving days for a whole year's stay and has him at the time of the General Assembly, a male helper, twelve winters old or older, so able-bodied that he can earn at least his food.[52] For all callings that are to be made before the moving days a man is only counted single-handed if the youth of twelve winters or more then with him was with him the preceding summer.[53]

Choice among joint householders

(p. 160) If two householders live in the same house, it is right to call them both if needed, but the one who lives closer if both are not needed.[54] Now if they keep one shepherd between them and no other men, they are both counted single-handed, but if one of them alone feeds the shepherd, he is right to have on a panel.[55]

If two men share a farm and one of them owns the land and the other is a tenant, the landowner is to be called.

If two landowners share a farm or two tenants who are rightly called to

---

51. A new law according to St ‡ 288 (II 320).

52. Add. ‡ 58.

53. The sense of this is doubtful and the *lectio facilior* of St ‡ 288 (II 320) may be preferable: "For all callings that are to be made before the moving days, he is only qualified to be called if the man of twelve winters or older who is then with him was there the previous summer as well, unless his keep is paid for."

54. Cf. Add. ‡ 110; "the one who lives closer" is more precisely defined there.

55. I.e., he is not counted single-handed but the other, who shares the shepherd but does not support him, is counted single-handed and so not eligible for panel service unless qualified by other wealth.

serve on a panel, he is to call the one who has the major holding, but if they have equal holdings, then he may call whichever he pleases, even though they keep no serving man.

If two men who have to pay assembly attendance dues share a farm and do not keep a serving man, then one of them is rightly called to serve on a panel. The other — given that he is capable of earning at least his food — is to contribute to all the necessary outlay in proportion to the size of his holding in the farm.

That man is not to be called who is not assembly-fit. A man is assembly-fit when he can ride full days' journeys and bring in his own hobbled horse after baiting and find his way by himself where the route is known to him. It is prescribed that it is not right to call him if he has that ailment which does not seem likely to be cured in time to make him assembly-fit. *The householder called must be fit*

On behalf of the household of an unfit man these four men may be rightly called if they have their settled home there: one is his son, two his stepson, three his close kinsman by marriage, married to his daughter, and four is his legal foster-son, whom the householder has brought up. These are rightly called only if they are of such age and such mental capacity that they are rightful assembly participants in those respects, and further both (p. 161) the householder and the man among them who is called in his place are to be qualified in terms of connection and legal involvement.[56] Legal fostering is when a man takes a child of eight winters or younger and brings him up until he is sixteen. The same men are rightly called on behalf of a household led by a woman as on behalf of the household of an unfit man, and in addition her husband, if he has his settled home with her, makes a fifth person qualified to be called. *Four men who may be called on behalf of an unfit man's household*

Definition of legal fostering

Five men who may be called on behalf of a woman's household

It is prescribed that where an unfit man or a woman is the householder who is covered by the call to serve on a panel and he or she has a household man at the time of the General Assembly — one taken on for a whole year and capable of earning at least his food — and then there arrives in the country a man who is assembly participant on behalf of the household, his or hers, where the calling needs to be made, then it is right to call him if he arrives before the calling is begun, given that he has his settled home there.[57] *A rightful assembly participant may be called for such households*

If a man doubts whether a man is qualified to serve on panels or not, then he is to name two witnesses or more to witness that "I ask you," and name him, "whether you are a rightful assembly participant or not," or whether he has the right to fulfil legal duties on behalf of his household *In case of doubt over a man's qualifications*

56. Add. ‡ 59.

57. Add. ‡ 59 (ii).

or the household of an unfit man or the household of a woman, should these questions rather be necessary — ask[58] a legal asking. It is then right for him to carry out the calling in accordance with the other's answer, but the latter is fined three marks if he replies falsely or if he makes no answer and the suit lies with the man who asked him. If he is not willing to prosecute, then the suit lies with the neighbor called instead of him, and if he is not willing then any one of the neighbors who wants to is to prosecute,[59] and the prosecutor is to call five neighbors of the man prosecuted at the assembly.

If father and son(s) are in one household

Wherever men call neighbors locally and father and son are together in a household, then even though only one of them has a holding in the farm, it is lawful to call whichever one wishes when both are qualified, and call the eldest of his sons if there are more than one. (p. 162) It is right for the one to serve on the panel who comes to the assembly even though the one who stays at home was called.[60] But if neither of them comes, the one who was called is to be prosecuted for staying at home; but if one of them sets out, the prosecution is against him, whatever went wrong afterwards.

Time and order of calling

[61]It is prescribed that calling is to begin in the morning and one after another are to be called until all are called. The caller is to call them all on one day if he can contrive it. A man has to call nine neighbors.

Counter-charges of assault: each side must call the same neighbors

When men accuse each other of assault, those who are later in starting the calling are to call the same neighbors as the others, but theirs is also the right to challenge them. If men are using neighbor-calling against each other and each side sets out to do it from opposite ends and they meet, then each side is required to tell whom they have called and also whom they intend to call. It is prescribed that they must all call the same neighbors and those making the later call on either side have the right to

Possible disputes

challenge the householders they are second in calling. If they meet and do not agree which neighbors so far uncalled by either side are to be added, then those who began the calling first are to decide and those who have called more neighbors by the time they meet are to decide.[62] But if they have called the same number of neighbors and also disagree as to who started the calling first, then nine neighbors of the place of action, those best qualified to serve on the panel for the original suit, are to decide which of them began the calling first, and the cases of those to whose disadvantage they give their verdict are void.

58. Reading *spyrja* for *spyrning* [sic].
59. Add. ‡ 59 (iii).
60. Cf. ‡ 77 (p. 123).
61. Cf. Add. ‡‡ 109-10.
62. Those who have called more householders are assumed to have begun first.

If the two sides meet at a time when each has got so far with the calling that, if they now follow up each other's calling as prescribed, more than nine neighbors of the place of action will be called in all, then those who when they met had less right to decide how the calling should go thereafter are to go to the houses of those neighbors whom they alone have called and name witnesses that they lift the call from them because they make more than nine called locally for that place of action, and speak so that men legally resident there may hear; (p. 163) and proceed with that speech as with the calling.⁶³ If they do not lift the call from the neighbors, then every case for which they have called neighbors is void, and staying at home carries no penalty for the neighbors if the panel gives a verdict to those callers' disadvantage and decides that they began the calling later. ⁶⁴Even if the other side lifts the call from their neighbors, which they were not required to do unless they wished, the cases of their opponents are still void if the panel gives a verdict to their disadvantage and decides that they did not lift the call from their⁶⁵ neighbors before the third sunrise from the time they were called.

Lifting the call from neighbors in excess of required number

Consequences of not lifting the call

If they agree which of them have to lift the call from the neighbors, then it is for them to decide from whom they will lift it and who the others are to call. If they agree which of them has to lift the call from the neighbors, their case is not spoilt even if they have at first called more than nine neighbors as long as they can lift the call from the extra men before the third sunrise.⁶⁶

Prosecutors are fined three marks if they conceal the calling or lie about it when asked, and moreover every case for which they have called neighbors is void. Neighbors are liable to lesser outlawry if they do not tell whether they are called or not and similarly if they lie about it.⁶⁷ But those who call second without knowing who the others have called — it is lawful for them to call those who they think are best qualified.

If men conceal or lie about calling

If a man delays a calling or hastens it unduly to the day when he knows that other men mean to call neighbors, because by doing so he wants to balk their suits, he spoils the case for which he himself is calling neighbors and his penalty is lesser outlawry. It is a summoning case and nine neighbors of the man prosecuted are to be called at the assembly.⁶⁸

Delay or haste in calling in order to balk others' suits

---

63. Add. ‡ 59 (iv).
64. Add. ‡ 59 (v).
65. Reading *sinum* for *hinum* "the other."
66. Add. ‡ 60.
67. Add. ‡ 60 (ii).
68. Add. ‡ 60 (iii).

(p. 164) It is prescribed that if a man wishes to call neighbors in a case of wounding.[69]

If a man calls neighbors locally in the moving days.[70]

If men are sent to oppose men.[71]

K ‡ 90

Women on whose account a man has the right to kill

There are six women a man has the right to kill for. One is a man's wife, two a man's daughter, three a man's mother, four is his sister, five is the foster-daughter a man has brought up, six is the foster-mother who brought a man up. It is prescribed that if a man arrives to find another man forcing a woman to lie with him there, a woman he has the right to kill for, and the man has forced her down and lowered himself down upon her, then he has the right to kill on her account there at that place; or likewise if he finds him in the same bed as the woman, so that they lie side by side, because it was his will to have wrongful intercourse with her; then a man has the right to kill on her account in both instances even if intercourse has not taken place.

Which panels are to decide what

Where a man kills on account of a woman or inflicts injury on a man when wrongful intercourse did not take place but was intended, then neighbors of the place of action alone are to decide on both matters, on the killing or on what injuries there are, and also on (p. 165) whatever he wishes to bring forward to prove the forfeit immunity of the man killed. But if the wrongful intercourse took place,[72] then neighbors of the killing place are to decide on the killing or on what injuries there are, but other neighbors are to decide on the intercourse, those who live nearest that place, but if everything occurred at one and the same place, then the same neighbors are to decide on both matters, his immunity or his forfeit of it.

If the killer and the principal are not the same man

It is prescribed that where a man kills a man on account of a woman for whom he has the right to kill, but some other man is the principal in the intercourse case, and the latter will not prosecute the case [then it is lawful for the one] who did the killing [to prepare the case] and to prosecute it and to transfer it to someone else [as if] he were the rightful principal.

Panel of five to give clearing verdicts

Those men who are to defend the case, on behalf of men who were at the killing with the killer or on behalf of the killer himself, they are to call five neighbors of the place of action, those living nearest to it, drawn

---

69. It is uncertain what article this introduced, possibly matter similar to that in Add. ‡ 56.

70. Add. ‡ 111.

71. See ‡ 77 (p. 125).

72. Add. ‡ 63.

from the prosecution panel which gives a verdict on the killing or the wounds, to give all clearing verdicts[73] on whatever they wish to bring forward to prove the dead man's forfeit immunity or to use as grounds of defense.

If a man has killed a man on account of a woman for whom he has the right to kill, he is to summon the dead man and speak thus: "I name witnesses to witness that I summon him" — for what he decides to state. "I claim that all his goods are under penalty. I claim that he fell with forfeit immunity," and, if he wishes to state it in these terms, that he has no right to church burial; and he is to state to which assembly he summons the case. If he wishes, he also has the right to summon him, if he is still alive, to full outlawry and claim that his wounds have no legal redress.

Summon dead man as one who had forfeited immunity, or wounded man to outlawry

K ‡ 91; p. 166

It is prescribed that if a man younger than twelve winters old kills someone, [he] is not under legal penalty for the killing but his kinsmen are to make restitution with kindred payments.[74] If a man younger than twelve winters old inflicts injury on someone, then the latter should ward him off as he would do if he were his foster-father or father, and he is not to do him any lasting injury. But if the grown man does him a lasting injury, the young man's immunity is not forfeit.

Killing or wounding by someone under twelve

K ‡ 92

It is prescribed that there shall be no such things as accidents. A man who holds a weapon is not under penalty if he holds it still and a man lurches against the weapon and gets scratched, wherever a panel gives a verdict that he did not intend the other to be scratched by it.[75] Wherever a man may have put his weapon, he is not under penalty if another man is scratched by it when he himself was not holding on to it, if a panel gives a verdict that he did not intend him harm from it [and that] he had put the weapon in a place where he had not anticipated harm to anyone from it. But all these panels to give clearing verdicts are to be drawn from the prosecution panel with which he is prosecuted, and five neighbors are to be drawn from it.

Defense in case of unintentional hurt

If a man (p. 167) fastens his weapon in a place where it falls down by

Responsibility for weapons that have been hung up

---

73. Reading *kveðja til bjargkviða allra fimm vettvangsbúa* for *kveðja bjargkviðar alla vettvangsbúa*, "call all neighbors of the place of action for a clearing verdict"; cf. St ‡ 293 (II 332).

74. The corresponding passage in St ‡ 294 (II 333) has "younger than sixteen winters." On kindred payments see ‡ 113 (pp. 175-83).

75. Add. ‡ 65.

itself and someone is harmed by it, the man who fastened it up is responsible.[76]

Responsibility in games

Whenever a man goes to wrestle of his own accord or to play a game, let him stay no longer at it than he pleases. Then he is responsible for himself as long as any harm he gets was not intended by his opponent; but if he gets lasting injury or death, it is assessed as if it was not a game.

K ‡ 93
On Deeds of Insanity

Definition

It is prescribed that if an insane man does injury to someone, it shall only be deemed a deed of insanity if he has previously done injury to himself[77] with injuries that put him in peril of death or of lasting injuries, and even so it only becomes a deed of insanity if neighbors are willing to give such a verdict.

No prior leave needed to settle

It is prescribed that where the panel verdict is of a deed of insanity the man in question may be sustained[78] pending judgment, but in other respects he then falls under the same penalty for inflicting injury as if he were a sane man; but men have the right to settle in such a case without prior leave.[79]

K ‡ 94
On Being Principal

A man's son is the principal in a killing case, sixteen winters old or older, freeborn, and a lawful heir, of such mental capacity that he can take charge of [his inheritance]. If there is no son or if he is younger than this, then the case lies with a man's father next, then next with a brother born of the same father, then next with a brother born of the same mother. If there are more brothers than one born of the same father, (p. 168) they all have equal shares in whatever they get from the case.

Succession of responsibility

If joint principals disagree or proceed differently

If some want to prosecute and some to settle, then whoever wants to prosecute to the limit of the law is to have his way.

It is prescribed that it is right for them all to prepare a case and none of them need transfer his case to another. But if they all want to prosecute to the limit of the law, judgment is to be given in the suit of the oldest of those who want to prosecute to the limit of the law. But if an elder brother transfers his suit to someone else and a younger brother conducts

---

76. Add. ‡ 88.

77. Add. ‡ 64.

78. Reading *er . . . œll* for *er . . . óœll*, "may not be sustained;" cf. St ‡ 295 (II 333) *er . . . þó œll*.

79. I.e., of the Law Council.

his suit in person, then judgment is to be given in the suit conducted in person.

If a man has taken a transferred case from a man as closely related to the dead man as some other principal who wants to settle, judgment is to be given in the former's suit if he is more willing to prosecute to the limit of the law than principals who conduct their suits in person.[80]

These men are on the list for being a principal. After brothers an illegitimate son is principal, then an illegitimate brother born of the same father, then an illegitimate brother born of the same mother. If these men do not exist, then the suit lies with the nearest descendant among those who are freeborn, lawful heirs, and present in the country. If several men are equally close kin, then the one among them who wishes to prosecute according to the law's rigor is to have his way.[81] Age is not decisive among equally close kin except among brothers. *Further succession of responsibility*

A killing case, and compensation too, is divided among the branches of a family in the same way as inheritance, even though there is one man from one branch and more than one from another branch.[82] *Killing cases and compensation go like inheritance*

It is lawful for a son to prosecute a killing case if he is between twelve and sixteen winters old if the principal permits it, but he does not need to take over the case formally from anyone.[83] *Sons between twelve and sixteen may prosecute a killing case*

A widow or an unmarried girl of twenty.[84]

If a principal in a case will not prosecute a suit involving personal compensation, belonging to a young man under sixteen winters, then it shall be (p. 169) lawful for the young man when he is sixteen winters or older to take up the case and so prepare it as if he had just heard of it for the first time, if he knows that the other had balked his case for him. It is lawful for him to transfer the case to someone else if he wants to. *Cases may be taken up when minors reach the age of sixteen*

If a man is not of age and a case arises in which he would be principal if he were old enough, then the suit falls to the man next of kin who is of age. If he has not prosecuted the case or transferred it or prepared it on the first Thursday of summer[85] after the young man becomes sixteen winters old, then the suit lies with the young man to prosecute and to settle.[86]

If a foreigner from Norway is killed.[87]

80. Add. ‡ 66.
81. Add. ‡ 66 (ii).
82. Add. ‡ 66 (iii); and cf. ‡ 118.
83. Add. ‡ 66 (iv).
84. See p. 158, ll. 16-19.
85. April 9-15.
86. Add. ‡ 101 (ii).
87. p. 158, ll. 20-23.

Injuries to minors

If killings happen at the General Assembly.[88]

If injury is inflicted on anyone under sixteen winters, then the principal in the case is the man who would be principal in the killing case if the young man were killed.[89] It is lawful for the young man to prosecute that case himself if the principal permits it, but he does not need to take over the case formally from any one.

If a man is killed who is not a lawful member of his father's family

If a man is killed who has not joined a family in accordance with law, even though he is openly fathered on a particular man, the killing case lies with his mother's kinsmen and the atonement as well — that is the way inheritance goes too.[90]

Injury suffered by person lacking mental capacity

If injury is inflicted on a man who is of age but of such mental incapacity that he does not have charge of his own property, the case lies with the man who is his lawful spokesman. The conduct of suits brought against him is to be as now rehearsed in the case of (p. 170) injuries done him.

Widows and women of twenty have charge of their own lawsuits for assault and minor wounds

A widow or an unmarried girl of twenty or more is to have charge of her own lawsuits if they are assaulted or wounded with minor wounds, whether they wish to transfer or settle. They must not take less than the personal compensation fixed by law.

If a Norwegian married in Iceland is killed

If a foreigner from Norway or the realms of the king of Norway[91] who is married in Iceland is killed, then the killing case after him lies with those men who would have it after his wife if she were killed.

Fourth cousins or nearer kin.[92]

If a man is killed or loses his power of speech.[93]

K ‡ 95

If a married woman is killed

If the wife of a man is killed with whom he has had children born as lawful heirs, the woman's husband is principal in that killing case. If such a woman has sons born as lawful heirs and they are of age, they are principals in the killing case on equal terms with her husband, and they and he have half the compensation each. If there is no son but the woman's father is alive or a brother born of the same father, then one of them becomes principal in the killing case on equal terms with the woman's husband.[94] If these men do not exist, the case lies with the woman's husband, but if there is another man so related to the woman that he would

---

88. It is uncertain what article this introduced, cf. ‡ 101 (p. 164).

89. Add. ‡ 101.

90. Add. ‡ 102.

91. Hebrides and Man, Orkney, Shetland, Faroes.

92. It is uncertain what article this introduced.

93. Cf. ‡ 101 (p. 164).

94. Add. ‡ 66 (v).

by law be counted her heir, then he shares compensation equally with the woman's husband.

A man has no right to kill a woman with a live child in her womb (p. 171) even if she has forfeited immunity by her own act or she is outlawed, and in such a case she does not fall with forfeit immunity.

If a woman with a live child in her womb is killed, then there are two killing cases and the case for killing the child is to proceed like other killing cases.

Heirs whether men or women have all the compensation in killing cases, no matter who prosecutes the case or who the principal is; and the lawful prosecutor is the man who can lawfully transfer it.

A mother takes one-third of killing compensation after her legitimate children, sharing with the dead man's brothers born of the same father; and in the same way she takes one-third of the compensation paid on account of her daughters, sharing with their brothers born of the same father.[95]

[96]If a man other than the principal prosecutes a case involving personal compensation because he thinks he is the principal and the proper principal pays no heed because he thinks someone other than himself is the principal, then he, the proper principal, is to have three-quarters of the settlement sum and the man who did the prosecuting one-quarter. If he needs to lay out money in bringing the prosecution or for support, then this is first to be subtracted from the settlement sum and they are to divide the rest between them. Now if he who prosecutes knows that he is not the principal, then the other, the proper principal, rightly claims the whole settlement sum awarded.

A pregnant woman, even of forfeit immunity, is not to be killed

Death of a pregnant woman means two killing cases

Rights to compensation of heirs and of mothers

If a man acts in error as a prosecution principal

K ‡ 96

It is prescribed that wherever a bounden debtor is the heir of a man killed he is not to conduct the case but he takes as much cash from the compensation as he is bound by debt for. If a bounden debtor is killed, then the case lies with his kinsmen. They are to offer the man who had money owed him as much cash as he may have been bound by debt for. But if (p. 172) they make no offer, then the case lies with [the man] who had money owed him by the man killed.[97]

It is prescribed that if a freedman is killed, then the case lies with his freeborn son, but otherwise with his freedom-giver. But if the freedom-giver kills his freedman and the freedman has no son, then the case lies with the chieftain[98] to whose assembly group the man killed had be-

Position of a debt-slave in killing cases

If a freedman is killed

---

95. Add. ‡ 87.
96. This section repeats ‡ 77 (p. 124).
97. Add. ‡ 67.
98. Add. ‡ 67 (ii).

longed. But if he is one and the same, then the case lies with the other chieftains of the same assembly. But if they disagree, they are to draw lots.⁹⁹ If the freedman of a freedman is killed, the case lies with the superior freedman.¹⁰⁰

K ‡ 97
On Killing of Foreigners

Danes, Norwegians, Swedes; other foreigners

If foreigners are killed here in the country, Danish or Swedish or Norwegian, then in the case of these three kingdoms that share our language the suit lies with the kinsmen of the dead man if they are here in the country. But cases for killing foreigners from all lands other than those with the languages I just told may be prosecuted here on grounds of kinship by nobody except father or son or brother, and only these if they themselves had previously acknowledged the kinship here in the country.

If a man without kin in Iceland is killed at a ship
Definition of a partner
Succession of rights of prosecution

If a man is killed at a ship and has no kinsmen here in the country, the case lies with his partner. A partner in accordance with law is one of a pair of whom the less well-endowed puts all he has into the partnership. But if no partner exists or if it is his partner who does the killing, then the case lies with his messmate, the man who most often shared with him over food. Now if there are more messmates than one who equally often shared with him over food, then they are to draw lots for the suit but all have equal shares in the compensation. But if no messmates exist,¹⁰¹ then the case lies with the ship's masters, and the one who owns the biggest share in the ship has the suit, but if they (p. 173) own equal shares in the ship, then they are to draw lots to see who is to conduct the suit but they all have equal shares in the compensation.

If a ship's master kills a man who has neither partner nor messmate, then the case lies with those who have shares in the ship with him; they have equal shares in all the compensation. The case lies with the one who owns the biggest share in the ship. They are to draw lots among themselves if they own equal shares in the ship.

If a ship's master who messes on his own is killed or if there is only one master and it is he who does the killing [of a man without partner or messmate], then the case lies with the chieftain to whose assembly group the man belongs who owns the land on which they are living.¹⁰²

If he is killed as he goes from ship to lodgings, the procedure is the same as if he were killed at the ship.

If he is killed while lodging with a householder, the case lies with the

---

99. Add. ‡ 67 (iii).
100. Add. ‡ 67 (iv).
101. Add. ‡ 68.
102. Add. ‡ 68 (ii).

householder.¹⁰³ But if the householder kills him, the case lies with the chieftain to whose assembly group he belongs. But if he is one and the same, the case lies with the other chieftains of the same assembly.¹⁰⁴

If he is killed in lodgings or on his way back to a ship

If he is lodging with a woman and is killed there — now if someone lodges with her who is a lawful assembly participant on behalf of her household, the case lies with him but she has the compensation; but if no one of this kind exists there, or if it is a man of this kind who kills him, then the case lies with the chieftain to whose assembly group the woman belongs.¹⁰⁵

The procedure is to be the same as if the man were killed in his lodgings until he rejoins his ship for good and all. But at the ship the procedure is to be the same as was told for the preceding summer.¹⁰⁶

If a foreigner lives here as a householder and has no kin and is killed, the case lies with the chieftain to whose assembly group he belonged. But if that chieftain kills him, the case lies with the other chieftains of the same assembly, unless the man killed has freeborn children, and the case then falls to that man who is next of kin to the children and of age and can take charge of it.¹⁰⁷

If a foreign householder without kin is killed

The procedure in cases of killing foreigners is to be as here rehearsed unless kinsmen of the men killed who share our language are here in the country, that is fourth cousins (p. 174) or closer. They have the right to prosecute killing cases here and to take compensation. If they come to the country later, all compensation from a killing case is still to be paid out but not with interest.

If kinsmen of a dead foreigner are in Iceland or come later

K ‡ 98

For all the killings I have now told and also for major wounds men are not to settle without prior leave of the General Assembly. Lesser outlawry is the penalty if men settle in cases which ought not to be settled without prior leave. The nearest kinsmen should first prosecute when men settle in a killing case without prior leave, but if they will not, then the case lies with anyone who is willing to prosecute to the limit of the law. It is a summoning case and nine householders are to be called at the assembly.¹⁰⁸

Penalty and procedure in case of settlement without prior leave

Lesser outlawry is the penalty for assisting such men.¹⁰⁹

103. Add. ‡ 69.
104. Add. ‡ 69 (ii).
105. Add. ‡ 69 (iii).
106. The procedures are those given above, p. 160. ll. 13 ff.
107. Add. ‡ 69 (iv).
108. Add. ‡ 70.
109. Add. ‡ 71.

Assistance to that man carries no penalty further.¹¹⁰
Sustenance of men carries no penalty.¹¹¹

K ‡ 99

Loss of right to attend assemblies

It is prescribed that those men who have had wounds or mortal wounds lawfully published as charges against them have no right to attend an assembly, but if they go to a formally inaugurated assembly (p. 175) the penalty is lesser outlawry, and all their cases are void; and so are all the defenses in which such a man is principal at the assembly, and also every suit and defense which he has prepared for that assembly — even though they are transferred cases — if he conducts them.¹¹²

Procedure and penalty if that loss of right is ignored

But if such men go to the General Assembly, the summons for that offense is to be made at Lögberg. But if they go to other formally inaugurated assemblies the summons for that offense is to be made locally and nine neighbors of the man prosecuted are to be called at the assembly to decide whether he has come to a formally inaugurated assembly since wounds or mortal wounds were published as charges against him; but if the case has been prepared for that assembly, then he may be summoned there to judgment if so desired. A panel is to be similarly called if it is a matter of attendance at the General Assembly.

Lesser outlawry is the penalty for all those men who ride with him because they wish to back him up in his attendance at the assembly.¹¹³

Forfeit of immunity

If those men go to an assembly who have no right to or they are at a formally inaugurated assembly, they forfeit their immunity in respect of injuries, and similarly all the men who are there in their party because they wish to give them help.

If a man meets someone at an assembly who has no right to be there

Where a man meets such a man at a formally inaugurated assembly who has no right to be there, he may choose to name witnesses to witness that he has met him at a formally inaugurated assembly, and he is to prosecute with that testimony.

Defense in such a case

If a panel gives a verdict of assembly attendance against a man, he has the right to call a panel of five of his neighbors to give a clearing verdict as to whether the other man had published wounds or mortal wounds as charges against him because he had wanted to balk his assembly-going but not because he thought him guilty of the charge; and if he gets the verdict that that was the other's reason, then he has a defense in the assembly-going case.

110. How this article may have continued is unknown.
111. Add. ‡ 73.
112. Add. ‡ 83.
113. Add. ‡ 70 (ii).

All these cases here told concerning injuries are to come to the Quarter Court for the Quarter the injuries were done in. But if men fight on a Quarter boundary, then the cases [are to] come to the Quarter Court for the Quarter which provides the majority of the neighbors called.

Which Quarter Court cases should come before

K ‡ 100; p. 176

At spring assemblies formally inaugurated and at autumn meetings men are to publish wounds on the assembly slope at the place where men customarily make announcements. Men may settle for no woundings that happen there without prior leave.[114]

Publishing wounds at spring and autumn assemblies

If men who have inflicted injury on others run into booths there, the penalty is lesser outlawry for men who shield them, if it is not at the place of action. But if it is at the place of action the penalty is full outlawry. But if those men shield them who own the booth there, the booth of those men loses its immunity in case of damage if they are first asked before witnesses to stand aside. But the neighbors to be called are those who live nearest the place of action from among those who have none of the injuries inflicted laid to their charge.[115]

Shielding; booths not sacrosanct

K ‡ 101

It is prescribed that where men give and receive injuries at the General Assembly, a booth-panel is to be called from the nearest three booths that can each provide three men not disqualified by their connections. No call is to be made on booths of shoemakers or sword cutlers.[116] But the first men to be called are those who own booths if they are qualified for the calling; and those first who have the largest share in the booth if all are not needed. Then other householders are to be called if the booth-owners are not qualified or if more are needed, but if it will not (p. 177) otherwise suffice, household men are to be called. All injuries and assaults and attempts and all lawbreakings which men commit [at the] General Assembly, at a place of action where men get wounds, are to be decided by a booth-panel, but assault and injuries that happen at the General Assembly are to be published at Lögberg.

Booth-panels to be called in case of injury at General Assembly

Publishing at Lögberg

When men are called to give a booth-verdict at the General Assembly and have not done so, they are required to go to the General Assembly the following summer just as if they had been called locally.

Booth-panel members are to attend the following summer

If a man dies from the wounds he got there at the General Assembly, it is possible to publish it before the five neighbors who live nearest the place where he dies.

Publishing death from wounds received at the General Assembly

---

114. I.e., of the Law Council; cf. Add. ‡ 89.

115. Cf. Add. ‡ 85.

116. Add. ‡ 76.

If a man strikes or wounds someone at assemblies.[117]

Injuries at the close of the General Assembly

If injuries are inflicted at the General Assembly at the time when new laws have been recited,[118] then it is not required that the courts be brought out, and those neighbors are to be called in the case who live nearest the assembly ground, from those who are qualified in terms of relationship (p. 178) and of attachment.[119]

Principal in case of a man killed or made speechless or senseless at the General Assembly

If a man is killed or loses his power of speech or becomes senseless as a result of injuries received at the General Assembly, the prosecution principal is his nearest male kinsman who is at the Assembly.

K ‡ 102

Prices on heads of outlaws

If a man is outlawed for killing at the General Assembly, the price on his head is three marks in legal tender. The second with the same price on his head is the man who burns people inside a house. The third is the slave who kills[120] his master or his mistress or their children or foster-kin. Fourth is the murderer.[121] But all other outlaws have a price of eight ounce-units.[122]

Prosecutor must choose one man as the killer; kindred payments and challenging depend on the choice

Where men are outlawed for killing, then the prosecutor is to choose one as the killer at the court or before the arbitrators at a settlement, whichever he likes of the men who were present at the killing, and he is to claim atonement from the kindred of that man,[123] and likewise he has the right to challenge on grounds of connection with that man. But if he does not choose anyone, there is no claim then to atonement nor right to challenge.

K ‡ 103

Prosecution for murder

It is prescribed that for murder a man is to make a summons and call on the chieftain to whose assembly group the man prosecuted belongs to form a panel of twelve. It is also possible to call locally nine neighbors of the man prosecuted, and to publish the charge at the assembly he called the neighbors to appear at. The third possibility after the discovery of a corpse is to call neighbors of the place where the corpse lies and publish the charge at the assembly.[124]

---

117. Add. ‡ 85.

118. Apparently the closing stage of the Assembly. New laws seem to have been announced separately after their adoption by the Law Council and collectively by the Lawspeaker near the end of the Assembly. Cf. ‡‡ 116, 117 (pp. 187-88, 192).

119. Cf. Add. ‡ 85 (ii).

120. Add. ‡ 77.

121. Cf. ‡ 88 (p. 146).

122. On claiming these rewards see ‡ 110 (pp. 171-72), Add. ‡ 133 (vii).

123. Cf. ‡ 113 (pp. 175-76).

124. Add. ‡ 78 (ii).

All these cases here told are to be published at the assembly and (p. 179) neighbors called locally;[125] indeed, all cases for which neighbors are called locally may lawfully be published; and finally, wherever it is lawful to publish, it is lawful to summon.

Publishing at the assembly; calling in the locality

K ‡ 104

In all those cases of which the principal has learnt when four weeks of summer have passed[126] or sooner, he must have done the summoning[127] by the Wednesday which is the day before six weeks of summer are over,[128] but neighbors are to be called by the following Saturday, the one in the seventh week of summer.[129] But if the principal learns of the suit later or the offense occurs later than that but before the last of the moving days,[130] then it is lawful to make the summons right up to the end of the seventh week of summer at the latest,[131] and neighbors are to be called by the time eight weeks of summer are over.[132]

Summoning times

But where it is a question of a counter-calling and one side have done their calling before the moving days and the other side want to do theirs after the moving days, then nevertheless they are to call the same neighbors. But if neighbors have moved house in the interval, then they are to call them at the place where they were living at the time of the first calling.[133] But the man who begins the calling of neighbors after the moving days is to call those who are going to live in the coming year nearest the place he makes his call for.

Calling before and after moving days

If a man learns of a case in which he is principal on Sunday in the moving days or later, he may choose not to prepare that case for prosecution that summer, but he may also choose to prosecute it at that summer's General Assembly; and if it is a case for which neighbors are to be called locally, then, if he thinks of prosecuting that summer, he must have made the summons at the latest by the Thursday when eight weeks of summer have passed[134] and also have called neighbors by then. The neighbors to be called must either all have been living there before the Thursday in the moving days or all be living there after the moving days.

If a principal learns of a case in the moving days

125. Add. ‡ 94.
126. With the arrival of Thursday, May 7-13; cf. ‡ 77 (p. 123).
127. Add. ‡ 95.
128. Wednesday, May 20-26.
129. May 23-29.
130. Sunday, May 24-30.
131. Wednesday, May 27 - June 2.
132. Eight weeks had passed with the arrival of Thursday, June 4-10.
133. Add. ‡ 96.
134. Thursday, June 4-10.

If cases arise within two weeks of the General Assembly

It is prescribed that in all suits which become known after (p. 180) eight weeks of summer have passed and do not require local calling — and so also in suits which become known so late that, even though local calling is required, a man could not get neighbors called by the time eight weeks of summer have passed — then he may do his summoning in such suits as near the General Assembly as he likes, should he in fact want to prosecute at the forthcoming General Assembly. But if local calling would have been required for a suit, had it become known earlier, then he is to call those nine neighbors at the assembly who live nearest the place for which he should make his call if he called neighbors locally for the same suit.

A new law. If a principal learns so late of a killing-case.[135]

If a principal is in a different Quarter

If a principal is outside the Quarter, it is lawful for him to prepare the suit by publishing it at an assembly, and call neighbors locally, [but it is also lawful for him to make a summons locally] and call nine neighbors of the place of action at the assembly. If it is so close to the General Assembly that someone from a different Quarter thinks there is not time enough to prepare a prosecution that summer, whatever the shortcoming may be, then it is lawful for him, if he wishes, to publish it at the close of the Assembly for prosecution the following summer. He is further to call nine neighbors, either locally or at the Assembly as he prefers.[136]

K ‡ 105

Procedure in cases of assault, wounding, or killing on the way to the assembly

If men assault each other or wound each other or if men are killed as they go to an assembly, it is right to publish it before nine or more neighbors, if such men are there as a prosecutor thinks will not have lawbreaking at that place of action laid to their charge. It is also right (p. 181) to publish before five neighbors of the place of action who in terms of distance would qualify to serve on a panel of nine. A third possibility is to publish it at Lögberg once the Assembly has been formally inaugurated, if the General Assembly is so close at hand that a prosecutor can publish it there before the third sunrise. A summons in such a suit is to be made locally at the home of the man prosecuted or else at a place where he himself hears it, and nine neighbors of the place of action called at the assembly. [137]It is moreover lawful for a man to do his summoning before he publishes assault or injury.

It is lawful to publish that charge at the Assembly and prosecute the same summer, and call neighbors of the place of action at the Assembly

---

135. This perhaps introduced an article like ‡ 107, cf. p. 167, ll. 11-12.
136. Add. ‡ 96 (ii).
137. A new law according to St ‡ 310 (II 346).

if there is time enough for that before the courts go out. If injuries that happen while going to the Assembly are published at Lögberg as a charge against someone, then if he is already at the Assembly he no longer has the right to be present at an assembly and he is to leave the Assembly the same day as a charge is published against him.[138]

Men charged must leave the assembly

K ‡ 106
In every suit which becomes known during the General Assembly, so that it is only then that a principal comes to learn of it, it is lawful for the summons to be made locally, whenever a man can call men to provide formal means of proof before the courts go out.

If a suit only becomes known during the assembly

K ‡ 107
It is prescribed that if cases are prepared against a slain man to maintain that he was a man of forfeit immunity, and the principal hears of the killing at the assembly or so late that he is not required to prepare a case for prosecution that same summer unless he wants to, it is nevertheless lawful for him to publish it straightway for prosecution and prosecute that same summer. If neighbors of the place of action where he (p. 182) got his death wound have been called locally by the other side, then he is to call the same neighbors at the assembly as the other side has called locally. If they prepare their case later and only at the assembly call neighbors of the place of action where he got his death wound to give a verdict of forfeit immunity against the man killed, they are to call them not later than the night before the courts go out to hear prosecutions. And the man prosecuting for the killing is to call the same neighbors as his opponent has already called, and the right of challenge lies with the one who called them second. Now, if it turns out that those called by the one side are not the same as those called as neighbors of the place of action where the man got his death,[139] then the man prosecuting for the killing is to call at the assembly those neighbors of the place of action whom he thinks best qualified. If previously and at some other place of action, the killer by his own act had forfeited his immunity in relation to the man now killed, and the prosecution principal is at the Assembly and a case is prepared to maintain that the man killed was a man of forfeit immunity at the place of action where he got his death wound or injury, then the prosecution principal of the killing case is to publish for prosecution against the killer both the killing and the lawbreaking which he had previously committed to the forfeit of his immunity in relation to the man killed, and he is to call neighbors at the assembly for that place of action where the killer

Case of forfeit immunity against a man who has been killed

Forfeit of immunity at place of action; calling neighbors

Earlier forfeit of killer's immunity at another place of action; calling neighbors

---

138. Add. ‡ 75.
139. Omitting *á þingi* "at the assembly."

had by his own act forfeited his immunity in relation to the man killed.

If a principal is not present when forfeit of immunity is pleaded against a dead man

If the prosecution principal is not at the assembly and a case is prepared to maintain that the man killed was a man of forfeit immunity — now, if his kinsmen are at the assembly, second cousins or closer, then any one of them who wants is to prosecute the killing case as if he were the rightful principal. But if they disagree about it, it lies with the man most closely related to him.[140] But if there is no one at the assembly who is related to him in this way or if they will not prosecute, then the conduct of the case lies with the chieftain to whose assembly group the prosecution principal belongs.

Wherever a man is killed, or wounded so that he is not himself fit to prepare a case and gets no one else to do it, then his kinsmen have the same choices of action in everything to do with the case as the prosecution principal if he were at the assembly; and the same is prescribed for the chieftain.

If forfeit immunity is not proved

It is prescribed that (p. 183) whichever one of the men now told does the prosecuting, then if the formal means of proof go in favor of the man killed, he is to be judged not under penalty for the charges prepared against him, but the killer under the fullest penalty. If the principal in the killing case is not at the assembly nor any one of those now told and it happens that a case is prepared to maintain that the man killed was a man of forfeit immunity but the killing case is not prepared,[141] then anyone who wants has the right to call for all the clearing verdicts needed for the man killed. He is to call neighbors as rehearsed earlier, in the same way as a man who was preparing the case for prosecution there at the assembly.

Clearing verdicts and verdicts in the dead man's favor

If any verdict is given in favor of the man killed of such a kind that the killer would be under penalty for it if the case against him had been prepared locally in accordance with law, then the man killed must be judged not under penalty for those charges and his property also.[142]

Case of a man killed at the assembly

The same procedure is to be followed when a man is killed at the assembly as was earlier rehearsed in the case of a prosecution principal who is not at the assembly and a case is prepared to maintain that the man killed was a man of forfeit immunity.

K ‡ 108
On Plots to Disfigure

Lesser outlawry is the penalty if a man asks another to go with him to inflict injuries or if he plots to disfigure someone. The same penalty applies

---

140. Add. ‡ 97.
141. Add. ‡ 97 (ii).
142. Add. ‡ 97 (iii).

to anyone who promises to go. It is a summoning case and nine neighbors of the man prosecuted are to be called locally.

If they make an ambush for anyone, then neighbors of the place of ambush are to be called locally. It is an ambush when men wait somewhere because they intend to inflict injuries on men at that place or to set out from there in order to do so. But if two groups meet, then even if those who were ambushed make the first assault, the others who (p. 184) lay in ambush fall with forfeit immunity. *Ambushes*

It is prescribed that all plots to disfigure carry a penalty of lesser outlawry even if they do not succeed, but full outlawry if they do. *Penalties*

If a man plots to strike someone.[143]

It is a plot to disfigure if a man deceitfully contrives that a weapon should fall on someone or fly at him, or contrives some other danger. Similarly, if a man sends someone towards perilous places or to where fierce animals are. In all such cases neighbors are to be called locally from the place where the man was harmed. But if he was unharmed, but it was nevertheless intended, then neighbors of the man prosecuted are to be called. *Disfigurement plots: definition and procedure*

Guðmundr[144] said it was law that nine neighbors of the place of action are to be called for plots to disfigure that are plotted at that place of action and there given effect,[145] but nine home neighbors for all plots to disfigure that are not given effect, and it is nine neighbors of the man who plotted the disfigurement plot who are to be called. *Guðmundr's statement on procedure in case of disfigurement plots*

K ‡ 109
On Burnings

It is prescribed that if a man asks another to go with him to burn a building with people or people's property in it, the penalty is lesser outlawry; (p. 185) and the same applies to anyone who promises to go, and nine neighbors of each one of them are to be called locally. If they set out and have fire with them, then neighbors are to be called from the place where they took the fire. But once fire is taken for burning they fall with forfeit immunity and the penalty is outlawry. But if they burn a building with people or people's property in it, the penalty is outlawry, and neighbors [of the place burnt] are to be called locally.[146]

---

143. Add. ‡ 106 (ii).
144. Guðmundr Þorgeirsson, Lawspeaker 1123-34.
145. Add. ‡ 106.
146. Here there is a lacuna in K, probably of two leaves. K begins again with matter corresponding to the parallel (though not identical) text given as Add. ‡ 133 (ii), cf. St ‡ 382 (II 399/17). The text immediately preceding this in St, also not found in K, is given in Add. ‡‡ 131, 132, 133 (i). If K had this same text it would have filled about a quarter of the postulated two-leaf lacuna.

K ‡ 110; p. 187, l. 17

Killing outlaws to win reprieve

[It is lawful] to kill outlaws for the reprieve of other outlaws who would have had the right to settle in the cases they were outlawed for, other than thieving cases. If a man not himself under legal penalty kills an outlaw for the reprieve of another outlaw, the last becomes an outlaw who may be given passage as soon as one outlaw is killed for his reprieve. If he kills yet another outlaw for his reprieve, then he becomes a lesser outlaw. And if he kills a third, then his reprieve becomes complete. There are the same steps of reprieve for an outlaw who himself kills other outlaws for his own reprieve.[147]

Killer must announce that he wants the reprieve of a named outlaw

Whether a man not himself under legal penalty kills (p.188) for an outlaw's reprieve or whether an outlaw kills for his own reprieve, whichever of them does a killing, he is to say that he wants the reprieve of that man or of himself instead of the outlaw's price[148] and they are to say it to five neighbors[149] at the same time as they publish the killing. He is always to announce the degree of reprieve for which the killing was done.

It is prescribed that more than one man may kill for the reprieve of a single outlaw if they so wish. Each of them is to publish before five neighbors that they wish their killing to be for that man's reprieve. He is moreover an outlaw who may be given passage when one is killed, and a lesser outlaw when two are killed, and completely reprieved when three are killed. But before it is published at Lögberg he is only reprieved in relation to men who have heard of the reprieve for which the killing was done; for it is to be announced in the coming summer for what degree of reprieve the killing was done.

Reprieve universally effective only after publishing at Lögberg

If a slave outlawed for killing his master or mistress is captured

When a slave becomes an outlaw because of killing his master or mistress,[150] then those who capture him are to take him, given it is within the same Quarter, to the man who got that outlaw condemned, and he is to cut off the outlaw's hands and feet[151] and let him live as long as he may. If the man who got him condemned will not cut off the outlaw's hands and feet, his penalty is lesser outlawry, and the case lies with those who brought him the outlaw. If they will not prosecute, the case lies with

---

147. Add. ‡ 133 (ii). A note in a seventeenth-century source, but probably derived from a text written *ca.* 1300, says of a famine winter in pagan times (*ca.* 975): "Many people starved to death, and some took to robbing and were outlawed and killed because of it. Outlaws then killed each other because it was made law on the initiative of Eyjólfr Valgerðarson that anyone who killed three outlawed men redeemed himself." See Jakob Benediktsson, *Skarðsárbók* (1958), p. 189 and pp. xxxix-xl.

148. Cf. ‡ 102 (p. 164).

149. Add. ‡ 133 (iii).

150. Add. ‡ 133 (iv).

151. Add. ‡ 133 (v).

anyone willing to prosecute the case in accordance with the law's rigor.

If men beat such an outlaw to death within the same Quarter and will not take him to the man who got him condemned, when it was in fact possible for them to overpower him by other means than weapons, their penalty is lesser outlawry. That case lies with the man who got the outlaw condemned.

Men not in the same Quarter have the choice whether they prefer to maim the outlaw in the same way as the man who got him condemned should or alternatively to take him to him. (p. 189) They are required to torture him to make him talk[152] and get the five nearest neighbors to come. The penalty for those who torture him is lesser outlawry if they do not tell the truth about his words or conceal them. The same procedure is to be followed in the case of bounden debtors who are taken into service because of debt in accordance with law and have been announced as such at Lögberg. There is the same right to prosecute men not in the same Quarter as men who are in the same Quarter, if they do not do one thing or the other, and nine neighbors are to be called at the assembly. *A debt-slave is treated the same way*

A man is not required to kill an outlaw, unless he was the one who got him condemned, even if he happens to meet him to speak to, as long as he does not capture him and gives him no saving advice.[153] *One is not necessarily required to kill an outlaw*

The man who has killed an outlaw is to publish a suit on the assembly slope or at Lögberg for the outlaw's price, a mark in legal tender, as a charge against the chieftain to whose assembly group he belongs and the other chieftains of the same assembly and all their assembly men, publish for the price and for the payment.[154] He is to get two men who give their word of honor that they were acquainted with that outlaw, and that man was killed who he says was killed. If he does not have men to vouch for this, then he is to call five of his neighbors to give a verdict whether it was he who did the killing there or not. The court has to enjoin the chieftains by judgment to pay a mark in legal tender, and each of the three and their assembly men to pay an equal part of that mark, and judge the settling day as the day after men have been one night at the [appropriate] assembly, for payment of that money at the booth doorway of each of those chieftains. But a chieftain who does not own a booth is to pay at the booth doorway of one of the other chieftains of the same assembly. But a chieftain is to claim the money from his assembly men and they are to pay it along with their assembly attendance dues. *Claiming the reward for killing an outlaw*

Where and when the reward is to be paid

If a man kills an outlaw, one of the four[155] with a bigger price on his

---

152. Cf. Add. ‡ 133 (vi).
153. Cf. Add. ‡‡ 131, 133 (viii).
154. Cf. Add. ‡ 133; ‡ 102 (p. 164).
155. Reading *iiii* for *iii*, "three;" cf. ‡ 102 (p. 164) and St ‡ 382 (II 401/26).

Claiming the reward for killing higher-priced outlaws

head, he is to publish the suit (p. 190) at Lögberg for the outlaw's price, three marks in legal tender, as a claim on all the chieftains here in the country and their assembly men,[156] publish it for judgment in the Quarter Court for the Quarter he himself comes from, and it is to be enjoined by judgment that that money be paid in the householder's churchyard[157] the following summer on the day that falls halfway through the assembly.

All formal means of proof are to be presented just as in other suits for outlaws' prices.[158]

K ‡ 111

Killing a man's slave

Servant killings are if a man kills another man's slave or bondwoman and the penalty is lesser outlawry.[159] It is to be prosecuted like any other killing save that neighbors are to be called at the assembly. If there was more than one man at his killing, the master of the man killed is to select one man as the killer, whichever he pleases from those who were present. If he is outlawed for the killing, the prosecutor is to have from his property the price of the slave at the value put on the slave by five neighbors of the prosecutor by oath on a book[160] at court.

Where the man who kills a slave is on grounds of relationship a rightful assembly participant on behalf of the household of the person who owned the slave, he is not under penalty but he must pay for the slave.[161]

A slave forfeits immunity

A slave forfeits his immunity if he says something to a man which between free men requires full personal compensation or if he does something which between free men requires half personal compensation.[162]

A man who kills a slave forfeits immunity in certain circumstances

If the master of a slave happens to be present when the slave is killed, then the man who kills the slave forfeits his immunity at that place of action as far as the master and any men who may be assembly participants on behalf of his household are concerned, unless the slave has forfeited immunity by his own act. Men have the right to avenge the slave at the place of action where he is killed but not afterwards.

---

156. Add. ‡ 133 (vii).

157. See p. 29, n. 17.

158. Add. ‡ 133 (viii).

159. In *Egils saga*, ch. 81, it says that the penalty was not incurred if the price of the slave was brought to the owner "before the third sunrise," and in *Eyrbyggja saga*, ch. 43, that it was not incurred if the men paying the price, specified as twelve ounce-units of silver, began their journey before that time. Cf. *Íslenzk Fornrit* II (1933), p. 282 and n. 2, IV (1935), p. 118 and n. 3.

160. A sacred book, its nature and size unspecified (Gospel, psalter, or missal were commonly used); cf. ‡‡ 42, 46 (pp. 82 and n. 77, 86).

161. Add. ‡ 130.

162. Add. ‡ 130 (ii).

If a slave runs under men's weapons to protect his master then the penalty is outlawry (p. 191) for his killing if he gets his death by it.

Full outlawry for a man who kills a slave defending his master

If a master kills his own slave he is under no penalty unless he kills him in an established holy season or in Lent,[163] when the penalty is lesser outlawry, and nine neighbors are to be called at the assembly and the case lies with the chieftain to whose assembly group the killer belongs. If he will not prosecute, then the case lies with anyone who wants to. He is under no penalty for killing the slave, whenever he kills him, if he kills for offenses for which a free man would fall with forfeit immunity.[164]

If a master kills his own slave

If a man gives another man's slave a blemishing blow, the master takes six ounce-units and the slave three.[165] Now, if he gives the slave a crippling beating or wounds him, then he is to pay the price of the slave to the man who owned him at the value set on him by neighbors by oath on a book, and further pay for his disadvantage, as assessed by neighbors, if the slave becomes incapable as a result of that beating.

Giving another man's slave blows or beatings

If men's slaves come to blows, then the one who strikes is to pay six ounce-units[166] to the master and three to the slave if he has the means to do so, otherwise nothing.

If slaves of different owners fight or kill each other

If men's slaves fight to the death, then the man who owns the slave who has done the killing has the right to do whichever he prefers, either let the slave be prosecuted or else pay for the killed slave at the value set on him by neighbors by oath on a book.[167]

If slaves give each other a crippling beating, then both owners are to profit from the healthy slave and both maintain the crippled one.

A slave has more right than a free man in one respect. A slave has the right to kill on account of his wife even though she is a bondwoman but a free man has no right to kill on account of his bondwoman even though she is his wife.[168]

A slave may kill on account of his wife

K ‡ 112
On Freedom for Slaves

The man who gives someone freedom is to maintain his children. It goes in the same way as inheritance. With (p. 192) slaves it is prescribed that the man who has money owed him by them is to maintain them.

Maintenance responsibility for freedmen's children and slaves

---

163. Cf. ‡‡ 8-15 (pp. 39-47).

164. Add. ‡ 130 (iii).

165. Add. ‡ 130 (iv).

166. Reading *gjalda sex aura* for *gjalda þrælinn* "pay for the slave," cf. St ‡ 379 (II 396).

167. Cf. p. 172, n. 160; Add. ‡ 130 (v).

168. Or his "woman." A bondwoman could not be a free man's legal wife in the sense that their children would be naturally regarded as legitimate and with rights of inheritance; cf. ‡ 118.

When a slave becomes free and when fully free

His oath

Rights to personal compensation

Fee to chieftain

If a man frees a slave he has not fully paid for

Buying a concubine

A slave freed but not fully freed

If livestock damage each other

A slave does not become free until the other has paid half his price or more. A man is given full freedom when he is led into the law. The chieftain to whose assembly group he belongs is to lead him into the law. He is to take a cross in his hand and name witnesses to witness that he swears an oath on the Cross, a lawful oath, and "I say before God" that he will keep the laws like a man who keeps them well, and it is his wish then to share in the laws with other men. "God be harsh on him who denies him that unless he atones for it with his goods." The man who was given freedom young does not need to swear that oath.

He is to take half personal compensation when he holds an earl's farm but total and complete compensation when he holds a king's farm.[169]

He is to give a penny to the chieftain who leads him into the law — that is to be the tenth part of an ounce-unit.

A man is to give freedom to the slave for whom he has provided the full price. If he gives freedom to a slave for whom he has not paid the full price, he makes himself but not his kinsmen responsible for him when the freedman becomes incapable.

It is lawful for a man to buy a bondwoman as a bedfellow for twelve ounce-units without prior leave.[170]

If a slave is given freedom but not led into the law or brought onto the assembly slope, then he is to take neither a free man's personal compensation nor a slave's; and he is then called a "spade-freedman."[171]

[172]If livestock do hurt to livestock, then half the damage as assessed by five neighbors is always the sum to be made good.

---

169. The import of this in Icelandic laws is obscure and debated. Probably conditions in Norway are reflected, or other parts under Norwegian dominion (cf. p. 158, n. 91). In those areas, estates belonging to king or earl were not infrequently managed by stewards who were slaves or freedmen.

170. Slavery proper seems to have disappeared in Iceland by *ca.* 1100, and soon after 1200 in Denmark and Norway; in Sweden it does not seem finally to have disappeared until the fourteenth century. Cf. p. 10, n. 10.

171. Apparently "freed from the spade," figurative of relief from some of the heaviest work normally done by slaves.

172. Add. ‡ 107.

The Wergild Ring List

K ‡ 113; p. 193

There are four wergild rings fixed by law. The first is of three marks. The second of twenty ounces. The third of two marks. The fourth of twelve ounce-units. A supplement of six ounces goes with the main ring, and forty-eight bits. A supplement of half a mark goes with the twenty-ounce ring, and thirty-two bits. A supplement of three ounces goes with the two-mark ring, and twenty-four bits. A supplement of two ounces goes with the twelve-ounce ring, and sixteen bits. Three men are both payers and receivers of the main ring: father and son and brother. Four men are both payers and receivers of the twenty-ounce ring: father's father and son's son, mother's father and daughter's son. Four men are again both payers and receivers of the two-mark ring: father's brother and brother's son, mother's brother and sister's son. Male first cousins take the twelve-ounce ring and also pay it. With that the wergild rings are disposed of.

Four wergild rings, with supplements and bits

Payers and takers of wergild rings

Those men who are first cousins once removed of the man killed are to take a mark from the killer's kinsmen of like degree (p. 194). Second cousins of the killer are to pay five and one-third ounces as atonement to second cousins of the man killed. Those men who are second cousins once removed of the killer are to pay three and one-half ounces to the dead man's kinsmen of like degree. Third cousins of the man killed are to take two and one-third ounces from third cousins of the killer. Those men who are kinsmen of the killer at one remove from that are to pay one and one-half ounces to the dead man's kinsmen of like degree. Fourth cousins of the man killed are to take one ounce from fourth cousins of the killer. There ends the atonement list.

Further payers and takers on the atonement list. Down to one ounce the dues make cases conferring rights of veto

All cases for which atonement of one ounce or more is appropriate are cases conferring rights of veto.[1]

If men of forfeit immunity are killed, there is no claim there to atonement.

Forfeit immunity, no atonement

If more men than one were present at the killing, the prosecutor is to choose one man as the killer at the court or before the arbitrators at the settlement, whichever he likes of the men who were present at the killing, and he is to claim atonement from the kindred of that man. If he does not

Prosecutor is to choose one man as the killer

---

1. Cf. ‡ 80 (p. 132), and pp. 182-83 below.

choose anyone, there is no claim then to atonement.²

If a prosecuting principal settles without prior leave or does not press the case to the limit

If the principal in a killing case settles for the killing without prior leave of the General Assembly, he has no right to any share with other kinsmen in the kindred payments. A principal in a killing case is to take a wergild ring only if killing compensation is not due to him. Similarly he may take ring-atonement as long as he does not accept money for such mitigation of the killer's penalty that he is not at least made a lesser outlaw. A principal disqualifies himself from ring-atonement if he pursues the case less rigorously at law or to a worse settlement than he would have done had the money been due to himself and if a panel gives this verdict on him.

If a killing is done by someone under twelve

If someone younger than twelve winters kills someone and no one else is found guilty of complicity in it, then the principal alone has all the kindred payments.

Atonement claims stand even if a case is spoilt by procedural defects

If a killing is not published or is published wrong, the claim for atonement remains the same; and likewise if the killing case becomes void, as long as this is not because forfeit immunity is accepted as grounds of defense. If the killer is (p. 195) outlawed or killed, the claim for kindred payments remains just the same.

Payment of wergild rings

All wergild rings are to be forthcoming, no matter how many payers there are and no matter how many the receivers, but no one is to pay bigger rings in atonement than he would take.

Proper payers and receivers of the biggest ring

Father, son, and brother of the man killed are to take the biggest ring and take it from the father, son, and brother of the killer, and each of them is to take one mark from the ring and two ounces of the supplement and sixteen bits, and that is how each of the others is to pay, given that all these classes of kinsmen exist on each side. If there is a single son of the man killed but many brothers, the brothers nevertheless are to take only a mark; and sons only a mark should there be many of them but only a single brother; and kinsmen of the slayer are to divide the payment between themselves in the same way even though there are not the same number of brothers as sons. If the dead man has a brother born of the same father and another brother born of the same mother, the brother born of the same mother is to take two-fifths of the mark and the one born of the same father³ three-fifths and he alone is to have the supplement and bits. A father is to take two shares in the wergild ring if there is no son and a son two shares if there is no father. If only one proper receiver of the main ring is alive, whichever of them it is, then he is to take the whole ring with its supplement and bits. Now if neither father

---

2. Cf. ‡ 102 (p. 164).
3. Reading *samfeðri* for *sammœðri* "born of the same mother."

nor son of the man killed is alive, but brothers of his are alive, some born of the same father and some of the same mother, then brothers born of the same mother take two-fifths of the ring and brothers born of the same father three-fifths and these are to have the supplement and all the bits. If father or son is alive and the only brother is one born of the same mother, then he is to take a full brother's share of the ring, just as if he were born of the same father, given that only one of the two, either father or son, exists. But if both father and son exist, and the only brother is one born of the same mother, then this brother is to take half a pennyweight less than five and one-half ounces from the wergild ring with a one-ounce (p. 196) supplement and eight bits. If there is no proper receiver of the main ring other than a brother born of the same mother, he is to take the whole ring and the supplement but no bits. But if there are no proper payers of the main ring, then all receivers are to suffer the same proportional reduction, always according to their place on the list.

The second wergild ring is of twenty ounces and the dead man's father's father and son's son, mother's father and daughter's son are to take that ring, and take it from the four men who are kin to the killer in like degree. That ring is to be split five ways among them, and father's father and son's son are to have three-fifths of the ring and all the supplement and bits, and mother's father and daughter's son two-fifths. If there is only either father's father or son's son but both the other kinsmen, and similarly if there is only either mother's father or daughter's son but both the other kinsmen, then the ring is nevertheless to be divided as was rehearsed earlier. And the payment men take whose kinship is traced through men is called ring payment, while the payment men take whose kinship is traced through a woman is called cognate payment.[4] Even though there are very many son's sons or daughter's sons, they do not take a greater share in the wergild ring, and similarly in the case of other ring receivers it is to be divided equally between all branches of a family, even though there is only a single man from one branch and many from another, provided that the branches are both ring-payment branches or both cognate-payment branches.[5]

Proper payers and receivers of the second ring

Ring payment and cognate payment

If there are no proper receivers of the twenty-ounce ring other than father's father or son's son, then he is to take the whole ring with supplement and bits. But if none exists other than mother's father or daughter's son, then they are to take the whole supplemented ring but no bits.

---

4. Icelandic *nefgildi*. The compound covers the compensation to the wider (cognate) kindred, traced through both male and female links.

5. Equal division within branches of the same kind of descent, but three-fifths and two-fifths between branches of male and cognate descent.

Proper payers and receivers of the third ring

The dead man's father's brother and brother's son, mother's brother and sister's son are to take the two-mark ring from the (p. 197) four men who are kin to the killer in like degree, and mother's brother and sister's son are to have two-fifths of the ring and father's brother and brother's son three-fifths and these are also to have the supplement and bits. Now if only a father's brother or a brother's son [is] in line for ring payment, he is to take the whole ring with supplement and bits. But if only a mother's brother or sister's son is in line for ring payment, he is to take the whole ring supplemented but no bits. That ring is to be divided for cognate payment in the same proportion as the twenty-ounce ring.

Proper payers and receivers of the fourth ring

Male first cousins of the man killed are to take the twelve-ounce ring and take it from all the men who are kin to the killer in like degree. That ring is also to be split five ways among them, and sons of father's brothers take three-fifths of the ring and the supplement and bits, and sons of father's sisters and sons of mother's brothers and sisters two-fifths of the ring. Even should there be only one father's brother's son and very many cognate cousins, he is nevertheless to take all the share allotted to father's brothers' sons. If there is only one mother's sister's son and very many sons of father's brothers, he is to have all the share allotted to mother's sisters' sons. Sons of father's sisters and of mother's brothers are to take as much of that cognate payment as sons of mother's sisters. If none exists other than a single father's brother's son, he is nevertheless to take the whole ring with the supplement and bits. Now if none of them exists other than a single mother's sister's son, he is nevertheless to take the whole ring and the supplement too but not the bits.

If there are proper payers but no proper receivers

If no proper receivers of the three-mark ring exist but proper payers exist, then father's father and son's son, mother's father and daughter's son are to take the main ring reduced by half a mark and that ring is to be divided for cognate payment like the twenty-ounce ring. They are each to take their own ring with supplement and bits but supplement and bits never go with a reduced ring. Now if there are no proper receivers of closer kin (p. 198) than father's brother and brother's son [and mother's brother] and sister's son, then they are to take three rings. They are to take their own ring whole and supplemented and with bits, and the main ring reduced by one mark and the twenty-ounce ring reduced by half a mark. Then all the rings come to two marks each. They only take ring payment in this way if proper payers of each ring exist. Moreover they are to take payment in the same way even though only cognate kin exist to receive it or similarly to pay it.

Supplement or bits never accompany reduced ring payment

If proper payers exist at every level but only some receivers

If the only living ring-receiving kin of the man killed are first cousins and proper payers exist at every level, then they are to take four rings. They are to take their own ring whole and the supplement too and bits.

They are also to take the main ring reduced by half. Thereby the biggest ring becomes the same as the smallest. Then they are to take twelve ounces for the father's father's ring, twelve ounces for the brother's son's ring: that is the twenty-ounce ring reduced by a mark and the two-mark ring by half a mark. Supplement and bits are to go with none of the rings save the cousin's ring. All those rings are to be split five ways and three-fifths fall to the father's brothers' sons and two-fifths for the cognate payment. If there is a single mother's sister's son but no father's brothers' sons, he is nevertheless to take all the rings.

If no ring receivers are alive other than father or son or brother while all the killer's kinsmen who are to pay rings in atonement exist, then father and son and brother, whether they all exist or only one of them, are to take all the rings whole. They are to divide the other rings among themselves like their own ring, and supplement and[6] bits are to go only with the main ring.

If a father's brother's son exists but no cognate cousins, he is nevertheless to take all the rings just the same.

If the only living (p. 199) ring-receiving kin of the dead man are father's father or son's son, mother's father or daughter's son, but all the ring-paying kin of the killer are alive, then whether they all exist or only one they are to take all the rings whole except the main ring — it is to be reduced by half a mark. Supplement and bits are to go with no ring save the twenty-ounce ring.

If the only living ring-receiving kin of the man killed are father's brother or brother's son, mother's brother or sister's son, while payers exist at every level, then they, whether all exist or only some, are to take all the rings. They are to take the main ring reduced by a mark and the twenty-ounce ring reduced by half a mark. They are to take their own ring whole and the first cousins' ring. Supplement and bits are not to go with any ring except the two-mark ring. And if there are no ring-receivers of closer kin than first cousins, then the procedure is to be as previously rehearsed.

If there are receivers of the main ring and of the two-mark ring but none of the twenty-ounce ring, then it shall go with the main ring if atonement-payers exist. But if there is any ring for which neither proper payers nor proper receivers exist, then that ring lapses.

Kinsmen of the killer are proper ring payers and for each ring according to their place on the list. Ring-payment kinsmen of the killer are to pay the same amount more than cognate-payment kinsmen towards each ring as ring-payment kinsmen of the dead man take more than his *Ring-payment kinsmen take and pay proportionally more than cognate-payment kinsmen*

---

6. Reading *ok* for *né* "nor."

Division of payment and receipt among kindred

cognate-payment kinsmen. And those men who are kinsmen of the killer, whether many or few exist to pay each ring, are to divide the total among themselves and provide their due share at all payments, even though the only proper atonement payers are cognate-payment kinsmen. Kinsmen of the man killed are to divide the amount taken among themselves at every level.

In absence of proper payers the killer pays the main ring

If payment by killer is not available and if further payers are lacking in closer degrees

If there are no proper payers of the main ring but receivers exist, then the killer himself is to pay the whole main ring in atonement with supplement and bits, given that he is not under legal penalty and is in the country, but then he is not to pay any other rings in atonement (p. 200). But if he does not exist, then those who are on the list to pay the twenty-ounce ring are to pay two rings in atonement, their own ring whole and the main ring reduced by half a mark.[7] If there are no closer atonement payers than father's brother and brother's son, mother's brother and sister's son, then they are to pay three rings in atonement, their own ring whole and two marks of the three-mark ring and two marks of the twenty-ounce ring, if receivers exist. If there are no closer ring-payers than first cousins, then they are to pay four rings in atonement, if receivers exist: twelve ounces for every ring. Supplement and bits are to go with no ring save the first cousins' ring.

If payers are lacking in remoter degrees

If the only living ring-payers are father and son and brother, then they are to pay all the rings whole if receivers exist and supplement only the main ring. But if no atonement-payers exist other than father's father and son's son, mother's father and daughter's son, then they are to pay four rings in atonement. The main ring is to be paid reduced by half a mark and then three rings whole, supplementing only the twenty-ounce ring, given that receivers for all of them exist. If no atonement-payers exist other than father's brother and brother's son, mother's brother and sister's son, while all the ring-receiving kin of the man killed are alive, then they are to pay four rings in atonement. They are to pay two marks for the main ring and two marks for the twenty-ounce ring and their own ring whole, and supplement that one only, and twelve ounces for the smallest ring. If atonement-payers of the biggest ring and the smallest are alive, and receivers exist[8] at every level, then father and son and brother are to pay three rings whole; supplement and bits are to go only with the main ring. If none of them exists other than a brother born of the same mother, then he shall provide the whole atonement in just the same way but without the bits.

7. Reading *sínum baugi fullum ok höfuðbaugi skerðum mörk* for *sínum baugi skerðum hálfri mörk* "their own ring reduced by half a mark."

8. Omitting *eigi* "not."

There is also one woman who is both to pay and to take a wergild ring, given that she is an only child, and that woman (p. 201) is called "ring-lady." She who takes is the daughter of the dead man if no proper receiver of the main ring otherwise exists but atonement payers are alive, and she takes the three-mark ring like a son, given that she has not accepted full settlement in compensation for the killing, and this until she is married, but thereafter kinsmen take it. She who pays is the daughter of the killer if no proper payer of the main ring otherwise exists but receivers do, and then she is to pay the three-mark ring like a son, and this until she enters a husband's bed and thereby tosses the outlay into her kinsmen's lap.

One woman who pays and receives a wergild ring

There are also five men who are called "atonement extras". One is a son born of a bondwoman or illegitimate, second is a step-son, and then there are three close kinsmen by marriage, a man married to the mother of the man killed or to his daughter or to his sister. They are to take collectively twelve ounces and five pennyweights, and take it whether one or all of them exist, and each of them an equal share, and take it from those five men who are related in like fashion to the killer, and these are then to pay equal shares in atonement whether one or all exist to make payment. But if they exist on neither side, then that atonement lapses.

Men called "atonement extras"

But if no first cousins once removed of the man killed exist to take atonement, then second cousins are to take their share, less by a third, along with their own share whole. Wherever beyond the wergild ring degrees there is no one to take atonement, then the next kinsmen more closely related to the dead man are always to take the whole of their share, but if there is nobody who is more closely related, then the next kinsmen more remotely related are to take the others' share — the share their fathers would have had — reduced by a third, given that payers exist.

If some kindred degrees do not exist

If some proper payers beyond the wergild ring degrees do not exist, then those who are more closely related to the killer are to pay the whole atonement. If there is nobody more closely related, then those who are more remotely related are to pay the atonement of those who do not exist — the share their fathers would have paid — reduced by a third (p. 202). But if none of these exists, that atonement lapses.

Payments beyond the wergild ring degrees are all to be divided equally among all branches of the family.

Equal division beyond the wergild ring degrees

If a freedman is killed, twelve ounces are to make the biggest ring and two ounces the supplement; ten ounces the second ring and one and one-third ounces the supplement; one mark the third ring and one ounce the supplement; and six ounces the smallest ring and two-thirds of an ounce the supplement.

Atonement for freedman

There shall be slave rings for when the proper receivers are slaves.

Atonement among slaves if they have means to pay

Now will be told the minimum rings which a slave is to pay in atonement for a slave. Twenty-four bits make the main ring and six[9] bits the supplement; twenty bits the father's father's ring and four[10] bits the supplement; sixteen[11] bits the father's brother's ring and three bits the supplement; twelve the first cousins' ring and two bits the supplement. Beyond the wergild ring degrees the atonements are to be eight bits, five and one-third[12] bits, three and one-half bits, two and one-third bits and one and one-half bits. Fourth cousins are to take one bit and likewise pay it, and that is the smallest atonement there is. Slaves are only to pay atonement when those who should pay have the means.

Four living men who must be atoned for by kindred payments

There are another four men who are called corpses even though they are alive. If a man is hanged or throttled or put in a grave or on a skerry or tied up on a mountain or below high-water mark, he is called "gallows-corpse" or "grave-corpse" or "skerry-corpse" or "mountain-corpse". Those men are all to be atoned for by kindred payments as if they had been killed even though they are alive.

Claims for kindred payments

It is prescribed that the claiming of kindred payments is to begin in the same summer as the killing case is settled or prosecuted or ought to be prosecuted, and it is then lawful to publish straightway for prosecution of the claim against all those who have heard of the killing. At court the prosecutor is to enumerate the kinship between the man prosecuted and the killer and between himself and the man killed (p. 203). Afterwards he is to name witnesses "to witness," he shall say, "that I give my word of honor that the enumeration of kinship between the two pairs of us now made is true and right, and the cases between N.N. and me are such-and-such." He is also to have two men to vouch for him who give their word of honor that they think that enumeration of kinship is right, but otherwise the procedure in these matters is as for other money penalties.

Enumeration of kinship with two men in support

It is also lawful to make a summons locally for atonement payments. But if the man prosecuted claims that someone else is as closely or more closely related, then he is to enumerate the kinship before the prosecutor and swear an oath to it, and then payment is to be adjudged from each of them as the law provides. Peace guarantees[13] are always to be forthcoming in return for atonement payments — otherwise there can be no claim for them.

Peace guarantee must come in return for atonement payment

If cases conferring rights of veto are unatoned, then a kinsman of the

---

9. The text has seven.
10. The text has three.
11. The text has fifteen.
12. The text has four and one-third.
13. Cf. ‡ 115 (pp. 184-85).

killer is nowhere to share living quarters with a kinsman of the man killed, save only if the former has come to a place to stay or visit without knowing any likelihood of the latter's coming there at that time. But if that is not so, then the latter may choose to forbid by veto his sharing the same living quarters. And if he does not go away, the penalty for him is lesser outlawry, and the summons for that case is to be made locally and nine neighbors of the home of the man prosecuted are to be called at the assembly to give a verdict as to whether he had shared living quarters with the other man after it was forbidden by veto or not, but kinship is to be proved in the way rehearsed earlier.[14]

Cases conferring rights of veto

If a man breaks a peace guarantee after atonement is paid, the personal compensation of every one of the payers is doubled in relation to that man, and moreover no one is to settle in such suits without prior leave.[15]

If a peace guarantee is broken after atonement is paid

If men who have the right to atonement are not of age or have left the country, then they are to claim what is theirs from those who took their share. But if atonement was made with reduced sums, then the kinsmen of the killer are to pay what was deducted.

Claims and payments by minors or people abroad

If kinsmen of the killer were not of age or were (p. 204) abroad when rings were paid in atonement, they are to pay their share when they are of age or come to Iceland and arrange it as has just been rehearsed.

The silver valid as atonement in rings, and in supplements and bits, is such as is no worse than the ancient legal silver was, with ten pennies making an ounce, looking more like silver than brass, standing up to the test of a nick, and of one quality inside and out. It is moreover lawful to make the payments in any form of legal tender.

Valid silver; payment in legal tender

K ‡ 114
Truce Speech

All know the events of the discord between A and B[16] but now their friends have intervened and seek to reconcile them. Now A, on behalf of himself and his heir and all the people for whom he has the right to give truce, gives truce to B until the settlement meeting they have appointed, and B accepts truce from A for himself and his heirs and all the people for whom he needs to accept truce. And first in this truce is God Himself, who is supreme, and all saints and every sacred relic, the pope in Rome and the patriarch,[17] our king and our bishops, and all clerics and all Christian people. I nominate twelve men to join in this truce between A

Twelve men nominated to join in the truce

---

14. Cf. ‡ 80 (p. 132), and p. 175 above.
15. I.e., of the Law Council.
16. In ‡‡ 114-15 A and B are used for N.N. in the Icelandic.
17. Probably the bishop of Jerusalem is meant, rather than the bishop of Constantinople.

and B who now stand on opposite sides in these matters; and he is to name the twelve men.

After that the man who makes the truce speech is to name two or more witnesses "to witness that this truce which has just been (p. 205) set shall be full and firm between all men who come to this gathering and for as long as men remain at this meeting and until each man comes back to his home, and if further meetings are arranged for the matters between them, this truce is to be kept all the same until matters between them are brought to the best possible end they can have. Now the earth upholds the truce, on high the sky bounds it, and around it is the red ocean[18] which encompasses all lands we have knowledge of. And within these borders that I have now told before men may that man nowhere thrive who breaks this truce which I have now set. And may he bind on himself so heavy a burden that he never gets from under it, and that is the harshness of the Lord God and the name of "truce-ravener." But may all the men who keep the truce well have God's mercy and the intercession of every saint with almighty God for all their needs. May God be gracious to him who keeps truce but harsh to him who breaks truce, gracious to him who keeps it. Take it and prosper. Truce is given."

Truce-breaking gives the twelve men right to personal compensation

Truce-breaking means outlawry throughout Norway

It is ancient law in our country that, if a man is put under penalty for truce-breaking, then the twelve men who were nominated to join in the truce have the right to take personal compensation from his goods, forty-eight ounce-units. But in Norway and wherever the Norse language is spoken it is law that if any man does not respect a truce, then such a man is outlawed from one end of Norway to the other, and forfeits both his lands and his goods, and shall never come to the country again.

K ‡ 115
Peace Guarantee Speech

There were causes of dispute between A and B but now they are settled and atoned with money, as the valuers valued and the tellers told (p. 206) and the judges judged and the receivers received and carried it away, the cash in full and each ounce produced, handed to him who should have it.

You two are now to be men reconciled and able to keep company over beer and board, in assembly and array, in coming to church and in the king's house, and wherever there are meetings of men you shall be as much at one as if this had never arisen between you. You shall share knife and meat-bit and all things with each other like family and not like foes. If matters later come up between you that are other than smooth, you shall redress with cash and not redden the spear. But the one of you who tramples on treaties made or smites at sureties given, he shall be an

---

18. The illimitable ocean is often called "red" in classical and medieval European usage.

outcast despised and driven off as far and wide as ever men drive outcasts off, Christians come to church, heathens hallow temples, fire flames, ground grows, son calls mother, mother bears son, men make fires, ship glides, shields flash, sun shines, snow drifts, Lapp skis, fir tree grows, falcon flies a spring-long day with a fair wind beneath both wings, heavens revolve, world is inhabited, wind whistles, waters flow to the sea, men sow seed. He shall shun churches and Christian people, house of God and man, every home save hell.

Now the pair of you hold the same book — and on the book now lies the money which A pays in atonement for himself and his heir born and [not] born, conceived and not conceived, named and not named. B takes guarantees of peace and A gives everlasting guarantees of peace which shall be kept while mold and men survive.

Now A and B are agreed and of one mind wherever they meet on land or water, on ship or ski, at sea or on steed, sharing oars or bailer, thwart or (p. 207) deck plank if need be, each reconciled with the other as father with son or son with father in all their dealings. Now they put their hands together, A and B. Keep the peace well in accordance with the will of Christ and of all those men who now hear the guarantee speech. May he who keeps the peace have God's grace but let him who breaks true guarantees of peace have His wrath, but His grace him who keeps them. Be prosperous your reconciliation and let us be witnesses of it who are here present.

The Lawspeaker's Section

K ‡ 116; p. 208

It is also prescribed that there shall always be some man in our country who is required to tell men the law, and he is called the Lawspeaker. And if a Lawspeaker dies, a man from the Quarter in which he last had his home is to be selected to recite the assembly procedure¹ the following summer. Men² are then to appoint a new Lawspeaker and make the decision who it is to be on Friday before suits are published.³ It is good if all agree on the same man, but if any Law Council man opposes what most want, lots are to be drawn to decide to which Quarter the Lawspeakership should fall. The men of the Quarter in whose favor the lot is drawn are to appoint the Lawspeaker they agree on from among those they can get to do it, whether he is from their Quarter or some other Quarter. If the men of the Quarter do not agree, it is decided by majority. But if there are equal numbers of those with seats on the Law Council who each want their man as Lawspeaker, those are to prevail whom the bishop in that Quarter joins in supporting.⁴ If there are Law Council men who refuse what others want (p. 209) but do not themselves put forward a man for the Lawspeakership, their votes are to be deemed worthless.

Temporary replacement and new election of Lawspeaker

Contested choice left to members from one Quarter decided by lot

Bishop has casting vote

When men have decided who it is to be, the Lawspeaker is to be appointed in the Law Council, and one man is to announce it and the others give their assent, and the same man is to have it for three summers continuously unless men do not wish to change then. From the Law Council at which the Lawspeaker is appointed men are to go to Lögberg and he is to go to Lögberg and sit down in his place and give men places at Lögberg as he wishes, and men are then to make their speeches.

Appointment in Law Council and seating at Lögberg

It is also prescribed that a Lawspeaker is required to recite all the sections of the law over three summers and the assembly procedure every summer.⁵ The Lawspeaker has to announce all licenses for mitigation of

Recital of laws

---

1. Some of the material from the Assembly Procedures Section above, ‡‡ 20-85 (pp. 53-138), probably with some of the present and following sections too, ‡‡ 116-17 (pp. 187-93).

2. I.e., men of the Law Council.

3. The first Friday of the Assembly, 19-25 June. Cf. ‡ 21 (p. 54).

4. Cf. p. 30, n. 20.

5. Cf. ‡ 117 (p. 193).

Other announcements by Lawspeaker

penalty, at Lögberg, and at a time when most men are present if that can be done, and the calendar, and also if men are to come to the General Assembly before ten weeks of summer have passed, and rehearse the observance of Ember Days and the beginning of Lent, and he is to say all this at the close of the Assembly.[6]

If the Lawspeaker's knowledge is inadequate

It is also prescribed that the Lawspeaker shall recite all the sections so extensively that no one knows them much more extensively. And if his knowledge does not stretch so far, then before reciting each section he is to arrange a meeting in the preceding twenty-four hours with five or more legal experts, those from whom he can learn most; and any man who intrudes on their talk without permission is fined three marks, and that case lies with the Lawspeaker.

Lawspeaker's fees

Every summer the Lawspeaker is to have 240 ells of homespun from the Law Council's funds[7] for his work. Half of all the fines imposed by judgment at the General Assembly are also due to him,[8] and payment of all of them is to be enjoined by judgment on a settling day which is to be in the following summer on the Wednesday in the middle of the Assembly, here in the householder's churchyard.[9] Everyone who gets a judgment awarding money is fined three marks if he does not report it to the Lawspeaker and tell him who (p. 210) the witnesses of the announcement of judgment were.

End of three-year term

It is also prescribed that when the Lawspeaker has had the Lawspeakership three summers he is then to recite the assembly procedure on the first Friday of the Assembly in the fourth summer but then, if he wishes, he is free from the Lawspeakership. If he is willing to keep the Lawspeakership longer, provided others are content that he should, then the Law Council is to decide that by majority.

If the Lawspeaker does not attend at the proper time

It is also prescribed that the Lawspeaker is fined three marks if, without legitimate excuse, he does not come to the General Assembly on the first Friday before men go to Lögberg, and men may then appoint another Lawspeaker if they want to.

---

6. Cf. ‡‡ 55, 61 (pp. 97-98, 111-12); p. 35, n. 37.

7. Payment was made for leave to marry within the remoter degrees of kinship, cf. ‡‡ 144, 147, 163, but other sources of revenue for the Law Council are nowhere defined. Possibly all licenses were paid for.

8. Cf. ‡ 41 (p. 80) for an exception and ‡ 117 (p. 193) where it is prescribed that the Lawspeaker may himself be fined and that he shares in fines imposed at the spring assembly he participates in.

9. Cf. p. 29, n. 17.

The Law Council Section

K ‡ 117; p. 211

We shall also have a Law Council and hold it here at the General Assembly each summer, and it is always to sit in the place where it has been long since.[1] There are to be three benches around the Law Council place, long enough for four dozen men to sit commodiously on each. That is twelve men from each Quarter who have seats on the Law Council to decide there on laws and licenses and the Lawspeaker in addition. They are all to sit on the middle bench, and there our bishops rightly have places too. *Law Council arrangement*

The twelve men from the Northern Quarter who have seats on the Law Council are those who act in the twelve chieftaincies which were had there when they had four assemblies and three chieftains to each assembly. But from all other Quarters those nine from each have seats on the Law Council who act in the full and ancient chieftaincies, of which there were three to every assembly when there were three assemblies in each of those three Quarters. However, these are all to have one man with them from each ancient assembly, so that nevertheless twelve men from each Quarter get a seat on the Law Council. In nominations at the General Assembly the powers of the ancient chieftaincies of the Northerners are all reduced by one-fourth compared with all the other full chieftaincies here in the country. *Men owning or acting in chieftaincies have seats*

It is also prescribed that each one of all the men with seats on the Law Council as now rehearsed must appoint two men (p. 212), assembly men of his, to join the Law Council for discussion with him, one in front of him and one behind him. Then the benches are fully manned, with four dozen men on each bench. *Each of them is to have two advisers with him*

When the Law Council has been cleared for a meeting, no one is to sit in the space inside the benches unless they have matters in dispute, but people may sit there at all other times. The Lawspeaker has the right to give men places there. The general public have to sit on the outside of the benches. Standing up at the Law Council is only lawful for men who are to speak on men's affairs when laws and licenses are in debate, and for those others who are outermost of the people who come there. Whoever does otherwise is fined three marks and the case lies with anyone who wants it. But if men so trample on each other at the Law Council, and do *Who is permitted to stand at the Law Council*

Penalty for disturbance

1. See Map II.

it on purpose, or cause so much riot or row that men's cases are balked because of it, the penalty is lesser outlawry as for every kind of assembly balking.

If someone finds his seat occupied

If men come to the Law Council who have seats there and other men have sat down in their places, they are to ask for their places and there is no punishment for the others if they then leave, but if they linger when a place is asked for, the penalty for that is a fine of three marks. Then the owner is to ask for his seat with witnesses, and if it is then refused the penalty is lesser outlawry. These are all summoning cases and nine neighbors of the man prosecuted are to be called for lesser outlawry cases and five for fining cases.

When the Law Council is to meet

The work of the Law Council

Granting licenses

It is also prescribed that the Law Council shall go out on both the Sundays in the assembly and on the closing day of the assembly and at all other times when the Lawspeaker or the majority wish it and on every occasion when men want to clear the Law Council for a meeting. Men are to frame their laws there and make new laws if they will. All licenses for mitigation of penalty and all licenses for settlements for which special leave must be asked and many other licenses as rehearsed in the laws are to be asked for there.[2] Leave is to be deemed given in the Law Council for everything which no one (p. 213) with a seat on the Law Council refuses and for which no veto comes from outside the Law Council. Each man who has a seat on the Law Council must do one thing or the other about every license, consent or refuse, otherwise he is fined three marks. If men ask for licenses in the Law Council when the men who have seats on the Law Council have either not all come or not all left but there are four dozen men or more there nevertheless, the Lawspeaker can complete it by giving the empty seats of those who have places there to other men, and anyone who refuses is fined. When the middle bench is fully manned, the Lawspeaker is to name witnesses "to witness," he shall say, "that these sit in the Law Council on my direction and are qualified to enact laws and licenses. I name these witnesses in accordance with law for the benefit of anyone who may need to use their witnessing." And all licenses shall then be as firmly enacted as if the chieftains were sitting there themselves, and it is only on their arrival that the men who were sitting there are to withdraw.

Authority of written law texts

It is also prescribed that in this country what is found in books is to be law. And if books differ, then what is found in the books which the bishops own is to be accepted. If their books also differ, then that one is to prevail which says it at greater length in words that affect the case at issue. But if they say it at the same length but each in its own version,

2. Cf. ‡‡ 55, 93, 98, 100, 113 (pp. 98, 156, 161, 163, 183); ‡‡ 59, 61 (pp. 108, 111); Add. ‡ 133 (ii); and probably ‡ 83 (p. 136, "permitted at Lögberg") and ‡ 84 (cf. p. 137, n. 251).

then the one which is in Skála[holt] is to prevail.³ Everything in the book which Hafliði⁴ had made is to be accepted unless it has since been modified, but only those things in the accounts given by other legal experts which do not contradict it, though anything in them which supplies what is left out there or is clearer is to be accepted.

If there is argument on an article of law and the books do not decide it, the Law Council must be cleared for a meeting on it. The procedure for that is to ask all the chieftains and the Lawspeaker at Lögberg before witnesses to go to the Law Council and take their seats to make plain this article of the law as it is to be henceforth. "I request with a legal request," the man who wants to test it is to say. (p. 214) If some of the men who have seats do not go to their places when they know the Law Council is to be cleared for a meeting, the penalty is lesser outlawry as for other kinds of assembly balking; and it is moreover lawful to claim that each such chieftain owes a three-mark fine and forfeits his chieftaincy.⁵ The penalty is the same for all men who have to take seats in the Law Council and do not do so at any Law Council meeting the law requires them to attend. After the chieftains have come into their seats, each of them is to give one man a place on the bench in front of him and another a place on the outer bench for discussion with him. Then those men who have matters in dispute are to rehearse the article of the law on which they differ and report what causes the rift between them. After that men must assess what they have said and make up their minds on the matter, and then all the Law Council men who sit on the middle bench are to be asked to explain what each of them wants accepted as law in the case. Then each chieftain is to say what he will call law and whose side he will take in the matter, and it is decided by majority. But if the Law Council men are in equal numbers with each group calling their version law, then those with the Lawspeaker among them are to prevail, but if there are more in the other group, they are to prevail. And each group is to swear a divided judgment oath⁶ on their version and make it hang on their oath that they think that the version they side with is law in the case and state why it is law.

If any Law Council man is so sick or wounded that he cannot be out of doors, both groups are to fetch his vote from his booth, and tell him what the rift between them is, and he is to swear the same oath as the others and state whose side he will take. (p. 215) If a Law Council man has lost

If books do not decide an article of law, the Law Council meets

Having heard the disputants, each chieftain says which he will support and why

If votes are equal, or if the Lawspeaker's side is the minority

If a member cannot be present or cannot act

---

3. Cf. p. 35, n. 40; p. 30, n. 20.

4. It was at the home of Hafliði Másson that the codification of the laws was begun in the winter 1117-18, cf. Introduction, pp. 4-5.

5. These are presumably alternative penalties but as such seem to have no precise parallel.

6. Cf. ‡ 42 pp. 82-83.

power of speech or is senseless or has died when these words are needed from him, then the man who would have the right to take up court nominations in case of his death is to speak instead of him.[7]

Oaths if the minority is twelve or more

If, when the Law Council men have expressed their opinions, there are twelve or more in the minority, then those who are fewer in number are to swear oaths on their version of the matter. Those in the majority are then also required to swear oaths on their version of the matter so that the number of them swearing is one more than the minority and at least two more if the Lawspeaker is in the minority group. If the majority all leave it to each other to swear the oaths, they are to draw lots among themselves unless they are all willing to swear. If the minority turn out to be fewer than twelve, they have no case to stand on, and no men from the majority are required to swear oaths in response to the oaths of a group with fewer than twelve in it.

If members balk proceedings

If there are any Law Council men who say they will be on neither side or refuse other duties in such matters, that all incurs the same penalty as rehearsed before,[8] and the cases lie with whichever of the men with matters in dispute is the more willing to prosecute to the limit of the law. If neither will prosecute, the case lies with anyone who will. The Lawspeaker is to give the places of those who do [not] do their legal duties to other men, and take some member of the same spring assembly as the balking comes from if that is possible, and the penalty for anyone who refuses is lesser outlawry. But if the Lawspeaker does not know anyone present from that part of the country, he is to ask the chieftains of the same assembly as the man who refuses his duties to provide someone instead so that the Law Council can be completed, and the penalty for a man who refuses that is the same as for the man who balked the assembly. If none of the chieftains from the same assembly will do his duties, men are to be asked for from another assembly and from a third if they get no one before that. Their words shall then count as much as those (p. 216) of other Law Council men.

Once decided, an article of law is to be rehearsed in the Law Council and announced at Lögberg

It is also prescribed that one[9] man is to rehearse with witnesses the article of the law for which there is a majority, but all the Law Council men are to give their assent to it. Afterwards it is to be announced at Lögberg.

Duty to listen to Lawspeaker's recital

All men with seats on the Law Council are also required to be always present at the reciting whenever the Lawspeaker wishes to recite the laws, whether that is at Lögberg or in the Law Council or in the church if the weather out of doors is unpleasant. If some Law Council men do not have time for this, two men selected from those who sit on the inner and

---

7. Cf. ‡ 84 (pp. 136-37).
8. See p. 191, ll. 11-15.
9. Reading *einnhverr* for *hverr* "each."

outer benches in the Law Council are to listen to the reciting for each of them. If no heed is paid to either of these prescriptions, the words of Law Council men who act in that way cannot count that summer in any argument on an article of law recited at that time. There is also a three-mark fine as penalty and the case lies with other Law Council men, and the summons is to be made at Lögberg, and nine neighbors of the man prosecuted are to be called.

The Lawspeaker has the right to give people places at Lögberg, and people who sit there without his leave are fined three marks. If men behave so improperly towards the Lawspeaker that they do not let him get to his seat, or those men he has individually named to sit at Lögberg with him, the penalty is lesser outlawry and it is to be prosecuted like other kinds of assembly balking. *Lawspeaker allocates places at Lögberg*

The Lawspeaker is required to tell everyone who asks him what the article of the law is, both here and at his home, but he is not required to give anyone further advice on lawsuits. He is also to recite the assembly procedure every summer and all the other sections so that they are recited every three summers (p. 217) if the majority wish to hear them. Assembly procedure is always to be recited on the first Friday of the assembly if men have time to hear it. *Duties of Lawspeaker*

A fine of three marks is the Lawspeaker's penalty if without legitimate excuse he does not discharge all the duties required of him. Half that fine is due to the man who prosecutes and half to the judges. And if the Lawspeaker commits any trespass which the majority are prepared to call assembly balking, his penalty for that is lesser outlawry. *Penalties if the Lawspeaker fails in his duties*

It is also prescribed that the only spring assembly where fines are due to him is the one in which he himself participates.[10] *Spring assembly fines due to Lawspeaker*

---

10. Presumably the same half share as prescribed for General Assembly fines, cf. ‡ 116 (p. 188).

ADDITIONS

Christian Laws Section

1. (From St ‡ 2; II 3/8–11; + K p. 24) If a priest is staying in a household, he incurs no legal penalty if he leaves the house without having with him the things needful to baptize a child, provided he returns to the same lodging in the evening. — *Baptism*

2. (From St ‡ 4; II 4/14–18; cf. K p. 25) — and dip the child into the water straight in front of him — "and the Son" — and dip the child's head in a second time towards the left — "and the Holy Ghost" — and dip the child's head in a third time towards the right so that it gets wet all over each time.

3. (From St ‡ 4; II 5/4–9; + K p. 25) It is lawful for a woman to teach him how to baptize a child but a woman is not to baptize a child unless no other possibility exists. A woman is to baptize a child only in case of utmost need, when there is no male present, not even a baby boy whose hands she can lay on the child to baptize it, and when the child itself is on the brink of death. A father is to baptize his child only if no other man is at hand.

4. (From St ‡ 5; II 7/2–3; + K p. 26) A priest is always to have available the things needful to baptize a child when he is at his legal home.[1]

5. (From St ‡ 7; II 7/19–9/6; cf. K pp. 27–30) A body is to be taken to a church at which the bishop permits burials. The householder who lives there must allow the burial and the body is to be buried where he permits or where the priest who serves the church permits if the householder is not present or gives no direction. If neither of them gives him any direction, he may bury him where he likes, though it is not to be immediately next the church. If he buries a body immediately next the church without their consent, he is fined three marks for it. But if the householder does not allow the burial, he is fined three marks, and each of them has a case against the other, but the body is to stay where it is buried. — *Burial*

If there is a burial church inside the commune, then people who live at a burial church farther off are not required to accept a corpse if it was possible for it to be buried at the nearer place.

If a man builds himself a church and says at once that he will not allow anyone to be buried there before himself or his children or his wife, it is lawful for him to do so if the bishop permits, even though it is a burial

---

1. See p. 24, n. 1.

church. But as soon as he has allowed someone else to be buried there, he is required to accept every corpse from then on.

A body is not to be buried naked. A man who does that is fined three marks.

It is prescribed that if a man who is bringing a body for burial or a child for baptism is taken by boat, the same men are required to ferry him back again if he cannot go by land, and they are fined three marks if they will not.

If they have cases conferring rights of veto at issue between them, then he must pledge them the legal atonement he owes them if he wants to be ferried back again and pay the atonement before they finally part. They are not required to ferry him if they have such a case against him unless he is willing to do this. But if he has such a case against them, he does not invalidate his case by letting them ferry him.

If a man finds a body in the countryside, he is to cover the corpse so that beasts do not prey upon it and tell the man who lives nearest and who has two serving men over and above himself. And this man is to bring it to church as soon as possible, or else he is fined three marks, unless they know of no one not under legal penalty missing and think it is the body of an outlaw.

If a man dies on common land when other people are there, those he shared a hut with are to take his body to church.

(ii) (From St ‡ 8; II 12/3-4; cf. K p. 28)   If a man dies at an assembly or an autumn meeting, his booth-mates or traveling companions are to take his body to church.

Feast of dedication and summoning

6. (From St ‡ 12; II 16/5-10; + K p. 32)   If men go to make a summons in the homefield of a place where the feast of the church's dedication is that day being celebrated and want to summon the householder or members of his household or guests, and the people there also have cases against those who come, it is lawful for them to make a counter-summons if they wish, just as if it were an ordinary day, as long as they do not make a journey from home for this purpose.

Churches and their property and repair

7. (From St ‡ 14; II 19/12-20/23; cf. K p. 34)   Every church shall remain on the site where it was consecrated, together with all the property it was endowed with or has gained by purchase or donation. But if anyone disposes of that property, the penalty is lesser outlawry, and all the property is to be adjudged back to the church. If one man owns the land and another the church on it, and the man who owns the land disposes of church property, the case lies with the man who owns the church, but if the man who owns the church disposes of the property, the case against him lies with the landowner. If neither of them is willing to prosecute, the case lies with anyone who is willing.

If a man owns more than one church, he may divide equipment and property between them as he wishes with the bishop's permission. And a man may pay for services out of church property if he has no other means, again with the bishop's permission. The man who owns a church is to provide wax candles and not fewer than ten masses between one General Assembly and the next. He is to ask the priest who lives nearest to sing the established services and he is fined three marks if he does not do so.[2]

The man who owns a church is to keep it in repair so that services can be held in it in all weathers, and he may dig turf on his — the landowner's — land but not where there is arable land or meadowland. The man who is householder on that land is to board the priest and one man with him or a horse. That same man is also to provide three masses between one General Assembly and the next, or else he is fined three marks.

If a church becomes so dilapidated that services cannot be sung in it, then the householder on that land is to send word to the man who owns the church early enough in the summer for it to be repaired. If the latter will not repair it, then the man who owns the land is to call five neighbors to come and say whether they think services can be held in the church in that state. If they think services cannot be held there in all weathers and the man who owns the land repairs the church, it becomes his property. If he repairs the church without previously showing it to neighbors, it nevertheless becomes his property as long as he had earlier sent word to the man who owned it and a panel gives a verdict that services could not have been sung in it in all weathers in the state it was in.

If a church falls down, the man who owns the land must have rebuilt it within the next twelve months — and that church is his property — or he must have moved bones away with the bishop's permission.

If a man who owns a church will not pay for services, he is fined three marks and the church becomes the property of the man who does pay for services.

If a church owner is so young that he does not have charge of his own property or if he has left the country and those who have his property will not look after his church and other men repair it, then when he takes over his property he may choose whether he will give the people who repaired it what they spent or let the church become theirs.

8. (From St ‡ 15; II 22/20–22; + K p. 36) If a bishop refuses to do what he is required to do in accordance with law, they[3] may respond by withholding his tithes. *Tithe legitimately withheld*

---

2. Add. ‡ 26.
3. Skálholtsbók ‡ 9 (III 20/21) adds: "and their household men."

Seal of confes- 9. (From St ‡ 16; II 25/7–10; + K p. 37)   If a priest discloses anyone's
sional broken   confession without what his diocesan thinks legitimate excuse, the penalty is lesser outlawry. Nine of the priest's neighbors are to be called at the assembly.

Court of priests   (ii) (II 25/17–18; cf. K p. 38)   The bishop is to prosecute the case before a court of priests in the church at the General Assembly.[4]

Supplies from   (iii) (II 26/1–4; + K p. 38)   A bishop is required to provide all his
bishop   priests with chrism every year and consecrate their mass vestments. If they wish to have wine and wheaten flour,[5] they are each to pay him three ells every year.

Foreign priests 10. (From St ‡ 17; II 26/12–18; cf. K. p. 38)   If he cannot get another priest, it is lawful to pay foreign priests for services, if they have the writ and seal of the bishop who ordained them announcing that it is lawful to receive priestly offices and hear services from them. If a priest has no seal, it is lawful for him to have the testimony of two men who were present at his ordination and who report the bishop's words saying that it is lawful for people to hear services and receive all priestly offices from him.

Holy day 11. (From St ‡ 20; II 31/1–4; cf. K p. 40)   A man is not to begin his
traveling journey on a Sunday if he travels with pack horses. It is also prescribed that two men are to be boarded over a holy season if they have one pack horse and three if they have two horses.

Boarding 12. (St ‡ 21, II 31; cf. K p. 42)   People on wedding journeys are to be
travelers boarded, five including the bridegroom or bride, elsewhere three, to a total of thirty.[6] Men on journeys to make a summons are also to be boarded, five [including a principal in a case among them], elsewhere three, to a total of thirty, within a fortnight of Easter or within a month if they go out of the Quarter. Traders are also to be boarded, five including the ship's master, elsewhere three. Men going to a spring assembly or an autumn meeting are also to be boarded.

Assembly men, traders, people on wedding journeys, vagrants — these four classes of people are permitted to travel with pack horses on a Sunday.

The same is prescribed for boarding men who go to call neighbors or to publish killings or wounds as for boarding men who go to make a summons.

13. (From St ‡ 22; II 31/18–32/7; ÷ K)   If a man goes by rowing boat

---

4. Cf. p. 29, n. 17.

5. For the elements of the Eucharist.

6. If the party numbered more than thirty, the extra presumably had to camp and fend for themselves.

on a holy day, he is not to have a burden of more than forty pounds. It is lawful to bring a vessel to a landing place on a holy day and to unload it if it is in any danger. It is also lawful for men to come from Vestmannaeyjar[7] on a holy day if they have been kept there by the weather, but a pennyweight of the ancient legal silver[8] is to be given for each person. Men may also come with a laden vessel from any offshore island on a holy day if a penny is given for each person.

Lawful activities in holy seasons

A seal may be killed on a holy day if it has got into a net, but it is not to be taken out; if a man does anything more to it, he is fined three marks.

(ii) (II 32/10–20; + K p. 43)   It is lawful for the men of Mývatn[7] to put out their nets in the lake after *eykt* on a holy day if the following day is an ordinary day.

It is lawful to cook food on a holy day that is to be given away and also to prepare other food to be eaten then. It is lawful to make a fire and slice peat for it but firewood must be chopped in advance.

If anyone's clothing gets torn when it is a holy day, it may be stitched up again.

If a man is using wooden equipment or withe bindings and these break, or pack saddles or whatever gear it is, he is to tie it together if that will serve. But if it will not serve, he may cut a tree to get withes and make it all good by shaping and joining to serve his purpose even though it is a holy day.

14. (From St ‡ 23; II 33/1–13; + K p. 42)   If men are walking boundaries on a holy day, it is lawful to cut earth-crosses and to make other marks for that purpose.

Lawful activities in holy seasons

If a man's livestock strays from communal pasture or livestock wanders from a pound,[9] it is lawful to drive it back and to ride after it. It is lawful for a man to carry a single sheep on his back even though it weighs more than forty pounds.

Men who are going to a spring assembly or an autumn meeting may put up tents up to nightfall on a Saturday and they may go with pack horses until the sun is shaft-high.[10]

All nets are to be taken up before *eykt*.[11] Men who row out to sea are to fetch in their lines before *eykt* and then row to land and carry their catch above high-water mark and leave it in such a way that neither birds nor animals can ravage it. If there are men on the boat who have

---

7. See Map I.
8. Cf. ‡ 113 (p. 183).
9. For stray beasts; Icelandic *sveltikví* is literally "starving pound."
10. See p. 42, n. 66.
11. See p. 41, n. 62.

households of dependents and are without means, it is lawful for them to fish until the sun is shaft-high.[12]

(ii) (II 33/16-34/2; + K p. 42) If a man's slaves or bounden debtors work after *eykt* of their own accord, they are fined four ounce-units if they have the means to pay.

If livestock gets into arable land or meadow, it may be driven out even though it is a holy day. Horses may be caught and bridled and hobbled although it is a holy day. But if a man is traveling, he is not to drive more than one horse.

It is also lawful to cut wood for tent poles or for firewood if men are traveling in uninhabited parts, even though it is a holy day. A man may cut himself a switch even on a holy day.

But if a man does more work on an established holy day than now told, whatever day it is, he is fined three marks and the case lies with anyone who wishes to prosecute. But if it is a festival of higher degree,[13] the penalty is six marks. The summons in such cases is to be made locally and five neighbors of the man prosecuted called at the assembly.

15. (From St ‡ 25; II 36/1-3; + K p. 43) — and board those who come first.

Forbidden food 16. (From St ‡ 52; II 60/11-12; + K p. 48) The penalty is lesser outlawry if anyone eats livestock the cause of whose death is unknown and it is called "what may not be eaten."

Obligatory thank-offering 17. (From Skálholtsbók ‡ 16; III 35/8-10; + K p. 47) A fifth part of all whales moved or cut up on established holy days is to be given away.

Relaxed observance 18. (Skálholtsbók ‡ 18; III 36; + K) On days of relaxed observance.[14] These are days of relaxed observance: of Sebastian [20/1], Vincent [22/1], Blasius [3/2], Agatha [5/2], Johannes ante portam latinam [6/5], Barnabas [11/6], Vitus [15/6], Johannes et Paulus [26/6], Commemoratio Pauli [30/6], Septem fratres [10/7], Mary Magdalen [22/7], Ad vincula Petri [1/8], Inventio Stephani [3/8], Sixtus [6/8], Hypolitus [13/8], Octave [of the Assumption] of Mary [22/8], Augustine [28/8], Decollatio Johannis Baptistae [29/8], Maurice [22/9], Cosmas et Damianus [27/9], Remigius [1/10], Dionysius [9/10], Gereon [10/10], Luke [18/10], the Virgins [21/10], Severinus [23/10], Bricius [13/11], Theodore [9/11], Barbara [4/12]. It is permitted to eat two meals on Barbara's day if it does not fall on a Friday.

Fasts 19. (Skálholtsbók ‡ 19; III 36; cf. K p. 47, Add. ‡ 28) On fasts com-

---

12. See p. 42, n. 66.
13. See ‡‡ 11-14 (pp. 44-47).
14. Icelandic *leyfisdagar* "days of permission;" *leyfi* is used of dispensation both from rules for fasting and from rules for working.

manded for workmen and unattached men. These are commanded fasts: all Fridays except in Easter week; all Friday nights from the Winter Nights[15] to Easter except on the one next after Christmas; all Wednesdays from the Winter Nights to Christmas unless feast days cancel the fast; every other day in the nine-week Lent.[16] People who stay on the farm are to fast on Friday nights from Easter to Winter except between Ascension Day and Whitsun. No night fasts are commanded for workmen during the summer [sic] except the two of seventy-two hours legally required before All Saints' day [1/11] and before Christmas.

20. (From Skálholtsbók ‡ 22; III 38/1-5; cf. K p. 47) In autumn before Michaelmas [29/9] we are to observe Ember Days in such a way that the Saturday which occurs in the Ember Days is always the one next after Holy Cross day [14/9]. And before Christmas we are to observe them in such a way that there is one Sunday between the Saturday in the Ember Days and Christmas Day. *Ember Days*

21. (From Staðarfellsbók ‡ 2; III 63/27-64/2; cf. K p. 30) No corpse is to be buried at church which the bishop forbids to bury at church. That is the fourth class of corpse, and he is to have announced it beforehand so people know. *Burial*

22. (From Staðarfellsbók ‡ 9; III 79/11-13; K. p. 45) Work may be done on the Tuesday and Wednesday and all the week from then on. That was included among the country's laws in the days of Bishop Þorlákr and Bishop Brandr.[17] *Leave to work*

23. (From Arnarbælisbók ‡ 13; III 177/2-3; + K p. 46) or on the evening before Þorlákr's day [23/12]. *Obligatory food gift*

24. (From AM 173 c 4to ‡ 2; III 278/26-279/4; + K p. 27) "[I name witnesses to witness] that I summon N.N. because he carried or caused to be carried to church the body of that man N.N. when he had no right to church burial. I claim that he owes a fine of three marks for that and should atone to the church for its desecration with twelve ounce-units. I summon it to the assembly." *Unlawful burial*

25. (From AM 173 c 4to ‡ 8; III 287/21-25; + K p. 35) But if the agreement has been reported at Lögberg or in the Law Council but the priest's harboring not forbidden by veto at Lögberg, it is lawful for him to go to the place where he hears his priest is and there or at the place where he spent the night forbid by veto his harboring. *Veto on harboring priest*

---

15. Cf. p. 31, n. 23.

16. Starting in the week beginning Septuagesima Sunday; ordinary Lent, beginning on Ash Wednesday, is the seven-week Lent.

17. Brandr Sæmundarson, bishop of Hólar 1163-1201, was in office throughout the episcopate of St Þorlákr Þórhallsson of Skálaholt, 1178-93.

Priest's fee 26. (From AM 181 4to ‡ 6; III 318/11-12; + St ‡ 14, Add. 7, p. 199; ÷ K) Ten masses on ordinary days are to rate half an ounce-unit.

Fasting and work before feast days 27. (From AM 181 4to ‡ 15; III 345/9-16; cf. K pp. 45-46) It is not required to fast on any night before a feast day on which fasting is to be observed unless a fast is then required on account of some other service. It is a holy day from nones onwards before John the Baptist's Day [24/6] and before Peter's Day [29/6] and before the first Mary's Day [15/8].[18] Before all feast days with a twenty-four hour fast before them no work is to be done past mid-evening.[19] It is lawful to work to night-time[20] before all feast days that do not have a twenty-four hour fast before them.

Fasts 28. AM 347 fol. ‡ LXVII; Ib 251-2; cf. K pp. 45-50, Add. 19) On commanded fasts. Bishop Þorlákr[21] commanded the people to observe these fasts over and above those listed as established fasts.[22] All ordinary Fridays except Friday in Easter week — then it is permitted to eat two meals in the day. From the time winter comes people are to fast every Friday night until Easter except on the one next after Christmas. Then it is permitted to eat foods made from milk. From the time winter comes people are to fast every Wednesday until Christmas. A Wednesday fast is not commanded from Christmas to the nine-week Lent.[23] When the nine-week Lent turns into the seven-week Lent people are to fast on three days and one night each week. It is permitted to eat two meals on Mondays and Tuesdays in the seven-week Lent. People are to fast every day in the Christmas fast and on two nights in each week unless feast days cancel the fast. From Easter to winter people who stay on the farm are required to fast on Friday nights but not workmen. Everyone is allowed foods made from milk on the Friday night following Ascension Day. People who are not well-off for fasting food are permitted to have foods made from milk before Whitsun. People are to observe a seventy-two hour fast, one before either All Saints' day [1/11] or Simon's day [28/10] and one before Christmas, as close as possible to Christmas itself. These fasts are commanded for all healthy people not older than seventy and not younger than sixteen winters old. It is not required to fast on any night before a feast day on which fasting is to be observed unless a fast is then required on account of some other service. Two seventy-two hour fasts are commanded for everyone in the country, healthy people younger than seventy and older than sixteen winters old, and all these fasts as well.

18. The Assumption, cf. p. 45, n. 78.
19. About 1800 hours.
20. See p. 124, n. 207.
21. St. Þorlákr Þorhallsson, bishop of Skálaholt 1178-93.
22. Cf. ‡‡ 13-17 (pp. 45-50).
23. Cf. p. 203, n. 16.

Assembly Procedures Section

29. (From St ‡ 216; II 248/7-20; cf. K p. 122)   A new law. If men put their horses into someone's keeping at the General Assembly, one ell is to buy tending for one horse, and the settling day for that money is the Wednesday in the middle of the Assembly in the householder's churchyard,[24] and the penalty if it is withheld is four and one-half marks. The man who looks after horses is only to use them for riding to keep watch on them, and for driving them to the Assembly and to where they are kept, and he is to share the riding fairly among the horses and not ride any one of them so much that it does not stay well filled out, and take full responsibility for them and take care of them as he would if they were his own and meant to do it properly. At the close of the assembly he is to show the owner his horse alive or dead before the calendar is announced.[25] Otherwise he is fined three marks. That case is to be summoned to the next Assembly. It is lawful to make that summons at any time throughout that day. He has a defense in the case if the prosecutor gets his horse before most people have ridden away. If a horsekeeper pays for a lost horse with his own money, he becomes the principal and the claimant if the horse is caught.   *Tending horses at the General Assembly*

30. (From St ‡ 233; II 266/17-19; + K p. 127)   It is lawful for a man with dependents to leave his household and let others buy his labor. It is also lawful for his children to work for their food in the summer for what time they can.   *Householders as hired labor*

31. (From St ‡ 234; II 267/1-4; cf. K p. 127)   Those men have the right to make their own contracts who build kitchen buildings and living rooms or other buildings from Norwegian timber, or build bridges over waters where fish run that may be netted, or build booths at the General Assembly, or work as sword-cutlers.   *Craftsmen's contracts*

(ii) (II 267/21-22; cf. K p. 128)   If a trader joins someone's household or a man who goes fishing —.

32. (From St ‡ 237; II 269/7-9; cf. K pp. 37, 128)   — and report their homes to five neighbors or at times when people come to church if they serve a district.   *A priest's legal home*

33. (From St ‡ 241; II 271/17-18; + K p. 130)   If a man is laid up but   *Household men*

---

24. Cf. p. 29, n. 17.
25. Cf. ‡ 116 (p. 188).

not off work, the householder is to look after him until the moving days and claim for his keep.

(ii) (II 272/17-19; cf. K p. 131) — each of them is to stay in the place where they live if they are tied to particular jobs unless the householders permit otherwise.

Joining an assembly third

34. (From St ‡ 243; II 276/5-13; + K p. 135)   If a man says nothing about it in the spring he belongs to no assembly group until the assembly, but he is fined three marks if he does not say he is joining some assembly group. If a man promises to say that someone is joining an assembly group and does not keep his promise, he is fined three marks at the suit of the man to whom he gave the promise and at the suit of the chieftain whose assembly group the latter wanted to join. If a man who was previously attached to a household comes into an inheritance and takes over a household, he joins the assembly group where his predecessor was. He does not need to say he is joining it. If a man takes a share in a household with a man already a householder he joins the assembly group the latter is in, unless he says he is joining a different one.

(ii) (II 276/15-277/3; + K p. 134)   If they are both in the same assembly third, then both are to pay only one lot of assembly attendance dues. If a man who is householding comes into an inheritance and so takes over a second household and the two did not have the same assembly membership previously, he is to say that he and his household are leaving one of the assembly groups. He does not then need to say he is joining an assembly group. If a man who elsewhere has a household of dependents attaches himself to a household, he is to say that his own household is joining some assembly group but he belongs to the assembly group of the householder where he is now attached. If his wife is at home in the household, she belongs to the same assembly group as the household does.

A new law. As soon as a man gives up householding he is straightway out of his assembly group[26] even though he starts householding again the following year — then he is to say he is joining an assembly.

If a chieftain wishes to exclude a man from his assembly third

35. (From St ‡ 247; II 278/16-279/8; + K p. 136)   — that he should look for membership of a different assembly group. If the chieftain wishes to say at a spring assembly that a man no longer belongs with him, then the man is to leave his group at the same assembly but only if he then joins the group of a chieftain who belongs to the same assembly or the group of a chieftain whose assembly, albeit a different one, is held within the same assembly boundary.[27] Otherwise it is lawful to tell the

26. He will then belong without choice to the same assembly group as the householder he lodges with.

27. Cf. p. 91, n. 110.

man about it at a spring assembly, should the chieftain mean to say at some later time that he no longer belongs with him. If the man of his assembly third does not say he is leaving either at the spring assembly or at the General Assembly, it is lawful for the chieftain to say that he no longer belongs with him, at Lögberg after the courts have been held and while the Assembly is still in being.

36. (St ‡ 249; II 281; cf. K p. 109) If a man formally guarantees to accept outlawry, that is lawful only if he does so for an outlawry offense, and the offense is to be stated, and the imposition of outlawry is not to be delayed longer than the suit in true and [un]spoilt form would remain valid, and the penalty is not to be made heavier than the offense. The man who means to impose outlawry is to name witnesses and speak thus: "I name them to witness that I nominate these twelve men including myself to join a settlement court or an outlawry court and to impose such outlawry on N.N. as I wish imposed and we agree upon." He is to swear an oath and so shall all the men who sit in the court or are engaged in providing formal means of proof there. Testimony of his formal agreement to accept outlawry is to be brought before the court and witnesses named to witness that testifying. The man imposing the outlawry is to speak thus: "These are my terms of settlement or outlawry: that I impose that outlawry on N.N. that he shall be a lesser outlaw" — or whatever he decides to lay down — "and I announce that outlawry of N.N.'s and that judgment of outlawry, and it is the judgment of us all." They are to give their assent. Afterwards he is to name witnesses to the announcement of judgment. Testimony of the announcement of judgment is to be brought at the confiscation court and the testimony of those named to witness it when the testimony of his formal guarantee to accept outlawry was brought. But however it happens, if he falls short of keeping the terms of mitigation laid down for him, he falls under the fullest penalty, and then all those who know that his outlawry has been added to are under penalty if they assist him; and when assistance to him is prosecuted his penalty is to be added to or confirmed in a Quarter Court in every way as is prescribed for confirming the outlawry of a lesser outlaw.[28]

Outlawry by private settlement

Nomination of settlement court

Announcement of judgement

Assistance of a man outlawed by private settlement

37. (St ‡ 250; II 282; cf. K p. 93) If a man wants to ask at a ship for a passage for someone, he is to name witnesses "to witness that I ask N.N., the ship's master, and his crew to ferry N.N. out of the country. I request a legal request, and I invite you to hear testimony of the terms laid down for his outlawry." And end his speech in this way: "and we bring forward testimony in such form before N.N., the ship's master, and

Asking passage for an outlaw

---

28. Cf. ‡‡ 55, 73 (pp. 97, 120-21).

before his crew, where passage is asked for N.N." The testimony is to be brought for which witnesses were named when the "life-ring" was paid and the "sustenance pledge" and the money due at the confiscation court.

If neighbors or witnesses fail to attend an assembly

38. (From St ‡ 251; II 282/13-17; cf. K p. 71)   A new law. If one man calls neighbors or witnesses locally and another man conducts the case at the assembly,[29] cases to do with the staying at home of neighbors or witnesses, if they do not come as is required of them, lie with the man who conducts the case and not with the man who called them.

Exiled man not to be hindered from leaving but then liable to ordinary prosecution

39. (From St ‡ 253; II 283/21-284/1; ÷ K)   If on account of things for which special permission has to be asked it is laid down that a man must go away,[30] no ban is to be put on his journey that summer, but then he is to be prosecuted if necessary for all suits in the normal way.

Treatment of Homicide

If assault results in a hit

40. (From St ‡ 263; II 296/3-4; + K p. 139)   The penalty for all of them is lesser outlawry if he is not hit, outlawry if he is.

Cases of assault

41. (From St ‡ 264; II 296/12-18; + K p. 139)   If men argue about an assault, about whether a man was hit or not, it is to be a blow only if a panel gives a verdict that he would have been hit if he had stood defenseless in the way. But for the five assaults just enumerated with lesser outlawry as the penalty there is no prosecution case to be made unless they are published before five neighbors before the third sunrise[31] or else eye-witnesses are named at the same place of action.

Retaliation for assault

42. (From St ‡ 265; II 297/8-10; + K p. 139)   In the nine assaults now enumerated a man has the right to kill in retaliation for all of them at the same place of action but not afterwards.

Injuries on both sides

43. (From St ‡ 267; II 298/13-14; + K p. 140)   — but both sides may be sustained pending judgment.

To be a wound a blow must draw blood

44. (From St ‡ 268; II 298/17-19; cf. K p. 141)   If a man strikes someone between the shoulders or on the nose so that blood spurts from mouth or nostrils, it is not a wound if it does not bleed where the blow landed.

29. Cf. Add. ‡ 56.
30. This would usually imply away from Iceland.
31. Cf. p. 143 and n. 23.

45. (From St ‡ 269; II 299/2-3; cf. K p. 140) — whether the skull was cut or split or broken. *Wounds*

(ii) (II 299/5-6; cf. K p. 140) — is asunder as far as the marrow, whether it is cut or broken.

46. (From St ‡ 271; II 300/15-301/5; cf. K p. 140) A new law. If men save the life of an assailant who inflicted injury in his assault by defending him with cut and thrust, the penalty is lesser outlawry if it is elsewhere than at the place of action. If a man who has inflicted injury now runs into a place where there is only room for one and men shield him there, then those who pursue are to ask them to move away or give him up. Shielding carries the penalty just rehearsed if, in accordance with law, any one of the pursuers has the right to vengeance there on his own or someone else's behalf, but even so those who shield him do not forfeit their immunity in respect of injuries they receive if it is not at the place of action. Shielding not at the place of action carries penalty if the original injuries are such as to involve penalty for giving assistance to the man charged with them, whether they are published sooner or later.[32] All cases of shielding not at the place of action are summoning cases and nine neighbors of the place where the cause arose are to be called at the assembly. *Shielding assailants*

47. (From St ‡ 273; II 301/19-302/8; + K p. 142) and it is to be published if more follows from it such as felling or throttling and then the man who gave the blow forfeits his immunity. Prosecution for this blow is to be thus: a man is to summon the other for striking him and assaulting him with an assault deemed such by law and make outlawry the penalty. Two suits may not be made out of that blow even though two are published, but if desired one may prosecute for assault only, with lesser outlawry as the penalty, and call neighbors locally. If the man who gave the blow boasts that it left a visible mark where it did not, he forfeits his immunity to the same extent as a man who has inflicted injuries which do leave a visible mark. *Prosecution for blows*

48. (From St ‡ 274; II 302/19-303/1; + K p. 142) A summons for that blow is to be made in every way as for the previous one except that now personal compensation from his property is to be claimed.

(ii) (II 303/7-8; cf. K p. 142) If it is published, prosecution for assistance is as for assistance after major wounds.

(iii) (II 303/9-14; + K p. 142) There are two suits if two are published. If a man [wants] to prosecute for assault he is [to call] nine neighbors locally. For a blow: a summons is to be made and it is to be *Prosecution for assault and for a blow*

---

32. See p. 212, n. 35.

stated that the other gave him a broken bone by that blow and make outlawry the penalty and claim personal compensation from his property. If a man holds another while he is given a blow, the penalty is outlawry and nine neighbors of the place of action are to be called locally.

False charge of wounding

49. (From St ‡ 275; II 304/11–14; cf. K p. 141)   The case lies with the man he charges with the wounding or, if he has picked on no individual for it, then with anyone of those who were in the opposing party at the time he said he got the wound.

Asking for truce

50. (St ‡ 277; II 305–8; ÷ K)   Wherever killing cases remain unatoned between men, and participants on both sides — prosecutors and defendants and sympathizers — wish to settle in those cases as soon as possible, then, whatever delays their agreement and whatever things they are asking, each side must give truce to the other, if they wish to ask for it. That is ancient law in Iceland.

If a killer asks for truce for himself from the corpse's kin by blood or marriage, or if his kinsmen do so for him or for themselves, before the third sunrise after the killing, with witnesses and with a view to complete settlement with the kinsmen of the killer or his friends, men of age and free born, then they are not to refuse a truce if asked in accordance with law.

It is lawful for men to ask for truce wherever men find themselves at a place where injuries are given and received, even though no one is killed.

Witnesses

And truce is asked for in accordance with law when a man names five witnesses or more, lawful eye-witnesses, each a man of twelve winters or older, free and with a settled home, or a man of eighty winters or younger, so healthy and able-bodied that he is capable of dealing death and defending his life and property, of using a shield and shooting from bent bow. "I name witnesses to witness that I ask N.N. and his companions, friends and kinsmen, for truce to spare property and truce to spare life for me and my men, for safe conduct as passenger and traveler, for a good outcome and complete settlement."

Refusal or silence when asked for truce

Then the penalty is lesser outlawry if the other man refuses truce, however he words his answer and also if he makes no answer. Witnesses are then to be named to that refusal, but the penalty is the same however he refuses truce.

Precautions if motives are suspected

It is not a refusal of truce if the man asked names five or more witnesses — to be selected in all respects like the two sorts selected earlier when the truce was asked for. The man asked for truce names witnesses to witness that he inquires of the other witnesses — and he is to name the other man or his witnesses by name — whether they have concern and sympathy for both the parties who are on opposing sides in this case, with complete settlement and loyal help as their object, or whether they have not. If the witnesses answer nothing or not what is in their thoughts, their penalty is lesser outlawry and he is moreover not required to allow his opponents truce.

If the man asked for truce suspects that the other side does not want a complete settlement with him, he is to request with witnesses that, before he allows them truce, the man who asked him for truce, and his witnesses too, should swear an oath to guarantee that there is no treachery towards him on their part. If they are willing to swear he is to waive the oath, unless his side wishes to swear as well. Then they are to word it this way, with God and all His saints to witness: "God be gracious to me if I tell the truth, harsh if I lie. God be gracious to me." Then he is to allow them truce.

If they refuse the oaths, there is a lesser outlawry case for the oath-lapse. It is another lesser outlawry case against them if they try to beguile him in some way; that is called truce-evasion if it does not succeed, but the penalty for truce-breaking, if it succeeds, is outlawry. *Oath-lapse, truce-evasion, and truce-breaking*

These cases [against the man] who asked for truce and against his witnesses lie with the man from whom truce was asked, and if he will not prosecute he is liable to a fine of three marks. The principal in the case for truce-breaking or oath-lapse is then the man who has to prosecute in the killing case, unless the principal in the killing or injury case is the man from whom truce was asked. If he will not prosecute, then the penalty for the man with whom the case for truce-breaking and oath-lapse first lay is lesser outlawry. [The case then lies with the men] who were witnesses of the asking for truce[33] but if they will not prosecute, the penalty is outlawry for the man with whom the case for truce-breaking first lay. The case against him lies with the man who asked for truce. But he is under no legal penalty if he does not summon for the lapse of the suit.

The only way[34] a man [A] has of invalidating cases brought by the other [B] in which judgment has been given against him, is by sum- *How in some circumstances of truce-breaking a*

---

33. Reading *þess er griða var beitt* for *þess er griða var beiddr* "of the man who was asked for truce."

34. In what follows it seems to be envisaged that an offender has been refused truce in some way, a case is brought against him and he is condemned. The refusal of truce can, however, be used to invalidate that case and judgment under certain conditions. If the man's offense allows him to be sustained pending judgment, and he is not responsible for truce-breaking or oath-lapse, his defense is clear (p. 212, ll. 1-3). If he is not responsible for truce-breaking or oath-lapse, but his offense does not allow him to be sustained (this latter would doubtless usually obtain, cf. n. 35 below), he may automatically attain the right to be sustained by asking for truce. This may be asked for by himself or someone else and it may be asked for anywhere, and he may then use the refusal of truce as a defense (p. 212, ll. 7-11). Finally, even if he was both responsible for truce-breaking or oath-lapse and guilty of an offense which did not allow him to be sustained, the refusal of truce could still be used in his defense if, elsewhere than at the place of action, one of his witnesses summoned his opponents to lose their right to proceed at law against him because of that refusal (p. 212, ll. 4-7).

killer may win the right to be sustained pending judgment

moning him [B] to lose his right to proceed at law, given that he [A] was a man who could be sustained pending judgment.[35] This suit of his [A] is only valid if he [A] was not guilty of the truce-breaking or oath-lapse. But if the man who asked for truce [A] may not be sustained and is also guilty of the truce-breaking, then one of his witnesses should summon him [B] to lose his right to proceed at law so that he [A] may be sustained pending judgment. That only helps him [A], however, if it is not at the place of action, but if he is not guilty of truce-breaking, then it does not matter whether they are at the place of action or elsewhere as long as truce is asked for in accordance with law and no matter who does the asking, the killer [A] may be sustained pending judgment. The exception is in the case of those men who have a price of three marks on their heads if outlawed.[36] There is no legal penalty if they are refused truce.

Prosecution for refusal of truce

It is lawful for the man who asks for truce to summon for refusal of truce at the place where the asking was done, and similarly for everything that follows from it, but otherwise he may name witnesses to it and make the summons at the home of the man prosecuted. And if there was no summons, the prosecution is to proceed using the testimony of the witnesses then named; but if a summons was made at the place where the asking for truce took place, then the prosecution is always to proceed by using the previous testimony in the case, other than testimony of the summons itself. But if it was at the place of action, then nine neighbors of the place of action qualified to give verdicts on killings or injuries are to decide on cases of lesser outlawry and full outlawry, but if it was elsewhere five neighbors. If it happens that they do not know whether neighbors will be called locally in cases of killing or injury, they are to ask with witnesses before they separate whether the others intend to call them locally or not or whom they mean to call. If they answer nothing or improperly, then nine witnesses are to be named, and the penalty for this deception at law is the same.

Publishing

51. (From St ‡ 278; II 308/10-12; cf. K p. 143)   But if it is not published or published wrong, then those who inflicted the injuries may be sustained pending judgment and have the right to attend assemblies.

(ii) (II 309/5-6; cf. K p. 143)   — if he himself does not wish or is not able to publish his wound.

(iii) (II 309/16-18; + K p. 144)   If he now transfers to another man the publishing of his injury at a time when he himself has set out to do it

---

35. A man against whom a charge of killing or wounding was published could not normally be given assistance or sustained pending judgment without penalty for those who helped him, see ‡ 86 (pp. 141, 142), Add. ‡ 51, and ‡ 98 (p. 161), Add. ‡‡ 71, 73.

36. See ‡ 102 (p. 164).

and the other man does it wrong, then he has no right to undertake the publishing a second time.

52. (From St ‡ 280; II 310/15-20; + K p. 144) — and state for which mortal wound he names as witness each of them he wishes to name. "I name this mortal-wound witness in accordance with law," he is to say, "for myself or for anyone who needs to use this witnessing." It is lawful for him to have a collective naming of witnesses when he names witnesses to mortal wounds but it is also lawful to name one witness to each mortal wound if he wishes. *Mortal-wound witnesses, and panels*

(ii) (II 310/25-311/3; + K p. 144) — and nine neighbors of the place of action, called locally, are to decide who are guilty of the wounds, and five neighbors from that prosecution panel, those who live closest to the place of action, are to decide how many mortal wounds there are.

53. (From St ‡ 281; II 311/4-7; cf. K p. 144) Those wounds found on a dead man which should be deemed major wounds if he lived are to be published as mortal wounds, but not such wounds as are smaller save only if a panel gives a verdict that the smaller-looking wound was the cause of death. *Wounds and mortal wounds*

(ii) (II 311/20-21; + K p. 145) Witnesses are to be named to wounds in the same way as to mortal wounds, and witnesses are to be selected on the same grounds.

54. (From St ‡ 282; II 313/5-6; cf. K p. 146) — where he thinks his life is no danger on that or any other account. *Publishing when survivors are on one side only*

55. (From St ‡ 283; II 315/7-18; + K p. 148) He is to name both the man against whom he publishes the injury and the man on whom it was inflicted and, third, the man before whom he published it. If a man wants to make two cases out of killing and assault, he is to name two or more witnesses. "[I] name witnesses to witness," he shall say, "that I publish an assault deemed such by law as a charge against N.N. in that he assaulted N.N. at that place of action where he wounded N.N. with the wound which proved mortal and N.N. got his death from. I publish it before N.N. I publish a legal publishing." Then he is again to name two or more witnesses to witness that "I publish as a charge against N.N. that he gave N.N. that wound which proved mortal and caused death at that place of action where N.N. made an assault deemed such by law on N.N. I publish a legal publishing." *Publishing assault and killing*

(ii) (II 315/22-316/5; + K p. 148) When a man wants to transfer to another the publishing of assault or injury he is to name witnesses to witness between them that he transfers to the other the publishing of assault or injury as a legal publishing. He transfers it in accordance with law and the other takes it in accordance with law. *Transfer of publishing*

A new law. If injuries are not published, then one case is to be made *If injuries are not published*

of it, and neighbors are to be called locally to decide whether he made an assault deemed such by law on him and wounded him with the wound he received and it is to be stated what wound it is.

Calling neighbors 56. (St ‡ 285; II 317-18; ÷ K) If a man wants to call neighbors, he is to name two or more witnesses to witness it and he shall say that "I call you N.N. to give a panel verdict, to pronounce on that matter" — and he is to state what he calls him for and to what assembly he calls him — "I call you to pronounce that verdict at court and before the court where the case has previously been presented, with your eight fellow-members and you yourself the ninth, and pronounce it either against or for. I call a legal calling" — in such a way that he himself hears it or else at his legal home so that men legally resident there hear it — "I call in a transferred case" — if that is what it is. He is to proceed like that each time until all are called. It is lawful for him to call neighbors where he meets them to speak to and at their homes. If no legally resident men hear his calling, he is to publish the calling before three neighbors, than whom no nine live nearer, men who have legal households and are on his road, and name witnesses to witness that he publishes a calling, a legal publishing before N.N., and he is to state what matter he made the calling for and to what assembly he called him and that he called a legal calling.

Transfer of calling It is lawful for a man, whether he has a transferred case or not, to transfer calling of neighbors to someone else, as he likes either for all or for some, and similarly if witnesses require to be called.[37] He is to transfer it with witnesses and transfer only the calling part of the case, transfer it in accordance with law and the other man takes it in accordance with law.

Challenging; disqualification 57. (From St ‡ 286; II 318/22-319/2; ÷ K) A man is to challenge on grounds of kinship with himself and kinship by marriage but he is not to challenge on grounds of spiritual kinship.[38] A man is not to give a panel verdict on a member of his own household.

Legal involvement and attachment disqualify (ii) (II 319/6-16; cf. K p. 149) Where killing cases are at issue, challenge is only to be made on grounds of legal involvement with the man selected as the killer in accordance with law and not with other men, even though they were present at the killing. The man selected as the killer is ever afterwards disqualified from any panel deciding on matters to do with the principal in the case and his kinsmen and his three kinsmen by marriage, both of such near degree as was rehearsed earlier.[39]

37. Cf. Add. ‡ 38.
38. Cf. p. 149.
39. See p. 149.

But the procedure against them in case of attachment is to enumerate the kinship between the man called for the panel and the killer and between the principal and the man killed, and afterwards give one's word of honor that the family enumeration is true and correct as now enumerated between the two sides, and state that such-and-such cases came between the man called for the panel and the principal — and name them both.

58. (From St ‡ 288; II 320/13-14; + K p. 150) — and, if willing, drive in his sheep without harm to them. *Single-handed householders*

59. (From St ‡ 289; II 322/10-12; + K p. 151) Calling is to pass by a place where a woman is the householder unless one of those men who may be an assembly participant on behalf of her household is with her. *Calling neighbor.*

(ii) (II 322/22-323/2; + K p. 151) The man with whom a principal is lodging is not to be called, nor the man with whom the man charged is lodging, nor the man with whom the man killed was lodging. Those neighbors are to be called who are qualified in every respect and not named as inflictors of wounds or mortal wounds.[40]

(iii) (II 323/14-15; + K p. 152) — and if they disagree, they are to draw lots.

(iv) (II 325/6-8; + K p. 153) But if they do not meet and both make their calling on the same day but not of all the same neighbors, then the whole procedure in their case is to be as was previously rehearsed.

(v) (II 325/12-14; + K p. 153) The men who had the right to let their calling stand also have the same choice of action over their neighbors, and they should use all the same procedure as was prescribed for the other side.

60. (From St ‡ 290; II 326/1-6; + K p. 153) If things turn out so that there is such close coincidence in calling neighbors that a panel of neighbors would decide that they called simultaneously the two neighbors they called first, then neither side's case is spoilt wherever neither[41] side had the intention of balking the other; and then they arrange between themselves what is to be done if more than nine neighbors are called. *Calling neighbor*

(ii) (II 326/10-14; + K p. 153) — given that they are asked with witnesses. Both are summoning cases and nine neighbors of the man prosecuted are to be called at the assembly in a lesser outlawry case but five in a fining case. The cases lie with those men who asked them for legal information and had the conduct of those suits which were balked by them. *Balking legal procedure*

---

40. Cf. ‡ 87 (pp. 144-45).
41. Reading *hvárigir* for *hvárir* "either."

    (iii) (II 327/5–6; + K p. 153)   The case lies with the man who conducts any case he was trying to balk.

Calling witnesses   61. (From St ‡ 291; II 327/16–328/2; ÷ K)   He is to name two or more witnesses to witness that "I call you N.N. to bear witness of what I then named you as witness for" — and state what that was. "I call you to bear that witness with the company I shall provide for you at court and before the court where I shall present the prosecution against N.N." — or the defense for him if that rather is needful — "I call you with a legal calling." He is to state what assembly he calls him to, and he is to publish that calling like a summons if legally resident men do not hear it.

Claiming food due to a man called to attend the assembly   (ii) (II 329/6–11; cf. K pp. 69/37–70/2)   — and the man who called him is to have the assembly attendance dues which the man who is called gets. If he does not allow him the food when they come to the Assembly, he is to summon him for that at Lögberg and make the penalty a three-mark fine and call five neighbors of the man prosecuted. If it is possible he is to have the witnesses brought before the court whom he named to witness it when he claimed the food.

Transfer of sick man's testimony   62. (From St ‡ 292; II 330/23–331/2; + K p. 69)   If the others named as witnesses with him do not come to see the sick man, he is to frame the wording of the testimony in the presence of the man who called him and those men who take over his testimony.

Right to kill on account of a woman   63. (From St ‡ 293; II 332/7–9; + K p. 154)   — a man has the right to kill on that account up to the next General Assembly. The other man falls with forfeit immunity at his hands and at the hands of all who go with him to inflict injury on that man and give him help.

Insanity   64. (From St ‡ 295; II 333/20–21; cf. K. p. 156)   — if he has previously done or tried to do injury to himself —.

"Accidents"   65. (From St ‡ 296; II 334/6–8; + K p. 155)   and no one else intended it either. If a panel gives a verdict that he held the weapon still and did not move it away because he wanted the other to get scratched by it, his penalty is full outlawry.

Prosecution in killing cases   66. (From St ‡ 297; II 335/14–17; + K p. 157)   It is prescribed that if some principals or those who have the conduct of the cases have settled or want to settle and some do not want to, then those are always to have their way who want to prosecute to the limit of the law.

    (ii) (II 335/23; + K p. 157)   In no circumstances does a killing case fall to a woman.

    (iii) (II 335/24–6; + K p. 157)   If they all want to prosecute to the limit of the law, they are to draw lots to see whose case is to be judged unless they all agree on something else.

    (iv) (II 336/2–3; + K p. 157)   — neither shall anyone take it from him unless the boy gets an infirmity such as would make it right for him to transfer a transferred case.[42]

(v) (II 336/10-11; + K p. 158) — and [they take] the compensation also, but the husband first.

67. (From St ‡ 298; II 337/4-7; cf. K p. 159) If they do not agree how much cash the man killed was owing him, five of his neighbors are to make the reckoning with them. But if they do not offer the cash within the next half month, the case lies with the man who had money owed him by the man killed. *Claim for debt owed by a man who has been killed*

(ii) (II 337/9-11; cf. K p. 159) Children of a freedman always take the compensation if they exist. But if the freedom-giver kills his freedman and the freedman has no son or the son is not of age, then the case lies with the chieftain —. *Rights of freedmen's children*

(iii) (II 337/14-22; + K p. 160) If a childless freedman is killed and his freedom-giver is dead, the case and the compensation lie with the heir of the freedom-giver. If the heir is not a man of age, the case lies with the chieftain to whose assembly group the man killed belonged. If the chieftain is the killer, the case lies with the other chieftains of the same assembly, and they are to draw lots if they disagree. If a freedman is killed who lives in a hut and is nowhere attached to an assembly group, the case lies with the chieftain to whose assembly group the householder belongs who owns the land on which the other had his hut. But if it is this chieftain who does the killing, then the case lies with the other chieftains of the same assembly in every way as previously rehearsed. *If a childless freedman is killed*

(iv) (II 337/23-338/8; + K p. 160) If he does the killing or is not alive, then the case and the compensation fall to the freedom-giver who gave freedom to the first freedman or to that freedom-giver's heir, as long as the freedman's freedman was childless. If compensation goes to someone who is not a man of age, then the case falls to the chieftain as rehearsed previously. And the same happens if no children of the superior freedman are alive. Furthermore a freedwoman has the right to take compensation for her freedman in the same way as a freedman for his. If more men than one give freedom to a man, then each of them is to take such share of killing compensation for him as they gave towards his freedom. *If a freedman's childless freedman is killed*

Freedom-givers

68. (From St ‡ 299; II 339/2; + K p. 160) — or it is his messmate [who] has killed him —. *A shipman killed*

(ii) (II 339/12-14; + K p. 160) — or where most of them brought their belongings ashore if it happened before they got to land.

---

42. According to ‡ 77 (p. 123), this transfer could be made only if he fell sick on his way to, or at, the assembly.

A shipman killed in lodgings

69. (From St ‡ 300; II 339/18-19; + K p. 161) And if more than one share the ownership of the household, the case lies with the one who has the biggest share.

(ii) (II 340/2-3; + K p. 161) — and they are to draw lots for the case and both have equal shares in the compensation.

(iii) (II 340/7-9; + K p. 161) — but she has the compensation. If the chieftain does the killing, she has the compensation but the case lies with the chieftains of the same assembly. If she kills him, the chieftain to whose assembly group she belongs has the case and the compensation.

Foreigners killed in Iceland

(iv) (II 340/19-23; cf. K p. 161) If that foreigner leaves freeborn and legitimate children, the case if he is killed falls to the family of the children's mother, and the children have the compensation, and the case lies with the man next of kin to the children who is of age, free born, with a settled home and of such mental capacity that he can take charge of lawsuits.

Settlement without leave

70. (From St ‡ 301; II 341/11-16; + K p. 161) The man who prosecutes this case is to summon as he pleases either both or one of those who have settled, and he has also to take up the original suit and prosecute it in accordance with the law's rigor. But if men want to settle these matters locally, then the summons over leave to settle is to be made locally and outlawry made the penalty and nine neighbors called at the assembly.

(ii) (II 342/8-9; + K p. 162) — and it is to be prosecuted as was previously rehearsed.

Assisting men charged with killing or major wounds

71. (St ‡ 304; II 342-43; cf. K p. 161) Lesser outlawry is the penalty for assisting men against whom killing or major wounds are lawfully published, or who have made a raid or burnt people inside a house so that they suffered death or lasting injury, or whatever they have done to anyone for which they are required in accordance with law to make restitution by kindred payments.[43] They are all summoning cases and the chieftain to whose assembly group the man prosecuted belongs is to be called on to form a panel of twelve.

If a man charged with wounding is found in someone's house

72. (St ‡ 305; II 343; cf. Add. ‡ 104 and K p. 141; ÷ K) When a man has published a minor wound as a charge against someone and then comes to a house and finds that man indoors there, he is to name witnesses to witness that in the house of the householder N.N. he has come upon the man N.N. against whom he has published a wound, and that he names those witnesses in accordance with law for his own use and advantage. The penalty is then lesser outlawry for the householder and for all those with him in the house who have spent the previous night with him and are home-men there. That is a summoning case and the chieftain

---

43. Kindred payments are specified in ‡ 113 (pp. 175-83).

to whose assembly group the man prosecuted belongs is to be called on to form a panel of twelve to give a verdict whether the man had been there in the house the previous night or not. He is moreover to have the witnesses brought forward before the court whom he named to witness it when he came upon that man in the house.

73. (St ‡ 306; 343-44; cf. K p. 162) It is assistance to a killer, carrying a penalty for anyone who has heard that the killing was published, if he is given food or if [anyone has] shared living quarters with him at a place where people share sleep and meals with him. But saving advice carries no legal penalty. Sustenance of men who have done injury to men of forfeit immunity carries no legal penalty, nor does it if they attend formally inaugurated assemblies. *Assistance*

74. (From St ‡ 307; II 344/4-19; cf. K p. 123; Add. ‡ 98) A man may transfer a killing case to another man if he wishes, for full prosecution or settlement, and then the man who has taken it shall have charge of it just as if he were the rightful principal in the case; and a man may transfer to someone else any case he wants to transfer. And a case is to be transferred thus: they are to take each other by the hand, the one who takes the case and the one who transfers it, and name two or more witnesses to witness that the principal transfers that case to the other, to prosecute and to settle and to use every formal means of proof as if he were the rightful principal. He transfers the case in accordance with law, and the other takes it in accordance with law. *Transfer of killing cases*

A man is to take the original suit from someone and then in all cases that subsequently arise from it he is the prosecutor of them all and he has the right to transfer them to someone else, and he does not need to take them over formally. A man who has a transferred case may not transfer the original suit unless he transfers it to the principal who transferred it to him. The principal may then transfer it to whom he pleases and use whatever he likes of the preparations the other has made for the case.

(ii) (II 345/1-8; cf. K pp. 121, 123) If a man takes a case from someone and such hindrances arise that for reasons of necessity the case is not prosecuted, then the principal may himself take up his case and prosecute it the following summer. *If a transferred case is not prosecuted*

If a man takes a case from someone and then will not prosecute and so tries to make the case void, he is liable to lesser outlawry at the suit of the principal, and neighbors are to be called at the assembly, and he is then to prosecute his case himself if the panel gives a verdict that the other is guilty of the charge.

75. (From St ‡ 310; II 346/23-347/1; + K p. 167) The summons in that case is to be made at Lögberg and nine neighbors of the man prosecuted are to be called at the Assembly. *Cases of injury on the way to the assembly*

Booth panels 76. (From St ‡ 311; II 347/8-10; cf. K p. 163) No call is to be made on booths of shoemakers or sword-cutlers or players or vagrants,[44] and on no booths with less than five men in them.

Higher-priced outlaws 77. (From St ‡ 313; II 348/7; cf. K p. 164) The third is the slave or bounden debtor who kills —.

Murder 78. (From St ‡ 315; II 348/17-18; cf. K p. 146) And it is murder if a man hides it from the majority of the people in the commune —.

(ii) (II 349/8-11; + K p. 164) For wounds or mortal wounds or blows which accompany the murder, it is possible to call locally nine neighbors of the place of action and publish the suit at the assembly, or to make the summons locally and prosecute like other killing cases.

When there are survivors on one side only 79. (From St ‡ 316; II 349/16-18; + K p. 146) — though it is also lawful for him to explain it no further than to say he is the man's killer if he left a dead man.)

Burial of man killed 80. (St ‡ 317; II 350; cf. K p. 146) If the principal in the case is present when a man is killed, he is to take the corpse to church. If he is not there, then the companions of the man killed are to do so. If they cannot or if the only man present is the one who killed him, he is to cover the corpse with stones or turf or clothing or snow if nothing else is available. But if it is not covered to keep out animals or birds, nine neighbors of the place of action are to be called locally and the penalty is lesser outlawry.

Age of victim immaterial 81. (St ‡ 318; II 350; cf. K p. 140) Outlawry is the penalty if someone kills man or woman, whatever age the persons killed are.

Husband's compensation for wife's death If a woman who is killed had a husband, then her husband has a ring of two dozen ounces from the payment,[45] even if he has no children with her.

Penalties the same for men and women A woman is under the same penalty as a man if she kills man or woman or injures them, and so it is prescribed for all departures from the law.

Publishing when principal is in a different Quarter 82. (From St ‡ 319; II 350/18-351/4; cf. K p. 145) If the principal is outside the Quarter when a killing is done, he is to set off within a month of hearing of it and is to have published it before the third sunrise after his arrival at the place of action, and he is to add the publishing of the assault if that took place there too.

Loss of right to attend assemblies 83. (From St ‡ 320; II 351/8-10; + K p. 162) If one group goes to the assembly and one group stays at home when charges of killing or wound-

---

44. Cf. ‡ 82 (p. 135 and n. 244).
45. I.e. half full personal compensation. This is usually reckoned in ounce-units, but the word used here, *tvítylptarbaugr* "two-dozen-ring", suggests the provision is a relic from an age when it was reckoned in ounces of silver. Cf. the similar archaism in Add. ‡ 105 (see p. 226 and n. 50). The word *verr* "man, husband" used in this sentence also appears to be an archaism.

ing have been published against both sides, and a panel gives a verdict of assault against those who stay at home, both are under penalty.

84. (From St ‡ 321; II 351/17–352/6; cf. K pp. 140-41) It is a wound if it bleeds where a blow lands. But it is a blow if it bleeds somewhere else. It is always to be published, whether the wounds are major or minor. The penalty is lesser outlawry if someone accompanies of his own accord a man against whom major wounds or mortal wounds have been published as charges. They are major wounds if a man is brain-wounded or internally wounded or marrow-wounded. And a man is brain-wounded if a probe meets the brain membrane. A man is internally wounded if a probe meets membrane or cavity. And marrow-wounded is when a probe meets marrow. Not publishing and publishing wrong amount to the same thing.

holds even if a man's case is upheld

Definition of wounds

(ii) (II 352/12–13; ÷ K) A new law. A bowshot cordon is now 240 legal fathoms, on level ground.[46]

Bowshot

85. (From St ‡ 322; II 352/16–353/9; cf. K pp. 163-64) If a man strikes or wounds someone at an assembly or at a formally inaugurated autumn meeting, the penalty is outlawry and a man's right to personal compensation is doubled at such places. If a man tries to avenge himself but the man who has injured him has run into a booth and men shield him there, then those in pursuit are to ask that they may go into the booth. If the others are unwilling and shield him, the penalty is lesser outlawry if this is not at the place of action but otherwise full outlawry, and the booth also forfeits legal immunity, unless they wished to separate the two sides and would have acted in just the same way if the man who has now suffered had made the assault. Then neighbors are to be called, those who live nearest the assembly as long as no injuries are laid to their charge. If men strike or wound or kill each other at the General Assembly, the personal compensation of men who receive injury is doubled and, further, no penalty is incurred if men there shield others.

Injury and shielding at assemblies

(ii) (II 353/17–22; cf. K p. 164) If injuries are inflicted at the General Assembly at the close of the Assembly when men strike their awnings, it is not required to bring a court out unless the judges are willing, though it remains lawful to ask a court to go out as long as the calendar has not been announced. But if it is prosecuted at the next Assembly those neighbors who are qualified in terms of attachment and live nearest the Assembly ground are to be called.

Injuries at the close of the General Assembly

86. (St ‡ 323; II 353-54); cf. K p. 141) It is prescribed that when a man is wounded he is to name witnesses to his wounds and show them

Wound witnesses and self-inflicted wounds

---

46. Cf. p. 30, n. 22.

what wounds he is wounded with. Neighbors of the place of action are to decide what wounds he was wounded with if witnesses are not named. If a man wounds himself on purpose or lets another man wound him, the penalty is lesser outlawry. Neither may he or his companions be sustained pending judgment any more than before, even though that was what he wanted to gain by his action. There is no legal penalty if a man lets himself be struck by someone else, if he wants to be.

Challenging and compensation when heirs are minors or women

87. (St ‡ 324; II 354; cf. K p. 159) If a man is killed and his heirs are men under age or women, all challenging is to be done on grounds of connection with them and they have all the money that comes out of the case.

Mother's share

A mother takes one-third of killing compensation after her legitimate children, sharing with the father and the dead man's brothers born of the same father.

Principal's share

A new law. Where killing compensation is due to a woman or to a man who may not prosecute his own suits, then the principal of the killing case has one-third of the killing compensation.

Responsiblity for weapons

88. (St ‡ 326; II 355; cf. K p. 156) The man who fastens up a weapon is responsible for it. If someone else moves the weapon afterwards, then whoever moves it is responsible for it, unless people stumble against it, or they are pushed against it — then those who do the pushing are responsible.

Wounding at assemblies

89. (St ‡ 327; II 355–56; cf. K p. 163) If a man wounds someone at an established assembly, formally inaugurated, they are not to settle even though it is only a minor wound, but both have the right to attend that assembly. All causes that arise within the assembly boundaries are to be published on the assembly slope and everything that is done against the law within the assembly boundaries is to be deemed in all respects as if done on the assembly ground itself.

At what assemblies cases may be brought

90. (St ‡ 328; II 356; cf. K pp. 99, 104) It is lawful to prosecute all cases that arise between men at the General Assembly. It is also lawful to prosecute at district assemblies, at Quarter assemblies when they are held[47] and all men of the Quarter may bring cases against each other there, and further at all spring assemblies when all principals and all the men against whom cases are brought belong to the same assembly. All injury cases on which neighbors of the place of action alone have to decide are lawfully prepared for a spring assembly only if the men who are in charge of the suits and are principals are all attached to that assembly or give leave for cases to be prepared for that assembly, even though they are not all attached to it, provided that all the men against

---

47. The only place in *Grágás* where Quarter assemblies are mentioned.

whom the cases are brought are attached to that assembly or else not attached anywhere.

If some want to prepare a case for a spring assembly and some for the General Assembly, then those who want it to be prepared for the General Assembly are to veto it at the spring assembly. If there are two principals in one case and one wants to prepare it for the spring assembly and the other for the General Assembly, then again the one who wants to prepare it for the General Assembly is to veto the case at the spring assembly. But if one wants to prosecute the case at the spring assembly and the other wants to settle, then the one who wants to prosecute at the spring assembly is to have his way, if it is right to prepare it for there.

A man is to forbid all these cases by his own veto, but if a case is prepared against him at a spring assembly to which he himself is not attached, then he is to get a chieftain's veto on the case at the spring assembly. *Individual's veto and chieftain's veto*

91. (St ‡ 329; II 357-8; cf. Add. ‡‡ 124-7; ÷ K) It is prescribed that if a countryman of ours is killed abroad, then it is lawful for the principal to publish that killing at Lögberg the summer after he hears of it, and from the moment he arrives in the country the killer may not be sustained, but shipmen are liable to penalty only after they have heard of the publishing. *An Icelander killed abroad*

If a countryman of ours is wounded or struck in Norway and does not return in three summers, while the man who inflicted injury on him does return, then it is lawful for the man who would be principal in the killing case after the other's death to prosecute that case. *An Icelander wounded or struck in Norway*

If a man wants to prosecute for a killing or injury done abroad, he is to ask at Lögberg whether any other men want to prosecute for that cause, and afterwards he is to ask if more men want to prosecute for any causes that have arisen in the realm of that king. If no other men wish to prosecute, then he is to prosecute before the court to which he himself belongs, as long as he is prosecuting for more than one cause arising in the realm of that king. If he prosecutes only for one cause, he is to prosecute it before the court to which the man prosecuted belongs. If he prosecutes more suits than one and the men prosecuted are all in the same Quarter, he is to prosecute before the court to which the men prosecuted belong. If others also wish to prosecute, they are to draw lots to decide before which of the Quarter Courts, to which the men prosecuted belong, they should prosecute all the cases. *Prosecution*

A new law. If a man is robbed abroad, the penalty is outlawry. The procedure for prosecution is to be as for killing abroad, except that the man was robbed and not killed.[48] *An Icelander robbed abroad*

92. (St ‡ 330; II 358; ÷ K) If a man slanders another before a king or *Slander abroad*

---

48. Cf. Add. ‡ 127.

earl or any man in authority abroad with the result that he is exiled or loses his property, the penalty is lesser outlawry. It is to be prosecuted with a panel of twelve. If grounds for defense that are offered in such suits and have to be assessed took place abroad, a scratch panel is everywhere to be used for them, but if the grounds for defense that are offered took place here, five neighbors of the man prosecuted are to be used. If grounds for defense are offered which took place at sea on the voyage to this country, five neighbors are to be used for the defense, those living nearest to the landing place where most men take their belongings ashore from the ship, or on board the ship if it occurs when they go from the country.

Scratch panel or panel of neighbors

Failure to cover a corpse

93. (St ‡ 331; II 358; cf. K p. 146 and Add. ‡ 80)   If a man does not cover the corpse when he leaves someone dead, the penalty is lesser outlawry. And that case is to go with the killing case when it is being prepared, and neighbors [are to be] called locally. If a man leaves someone dead who had previously been in his company, whether he died from sickness or cold or other men's weapons, or whatever caused his death so as to make it necessary for him to cover his corpse, the penalty is lesser outlawry [if he does not do so], and it is a summoning case and nine neighbors of the man prosecuted are to be called at the assembly.

Formula for publishing a killing

94. (From St ‡ 332; II 359/2-16; + K p. 165)   A killing is to be published in this way: a man is to name two or more witnesses "to witness," he shall say, "that I publish as a charge against N.N. that he made an assault deemed such by law on N.N. and in that assault gave him those wounds which proved mortal at that place of action where N.N. got his death. I claim that for that offense N.N. must become a condemned outlaw, not to be sustained, not to be given passage, not to be given any saving advice. I claim that all his property is under penalty. I claim personal compensation due to me from his property" — or to the man who is principal in the case — "forty-eight ounce-units in legal tender. Then I claim half of what remains for myself and half for all the men of the Quarter to whom property under penalty is due in accordance with law. I publish this case for the Quarter Court before which the case has to come in accordance with law. I publish it now for prosecution this summer and for the fullest penalty to fall on N.N. I publish a legal publishing. I publish it in men's hearing at Lögberg" — and as a transferred case if it is one.

Common knowledge

95. (From St ‡ 333; II 359/19-360/4; cf. K p. 165)   If all those cases of which the principal has learnt when four weeks of summer have passed or sooner and which are then common knowledge in the district — and cases are common knowledge in a district when the majority of assembly participants in the commune where the cases arise have learnt of them

and people think they are true, and when a case is common knowledge the principal must also have learnt of it, whether he is in that commune or a different one — the summoning must be done —.

96. (From St ‡ 334; II 360/14-15; + K p. 165)   — unless they meet them to speak to. *Preparing a suit*

(ii) (II 361/21-24; + K p. 166)   It is also lawful to publish the case the same summer as he hears of the killing and to prosecute that same summer, and then he is to call nine neighbors of the place of action at the assembly, those he thinks qualified on all grounds of connection.

97. (From St ‡ 335; II 363/10-11; + K p. 168)   If they are equally closely related, they are to draw lots among themselves. *Forfeit immunity pleaded against a dead man*

(ii) (II 363/23-24; + K p. 168)   — or if his kinsmen or his chieftain are unwilling, though present, —.

(iii) (II 364/4-5; + K p. 168)   It is to go the same way if the wounded man has lost his power of speech and a case is prepared against him to maintain that he is a man of forfeit immunity.

98. (From St ‡ 336; II 364/10-15; cf. K p. 123; Add. ‡ 74 (ii))   A new law. If a man takes a case from someone else and then will not prosecute and wishes by this to balk his case for him, the penalty is lesser outlawry and he is to make the summons in that case locally and call nine neighbors of the man prosecuted at the assembly. And the principal has the right to take up his case and prosecute it the following summer. *Willful neglect of a transferred case*

99. (St ‡ 338; II 365; ÷ K)   If a man shuts someone in a building so that he cannot get out without damaging the building in its locks or timber or turf, or if he holds someone or restrains his movement in any way so that the delay is such that he would otherwise have gone the length of a bowshot or more,[49] the penalty is lesser outlawry and nine neighbors of the man prosecuted are to be called at the assembly and the summons made locally. *Enforced restraint*

100. (From St ‡ 339; II 365/12-14; + K p. 147)   If a man strikes a horse with a rider, the penalty is a fine of three marks and he is to call five neighbors of the man prosecuted at the assembly but make the summons locally. *Offenses against a man on horseback*

(ii) (II 365/16-18; + K p. 147)   — and whatever a man does so that the other falls off as a result of his actions, the penalty is full outlawry —.

101. (From St ‡ 340; II 366/6-8; + K p. 158)   If women who are married have charge of the property of young people on whom injury is inflicted, the cases lie with their husbands. *With whom cases lie*

(ii) (II 367/4-8; + K p. 157, cf. p. 123)   If the man who is principal in

---

49. Cf. Add. ‡ 84 (ii); p. 30, n. 22.

a case dies before he has transferred the case or prepared it or settled it, but the case did arise in time for him to hear of it, then the case lies with the man who is next of kin and of age, but only the heir of the principal if no one else is more closely related.

No one can inherit from his victim

102. (From St ‡ 341; II 367/12–13; + K p. 158) No one shall ever take inheritance after the person he kills or whose death he successfully contrives.

103. (St ‡ 342; II 367–68; cf. K pp. 139-40, Add. ‡ 134) It is also prescribed that if men meet at a road junction and their encounter turns into an onslaught, then all those on the side from which the first assault was made forfeit their immunity in respect of injuries unless they are men who were lawfully trying to separate them. It is an onslaught when three men or more in all are killed or wounded and these are drawn from both sides.

Definition of an onslaught

Lawful separation

But men who lawfully separate them are those who set off from home knowing the intention of neither side, and who wished to separate them just as they would do if everybody at that place of action seemed to them of equal desert and if the assault had been made on those who had now made the assault, and finally who leave in company with neither side. A fight is separated when there is more than a bowshot between them.

Shielding

Whenever injuries of such extent as now rehearsed are given and received between two parties, from then on no legal penalty is incurred if men shield either side at that place of action. Moreover, both parties may be sustained pending judgment.

Penalty for an accomplice

If someone goes with a man to the place of action and in order to inflict injury on another, the penalty for him is outlawry and he forfeits his immunity in respect of injuries there. But if he goes away from the place of action with a man who has inflicted injury, the penalty is lesser outlawry.

A man who has inflicted a flesh wound may not be sustained

104. (From St ‡ 343; II 369/1–5; cf. K p. 141; Add. ‡ 72) A man may not be sustained in secret pending judgment if he has inflicted a flesh wound on someone. But if the latter catches him in a house and names witnesses to witness it, the penalty is lesser outlawry and it is to be prosecuted with that testimony.

Witnessing

In every kind of witnessing witnesses are to testify to what they have heard or to what they have seen.

Blows and personal compensation

105. (St ‡ 344; II 369; cf. K pp. 140, 146) If a man strikes another the penalty is outlawry, and if the blow leaves a visible mark, the latter has the right to take personal compensation from his property, two of the biggest rings;[50] and men have no right to shield a man who has struck

50. Cf. ‡ 113 (p. 175), where the "biggest ring" is of twenty-four ounces of silver. Ordinary personal compensation was forty-eight ounce-units of legal tender and presumably this

someone, but he may nevertheless be sustained pending judgment, unless the blow is so great that a bone is broken — then he is not to be sustained if it is published.

106. (From St ‡ 345; II 370/1-2; + K p. 169)   — and also those that are plotted elsewhere and given effect at the place of action —. *Disfigurement plots*

(ii) (II 370/3-10; cf. K p. 169) If a man plots to strike someone or to wound or to disfigure, whichever of these he plots, he is to be prosecuted in accordance with the result, even if a mortal wound results where he planned a blow or wound. *Prosecution for plots to injure*

If a man avenges an assault with a blow, neighbors of the place of action are to decide on the assault but a panel of twelve on the blow. *Decisions on assaults and blows*

Plots are when a man speaks in such a way of someone else that what he says to others brings that man closer to death and farther from good health, if what he spoke of comes about. *Definition of plots*

107. (From St ‡ 349; II 374/10-15; + K p. 174, cf. p. 116) If anyone is caught harming people's sheep, he falls with forfeit immunity at that place of action. Whatever livestock a man harms to someone else's loss, he is fined three marks for it and he is to make good the damage as assessed by neighbors. But if the damage amounts to five ounce-units or more, the penalty is lesser outlawry and nine neighbors are to be called at the assembly, but five if it is a fining case. *Harming livestock*

108. (St ‡ 350; II 374-75; cf. Add. ‡ 103; ÷ K) If a man wishes to prosecute for assault, he is to state which man made it on him, but if an onslaught occurs there, he is not required to state which man it was: then it is to be stated whether the assault on him was made from that side, or from which side the assault first came. If assault or injury occur between different sides, but not an onslaught, then a man is to state against whom it is published. If a man publishes assault or injury, he is to publish it so that neighbors hear it, though it is also lawful for him to publish it at the homes of neighbors so that legally resident men hear it. *Assault and onslaught*

109. (St ‡ 351; II 375; cf. K pp. 152, 125; Add. ‡ 111) If men call neighbors locally on the Saturday in the moving days or earlier, those neighbors are to be called who were living there the previous year. If those neighbors have left, it is lawful to call them at the house-sites. *Calling neighbors*

All neighbors are to be called on the same day if that can be done or with as little interval as possible if it cannot be done on the same day. If men do the calling in the moving days, it is prescribed that such callings are to be made on the same day if that can be done, unless men accuse each other of assault — the calling in such cases is always to be done like that, whatever time of year it is.

archaic phrase would have been interpreted in terms of this currency in the thirteenth century. Cf. p. 220, n. 45.

Calling and counter-calling

110. (St ‡ 353; II 376; cf. K p. 152 and p. 150)   If men accuse each other of assault, then those who wish to call neighbors first are to begin their calling so as to finish it in time for those who call second to make their calling by Saturday nones in the moving days.[51] If men start their calling so late that, if they wait until the others have finished, they will not be able to make it by Saturday nones in the moving days, then they are to wait until the others have finished, presuming that they know the others have started, and it is then lawful for them, if they have to make a counter-calling, to start on it after the moving days. They are to call the same neighbors as the others have called and at those houses where they had their households before the moving days, unless they should meet them to speak to.

A man lives closer to the place of action who lives in that part of a building which looks towards the place of action, if there is any question about it.

Prosecution for helping men charged with wounding

111. (From St ‡ 354; II 377/1-12; cf. K p. 154; Add. ‡ 109)   The procedure for prosecuting men who at a formally inaugurated assembly or on a journey to an assembly give help to someone against whom wounds or mortal wounds are published as charges is to be the same as for prosecuting the man himself except that they are not to be prosecuted with testimony.

Calling neighbors in the moving days

If a man calls neighbors locally in the moving days or earlier, he is to call those men who at the time of the preceding General Assembly were living at the houses he makes his callings at, if they are still alive and in the country. He is to call them at those houses even if they have left and he is to publish the calling before three men.

Rights of freedmen and illegitimate people in killing cases

Killing cases for their children lie with freedmen and men born illegitimate just as they do with men born as lawful heirs, and similarly they take all compensation for them, and finally freedwomen and women born illegitimate take compensation for their children just as men do.

Causing burns

112. (St ‡ 357; II 378-79; ÷ K)   If a man tips fire on someone or throws it or anything he would be burnt by if it landed on his bare skin, the penalty is outlawry, and similarly if he pushes someone into a fire or into any place where it is likely that the other will get burnt, or if he pours something so hot on him or puts it under him or however he contrives it that he is likely to get a burn from it, the penalty in every case is outlawry even if no burn results, and similarly if a man singes off someone's hair. These are summoning cases, and if no burn results nine neighbors of the man prosecuted are to be called at the assembly.

---

51. When the weekend holy time (*helgi*) began, cf. ‡‡ 9-10 (pp. 41-43).

113. (St ‡ 358; II 379; ÷ K) If a man binds someone or tortures someone he has no right to torture[52] or if he burns someone with those things just rehearsed so as to leave a visible mark, he is to publish that like other assaults, and if more follows from it, it is to be deemed to involve forfeit of immunity, and in that case nine neighbors of the place of action are to be called locally. *Binding and torturing*

114. (St ‡ 359; II 379; ÷ K) Wherever a man takes another or whatever place he gets him into or whatever thing he moves towards him with the idea that the other would get death or infirmity from it, or with the wish that the other's death might be brought about or contrived by it, and so also if he does something that brings about death or lasting injury or infirmity, however he sets about it, the penalty in every case is outlawry even though he does not wound him. And even though no killing results, nine neighbors of the place where the attempt was made on the person are to be called locally [*sic*] and the summons made locally. *Attempting to cause death, lasting injury, or infirmity*

115. (From St ‡ 360; II 379/17-380/7; ÷ K) If someone capsizes a man's boat or wrecks his vessel in deep water, the penalty is outlawry. If men sailing or rowing an ocean-going ship run down men and wreck their vessel, the penalty is outlawry. If they are on their way from the country, neighbors of the landing place where most of them carried their belongings on board are to be called. But if they have arrived from other countries, then he is to call neighbors of the landing place where most of them took their belongings ashore from the ship. If when sailing or rowing they run down men who go by boat along the coast, neighbors who live on the land nearest their encounter are to be called. Wherever men suffer loss of life as a result, these are all summoning cases and nine neighbors are to be called at the assembly. But if loss of life results, it is also lawful to publish it and neighbors are then to be called locally. *Capsizing or wrecking another man's vessel*

(ii) (II 380/17-20; ÷ K) If a man aims a blow at someone and stops it himself, the penalty is lesser outlawry. The other has no right to kill in retaliation. The summons is to be made locally and nine neighbors of the man prosecuted called at the assembly. *A blow checked*

116. (St ‡ 361; II 380-81; ÷ K) If a man cuts hair from someone's head or makes him dirty anywhere in order to disgrace him or tears or cuts clothing off him or takes anyone against his will the length of a bowshot or more, and for anything a man does to disgrace someone else, however he sets about it, the penalty in every case is outlawry. In such cases the summons is to be made locally and nine neighbors of the man prosecuted called at the assembly. *Humiliating actions*

If a man pulls someone towards him, the penalty is a fine of three *Pulling*

---

52. Cf. ‡ 110 (p. 171).

and pushing marks. If he then pushes him away, he is for that fined another three marks. But if he does both, that makes two cases, and five neighbors are to be called at the assembly. If a man pushes someone against stock or stone, or wherever he pushes him against something hard so that his skin is blue or red afterwards, or if he pushes him into water or urine or food or dirt, the penalty in every case is outlawry even if the man does not fall, and nine neighbors of the man prosecuted are to be called at the assembly.

Pulling hats off 117. (From St ‡ 362; II 381/14–18; ÷ K) If a man pulls the hat off someone's head, the penalty is a fine of three marks. If there is a chinstrap on the hat and he pulls it off forwards, the penalty is lesser outlawry. But if a chinstrap keeps the hat on and he pulls it back off his head, that is throttling[53] and he has the right to kill in retaliation and the penalty is outlawry.

Prosecution 118. (St ‡ 363; II 382; ÷ K) If a man bites someone or scratches or pinches so as to leave a blue or red mark, the penalty is lesser outlawry. It is a wound if it bleeds. If a man tips food or urine or dirt over someone, so that it is visible afterwards, the penalty is outlawry. But if a man pours water over someone, the penalty is lesser outlawry. If a man pisses on somebody, the penalty is lesser outlawry, outlawry if a man shits on somebody. In all these cases now told, except throttling and felling,[54] there is no right to kill in retaliation. The summons is to be made locally and nine neighbors of the man prosecuted called at the assembly in lesser outlawry cases, five in fining or three-mark cases.

Attempts to heal 119. (St ‡ 364; II 382; ÷ K) If a man cauterises someone or bleeds someone for the good of his health, and whatever a man does for the good of another person's health, as long as he wanted him to get improvement and not infirmity by it, then if he suffers death or harm from it, the man whose aim was to cure him is under no legal penalty.

Penalty for raiding 120. (St ‡ 365; II 382-83; ÷ K) It is prescribed that if men take to raiding in our country or make what a panel verdict decides is a raid, however they contrive it, going to islands or caves or fortified places or ships, wherever they take refuge when making raids, then they at once become men who may not be sustained and they forfeit their immunity in relation to everybody, they have a price of eight ounce-units on their heads[55] and their corpses are to be covered like outlaws' corpses[56] as soon

---

53. See ‡ 86 (p. 139).
54. Ibid.
55. Cf. ‡ 102 (p. 164).
56. Cf. ‡ 2 (p. 30), Add. ‡‡ 5, 131.

as men have heard of a raid, and they may not be sustained even if it has not been published. But raiding is when men take people or people's property from them against their will or beat or bind or wound people if they have the power. If they are not killed in their raiding, it is lawful to do whichever is preferred, either summon them locally for raiding or publish it at the assembly and prosecute the same summer, making outlawry the penalty. Those men who are the first victims of their raiding in the Quarter are to call nine neighbors locally from around the place where the raiding began in that Quarter. But all the other men in the Quarter who were later victims of those men's raiding are to do as they prefer, call neighbors locally from around the place where the raiding began in the Quarter or else call neighbors at the assembly from around the place where the raid for which they prosecute them was made. Cases are to be prosecuted before the court for the Quarter from which the majority of neighbors are called. But if the same men go raiding in more Quarters than one, the prosecution against them is to proceed in every Quarter in the same way as now rehearsed for one. *What constitutes raiding* *To summon for raiding*

121. (St ‡ 366; II 383–84; ÷ K) If men plan raids with those who go raiding, whether they are there with them or elsewhere, or if a man knowingly receives something that they took on a raid, although not there himself, the penalty in both cases is the same as if they had accompanied them on their raiding. *Complicity in raiding*

If a man kills a man who is on a raid, he is to call neighbors of the place of action to give a verdict as to whether the other had been raiding since the last General Assembly. If the panel gives the verdict that he was on a raid, then the court judgment is to be that he fell with forfeit immunity and all his property is under penalty, a price of eight ounce-units on his head, and damages are to be adjudged from the brigand's property now under penalty to the men he had robbed, such a share to each as each had lost. If it does not amount to so much, each sum is to be proportionally reduced. But if it amounts to more, then the outlaw's price is to be taken from the extra. But if there is not enough for this, he is to claim it in the same way as any other outlaw's price.[57] *If a raider is killed*

If a man wants to prosecute for raiding, he must prosecute before or at the third General Assembly from the time the principal heard of it, but it is never too late if news of it is kept from him. *Time limit for prosecution*

122. (St ‡ 367; II 384–85; ÷ K) If a man takes another man's property and commits theft thereby,[58] or it is found in his hands, then the one who took the property falls at that place of action with forfeit immunity if *Theft*

---

57. Cf. ‡ 110 (pp. 171-72).
58. Prosecution for theft itself is treated in ‡ 227.

killed by the man who owned the property that was stolen and also if killed by anyone who gives the latter help in this. They are not to avenge anything but the theft committed by the man who took the property found there in his hands at that place of action.

Prosecution for injury to thief; counter-charge of forfeit immunity

If a principal prepares a case against a man who inflicted injury on a man who was caught with stolen property in his hands, then the man against whom the case is prepared is to make a counter-summons against the man who took the property and maintain that he was a man of forfeit immunity if he was killed or under penalty of outlawry if he is alive and claim his wounds have no legal redress. Nine neighbors of the place of action called locally have to decide on killing and wounds and similarly whether stolen property was found in the hands of the man on whom injury was inflicted at that place of action or whether it was not. But if the panel gives a verdict that stolen property was found in his hands at the time when injury was inflicted on him and that they inflicted injury on him at that place of action for that reason, then he falls with forfeit immunity if that theft carried outlawry as its penalty. It is also lawful for the man who is to defend himself in the case to call neighbors locally to decide that the man who took the property forfeited his immunity and for him to publish the case at the assembly.

If a man is killed on board ship

123. (St ‡ 368; II 385; ÷ K)   It is further prescribed in our laws that if a man is killed on board a ship when men voyage here to the country, then until they arrive in our country men incur no penalty for sharing living quarters with the killer on that side of the mast where men have fewer differences with others. But they are immediately under penalty for sharing living quarters with the killer if they stay overnight with him when they come to the mainland. All other men incur no penalty for sharing living quarters with him or for assisting him until the killing is published. Neighbors of the landing place where they lay up their ship are to be called, but if they make a return voyage, then of the landing place where most of them brought their belongings ashore. But if men who leave the country give and receive injuries, neighbors are to be called from the landing place where most of them carried their belongings on board.

If an Icelander is killed abroad

124. (St ‡ 369; II 386; cf. Add. ‡ 91; ÷ K)   If a countryman of ours is killed abroad, the killer is under the same penalty for that killing as if the killing were done in our country. Prosecution may be undertaken here for a foreign killing even though it has been prosecuted or settled abroad, unless the man who settled in accordance with law there is the principal in the case, and then the settlement is to be kept here if they make that a point in their agreement there.

A prosecution is not to be started here before the third General Assembly from the time the news of the killing gets here, unless the killer comes to the country before then. The prosecutor of the case is to ask at

Lögberg before witnesses which assembly the killer is attached to and which assemblies the men who were at the killing and he wishes to prosecute are attached to.[59] He is also to ask before witnesses if any other men wish to prosecute the killer or those men he wishes to prosecute for presence at the killing. If all those prosecuted are from the same Quarter, then the cases are to come before the Quarter Court for the Quarter they are from. And if the prosecutors of cases are all from one Quarter while the others against whom cases are brought are from different Quarters, then the cases are to come before the Quarter Court for the Quarter the prosecutors are from. If no one admits the assembly attachment of the men prosecuted and the prosecutors do not all come from the same Quarter, then those who prosecute are to draw lots among themselves to decide before which of the Quarter Courts for the Quarters from which they come the cases are to be brought. But if men admit the assembly attachment of the men prosecuted and they are not all from the same Quarter, the prosecutors are again to draw lots to decide before which of the Quarter Courts for the Quarters from which the others come the cases are to be brought.

125. (St ‡ 370; II 387; cf. Add. ‡ 91; ÷ K) The prosecutor is also to publish a charge of foreign killing at Lögberg against the killer and state in which king's realm he killed him and publish it for prosecution and for the fullest penalty just as in any other killing case. If the killing has taken place in the realm of the king of Norway or of the king of the Danes or of the king of the Swedes, the prosecutor is to bring forward five of our countrymen and two of the five must have been in the realm of that king when the killing was done or been there subsequently. It will serve if three of them have stayed permanently in the country here but all must be qualified in terms of connection. These five men are to speak in these terms at the court and swear oaths beforehand and say that this man was killed in that kingdom — and name the man killed — "and that this man N.N. who is now prosecuted here was there at that time — and we give our word of honor on that and we pronounce this scratch verdict here before the court."

Further on procedure in case of killing in Scandinavia

Verdict of a scratch panel

126. (St ‡ 371; II 387–88; cf. Add. ‡ 91; ÷ K) The defender in the case is also to bring forward five men and he is to select them in the same way as rehearsed earlier. They are to give their word of honor that the man killed was none the closer to death because of the presence of that man in that kingdom. If there is no substance for that, they are to give their word of honor that he was on service with the king or some man in authority and could not be master of his movements, and that the man killed fell a

Defense by scratch panel

---

59. See ‡ 22 (pp. 55-57).

victim to their advance. If there is no substance for that, then they are to give their word of honor that the killer was defending his property or his life when the other man fell. If there is no substance for that, they are to give their word of honor that the man killed was on a pirate ship when he was killed. They are to pronounce one of these scratch verdicts before the court and speak in the terms previously rehearsed. But if none of these scratch verdicts comes forward for the defense, the killer is under penalty.

A man killed in Western Europe or the British Isles

127. (St ‡ 372; II 388–9; cf. Add. ‡ 91; ÷ K) If a man is killed in western Europe north of Valland,[60] then every man is equally well qualified to vouch in the case who has been in the realm of any king among those countries at the time of the killing or subsequently, in the realm of the king of the English or of the king of the Welsh or of the king of the Scots or the king of the Irish or the king of the Hebrideans.[61] If a man is killed south of the realm of the Danes, then every man is equally well qualified to vouch in the case who was in the realm of any king among those countries at the time of the killing or subsequently. The procedure for these killings is to be the same in both prosecution and defense and in all other respects as for foreign killings, and similarly for any wounds a man may get in those places. If a man gets a wound or is struck while abroad, the penalty is outlawry and he has moreover the right to prosecute his case here even though he also prosecutes it in accordance with law there, but not if he has settled there with a complete settlement, and the man who prosecutes for wounds he got in Norway, and the man who defends too, are to proceed as in cases of foreign killing except that he is not prosecuting on account of a dead man.

Robbery abroad

A new law. If a man is robbed of his property abroad, the robbery is to be prosecuted here with the same formal means of proof, and also defended.[62]

Plots plotted abroad

As for plots made abroad by someone who plots against a man's life or plots to disfigure, they are not liable to legal penalty here if they are not given effect, but outlawry if they are.

60. I.e., north of Normandy and the Lower Seine region.

61. Norway ceded Hebrides and Man to Scotland in 1266 and the title of "King of the Isles" lapsed thereafter. Ireland had many local kings and a High Kingship. Rule in Wales was usually divided among several princes who, though they had the power of kings, were seldom given the regal title. It is of interest to note that the codification of *Vígslóði* in 1117-18 (to which this passage is probably attributable) took place in the long reign of a ruler who would pass better than most as "king of the Welsh" — Gruffydd ap Cynan (1099-1137), partly Norse by birth and closely connected with Norse-Irish Dublin. (We are indebted to Professor H. Loyn and Dr Gwyn A. Williams for clarification of medieval Welsh regality.)

62. Cf. Add. ‡ 91, p. 223/38-40.

Blows struck abroad, plots to disfigure or plots against life given effect abroad, are all to be prosecuted with a panel of twelve and the prosecution is not to be started here sooner than in a case of foreign killing.[63] If grounds for defense that are offered in such suits and have to be assessed took place abroad, a scratch panel is everywhere to be used for them, but if the grounds for defense that are offered took place here, then a panel of five neighbors is to be used at the assembly. *Procedure for prosecution and defence*

128. (St ‡ 373; II 389; ÷ K) If a man is killed in Greenland,[64] that is also to be prosecuted here like other foreign killings except that men who vouch in the case are not required to have been there either at the time or subsequently. Regard shall only be had to their connections in selecting them. If the principal is in Greenland and settles there over a killing or prosecutes for it, then there is no prosecution case to be made here. If the principal is not over there and someone else prosecutes it to the limit of the law, the principal has nevertheless the right to prosecute here for assistance to the man in question, and he does not need to take over such cases formally from anyone else. But if a man who is not the principal prosecutes over there and not to the limit of the law, then a prosecution case may be made here. *If a man is killed in Greenland*

129. (St ‡ 374; II 389–90; ÷ K) If someone is outlawed in Greenland, then everyone is outlawed here who is outlawed there. And assistance for the outlawed man who over there was put under the fullest penalty is to be prosecuted as if he had been outlawed here at a spring assembly and before his outlawry is reported at the General Assembly.[65] A man may defend the suit for such a killing here by bringing forward at court five of our countrymen who give their word of honor that the man killed was none the closer to death because that man was there or else that that man had his property or his life to defend. *Outlawry in Greenland means outlawry in Iceland*

130. (From St ‡ 379; II 395/20–23; + K p. 172) — to the man who owned him as assessed by five neighbors and have offered the payment within the next half month. And if he does not offer the payment in this way, his penalty is lesser outlawry. *If a slave is killed*

(ii) (II 395/24–396/2; + K p. 172) And a man does something to another requiring half personal compensation when he commits such personal offenses as carry a penalty of lesser outlawry. *Half personal compensation*

(iii) (II 396/15–17; + K p. 173) If the man who kills his own slave has a chieftaincy, the case lies with the other chieftains of the same assembly. *Killing one's own slave*

---

63. See Add. ‡ 124 (p. 232).

64. The Greenlanders lived in two coastal settlements in southwest Greenland; the colonization was made from Iceland *c.* 985, but the Greenlanders were politically independent.

65. See ‡ 59 (p. 108).

Slave injures slave   (iv) (II 396/18–20; + K p. 173)   All that payment is to be made in objects of value and each of them shall appoint his own legal valuer.

Slave kills slave   (v) (II 396/28–397/5; cf. K p. 173)   One choice is to pay for the slave as assessed by neighbors. The second choice is to pay for the killed slave with half his price and for the other half pay over the one who killed him within the next fortnight. The third choice is to let the slave be prosecuted for the killing. But if slaves who fight to the death belong to the same man, he arranges it then as he pleases.

Execution of captured outlaw   131. (St ‡ 380; II 397-98; cf. K p. 171)   It is prescribed that if outlaws are killed the procedure is to be as will now be told. Where men capture an outlaw they are not to take him more than a bowshot from that place if they have to execute him. They are to cover his corpse in a place where there is neither arable land nor meadow land and from where no waters flow to houses, beyond bowshot from anyone's wall.[66] If they do not cover the corpse of an outlaw, the penalty is a fine of three marks.[67] And if they execute the outlaw in a forbidden place, the penalty is a fine of three marks and the court is to enjoin them by judgment to move the outlaw away in the next fortnight and that case lies with the man who owns the land. But they are only under penalty for taking an outlaw more than a bowshot if they earth his corpse on land in other ownership than that on which they captured him. But if they wish to take an outlaw to the man who got him condemned, it is lawful for them to do so, and they are to take him bound and offer their help in going with him to the place where he means to execute him.

Releasing or assisting an outlaw   If the man who got him condemned lets the outlaw go, the penalty is outlawry and the case lies with the men who took the man to him, and he further loses every right to proceed against people who assist the outlaw. If the man who got him condemned sends an outlaw to other men or assists him in any way, then he loses the right to proceed against anyone else who assists the outlaw, and his penalty is outlawry and the case lies with anyone who wishes to prosecute him for it on the grounds that he knowingly assisted an outlaw he himself had got condemned, and the prosecutor is to make outlawry the penalty and claim that he has lost all right to proceed against anyone who assists the outlaw and claim that such cases now lie with himself.

No one is under penalty for giving food to an outlaw when men are taking him to the man who got him condemned.

Reward for killing or capturing an outlaw   Where men kill an outlaw, the price on his head is due to the one who first hit him with a weapon. But if they chase him onto weapons or into

---

66. Cf. p. 30, n. 22, Add. ‡ 84 (ii).
67. Cf. ‡ 2 (p. 30), Add. ‡ 5.

perilous places, they all share the price equally, and similarly if they take him to the man who got him condemned, and they are to draw lots to decide which of them is to claim it.

132. (St ‡ 381; II 398-99; cf. Add. ‡ 133 (viii); ÷ K)   If outlaws run into abandoned buildings or into uninhabited shielings, men have the right to break into those buildings to get at them if they want, or to burn them if they cannot overcome them in any other way. They are to pay for the building to the man who owned it at the value set on it by five neighbors by oath on a book.[68]

Damage to property in pursuit of outlaws

If outlaws run away from people into buildings where men not under legal penalty are inside, then those who pursue them are to ask the men not under penalty to come out. If they will not come out, the penalty is outlawry if the outlaws are assisted thereby. If anyone breaks into a building to get at outlaws, the building loses its immunity and men previously not under legal penalty lose theirs if they shield outlawed men,[69] but they are to pay compensation for the damage to the man who owned the building, at the value set on it by five neighbors, if they do not come out. Buildings are not to be burnt to get at outlaws if they are not abandoned buildings. If outlaws have as many men or more as the others who are inside the building with them, and these cannot leave because of the outlaws, then their stay under the same roof puts them under no legal penalty if they can get a clearing verdict that they were unable to leave or did not dare to.

If slaves or bounden debtors kill an outlaw, the price is due to the men who have money owed them by those who killed the outlaw.

If a slave or debt-slave kills an outlaw

133. (From St ‡ 382; II 399/13-17; cf. K p. 171)   If a man kills an outlaw, he is to publish it within twelve hours and announce it to a legally resident man. But if he does not announce it within twelve hours, he may not claim the outlaw's price. But the killing of an outlaw is only to be murder if a panel gives a verdict that he tried to conceal it.

Publishing the killing to claim the reward

(ii) (II 399/17-400/5; cf. K p. 170)   All outlaws have the right to kill other outlaws for their own reprieve if they will, only not if they were outlawed for thieving cases or killing cases or for any case which may not be settled without prior leave unless special permission is asked.[70] If an outlaw has killed another outlaw for his own reprieve, he is to go to a house where he thinks he is in no danger, and announce to a man legally resident there that he has killed an outlaw and show the corpse. Then he is to be an outlaw who may not be sustained but who may be given passage

Outlaws who kill others for reprieve

---

68. Cf. p. 172, n. 160.
69. Cf. ‡ 100 (p. 163), Add ‡ 85.
70. I.e., of the Law Council, cf. ‡ 117 (p. 190 and n. 2).

without right of return to the country. And if a man kills two outlaws, he is then a lesser outlaw, and if he kills a third, his reprieve is complete. And similarly if he kills a single outlaw with the bigger price on his head,[71] then his reprieve is to be complete.

A slave outlawed for killing his master

(iii) (II 400/7; + K p. 170) — those who live closest to the corpse —.
(iv) (II 400/13; + K p. 170) — or fosterer or their children —.
(v) (II 400/16; + K p. 170) — at a road-junction —.
(vi) (II 401/1–2; cf. K p. 171) If they will not take him, they are required to torture him to make him talk.

Claim after killing higher-priced outlaws

(vii) (II 401/26–402/2; cf. K p. 172) If a man kills an outlaw, one of the four with a bigger price on his head, he is nevertheless to publish that suit at Lögberg as a claim for the outlaw's price, three marks in legal tender, on all the chieftains in the ancient chieftaincies, that existed in the Quarter he belongs to when the assemblies were undivided, and on all the men of their assembly thirds —.

(viii) (II 402/6–22; + K p. 172; cf. K p. 171; Add. ‡ 132) The penalty is lesser outlawry if it is not paid.

Meeting an outlaw

If men see an outlaw as they travel, they are under no legal penalty if they do not capture him as long as they have nothing to do with him. But if they barter with him or have any other kind of exchange, or give him advice so that he is then closer to saving his life than he was before, that is assistance for him and the penalty is lesser outlawry. Anything men do or any advice men give so that an outlaw is closer to saving his life than he was before is assistance to him, no matter whether whatever is deemed assistance is large or small.

Buildings must not be burnt in pursuit of outlaws

Men are not to burn a building which has other men's livestock in it in order to get at outlaws, even when it contains nobody who is not under penalty or they cannot get at the outlaws in any other way — they are still not to burn the building. And if they burn the building despite the fact that other men's livestock are inside, that is to be prosecuted like any other burning. If they do not offer the men who owned the house they broke into or burnt such compensation as five neighbors assess the building to be worth within the next half month, it is to be prosecuted like any other burning, or as malicious damage if it is broken.[72]

Definition of a bowshot

134. (From Troilsbók, fol. 189v; III 716; cf. K pp. 141-42; Add. ‡ 103) And a bowshot is when an arrow is placed on a bowstring and so shot from the place of the last encounter and from there to the place where the arrow comes down of itself if there is no obstruction to impede it.

---

71. See ‡ 102 (p. 164).
72. See ‡‡ 109, 63 (pp. 169, 116).

Guide to Technical Vocabulary

I
Annotated Glossary

The Icelandic equivalents of the English headwords will be found against the same headwords (designated by an asterisk) in the Guide to Technical Vocabulary section II, pp. 262-69.

Cross-references in the entries are indicated by italic.

For the system of reference numbers see Introduction, p. 18.

Where appropriate, page-references are included to *IS*, i.e., to *A History of the Old Icelandic Commonwealth: Íslendinga saga* by Jón Jóhannesson, translated by Haraldur Bessason; University of Manitoba Icelandic Studies II (1974).

AGREEMENT See *Formal agreement*.

ARBITRATORS Men put up from each side to arrange the terms of a *private settlement*. Cf. pp. 109-10, Add. ‡ 36; further ‡ 244.

ASSEMBLY ATTACHMENT See *Assembly third*.

ASSEMBLY ATTENDANCE DUES A sum agreed between the *chieftain* and his assembly men to be paid by every *householder* with means above a prescribed level if he or a proper representative did not attend the *General Assembly* and to be received by *assembly participants* who did attend. A householder with means above the level at which dues became payable (it was higher for the man who farmed single-handed) was affected by his status in several ways: it made him an assembly participant, qualified him to serve on *panels,* gave him full membership of the *commune*, made him responsible for lodging travelers, ruled him out as a receiver of charity. Cf. pp. 41, 48, 57-58, 71-73, 125, 150-51, 171, Add. ‡ 34 (ii). *ÍS* 61.

ASSEMBLY-BALKING Any manipulation, disturbance, or delay of assembly procedures that hinders their effective working. The standard penalty is *lesser outlawry.* See pp. 58, 61, 74, 77, 79, 81-82, 102, 189-90, 191, 193.

ASSEMBLY GROUP See *Assembly third*.

ASSEMBLY MAN See *Assembly third*.

ASSEMBLY MEMBERSHIP   See *Assembly third*.

ASSEMBLY PARTICIPANTS   *Chieftains* and *householders* liable to pay *assembly attendance dues* were assembly participants. Qualified men could act as substitutes for householders as long as their *settled home* was in the household they represented. The same men were qualified to act on panels of *neighbors*. At *spring assemblies* a *household man* could meet for his householder. At an assembly the participants' number was augmented by those called locally to provide *formal means of proof*. For full participation in the business of an assembly all such men had to arrive at a spring assembly not later than one night after it began and at the *General Assembly* not later than the first Sunday. See pp. 43, 58, 64, 73, 100, 107-08, 125, 151, 161, 172, Add. ‡ 12.

ASSEMBLY SLOPE   The place at *spring assemblies*, corresponding to *Lögberg* at the General Assembly, where announcements, *publishings*, and *summons* were made. Cf. pp. 101, 108, 122.

ASSEMBLY THIRD   Each *spring assembly* was held under the supervision of three *chieftains*. The assembly to which a chieftain belonged dictated the assembly attachment and attendance of the men who were his supporters; they belonged to his "assembly group" or "assembly third". Everyone had to belong to some chieftain's assembly group, *householders* independently and others through their householders, but it was a matter of contract: a man said publicly that he was joining the assembly group of a given chieftain, and if the chieftain concurred, his "assembly membership" or "attachment" was fixed. He could also say that he was leaving an assembly group or a chieftain could say that a man no longer belonged to his assembly group; he then had to join another. Permission from the *Law Council* was needed to have an assembly man in a *Quarter* other than the one the chieftain lived in (except over the fjord in Hrútafjörðr, see Map I). Change of *residence* would often necessitate change of assembly attachment and in some cases this was prescribed, with or without choice. Men of a chieftain's assembly third had to attend spring assemblies (or send a representative) and at least one in nine of them had to attend the General Assembly; it was from among them that the chieftain selected men to act as *judges*, and as members of *panels of twelve*, and for other legal duties. Cf. pp. 55, 58, 62-63, 132-36, Add. ‡‡ 34 (ii), 35.

ASSISTANCE   A general term for assisting (sheltering, sustaining, ferrying, advising, or simply sharing food and living quarters with) people who could not be assisted without liability to penalty: either after they had committed an offense and the charge against them was *published* but not yet judged ("not to be sustained pending judgment") or after they had been made *outlaws*. Ignorance might be allowed as a total or partial defense. Cf. pp. 119, 124-25, 141, Add. ‡‡ 71, 73, 103-05, 133 (viii).

ATONEMENT   See *Wergild ring*.

AUTUMN MEETING   A meeting lasting not less than one night and not more than two days in the autumn between the outside dates of 16 July and 23 August (cf. p. 111, n. 157). It was held on the site of the *spring assembly*, or elsewhere by arrangement, under the superintendence of the three *chieftains* of the assembly. It was especially intended to bring knowledge of General Assembly proceedings and announcements (including the calendar) to those members of the local assembly groups who had stayed at home, but it could also be the occasion for other business. Cf. pp. 37, 51, 90, 111-12, 128, 136, 163. *ÍS* 82-83.

BITS   See *Wergild ring*.

BOOTH-PANEL   In cases arising from conflict at the *General Assembly* nine qualified men were called from the nearest booths able to provide three apiece to give *verdicts* as required, like a panel of *neighbors*. Cf. p. 163, Add. ‡ 76.

BOUNDEN DEBTOR   A person taken into bondservice because of debt (which might arise as a result of legal penalty). Bondservice was obligatory for someone who could not maintain his parents; if he could not maintain his children he could either go into bondservice himself or put them into bondservice. A bounden debtor is classed with the *slave* in provisions concerning flight and harboring, in absence of responsibility for offenses and of interest in certain rewards. Bondservice ended with payment of the debt. Cf. pp. 42, 46, 84, 159, 171, Add. ‡‡ 14 (ii), 132; further ‡‡ 128, 158. *ÍS* 354.

BOWSHOT (CORDON)   A standard distance (see p. 30, n. 22) applied in a variety of circumstances (separation of hostile parties, location of *confiscation courts*, of graves of malefactors, immunity for lesser *outlaws*, impeding someone's movement). Cf. pp. 30, 89, 112, 141-42, 146, Add. ‡‡ 84 (ii), 103, 131, 134.

CALL, CALLING   A *witness* or a neighbor needed on a panel of *neighbors* had to be formally told that he was required to attend a given assembly or *court*, there to perform his legal duties as part of a litigant's *formal means of proof*. He was "called" by the *principal* or the man to whom he had *transferred* the calling. If there was error in the number of neighbors called, the extra men had to be formally told they did not need to attend — the call was "lifted from them." Calling was done in set form locally, or at the assembly as prescribed, or in accordance with circumstances (cf. *Summon*). If he was a *household man* or a *householder* who did not pay *assembly attendance dues*, the man called might lawfully ask for means (horse and food) to attend the *General Assembly*. In certain cases undecided at one assembly the men required to provide formal means of proof were automatically called to attend the next assembly where the case would be heard. "Reliance witnesses" (of a man's calling) were men who might be expected to attend an assembly without being specifically called. Cf. pp. 23, 63-64, 67, 69-70, 118, 149-54, Add. ‡‡ 56, 59, 60, 61 (ii), 109-11.

CASE CONFERRING RIGHTS OF VETO See *Veto*.

CHALLENGE A man nominated as a *judge*, named and called as a *witness*, or called to serve on a panel of *neighbors* had to be qualified in various ways and if he were not he could be challenged and dismissed. The chief grounds for challenge were kinship, kinship by marriage, spiritual kinship, legal involvement (all these in relation to *principals* in a case), lack of status as an *assembly participant*, and distance in the case of panels of neighbors. If a man was successfully challenged as a judge or panel member, he was normally simply replaced by someone else who was qualified. See pp. 59-62, 71-72, 149, 152, Add. ‡ 57. *IS* 67-69.

CHIEFTAIN, CHIEFTAINCY There were thirty-six "ancient and full" chieftaincies in Iceland; another three were instituted *c*. 965; the number was made up to 48 *c*. 1005 for the purposes of the *Fifth Court* (cf. p. 83, n. 80). It was the thirty-six ancient and full chieftaincies which gave their holders authority to nominate *judges* at the *General Assembly* but the additional three of *c*. 965 could, like them, nominate courts at *spring assemblies* and *confiscation courts*, form *panels of twelve*, provide a chieftain's *veto*, sit in the *Law Council*, and have certain rights of last-resort prosecution and claim. A chieftaincy was private property. It might be owned by one or more persons, but only one man could act in it at any time; he might be the owner or part owner, but could also be a man to whom the authority was formally *transferred* (in case of emergency the other chieftains of the same spring assembly might invest a man from the missing chieftain's *assembly third* with the authority). A chieftain's penalty for certain offenses included forfeit of the chieftaincy. Cf. pp. 53-54, 57, 61-63, 80, 83-84, 106-08, 116, 122-23, 132-33, 135-36. *IS* 56-63.

CHIEFTAIN'S VETO See *Veto*.

CLEARING VERDICT A *verdict* of a panel of *neighbors* which, if favorable, provided a valid defense for the man prosecuted. If prosecuted by means of a panel of five neighbors, that same panel should be called to give a clearing verdict; if by a panel of nine, five members selected from that panel; if by a panel of twelve, five neighbors of the man prosecuted. Cf. pp. 60, 74, 77, 155.

COMMUNE An association of whom at least 20 were *householders* liable to pay *assembly attendance dues*. The commune was responsible for arranging local affairs, chiefly the care of *incapable people*, allocation of charitable gifts (through an elected committee of five), and mutual insurance. They had regular meetings (*samkvámur*). See pp. 28 and n. 14, 41, 46; further ‡‡ 234-35. *IS* 83-88.

COMPENSATION "Compensation" usually means *personal compensation* (as also the phrase "killing compensation"). Compensation for damage (to property) was usually assessed by *neighbors* under *oath*. Cf. pp. 92, 116, 157, 158-61, 176, 181, Add. ‡‡ 67 (ii)-(iv), 87, 111.

CONFISCATION COURT When a man was outlawed a confiscation court was held, normally outside his home, a fortnight after the assembly at which he was outlawed or at which the appropriate *chieftain* was asked to nominate such a court. The court dealt with every matter concerning the outlaw's property: adjudging what was due to his wife, creditors, and the presiding chieftain, deciding what should be done for his dependents, and adjudging half of whatever was left to the man who got him condemned and half to the men of the assembly, if he was outlawed locally, or to the men of the *Quarter*, if he was outlawed at the *General Assembly*. According to ‡ 73 (p. 121) the confiscation court should also judge that the outlaw's sentence should now take effect (possibly only in the case of *lesser outlaws*). Sentence of lesser outlawry lapsed if no confiscation court was held. See pp. 88-93, 108, 112-21, 123.

CONTRARY TESTIMONY A *panel verdict* at odds with testimony offered by *witnesses*, or testimony at odds with a verdict (testimony had to precede panel verdicts in the procedure), is inadmissible contrary testimony and subject to penalty. See p. 77.

COURT See *Confiscation court, Debt court, District court, Fifth Court, Quarter Court, Private settlement*.

DEBT ASSEMBLY See *Spring assembly*.

DEBT COURT A court established to control the allotment of property when a man died insolvent. The procedure of such courts was also prescribed for the *confiscation court* held after a man had been outlawed. Cf. p. 90, n. 106.

DEPENDENT, INCAPABLE PERSON   Icelandic *ómagi* means someone incapable of maintaining himself or herself by working (because of childhood, old age, or other infirmity). For this the translation uses "dependent" when the responsibility for maintaining such a person lay with an individual, "incapable person" when the responsibility lay with the community (in the latter case such people were usually *itinerant*). Rules about working times and wage contracts might be relaxed for men with "households of dependents." The share of an outlaw's property that fell to the community was first devoted to maintenance of his dependents otherwise to maintenance of other incapable persons itinerant in the relevant district. Cf. pp. 41, 46, 78, 91-92, 101, 113-15; further ‡‡ 128-43.

DISTRICT COURTS   *Ad hoc* local courts not held at established assemblies. Among them were commune courts, outfield courts, communal pasture courts, courts for foreign traders. Cf. p. 109, n. 147.

DIVIDED JUDGMENT, GIVE DIVIDED JUDGMENT   If *judges* in a *spring assembly* court or *Quarter Court* disagreed and there were more than six in the minority (or possibly irrespective of the numbers involved), each of the two groups had to make a formal effort to procure unanimity. If this proved unsuccessful, each group then pronounced its judgment, and the case where such a divided judgment was given then went automatically to a Quarter Court from a spring assembly, to the *Fifth Court* from a Quarter Court. Judges who had sided with the judgment not confirmed by the court of second instance were liable to prosecution. The same expression but not the same procedure is used of disagreement in the Fifth Court and at district courts. Cf. pp. 82-83, 88, 103, 191. *ÍS* 69, 73-74.

ELL   The early Icelandic ell was *c.* 49 cm (19.4 inches); later a longer ell of *c.* 54-57 cm was also used. Standard *homespun* was measured in the latter: six ells of cloth, of given quality and two ells broad, provided the normal *ounce-unit*.

ENJOIN BY JUDGMENT   See *Judge*.

FIFTH COURT   A court of first instance at the *General Assembly* for certain specified offenses, of second instance in the case of *divided judgments* from *Quarter Courts*. In nominating *judges* for this court the men acting in the thirty-six ancient and full *chieftaincies* were supplemented by twelve acting in new chieftaincies (presumably the three additional chieftaincies established in the North *Quarter c.* 965 and three more from each of the other Quarters). Of the forty-eight judges nominated twelve had to be set aside by the litigants, so that only thirty-six gave judgment (*summing up* might be done by men from among the twelve set aside). Decisions were by majority; a tie normally decided a case in favor of the prosecution, but if it was a tie in a case of a previous divided judgment at a Quarter Court, a decision was reached by drawing lots. Cf. pp. 83-88. *IS* 70-74.

FINE   Fines are common penalties, imposed in consequence of a suit and *judgment* (summary punishment except on slaves did not exist). Whenever an unspecified fine is mentioned, it is the standard fine of three *marks* (twenty-four legal *ounce-units*) that is intended. Half a fine generally went to the prosecutor, half to the *Lawspeaker* (at the *General Assembly*) or to the men of the assembly (at a *spring assembly*). Payment of the fine was enjoined by judgment; failure to pay was *judgment breaking.* Cf. pp. 50, 80, 117, 188, 193.

FORBID BY VETO   See *Veto.*

FORMAL AGREEMENT, GUARANTEE   Formal agreement or guarantee (to pay on one's own or someone else's behalf, to accept outlawry as a penalty or possible penalty, to take over a case, to make a contract, etc.) was made by word of mouth and a handshake. In some transactions this was obligatory, as were witnesses to it. Cf. pp. 27, 92, 117, 122; 109, 119-20. Add. ‡‡ 36, 74.

FORMAL MEANS OF PROOF   These comprised, as necessary or as available, panels of *neighbors, witnesses,* and men to vouch on their *word of honor* for their belief in the truth of what was delivered; such men counted as *assembly participants.* In subsequent proceedings it might be necessary to provide formal means of proof (normally the attest of witnesses) that formal means of proof had been produced earlier. Where the first formal means of proof consisted of witnessing, the second is called "testimony of testimony." Cf. pp. 58, 66, 75, 80-81, 99, 101-02, 106, 108-09, 138.

FORMALLY INAUGURATE AN ASSEMBLY   An initial ceremony at an assembly established a higher degree of peacefulness for its duration and within the assembly boundaries. *Personal compensation* payable for injury was doubled as long as this extra *immunity* was in being. Various offenders were not permitted to attend formally inaugurated assemblies. See pp. 43, 99 (and n. 124), 111-12, 162-64. *IS* 45-46.

FREEDMAN   See *Slave.*

FREEDOM-GIVER See *Slave*.

FULL OUTLAW(RY) Full outlawry cast a man out of society. The outlaw forfeited his property and all rights, civil, family, and ecclesiastical. He could not lawfully be given any *assistance* — sustenance, passage, or any saving advice. He might be killed by anyone with impunity and had a price on his head; this applied for ever even if he escaped abroad. In certain cases he could win reprieve by killing other outlaws. Full outlaws whose sentence was imposed by *private settlement* might benefit from mitigation: passage from the country might be permitted for them, their banishment might be local or temporary. Cf. pp. 30, 96-98, 119-21, 170-72, Add. ‡‡ 131-33.

GENERAL ASSEMBLY The assembly for the whole of Iceland, held at Þingvöllr (see Maps I and II) between Thursday 18-24 June and Wednesday 2-8 July. It was a public meeting open to all free people and obligatorily attended by men acting in all the *chieftaincies* in the country (those of them with assembly groups accompanied by at least one in nine of their *assembly men*) and by all men who were *assembly participants* because of their legal duties. The General Assembly provided the setting for the election of the *Lawspeaker* and the recital of the laws; the work of the *Law Council* in framing laws and giving licenses; the judgments of the four *Quarter Courts*, the *Fifth Court*, and the special Priests' Court; payment of certain sums; publication of *new laws, judgments*, and the calendar for the coming year; and legal announcements of all kinds. Cf. pp. 37-38, 51, 57-58, 108, 187-93. *IS* 35-49.

GOOD MAN AND TRUE A free member of the community of recognized integrity who met the requirements of the law for nomination as a judge or for other legal duties. It is sometimes prescribed that a man should give his *word of honor* (literally "make his quality as a man of integrity hang on it" — *leggja undir þegnskap sinn*). This kind of asseveration contained no reference to religious sanction, but it seems to have been preceded by the general *oath*, sworn by anyone participating in processes of the law, which did contain such reference. Cf. 54, 60-61, 67, 71, Add. ‡‡ 125-26.

HEIR, NATURAL HEIR, LAWFUL HEIR A natural heir had various obligations, in taking a child for baptism or a corpse for burial, maintaining *dependents* and acting as a *principal* in a lawsuit. Cf. pp. 23, 26, further ‡‡ 118-27.

HOMESPUN Cloth of standard quality, two *ells* wide, which in pieces of set length served as a form of currency related to silver and other legal tender (generally as *ounce-units* of six ells). Cloth was the chief Icelandic product in staple demand abroad, and when "trade goods" are referred to, homespun is usually meant. Cf. pp. 32, 36-37, 126. *IS* 331-33.

HOUSEHOLD ATTACHMENT Every person was supposed to be attached to a particular household. This attachment implied a special relation between the *householder* and the person to whom he gave *lodging* in his household and between the latter and other people with places there. Members of a householder's immediate family were automatically attached to his household; others joined it by agreement, as workers (*household men*), or in other capacities. A man's household attachment would determine what his legal duties were, where he should be *summoned*, which *assembly group* he belonged to. Cf. pp. 125-32. *IS* 354-57.

HOUSEHOLD MAN (WOMAN) A free man or woman attached to a household by agreement with the *householder*, cf. *Household attachment*. A household man could act as a substitute for his householder in certain situations, but in some situations might be held to have less legal responsibility than him. If *called* to attend the General Assembly, he could claim aid (horse and food) from the man calling him. Cf. pp. 42, 63-64, 69, 100, 118, 125-32, 151-52. *IS* 354-57.

HOUSEHOLDER, HOUSEHOLD(ING) A householder was the head of a household counted independent either because he owned land or, if a tenant, owned milking stock. Joint householding was also possible. The householder represented the household in the performance of legal duties, but to be an *assembly participant* in the ordinary way he must have the means that make him liable to pay *assembly attendance dues*. A close relative whose settled home was in the household could act as a substitute for him, as was the rule in the case of a woman householder or an unfit householder, and in some circumstances a *household man* could act as his deputy. Cf. pp. 42, 63-64, 72-73, 100, 107, 124-25, 132, 150-52, Add. ‡‡ 59, 69. *IS* 344-49.

IMMUNITY, FORFEIT IMMUNITY Every free person not under legal penalty and everything animate or inanimate belonging to such a free person enjoyed immunity as of right. If that immunity was violated by injury or insult, redress could be had by legal process, or in some cases immediate physical retaliation was legally permitted (cf. *Right to kill*). In the latter case subsequent justification at law would require demonstration that the first offender or someone aiding him had forfeited his immunity by his own act and so lost his right to legal redress. A *full outlaw* lost his immunity totally; *lesser outlaws* and others with mitigation of their penalty lost theirs conditionally. Particular immunity was extended to assemblies when *formally inaugurated* for as long as they lasted and in the area they covered. Cf. pp. 139-42, 154-55, 167-69, Add. ‡‡ 46, 63, 85.

INCAPABLE PERSON See *Dependent*.

ITINERANT (JUDGE ITINERANT, BE ITINERANT) Incapable people (cf. *Dependent*) were *maintained* as a charge on the community. Efforts seem to have been made to find settled homes for them but generally they appear to have been made itinerant among the *householders* of the appropriate *commune* or *assembly group* or the whole country, moving from one allotted place to another and staying such time as agreed among those responsible for lodging them. Cf. pp. 91, 113-15. *ÍS* 83-84.

JUDGE, JUDGMENT Men were *nominated* (at assemblies usually by men acting in chieftaincies and following fixed rules) to act as judges. They could be *challenged* on various grounds and disqualified and replaced by others as necessary. Twelve acted together in *ad hoc* courts like *confiscation* and *settlement courts*, thirty-six in courts at *spring assemblies* and in *Quarter Courts* (though some scholars maintain there were only nine judges in Quarter Courts), forty-eight were nominated but thirty-six acted in the *Fifth Court*. The *formal means of proof* for prosecution and defense were presented before the judges; one of their number *summed up* the prosecution case, one the defense case. The man charged was then judged to have incurred or not to have incurred the penalty prescribed by the law and stipulated as the penalty by the prosecutor in presenting his case. Some courts required virtual unanimity of judgment (see *Divided judgment*), others a simple majority. In other cases it might be proper for the judges by their judgment to adjudge something (money, a dependent), to someone or to enjoin someone to do something. Cf. pp. 53-54, 59-63, 64-65, 79-82, 84-85, 87-88, 101-06. *ÍS* 66-69, 71.

JUDGMENT BREAKING This was failure to take some action or make some payment enjoined by *judgment*. It gave grounds for a new lawsuit with severer penalties where applicable. Cf. pp. 38, 92, 121.

KEEP Cost of and charge for board and lodging. For dependents it might be arranged by "fair agreement." For *household men* and women it was contracted for a year at a time (over the two seasons, summer and winter) and it could be withheld or claimed or adjusted for a variety of reasons. Cf. pp. 125-32.

KILLING COMPENSATION   See *Personal compensation*.

KINDRED PAYMENTS   See *Wergild rings*.

LAW COUNCIL   Ultimate legal authority rested with the Law Council at the *General Assembly*. It comprised the men acting in the thirty-six full and ancient *chieftaincies*, and in the three additional ones from the North Quarter, the supplementary members from the other three Quarters, the bishops (one 1056-1106, two thereafter), and the *Lawspeaker*, who presided. The name "Law Council" is also used of the fixed place where this body met. Each chieftain brought two men from his *assembly third* to advise him. The Council elected the Lawspeaker, decided what was law or what should be law (*rétta lög* and *gera nýmæli*), and granted licenses (for marriage within remoter forbidden degrees, *private settlements*, mitigations of *penalty*, reprieve of *outlaws*, matters to do with *chieftaincies*, local assemblies, and *communes*); some matters could not be arranged without prior *leave* from the Law Council. The Council regularly met on the two Sundays in the General Assembly session, and at other times when, in response to demand, they undertook to "clear the Law Council for a meeting." Cf. pp. 189-93. *ÍS* 63-66.

LAW RECITAL   This was undertaken by the *Lawspeaker* at the *General Assembly*, at *Lögberg*, in the *Law Council* or in the church (in bad weather). The section on assembly procedures was recited at the start of each Assembly, the remainder fitted in as convenient. It was laid down that all the laws should be recited in the course of the Lawspeaker's three-year tenure of office. Attendance at the law recital was obligatory for men with seats on the Law Council, though they could send as substitutes the two men they took with them as advisers into the Law Council. Cf. pp. 187-88, 192-93. *ÍS* 47-49.

LAWSPEAKER   The Lawspeaker was elected by the *Law Council*. His term of office was for three summers and included the start of a fourth session of the *General Assembly*; he could then continue in office if he and the Law Council agreed. He recited the laws, with the prior aid of others if his memory failed him, told men what the law was when asked, made official announcements, presided at meetings of the Law Council, led the procession to the places he appointed for the sessions of the *Quarter Courts*. He had a seat at *Lögberg* and the allotment of places there. He received a fee and a half of the fines imposed by judgments at the General Assembly and at the spring assembly he participated in. Cf. pp. 59, 187-93. *IS* 47-49.

LEAVE, LICENSE See *Law Council*, the chief source of dispensation from legal rigor. The terms may also be used of various kinds of permission from other sources of authority (chieftains, judges in court session, bishops). Cf. pp. 190 and n. 2; 30-31, 62, 65, 77, 98.

Household man, Membership of or attachment to a household gave legal domicile. The term is normally used of people other than householders and their families. Cf. *Household attachment, Household man, Legal home, Residence*.

LEGAL HOME This corresponds to *legal domicile* and probably has no wider application though it is extended for example to the lodging of a priest serving a district. A person was said to be "legally resident" or to have his "settled home" or to be "in settled lodging" at his legal home. Cf. *Household attachment, Residence*. Cf. pp. 37, 125-29.

LEGAL TENDER Normally means payment by the *ounce-unit* (six *ells* of *homespun*) or in other legally acceptable goods with their value fixed in ounce-units; some items could be subject to valuation by lawful valuers. Cf. *Objects of value, Price of a cow*. Cf. pp. 126, 183. *IS* 331-34.

LESSER OUTLAW(RY) Lesser outlawry involved payment of a "life-ring" (a mark in legal tender, one-eighth of which, i.e. one ounce, was called the "sustenance pledge") to a *chieftain* (waived if the chieftain was able to take an ox or cow from the estate as he was entitled to do), forfeit of other property, and banishment from Iceland for three years (starting within three years of the sentence). The procedure of the *confiscation court*, the lesser outlaw's permitted homes, and his efforts to get passage abroad were extensively regulated. Failure to abide by the rules meant total forfeit of *immunity*. While abroad the "lesser outlaw" enjoyed normal immunity. Cf. pp. 92-95, 98, 117-18, Add. ‡ 37.

LIFE-RING See *Lesser outlaw*.

LOCALLY See *Call, Summon*.

LODGING, BOARD AND LODGING Everyone was supposed to have a lodging (normally including board) which constituted his *legal home* and *household attachment*. Board and lodging were the usual return for ordinary farm or household work, and a value could be put on someone's *keep* by prior agreement or subsequent assessment. Special tasks, like shepherding, cattle tending, catering, commanded extra wages. Lodging had to be taken by priests and other people (visitors from abroad, for example) unattached or temporarily attached to households. Board and lodging had to be provided for certain kinds of travelers by *householders* liable to pay *assembly attendance dues*. Cf. pp. 23, 27, 33-34, 36, 40, 42-43, 125-32, Add. ‡‡ 11-12, 32-33.

LÖGBERG The place at the *General Assembly* (see Map II) where the *Lawspeaker* sat and where he had the allotment of other seats. *Publishings* and *summonings* and various announcements and formal requests were made at Lögberg (an audience of at least twenty was normally required) and the *law recital* could take place there. The procession of *chieftains* and *judges*, headed by the Lawspeaker, began here when the courts went out. Cf. pp. 51, 55-56, 59, 62-65, 68, 89, 187, 191-93. *ÍS* 43-44.

LOSE RIGHT TO PROCEED AT LAW This is the aim of a summons brought to invalidate the case of a man who has refused *truce* to an opponent and proceeded with a prosecution. Similarly, a man who does not proceed rigorously against an outlaw whom he himself got condemned loses his right to prosecute anyone else for *assistance* to that outlaw. Cf. Add. ‡‡ 50, 131.

MAINTAIN, MAINTENANCE *Dependents* and incapable people were maintained by those legally responsible for them, in the first place their natural *heirs* and then remoter members of their families. If these did not exist or were themselves poverty-stricken (sometimes because outlawry stripped them of their possessions), the dependents were a charge on the men of the *commune*, of the local *assembly*, of the *Quarter* or of the whole country, according to circumstances. If means allowed, they might be found settled homes; otherwise they were *itinerant*. Cf. pp. 91-92, 113; further ‡‡ 128-43.

MARK Eight ounces (just under half a pound avoirdupois, *ca.* 200 gm); eight *ounce-units*.

MEANS OF PROOF See *Formal means of proof*.

MITIGATION, TERMS OF MITIGATION See *Private settlement*.

MOVING DAYS Four established days (Thursday to Sunday) at the end of May in which a person's *legal home* might be changed. This was the time for making or renewing contracts as *household men* and tenants and for moving house. Such moving could affect the *calling* of *neighbors* for service on panels. Cf. pp. 125-26, Add. ‡‡ 109-11.

TO NAME (WITNESSES) To record action or speech, offensive or inoffensive or procedural (*calling, publishing, summoning, formal means of proof*), it was necessary to have suitably qualified *witnesses*. These were men present on the occasion and specifically named as witnesses by the man who thought he needed such a record. He named them "for himself," i.e. their testimony was exclusive to the formal means of proof that accompanied his case; if others wanted witnesses of the same thing, they had to name them separately. (The expression "name witnesses for oneself" is so regular in the laws that it is always shortened to "name witnesses" in the translation. In some matters witnesses might be named for general use, "for myself or for anyone who needs to use this witnessing," "for the benefit of anyone who may need to use their witnessing," cf. p. 190, Add. ‡ 52.) Witnesses named in this way and without valid grounds for excuse could not then lawfully refuse when subsequently *called* to give their testimony before a court. Cf. pp. 54, 63-64, 66-70, 89-90, 118-19, Add. ‡‡ 36, 61.

NEIGHBOR Five or nine neighbors, *householders* or their proper substitutes, living closest to the appropriate place (legal home of man prosecuted or prosecuting, *place of action*, some other specified place) and qualified in other respects, could be called to form a panel to deliver *verdicts* under *oath* on facts, motives, circumstances, as required, before a *court*. Neighbors were either *called* locally to attend an assembly for this purpose and were then the qualified men who really lived closest to the relevant place, or they were called at the assembly without prior notice and were then the nearest of those neighbors who happened to be present among the *assembly participants*. Panel members were subject to *challenge* and could be replaced for various reasons. Some or all of the same panel called for a prosecution could be asked to give *clearing verdicts*. Verdicts depended on a majority vote. Cf. pp. 50, 63-64, 69-77, 137-38, 142-43, Add ‡‡ 52 (ii), 56. Panel verdicts took second place to *witnesses*, but a man's case was not spoilt by absence of witnesses, if he could cover their lack by a panel verdict, cf. pp. 67, 70. A panel of five neighbors was used to assess the value of property, cf. pp. 33, 172-73, Add. ‡‡ 107, 130 (i) (v), 132, 133 (viii).

NEW LAW A number of articles in the manuscripts are marked as "new law." These were made by the *Law Council* and underwent a trial period before final adoption. Cf. pp. 5 and n. 9, 51 and n. 103.

NOMINATE It was necessary for men to be selected and formally nominated (normally one by each *chieftain*) to serve as *judges* in the various *courts*. Cf. pp. 53-54, 58, 62-63, 83.

OATH Oaths were sworn at the outset of litigation by men conducting cases and those participating in legal procedure in any capacity. Oaths were sworn on the Cross or a sacred book. The ordinary oath was the "lawful oath;" the "Fifth Court oath," used in the *Fifth Court* and sometimes in other circumstances, was more solemn. Oaths were also sworn by *neighbors* acting as valuers and by freed *slaves* when "led into the law." Cf. pp. 59-60, 61, 65-66, 68, 71-72, 75, 77-78, 79, 82-83, 84-87, 101-02, 174. Add. ‡ 50.

OBJECT OF VALUE Payment was permitted or prescribed in "objects of value," things which did not come within the ordinary lists of currency equivalents (cf. *Ounce, Price of a cow*) and whose worth was assessed by "legal valuers." Cf. pp. 93, 117, 119-20, Add. ‡ 130 (iv).

OUNCE, OUNCE-UNIT An ounce was a weight of just over twenty-seven grams, nearly one ounce avoirdupois (28.35 gm). An *örtug* was one-third of an ounce, a pennyweight (distinct from a penny counted) was one-tenth of an ounce (but one-sixtieth by later reckoning). These weights were especially used of amounts in gold and silver. An ounce-unit originally represented what an ounce of silver could buy in other media of exchange, generally in *homespun* cloth but also in other forms of *legal tender*. The ounce-unit of homespun came to have its own separate significance as a currency unit, normally accepted throughout Iceland as six *ells* of two-ell wide cloth of a certain quality, though three-ell and four-ell ounce-units could also be used by local or private agreement (cf. pp. 37, 119). The relationship in the values of the ounce-unit of cloth and the ounce of refined silver is estimated to have fluctuated as follows: *c*. 1000 3:1 (i.e. 18 ells to 1 oz.); *c*. 1100 8:1 (48 ells to 1 oz.); *c*. 1200 7.5:1 (45 ells to 1 oz.); *c*. 1300 6:1 (36 ells to 1 oz.). *IS* 331-34.

OUTLAW See *Full outlaw, Lesser outlaw*.

OUTLAWRY COURT See *Private settlement*.

PANEL See *Neighbors, Booth panel, Panel of twelve, Scratch panel, Verdict*.

PANEL OF TWELVE A panel formed at an assembly by a *chieftain* when called upon to do so and consisting of himself and eleven men of his *assembly third* nominated by him. A chieftain could not refuse to form such a panel. It was a *means of proof* chiefly used in cases where a greater degree of public interest was involved (e.g. sorcery, theft, and perjury), and in cases arising outside the country. Certain modifications were introduced when the chieftain was himself prosecuted. Cf. pp. 39, 50, 55-56, 63, 74-76, 121, 138, 149.

PASSAGE   See *Full outlaw*.

PAYMENT DAYS   See *Settling days*.

PEACE GUARANTEE   Mutual vows before *witnesses* to live peaceably after the conclusion of a settlement. See pp. 184-85.

PENALTY   See *Chieftain, Confiscation Court, Fine, Full outlaw, Lesser outlaw, Private settlement*.

PENNYWEIGHT   See *Ounce, ounce-unit*.

PERMISSION   See *Leave, license*.

PERSONAL COMPENSATION   For some transgressions personal compensation had to be paid, sometimes called "killing compensation" in case of death. The rate for all free people was the same, forty-eight *ounce-units* in *legal tender* (a *mark* of silver); a *slave* seems to have got three ounce-units (cf. p. 173). The compensation was doubled for injuries suffered at assemblies *formally inaugurated* or in spite of *peace guarantees*. Words and actions were also defined as requiring half or full personal compensation (cf. Add. ‡ 130 [ii]), but prosecution of words requiring half personal compensation could only be undertaken when aggravation had made full compensation the payment prescribed (cf. pp. 131, 172). Personal compensation was separate from legal penalties imposed by court judgment, but was among the first claims at an outlaw's *confiscation court*. In some instances it replaced a payment in the *wergild ring* system (cf. pp. 176, 181). Claim to it was forfeit if the offended person kept any sort of company with the offender. Cf. pp. 90, 99, 147, 158-61, 183, Add. ‡‡ 48, 67, 69, 87, 94.

PLACE OF ACTION   In some cases penalties for subsequent offense and the *right to kill* in retaliation depended on whether an original place of action, usually defined with reference to assault and conflict, remained the setting. The place of action often decided which *neighbors* were to be *called* to serve on panels. Cf. pp. 141-42, 148-49, 154, Add. ‡‡ 46, 50, 52 (ii), 85.

PREPARE A CASE   To prepare a case was to undertake at the proper times all that was necessary to present it before a court, using formulas and naming witnesses as prescribed for the *publishing, summoning*, and *calling* which the case required.

PRESCRIBED (IN THE LAWS)   This standard introduction to a statement of what the law is answers to Icelandic *mælt* (*í lögum*).

The original sense of the phrase is something like "spoken among the laws," i.e. included in the *law recital* undertaken by the *Lawspeaker*.

PRICE OF A COW A cow of specified age and condition represented a standard sum for valuation and exchange purposes, customarily but not always counted equivalent to two and one-half *ounces* of silver or twenty *ounce-units* (one hundred and twenty *ells* of *homespun*). Cf. pp. 116, 125, 150. *IS* 333-34.

PRIEST'S DISTRICT A priest could contract with one or more householders to serve his or their church or churches. That made his "district" but it might be geographically mingled with "districts" served by other priests. The limits of a *commune* seem generally to have set limits on a priest's obligations. The bishops also laid down to which churches people should pay their church tithe, and these came to have the status of parish churches, often specifically endowed (as well as having tithe income) for maintaining clergy who were also responsible, and paid, for officiating at churches, chapels, and oratories elsewhere in the neighborhood. Cf. Cf. pp. 28, 32-34, 37, Add. ‡ 32. *IS* 165-66, 168-69.

PRINCIPAL Every prosecution and defense required a principal, normally the person offended and the offender, but in case of death the succession was regulated and others had to act for women, minors (under 16 winters), and people without the capacity to manage their affairs. There could be joint principals in a case. The principal was responsible for preparing and presenting the case on his side. A principal could transfer parts of a case's preparation or the case as a whole to someone else, but *challenge* (of *judges, neighbors*) was to be on grounds of connection with him, not with the man who conducted a transferred case. Principals charged with acts of violence were usually automatically banned from attending assemblies, and their defence was necessarily transferred. No principal in a case could be nominated as a judge except in the *Fifth Court*. A prosecution for which no natural principal existed might fall to a *chieftain* or to anyone willing to undertake it. Cf. pp. 32, 53, 72, 121, 124, 156-61, 164-68, Add. ‡‡ 67-69, 74, 82, 97-98.

PRIVATE SETTLEMENT Cases could be settled privately and penalties imposed, even outlawry if accepted by *formal agreement* from the outset, or, if not, by a settlement or *outlawry court* consisting of the principal or his substitute on the one side and eleven men nominated by him. Private settlements allowed various mitigations of regular outlawry penalties (e.g. an otherwise full outlaw might be allowed passage abroad, a man otherwise treated as a lesser outlaw might be banished for life) but these had normally to be approved by the *Law Council*. In some cases prior *leave* of the Law Council was required, in others private settlement was expressly forbidden, Cf. pp. 98, 109-10, 119-20, 161, 163, 175-76, Add. ‡‡ 36, 66, 70, 74.

PROOF See *Formal means of proof.*

PROSECUTION ASSEMBLY See *Spring assembly.*

PUBLISH, PUBLISHING Making actions, charges or claims public knowledge was an essential legal formality in various instances. Thus, a man who killed someone or inflicted injury should publish it as his work within a given time and distance; offended parties should publish the offense as a charge against the offender before the third sunrise and before five neighbors; in certain circumstances the fact that a *summons* or *calling* had been made should be established by publishing it before three neighbors; various agreements should be published at *Lögberg*, in the *Law Council*, or at a *spring assembly*. In a number of cases publishing at the assembly for *judgment* at that assembly is prescribed as the proper prosecution procedure, with *neighbors* called locally beforehand to provide *formal means of proof*. (Some suits might be published at the end of one assembly for judgment at the next.) This procedure is sometimes prescribed as an alternative to summoning locally and calling neighbors at the assembly, but could apparently always be replaced by the latter mode of conducting a case. Cf. pp. 32, 35, 54, 83, 96, 125, 142-48, 164-65, 166-67, 182, Add. ‡‡ 47-48, 51, 55, 61, 78 (ii), 82, 84, 94, 96 (ii), 111, 133 (i) (vii).

QUALIFIED (NOT DISQUALIFIED) See *Challenge.*

QUARTERS These territorial divisions (see Map I) came into being *c.* 965. From 1106 the diocese of Hólar was coterminous with the Northern Quarter, the diocese of Skálaholt with the East, South, and West Quarters. With the division *c.* 965, the Northern Quarter's nine "full and ancient" *chieftaincies* were increased to twelve; the other Quarters kept nine, but the imbalance was leveled in various ways in *General Assembly* business. Choice of *Lawspeaker* might be left to the *Law Council* men of a single Quarter. Origin in a Quarter decided which *Quarter Court* should judge a case; possible differences of interest were regulated. A man might have households in more than one Quarter but was expected to decide where he belonged for the performance of legal duties. Except over the long and narrow Hrútafjöðr (see Map I), a man could not belong to the *assembly group* of a chieftain in a different

Quarter without permission of the Law Council. Cf. pp. 35-36, 83, 187, 189, Add. ‡‡ 91, 120. *IS* 49-52.

QUARTER ASSEMBLIES These were established with the division of Iceland into *Quarters*. It is said that the intention was to provide a more neutral ground for disputes between men of different *spring assemblies*, but people seem to have mostly preferred to take cases to the *General Assembly* (which was in any case the prescribed second instance in case of *divided judgment* at spring assemblies). Quarter assemblies are mentioned only in Add. ‡ 90. *IS* 49-52.

QUARTER COURT Four courts at the *General Assembly*. The *Quarter* to which the man prosecuted belonged or in which the *place of action* lay normally decided which Quarter Court heard the case. Each Court had thirty-six *judges*, one nominated by each of the men at the Assembly acting in the "full and ancient" *chieftaincies* (though some scholars have argued that Quarter Courts had only nine judges). The courts had no prescribed sites. The judges were led out by the *Lawspeaker* who appointed a place for their hearings (which in certain circumstances they could subsequently shift). They were protected by court-guards if necessary. Courts did not sit before the first Monday of the Assembly (22-28 June), then as necessary, and they could be called out to hear a case at any time up to the announcement of the calendar at the close of the Assembly. Cf. pp. 53-56, 80, 103, 163, Add. ‡‡ 90, 124. *IS* 66-70.

REPRIEVE See *Full outlaw*.

RESIDENCE A person's residence (cf. *Legal home*) decided various matters of legal importance: where he paid tithes, where he should be *summoned*, what *neighbors* were to be *called* to serve on a panel, what chieftain's *assembly group* he belonged to (independently or through his *householder*), where a *confiscation court* should be held. Cf. pp. 55, 125-29.

REVOKE JUDGMENT In prescribed cases a suit against *judges* could be brought in order to get their judgment revoked. Thus, in *divided judgments*, the judges on either side should *publish* the judgment of the other side as one to be revoked. If a court gave judgment in spite of protest against the *formal means of proof* produced, it was possible to summon that judgment to be revoked: similarly, if a man was summoned to a *spring assembly* to which he did not belong (and did not obtain a *veto* on the proceedings), or if judgment was given at a spring assembly rather than at the General

Assembly against the will of a joint *principal*. Cf. pp. 83, 103-04, 110, 121.

RIGHT TO KILL An aggrieved person automatically gained a right to vengeance for certain kinds of transgression, especially assault, injury, verbal or other insult, and sexual offenses offered or committed against those kinswomen for whom the laws gave a man the specific right to kill. The aggressor lost his *immunity*. The duration of this right to vengeance was limited according to the nature of the offense and sometimes restricted to the *place of action*. Cf. pp. 141, 142, 149, 154-55, 172, Add. ‡‡ 42, 46, 63, 121-22.

RING See *Wergild rings*.

SCRATCH PANEL An *ad hoc* panel of five men with prescribed qualifications acting like a panel of *neighbors*, assembled to give *verdicts* in cases arising outside Iceland. Cf. Add. ‡‡ 92, 125-27.

SETTLED HOME See *Legal home*.

SETTLED LODGING See *Legal home*.

SETTLEMENT COURT See *Private settlement*.

SETTLING DAY Days for settling debts could be fixed by private arrangement but in some instances and for payment of fines and rewards the law prescribed times and places. The "debt assembly" was the latter part of the *spring assembly*, and provided the normal occasion for settlement among its members: they "shared payment days." Cf. pp. 27, 36, 38, 92, 117, 122, 171-72.

SHARE LIVING QUARTERS See *Assistance*.

SLAVE A slave was his master's property. If the latter killed him outside Lent he was not answerable at law (though he doubtless would be to the Church). The slave's legal responsibility was consequently diminished. He had, however, a certain right to *personal compensation*, the *right to kill* on account of his wife, the possibility of acquiring some means, and of punishment by outlawry. His freedom could be given to him or bought for him; certain ties remained between the freedman and the freedom-giver. He was not fully free until he had been "led into the law." Cf. pp. 10 and n. 10, 42, 46, 172-74, 181-82, Add. ‡‡ 130, 132. *IS* 349-54.

SPRING ASSEMBLY A spring assembly is a named local assembly meeting at a specific place with fixed boundaries, whose site could not be altered without permission from the *Law Council*. For the places and names see Map I. The meeting took place under the leadership of three *chieftains* and was *formally inaugurated* by one of them; it lasted four nights or up to a week between the outside limits of 7 and 27 May. The first part was the "prosecution assembly" when a court was *nominated* and *judgments* given in any cases prepared for it. Cases between members of the same assembly where the prescribed penalties were *fines* had always to go to spring assembly courts and be decided there. Other cases could go to a spring assembly or the *General Assembly* as preferred; *divided judgments* at the former were automatically referred to the latter for new trial. Procedures at a spring assembly were to follow those of the General Assembly. The second part was the "debt assembly," the normal *settling days* between members of the same assembly, where a local scale for *ounce-units* might be employed. Cf. pp. 37, 43, 98-109, 116-17, 122, Add. ‡‡ 89-90. *IS* 74-82.

SUM UP Summing up was an essential part of judicial procedure. When prosecutor and defender had presented their cases and produced their *formal means of proof*, one of the *judges* in the court summed up the former's case and one the latter's. The same men announced the judgment of the court. Judges seem to have volunteered to undertake the summing up; if none did, lots had to be drawn. The judge in question may then have been the one marked by a pleader as his special auditor (cf. the formula p. 66 and n. 36). In the *Fifth Court* a man summing up could be one of the twelve judges dismissed by the litigants from the forty-eight nominated: these had to hear the case but passed no judgment. Cf. pp. 79, 81-82, 87, 103.

SUMMON, SUMMONING A common and often obligatory prosecution procedure was to summon the man prosecuted to answer for his offense before a *court*. This was usually done in set form at his *legal home* or as near to it as could be safely managed; this was to summon him "locally" (*heiman*, literally "from home"). In the ordinary way it had to be done within prescribed time limits, the "summoning days" (four weeks or less before the *General Assembly*, two before a *spring assembly*), but in some instances an immediate summons (irrespective of place) or a summons at the assembly was appropriate. When a case is specified as a "summoning case" it could only be prosecuted by summoning locally and *calling neighbors* at the assembly to serve on the necessary panel. Any case for which the prescribed procedure was to *publish* at the assembly and call neighbors locally could equally well be prosecuted by summoning locally and calling neighbors at the assembly. Sometimes the two procedures are prescribed as acceptable alternatives. Cf. pp. 50, 58, 65-67, 99-104, 123-24, 125, 128-29, 149, 161, 164-67, Add. ‡‡ 29, 50, 75, 78 (ii).

SUMMONING CASE See *Summon*.

SUMMONING DAYS See *Summon*.

SUPPLEMENT See *Wergild rings*.

SUSTAIN, SUSTENANCE See *assistance*.

SUSTENANCE PLEDGE See *Lesser outlaw*.

TESTIMONY See *Witness*.

TESTIMONY OF TESTIMONY See *Formal means of proof, Witness*.

TRANSFER A *principal* could transfer by *formal agreement* the conduct of a case to someone else, but *challenge* of *neighbors* and *judges* was done in relation to principals, and they also of course profited or suffered from penalties imposed as a result of judgments. Some preliminary steps like *publishing* and *summoning* could be transferred on their own. The man who took over a case had large independent authority, but the fact that it was a transferred case had to be made clear throughout the proceedings and he was not himself allowed to transfer it except back to the principal (to whom it reverted in case of death or default) or if taken ill at or on his way to the assembly. A person who owned a *chieftaincy* could transfer power to act in it to someone else. A man acting in a chieftaincy had to transfer power of *veto* in certain circumstances. Cf. pp. 121, 123, 143, 157, Add. ‡‡ 38, 55 (ii), 56, 66 (iv), 74.

TRUCE Temporary cessation of hostility, arranged in set manner and conferring certain rights; it could be a legal wrong to refuse an offer of truce. Cf. pp. 183-84, Add. ‡ 50.

VENGEANCE See *Right to kill*.

VERDICT, PANEL VERDICT The decision by majority vote of a panel of *neighbors*, a *panel of twelve*, and a *scratch panel* is their verdict. It is given "to the advantage" or "to the disadvantage" of one side or the other.

VETO, POWER OF VETO There were three major areas where a power of veto entered: (1) A man outside the *Law Council* could veto proceedings in the Council when leave was asked for *mitigation* of outlawry. (2) In specific circumstances a court process could be forbidden by a man using his own veto; but when it was at an assembly to which he had been wrongly summoned he could only do this with a "chieftain's veto," formally transferred by the *chieftain* in question. (3) A man might be entitled to forbid someone to share living quarters with him or to keep him any company. Cases conferring rights of veto in this way arose from non-payment of sums of one *ounce* or more under the *wergild ring* rules. Cf. pp. 61, 76, 98, 104-06, 132, 175, 182-83. Add. ‡ 5.

VOUCH In some circumstances a man enumerating kinship had to be supported by two suitably qualified men who vouched for their belief in the truth of his enumeration. They were also required in support of a man *challenging* on grounds of distance, in confirmation of the oaths of prosecutor and defender in the *Fifth Court*, and in some other situations. See *Oath, Good man and true*. Cf. pp. 61, 71-72, 78, 85-86, 171, 182, Add. ‡‡ 126-28.

WERGILD RING A wergild ring was the atonement to be paid by a member of a killer's family to the corresponding member of the family of the man killed; such atonement is also referred to as "kindred payments." They were to be paid irrespective of the success or failure of a lawsuit (unless the dead man was of *forfeit immunity*). The term "wergild rings" is restricted to the chief degrees; if unpaid, rights of *veto* were conferred. The "rings" were calculated in *ounces* of silver, though their value could be met in other forms of *legal tender*. The "main" ring was accompanied by a "supplement," also calculated in ounces of silver, and by "bits," whose weight and value are unknown. Cf. pp. 175-83.

WINTER Age is counted in the number of complete winters survived, cf. p. 31, n. 23, p. 49, n. 89.

WITNESS Witnesses were usually *named* on the occasion; they might then be subsequently *called* to give testimony before a court. Two made the usual minimum number but in some situations at least three or five were required. Witnesses had to get together in framing the wording of their testimony (immaterial deviation was allowed within certain limits) and gave it on *oath*. If a witness fell ill, his witnessing could be taken over by two other men (or three men could take over the testimony of two first-hand witnesses). In certain circumstances a witness could claim aid towards attending the assembly he was called to. If he failed to attend, he was liable to penalty; if wrongly called, he was supposed to attend and resign at the assembly. Absence of witnesses could be made good by suitable panel *verdicts*. Witnesses were to witness only to what they had seen and heard. Such included witnesses of assault and of wounds, mortal or otherwise. Steps in legal procedure were witnessed to ensure the record (hence "summons witnesses," "calling witnesses," "witnesses of announcement of judgment"). Witnesses were also named to witness that *formal means of proof* had been brought; they could then provide "testimony of testimony" if required. Cf.

pp. 32, 54-56, 59-60, 65-70, 89-90, 113, 118-19, 124, 141, 144-46, Add. ‡‡ 50, 52-53, 61-62.

WORD OF HONOR See *Good man.*

II
A Selection of Terms Normally Used as Equivalents

In the English-Icelandic list the headwords with an asterisk are those with entries in the Annotated Glossary, p. 239 ff.

Where the equivalent expression consists of a phrase, the alphabetical order normally disregards adjectives and adverbs and depends on the chief noun, the first of two if they are juxtaposed, or the verb if there is no noun. Some verbs denoting actions of central importance in procedure (e.g. "call," "publish") are given precedence over nouns. Natural association sometimes governs the clustering (e.g. entries connected with "assembly group"). Some duplication of entry has been introduced to make finding easier.

The equivalent phrases are sometimes given a degree of generalization which they do not have in the translation (e.g. *vera ór goðorði* "forfeit a chieftaincy"), where the translation will read "his" or "the chieftaincy."

The following abbreviations are used:

adj.	Adjective	*e-t*	eitthvert
e-r	einnhverr	*e-u*	einhverju
e-m	einhverjum	**pl.**	plural
e-n	einhvern	**sg.**	singular
e-s	einhvers	**vb.**	verb

English — Icelandic

accident *váðaverk*
adjudge *dœma*
legal administrator *lögráðandi*
affair *sök*
affect (a case) *skipta máli*
formally agree, make a formal agreement* *handsala*
(terms of) agreement *máldagi*
fair agreement *jafnmæli*

amount *aurar (*sg.* eyrir)*
announcement(s) *uppsaga*
announcement of judgment *dómsuppsaga*
appoint *kveða á*
arbitrator* *sáttarmaðr, sættarmaðr*
article of the law *lögmál*
legal asking *lögspurning*
assault *frumhlaup*

(established) assembly *(skap)þing*
attached to an assembly *þingfastr*
assembly attachment* *þingfesti*
have the right to attend an assembly
  eiga þingreitt
assembly attendance dues* *þingfararkaup*
assembly-balking* *þingsafglöpun*
assembly boundary *þingmark*
close of an assembly *vápnatak*
assembly ground *þingvöllr*
assembly group* *þing*
man of an assembly group
  þingmaðr
be in someone's assembly group
  vera í þingi með e-m
say someone no longer belongs to an
  assembly group *segja e-n á brott*
say one is joining an assembly group
  segja sik í þing
say one is leaving an assembly group
  segja sik ór þingi
assembly man* *þingmaðr*
man of a different assembly
  útanþingsmaðr
man of the same assembly (group)
  þingunautr
assembly membership* *þingvist*
assembly participant* *þingheyjandi (-há-
  maðr)*
assembly procedure(s) *þingsköp*
assembly slope* *þingbrekka*
assembly third* *þriðjungr*
man of an assembly third
  þriðjungsmaðr
assistance* *björg* (**pl.** *bjargir*)
lose the right to proceed against someone
  who assists an outlaw *vera af
  björgum*
in terms of attachment *at hreyrum,
  hrörum*
maintain (household) attachment
  varðveita grið
attestation that formal means of proof
  have been produced *gagnagögn*
atone *bœta*
atonement* *sakbœtr*
legal atonement *lögbót*
(established) autumn meeting* *(lög)leið*
avenge *hefna*

baiting verdict *egningarkviðr*
balk *glepja, afglapa*
balking *afglöpun*
bit* *þveiti*
blow *drep*
board (**vb**) *ala*
boarding *eldi*
board and lodging* *vist*
booth *búð*
booth-mate *búðunautr*
booth-panel* *búðakviðr*
booth-resident (**adj.**) *búðfastr*
bound by debt *skuldfastr*
bounden debtor* *(lög)skuldarmaðr*
bowshot* *ördrag, örskot*
bowshot (cordon) *örskotshelgi*
branch of a family *knérunnr*
break (an arrangement) with someone
  bregða (máli) við e-n
breaking *rof*

calendar *misseristal*
call* (locally) *kveðja (heiman)*
call neighbors *kveðja búa*
call on a chieftain to form a panel of
  twelve *kveðja goða tólftarkviðar*
automatically called *sjálfkvaddr*
qualified to be called (for the calling)
  réttr í kvöð
(legal) calling* *(lög)kvöð*
local calling *heimankvöð*
calling witness *kvaðarváttr*
make callings *kveðja kvaðir*
lift a calling from someone *nema kvöð
  af e-m*
case *sök*
case conferring rights of veto*
  lýritnæm sök
doubtful case *ifasök*
prepare a case *búa sök*
transferred case *handseld sök*
cause *sök*
challenge (**vb**) (on grounds of something)
  ryðja (at e-u)
challenge on grounds of connection with
  someone *ryðja við e-n*
words of challenge *(h)ruðningarmál*
have, take charge of *ráða fyrir*
chastise *ráða*
chattels *lausir aurar*

chieftain* *goði* (**pl.** *goðar*)
chieftain's panel *goðakviðr*
chieftain's veto* *goðalýritr*
chieftains of the same assembly
   samþingsgoðar
chieftaincy* *goðorð*
act in a chieftancy *hafa, fara með*
   goðorð
forfeit a chieftaincy *vera ór goðorði*
own a chieftaincy *eiga goðorð*
claim (**vb**) *heimta; telja*
claim *heimting*
rightly claim *eiga heimting*
make a claim for aid (in response to a
   calling) *kveðja í gegn*
clear (**vb**) *ryðja*
clearing verdict* *bjargkviðr*
close of an assembly *vápnatak*
cognate kin *nefgildingar* (**pl.**)
cognate payment *nefgildi*
cognate-payment kinsman *nefgildismaðr*
collect *heimta*
commit *vinna*
(established) commune* *(lög)hreppr; herað*
compensate *bœta*
compensation for damage* *skaðabœtr*
compensation for killing* *vígsbœtr*
personal compensation (fixed by law)*
   (lög)réttr
case which requires personal compensation *rétta(r)farssök*
full, half personal compensation *full-,*
   hálfréttr
condemned *sekr*
get condemned *sekja*
conduct *meðför*
conduct (**vb**) *fara með*
confirm *reyna*
confiscation court* *féránsdómr*
connection *tengðir*
consent *ráð*
be content someone has something *unna*
   e–m e–s
make one's own contracts *fara með*
   kaup sín
contrary testimony* *andvitni*
counter-calling *gagnkvöð*
make a counter-summons *stefna í*
   gegn (at móti)
(lawful) court* *(lög)dómr*
courts are sitting *dómar eru úti*

move courts out *fœra dóma út*
court-guarding *dómvarzla*
price of a cow* *kúgildi*

damage *skaði*
malicious damage *spellvirki*
damages *skaðabœtr*
(taken into service because of) debt
   (tekinn í) skuld
bound by debt *skuldfastr*
debt assembly* *skuldaþing*
debt bondage *skuldfesti*
debt court* *skuldadómr*
bounden debtor* *(lög)skuldarmaðr*
deception at law *lögvilla*
deceptive outlawry *breksekt*
decide *ráða*
decide on something *skilja um e-t*
deemed by the law *lögmætr*
defense, grounds of defense *vörn*
legal defense *lögvörn*
defense in a case *sakarvörn*
have a defense in the case *verjask máli*
defense oath *varnareiðr*
departures from the law *lagaafbrigði*
(inherited) dependent* *(erfða)ómagi*
desecration *löstr*
determine *ráða*
direction (i.e. instruction) *ráð*
dismiss *nema ór, upp*
not disqualified *réttr*
disqualify *ráða af, ór*
in terms, on grounds, of distance *at*
   leiðarlengð
district (priest's)* *(prests) þing*
district *herað*
district assembly *heraðsþing*
district court* *heraðsdómr*
be divided among the branches of a family
   hverfa í knérunna
divided judgment* *véfang*
matter concerning a divided judgment
   véfangsmál
divided judgment oath *véfangseiðr*
be with someone in giving a divided
   judgment *vera (saman) at (í)*
   véfangi með e-m
give divided judgments *véfengja*
join in giving divided judgment *ganga til*
   véfangs
legal domicile* *löggrið*

264 LAWS OF EARLY ICELAND

doubtful case   *ifasök*
be due to someone   *eiga at taka*
duties   *skil*
legal duties   *lögmæt skil, lögskil*

ell*   *alin, öln*
enjoin by judgment*   *dæma*
enumerate; enumerated   *telja; talidr*
enumeration of kinship   *frændsemistala*
enumerator   *teljandi*
established   *lögtekinn*
excuse oneself   *segjask ór*
without legitimate excuse   *at naudsynjalausu*
lawful eyewitness   *lögsjáandi*

fair agreement   *jafnmæli*
false verdict   *ljúgkvidr*
false witness   *ljúgvitni*
(established) fast   *(lög)fasta*
commanded fast   *bodfasta*
(legal) fee   *(lög)kaup*
feast day   *messudagr*
ferry (**vb**)   *ferja*
Fifth Court*   *fimtardómr*
fined, pay a fine (at the suit of someone)*   *útlagr (vid e-n)*
common fold   *rétt(r)*
foods made from milk   *hvitr matr*
one who can earn his food   *matlauni*
give food to   *ala*
forbid by veto*   *verja lýriti*
formally agree, guarantee*   *handsala*
formal means of proof*   *gögn* (see further under "means")
formally inaugurate an assembly*   *helga þing*
legal fostering   *lögfóstr*
found in someone's hands   *handnuminn*
frame (in words), frame the wording of   *rétta*
freedman*   *leysingi*
freedom-giver*   *frjálsgjafi*
full outlaw; full outlawry*   *skógar-, skóggangsmadr; skóggangr*

General Assembly*   *Alþingi*
good man and true*   *þegn*
grounds of defense   *vörn*
formally guarantee, give a formal guarantee*   *handsala*
without guile   *véllauss*

guilty of the charge   *sannr at sök*
guilty of complicity   *sannr at rádum*

harboring   *innihafnir* (**pl.**)
harm (to person)   *skadi*
have to   *eiga*
heir*   *arftökumadr*
(born) a lawful heir   *arfborinn, arfgengr*
born a lawful heir   *alinn til arfs*
natural heir   *skaparfi, skapörfuni*
hire out   *selja á leigu*
hold (a court)   *heyja*
established holy day   *lögheilagr dagr*
(legal) home*   *(lög)heimili*
from home   *heiman*
having a settled home*   *heimilisfastr*
home-man   *heimilis-, heimamadr*
homespun*   *vadmál*
(legal) household*   *(lög)bú*
household attachment*   *grid*
household man*   *gridmadr*
household helpers   *hjónalid*
household members who are a charge on the householder   *skuldahjón*
household people   *hjú*
household stock   *bú*
attach oneself to a household   *þiggja grid*
be attached to a household   *hafa, þiggja grid*
be in a household   *vera á gridi*
enter a household   *ganga, koma í grid (til grids)*
find a household to join   *fá sér grid*
join a household   *taka sér grid*
move into a household   *fara til grids*
householder*   *búandi, bóndi*
be a householder, continue householding   *búa*
give up householding   *bregda búi*
start householding   *gera bú*
hut   *búd*
live in a hut   *sitja búdsetu*
hut-mate   *búdunautr*

immune   *heilagr*
immunity*   *helgi*
establish immunity   *helga*
forfeit (**adj.**) immunity*   *óhelgi*
of forfeit immunity   *óheilagr*
forfeit (**vb**) immunity in relation to someone   *verda óheilagr vid e-n*

forfeit (**vb**) immunity in respect of something   *verða óheilagr fyrir e-u*
imposition of outlawry   *sektargerð*
formally inaugurate*   *helga*
formal inauguration of an assembly   *þinghelgi*
incapable person*   *ómagi*
become incapable   *verða at ómaga*
inflict   *vinna*
inflict injury   *veita, vinna áverk*
legal information   *lögfréttir* (**pl.**)
inheritance   *arfr*
come into, take an inheritance   *taka arf*
injury   *áverk(i)*
lasting injury   *örkuml*
(sexual) intercourse   *legorð*
wrongful intercourse   *misrœða*
invalid (**adj.**)   *ómætr*
invalidate one's case   *sitja sökum sínum*
in terms of legal involvement   *at sökum*
be (legally) itinerant*   *(eiga at) fara*
judge someone itinerant*   *dœma för e-m*

judge*   *dómandi*
seat a judge   *setja niðr dómanda*
judge (**vb**)*   *dœma*
(lawful) judgment*   *(lög)dómr*
judgment breaking*   *dómrof*
enjoin by judgment*   *dœma*

(cost of, charge for) keep*   *fúlga*
have the right to kill* (in retaliation)   *eiga vígt (í gegn)*
who may-be killed with impunity   *drœpr*
killing case   *vígsök*
killing compensation*   *vígsbœtr*
killing place   *vígsvettvangr*
kindred payments*   *niðgjöld*
kinship   *frændsemi*
kinship by marriage   *mægðir* (**pl.**)
spiritual kinship   *guðsifjar*

laboring work   *önnungsverk*
landing place   *höfn*
law(s)   *lög*
in accordance with (the) law   *at lögum*
lawbreaking   *lagalöstr*
Law Council*   *lögrétta*
clear the Law Council for a meeting   *ryðja lögréttu*

lawful   *réttr*
to the limit of the law   *til fullra laga*
law recital*   *uppsaga*
according to the law's rigor   *til laga*
Lawspeaker*   *lögsögumaðr*
lay down terms   *mæla (fyrir)*
leave*   *lof*
without prior leave   *fyrir lof fram*
legal asking   *lögspurning*
legal domicile*   *löggrið*
legal home*   *lögheimili*
legal tender*   *lögaurar* (**pl.**)
legitimate   *skírborinn*
lesser outlaw; lesser outlawry*   *fjörbaugsmaðr; fjörbaugsgarðr*
lesser outlawry case, offence   *fjörbaugssök*
license*   *lof*
life ring*   *fjörbaugr*
on the list of   *talið*
live   *búa*
livestock   *búfé*
share living quarters*   *vera samvistum*
locally*   *heiman*
(night) lodging   *gisting*
(be in) lodging*   *(vera á, vera í) vist*
in settled lodging*   *vistfastr*
lost the right to proceed at law*   *vera af sökum (björgum)*
Lögberg*   *Lögberg*

maintain*   *fœra fram*
have the duty to maintain someone   *eiga framfœrslu e-s*
maintenance*   *framfœrsla*
mark* (**i.e.** eight ounces, eight ounce-units)   *mörk*
lawful mark   *lögmark*
master of the house   *húsbóndi*
(ship's) master   *stýrimaðr*
may   *eiga*
means to pay   *órkostr*
(men to provide) formal means of proof*   *gögn*
formal means of proof for the defense   *varnargögn*
formal means of proof for the prosecution   *sóknargögn*
formal means of proof in an original suit   *frumgögn*
men to attest (attestation) that formal

means of proof have been produced *gagnagögn*
(make a) protest against some formal means of proof *kveða á gögn*
meeting *samkváma*
mentally deficient *óvitr*
messmate *mötunautr*
(terms of) mitigation* *sýkna*
mortal wound *ben*
(legal) moving days* *(lög)fardagar*

name (witnesses, men) to witness* *nefna í þat vætti*
necessity *nauðsyn*
for reasons of necessity *fyrir nauðsynjum*
neighbor* *heimilisbúi, (ná)búi*
new law* *nýmæli*
nominate (someone to join a court)* *nefna (e-n í dóm)*

(lawful) oath* *(lög)eiðr*
by oath on a book *við bók*
oath-lapse *eiðfall*
oath-swearing *eiðunning*
oath-taking *eiðspjall*
object of value* *gripr*
be an obstruction (to verdict, to judgment giving) *standa fyrir (kviðburð, dómi)*
offense *sök*
onslaught *hervígi*
established opening *löghlið*
ordinary day *rúmheilagr dagr*
ounce, ounce-unit* *eyrir* (**pl.** *aurar*)
outfield *engi*
outfield haymaking *engiverk*
(full) outlaw* *skógar-, skóggangsmaðr*
(full) outlawry* *skóggangr*
lesser outlaw* *fjörbaugsmaðr*
lesser outlawry* *fjörbaugsgarðr*
outlawed *sekr*
outlawed as the result of a private settlement *sekr at sátt*
deceptive outlawry *breksekt*
impose outlawry *gera sekt*
imposition of outlawry *sektargerð*
have something owed to one by someone *eiga e-t at e-m*

panel (of neighbors)* *(búa)kviðr*
qualified to serve on a panel (of neighbors) *réttr í (búa)kvið*

panel for an original suit *frumkviðr*
assemble a panel *setja kvið saman*
a panel gives a verdict *kviðr berr*
scratch panel (verdict)* *fangakviðr*
panel of twelve* *tólftarkviðr*
panel-of-twelve verdict *tólftarkviðr*
participate in *heyja*
passage from the country* *farning*
give passage to *ferja*
who may (not) be given passage *(ó)ferjandi*
pasture land *hagi*
communal pasture *afrétt(r)*
(legal) pay *(lög)kaup*
proper payer *skapbœtandi*
payment days* *gjalddagar*
peace guarantee* *trygðir*
the penalty* is *varðar*
make the penalty *láta varða*
be under penalty *varða; sekjask*
be under no legal penalty *varða eigi við lög*
incur, carry penalty *varða*
under (legal) penalty *(lög)sekr*
not under legal penalty *sýkn*
property under penalty *sektarfé*
pennyweight* *peningr veginn*
permission* *lof, leyfi*
personal compensation (fixed by law)* *(lög)réttr*
full, half personal compensation *full-, hálfrétti*
case which requires personal compensation *rétta(r)farssök*
pick out *ryðja upp*
place of action* *vettvangr*
place for summoning *stefnustaðr*
pledge *veðmál*
plot *ráð*
lose power of speech *verða ómáli*
prepare a case* *búa sök*
prescribed (in the laws)* *mælt (í lögum)*
present (**vb**) *segja fram*
presentation, presenting *framsaga*
prevail *ráða*
price of a cow* *kúgildi*
priest's district* *(prests) þing*
principal* *aðili*
private settlement* *sátt, sætt*
proceed (in something) *fara (at e-u)*
lose right to proceed against someone

TECHNICAL VOCABULARY 267

who assists an outlaw *vera af björgum*
lose right to proceed at law *vera af sökum*
stolen property *þýfð, þýfi*
prosecute *sœkja*
right to prosecute *sókn*
prosecution *sókn*
prosecution assembly* *sóknarþing*
prosecution at law *lögsókn*
prosecution panel (verdict) *sóknarkviðr*
make a protest at formal means of proof *kveða á gögn*
publish* *lýsa*
publish (as a charge) against someone *lýsa á hönd e-m*
publish as a claim on someone *lýsa á hönd e-m*
publish for judgment *lýsa til dóms*
publish a judgment as one to be revoked *lýsa dómi til rofs*
(legal) publishing *(lög)lýsing*

qualified (in terms of something)* *réttr (at e-u)*
qualified to be called (for the calling) *réttr í kvöð*
qualified to serve on a panel (of neighbors) *réttr í (búa)kvið*
Quarter* *fjórðungr*
Quarter assembly* *fjórðungsþing*
Quarter Court* *fjórðungsdómr*

raid(ing) *hernaðr*
proper receiver *skapþiggjandi*
without legal redress *óheilagr*
rehearse *tína*
reject *rengja*
rejection at law *lögrengð*
relationship *skuldleikar*
reliance witness *trúnaðarváttr*
remove *ryðja ór*
lawful reporter *lögsegjandi*
reprieve* *sýkna*
legal request *lögbeiðing*
(legally) required *(lög)skyldr*
residence* *heimilisfang*
legally resident *lögfastr*
resign *segjask ór*
be responsible for *ráða fyrir*

make oneself responsible for *ráða sér á hendr*
revoke (judgment)* *rofna*
to be revoked *til rofs*
have the right (to do something) *eiga (at gera e-t)*
have the right to kill (on account of someone)* *eiga vígt (um e-n)*
right(ful) *réttr*
(wergild) ring* *baugr*
(wergild) ring fixed by law *lögbaugr*
ring payment *bauggildi*

saving advice *bjargráð*
scratch panel (verdict)* *fangakviðr*
forcible seizure from someone's grasp *handrán*
(especially) select (vb) *vanda*
have regard to something in selecting *vanda at e-u*
senseless *óviti*
sentence *áfall*
give sentence against someone *dœma áfall e-m*
separate (vb) *skilja*
(established) services *(lög)tíðir*
serving man *húskarl*
settle *sættask (á)*
(private) settlement* *sátt, sætt*
settlement terms *sáttargerð*
settling day* *eindagi*
fix a settling day *eindaga*
share living quarters *vera samvistum*
shield someone *standa fyrir e-m*
legal silver *lögsilfr*
slave* *þræll*
speak *mæla (fyrir)*
malicious speech *illmæli*
spoil (vb) *spilla*
someone's case is spoilt by something *e-t verðr e-m at sakarspelli*
spring assembly *várþing*
state (vb) *kveða á*
stolen *þjófstolinn*
stolen property *þýfð, þýfi*
strike *drepa*
substance for something *efni e-s*
(original) suit *(frum)sök*
sum *eyrir* (**pl.** *aurar*)
sum up* *reifa*
summing up *reifing*

268 LAWS OF EARLY ICELAND

summon* *stefna*
summon someone to lose the right to proceed at law* *stefna e-m af sökum*
summoning case* *stefnusök*
summoning day* *stefnudagr*
(legal) summons *(lög)stefnustaðr*
(legal) summons *(lög)stefna*
go to make a summons *(fara) stefnuför*
summons witness *stefnuváttr*
supplement* *baugþak*
sustain* *ala*
who may be sustained (pending judgment) *œll (til dóms)*
not to be sustained (pending judgment) *óœll (til dóms)*
sustaining (an outlaw) in ignorance *óvísaeldi*
sustenance *eldi*
sustenance pledge* *alaðsfestr*

tell *telja*
legal tender* *lögaurar* (**pl.**)
lay down terms *mæla (fyrir)*
test (**vb**) *reyna*
testifying *vitnisburðr, vættisburðr*
testimony* *váttorð, vitni, vætti*
contrary testimony* *andvitni*
testimony of settlement *sáttarvætti*
testimony of testimony, men to witness testimony produced* *vættisvætti*
theft *þjófskapr*
thieving case *þjófsök*
throttle *kyrkja*
(legal) tithe *(lög)tíund*
trade cloak *vararfeldr*
trade goods *vara, varningr*
trader *farmaðr*
traders' hut *farmannabúð*
tramp *húsgangsmaðr*
transfer* (**vb**) *selja*
transferred case *handseld sök*
truce* *grið*
set a truce *nefna grið*
truce-breaking *griðarof*
true and unspoilt *sannr ok óspiltr*

unattached man *frelsingi*
utter *telja fram*

vagrant *göngumaðr*
valid *mætr*
legal valuers *lögmetendr*
vengeance* *hefnd*
(panel) verdict* *(búa)kviðr; kvöð*
verdict for an original suit *frumkviðr*
verdict-giving *kviðburðr*
false verdict *ljúgkviðr*
give, pronounce a verdict *bera kvið*
(power of) veto* *lýritr*
lawful veto *löglýritr*
veto (**vb**)* *koma lýriti fyrir*
forbid by veto* *verja lýriti*
case conferring rights of veto* *lýritnæm sök*
chieftain's veto* *goðalýritr*
void *ónýtr*
vouch (for)* *sanna*
man to vouch* *sannaðarmaðr*

wages *kaup, leiga*
have one's way *ráða*
whatever does duty for a weapon *vígvölr*
wergild ring* *baugr*
winter* *vetr*
withhold (testimony, etc.) *halda (vætti, etc.)*
witness(es)* *váttr, vætti*
name witnesses (men to witness)* *nefna vátta (í þat vætti)*
witness of the announcement of judgment *dómsuppsöguváttr*
witness of settlement terms *sáttargerðarváttr*
false witness *ljúgvitni*
give one's word of honor* *leggja undir þegnskap sinn*
words of challenge *(h)ruðningarmál*
directing one's words to N.N. *yfir höfði N.N.*
working season *annir* (**sg.** *önn*)
wound *sár*
wound classed as mortal *ben*

year, whole year *misseri* (**pl.**)

Icelandic — English

aðili principal
áfall sentence
dœma áfall e-m judge sentence should fall on someone
afglapa balk
afglöpun balking
afrétt(r) communal pasture
ala board, sustain, give food to
alaðsfestr sustenance pledge
alin ell
alinn til arfs born a lawful heir
áljótsráð plot to disfigure
alþingi General Assembly
andvitni contrary testimony
annir (sg. *önn*) working season
arfborinn, arfgengr (born) a lawful heir
arfr inheritance
taka arf come into, take, an inheritance
arftökumaðr heir
áverk(i) injury
veita, vinna áverk inflict injury

bauggildi ring payment
baugr (wergild) ring
baugþak supplement
ben mortal wound, wound classed as mortal
bera (kvið) pronounce, give a verdict
kviðr berr a panel gives a verdict
bjargkviðr clearing verdict
bjargráð saving advice
björg (pl. *bjargir*) assistance
vera af björgum lose the right to proceed against someone who assists an outlaw
boðfasta commanded fast
við bók by oath on a book
bregða (máli) við e-n break (an arrangement) with someone
breksekt deceptive outlawry
bú household; household stock
gera bú start householding
bregða búi give up householding
búa live, be a householder, continue householding
búa sök prepare a case
búakviðr panel of neighbors; panel verdict
búandi, bóndi householder
búð booth; hut

búðakviðr booth-panel
búðfastr booth-resident
sitja búðsetu live in a hut
búðunautr booth-mate; hut-mate
búfé livestock
búi neighbor
bœta compensate; atone, make good

dómandi judge
dómar eru úti courts are sitting
dómr court; judgment
dómrof judgment breaking
dómsuppsöguváttr witness of the announcement of judgment
drep blow
drepa strike
drœpr who may be killed with impunity
dœma judge, adjudge, enjoin by judgment

efni e-s substance for something
egningarkviðr baiting verdict
eiðfall oath-lapse
eiðspjall oath-taking
eiðunning oath-swearing
eiga at taka be due to someone
eiga e-t at e-m have something owed to one by someone
eindaga fix a settling day
eindagi settling day
eldi sustenance, boarding
engi outfield
engiverk outfield haymaking
erfðaómagi inherited dependent
eyrir (pl. *aurar*) ounce, ounce-unit; sum, amount

fangakviðr scratch panel (verdict)
fara be itinerant (of incapable people)
eiga at fara be legally itinerant
fara (at e-u) proceed (in something)
fara með conduct
fara með goðorð act in a chieftancy
fardagar moving days
farmaðr trader
farmannabúð traders' hut
farning passage from the country
féránsdómr confiscation court
ferja ferry, give passage to
ferjandi who may be given passage

fimtardómr Fifth Court
fjórðungr Quarter
fjórðungsdómr Quarter Court
fjórðungsþing Quarter assembly
fjörbaugr life ring
fjörbaugsgarðr lesser outlawry
fjörbaugsmaðr lesser outlaw
fjörbaugssök lesser outlawry offense, case
framfærsla maintenance
eiga framfærslu e-s have the duty to maintain someone
framsaga presenting, presentation
frelsingi unattached man
frjálsgjafi freedom-giver
frumgögn formal means of proof in an original suit
frumhlaup assault
frumkviðr panel (verdict) for an original suit
frumsök original suit
frændsemi kinship
frændsemistala enumeration of kinship
fúlga (cost of, charge for) keep
fullrétti full personal compensation
færa dóma út move courts out
færa fram maintain
dæma för e-m judge someone itinerant

gagnagögn attestation (men to attest) that formal means of proof have been produced
gagnkvöð counter-calling
gisting (night) lodging
gjalddagr payment day
glepja (vb) balk
goðakviðr chieftain's (panel) verdict
goðalýritr chieftain's veto
goði chieftain
goðorð chieftaincy
eiga goðorð own a chieftaincy
hafa, fara með goðorð act in a chieftaincy
vera ór goðorði forfeit a chieftaincy
(1) grið truce
griðarof truce-breaking
(2) grið household attachment
fá sér grið find a household to join
fara til griðs move into a household
ganga í grið enter a household
hafa grið be attached to a household

koma í grið (til griðs) enter a household
taka sér grið join a household
varðveita grið maintain (a household) attachment
vera á griði be in a household
þiggja grið attach oneself, be attached to a household
griðmaðr household man
gripr object of value
guðsifjar (**pl.**) spiritual kinship
gögn (men to provide) formal means of proof
göngumaðr vagrant

halda (gögnum, vætti) withhold (formal means of proof, testimony)
handnuminn found in someone's hands
handrán forcible seizure from someone's grasp
handsala formally agree, guarantee; make formal agreement, give a formal guarantee
handseld sök transferred case
hefna avenge
hefnd vengeance
heilagr immune
heiman locally; from home
heimankvöð local calling
heimili home; house
heimilisbúi neighbor
heimilisfang residence
heimilisfastr having a settled home
heimilis-, heimamaðr home-man
heimta collect; claim
heimting claim
eiga heimting rightly-claim
helga inaugurate formally; establish immunity
helgi immunity
herað district; commune (= *hreppr*)
heraðsdómr district court
hernaðr raid(ing)
heyja participate in; hold (a court)
hjónalið household helpers
hjú household people
hreppr commune
at hreyrum, hrörum in terms of attachment
(h)ruðning challenge
eiga (h)ruðning have the right to challenge

TECHNICAL VOCABULARY

(h)ruðningarmál words of challenge
húsbóndi master of a house
húsgangsmaðr tramp
húskarl serving man
hverfa í knérunna be divided among the branches of a family
hvítr matr foods made from milk
höfn landing place
yfir höfði N.N. directing one's words to N.N.

ífasök doubtful case
illmæli malicious speech
illvirki malicious damage
innihafnir **(pl.)** harboring

jafnmæli fair agreement

kaup wages, fee, pay
fara með kaup sín make one's own contracts
knérunnr branch of a family
kúgildi price of a cow
kveða á state; appoint
kveða á gögn make a protest at some formal means of proof
kveðja call
kveðja (ná)búa call neighbors (to serve on a panel)
kveðja goða tólftarkviðar call on a chieftain to form a panel of twelve
kveðja kvaðir make callings
kveðja í gegn make a claim for aid (in response to a calling)
kviðburðr verdict-giving
kviðr panel; (panel) verdict
kvöð calling; verdict
kvaðarváttr calling witness
kyrkja throttle

lagaafbrigði departures from the law
lagalöstr lawbreaking
láta varða make the penalty
lausir aurar chattels
legorð (sexual) intercourse
leið autumn meeting
réttr at leiðarlengð qualified in terms of distance
ryðja at leiðarlengð challenge on grounds of distance

leiga wages
selja á leigu hire out (at a rate)
leysingi freedman
ljúgkviðr false verdict
ljúgvitni false witness
lof leave, license, permission
fyrir lof fram without prior leave
lýritnæm sök case conferring rights of veto
lýritr (power of) veto
koma lýriti fyrir veto
verja lýriti forbid by veto
lýsa publish
lýsa á hönd e-m publish (as a charge) against someone; publish as a claim on someone
lýsa dómi til rofs publish a judgment as one to be revoked
lýsa til dóms publish for judgment
lög law(s)
at lögum in accordance with law
lögaurar **(sg.-eyrir)** legal tender
lögbaugr (wergild) ring fixed by law
lögbeiðing legal request
lögbót legal atonement
lögbú legal household
lögdómr lawful court; lawful judgment
lögeiðr lawful oath
lögfardagar legal moving days
lögfasta established fast
lögfastr legally resident
lögfóstr legal fostering
lögfréttir legal information
löggrið legal domicile
lögheilagr dagr established holy day
lögheimili legal home
löghlið established right of way
löghreppr established commune
lögkaup legal fee, legal pay
lögkvöð legal calling
lögleið established autumn meeting
löglýritr lawful veto
löglýsing legal publishing
lögmál article of the law
lögmark lawful mark
lögmetendr legal valuers
lögmætr deemed by law
lögmæt skil legal duties
lögráðandi legal administrator
lögrengð rejection at law
lögrétta Law Council

lögréttr   personal compensation fixed by law
lögsegjandi   lawful reporter
lögsekr   under legal penalty
lögsilfr   legal silver
lögsjáandi   lawful eyewitness
lögskil   legal duties
lögskuldarmaðr   bounden debtor
lögskyldr   legally required
lögsókn   prosecution at law
lögspurning   legal asking
lögstefna   legal summons
lögsögumaðr   Lawspeaker
lögtekinn   established
lögtíðir   established services
lögtiund   legal tithe
lögvilla   deception at law
lögvörn   legal defense
löstr   desecration

máldagi   (terms of) agreement
matlauni   one who can earn his food
meðför   conduct
messudagr   feast day
misrœða   wrongful (sexual) intercourse
misseri   season; (**pl.**) (whole) year
misseristal   calendar
mægðir (pl.)   kinship by marriage
mæla (fyrir)   speak; lay down terms
mælt (í lögum)   prescribed (in the laws)
mætr   valid
mörk   mark (8 ounces)
mötunautr   messmate

nábúi   neighbor
nauðsyn   necessity
fyrir nauðsynjum   for reasons of necessity
at nauðsynjalausu   without legitimate excuse
nefgildi   cognate payment
nefgildingar   cognate kin
nefgildismaðr   cognate-payment kinsman
nefna dóm   nominate a court
nefna í dóm   nominate to join a court
nefna grið   set truce
nefna vátta (í þat vætti)   name witnesses, men (to witness)
nema kvöð af e-m   lift a calling from someone

nema ór, upp   dismiss
niðgjöld   kindred payments
nýmæli   new law

óferjandi   who may not be given passage
óheilagr   of forfeit immunity; without legal redress
verða óheilagr fyrir e-u   forfeit (**vb**) immunity in respect of something
verða óheilagr við e-n   forfeit (**vb**) immunity in relation to someone
óhelgi   forfeit (**adj.**) immunity
ómagi   dependent; incapable person
verða at ómaga   become incapable
verða ómáli   lose power of speech
ómætr   invalid
ónýtr   void
órkostr   means to pay
óvísaeldi   sustaining (an outlaw) in ignorance
óviti   senseless
óvitr   mentally deficient
óœll (til dóms)   not to be sustained (pending judgment)

peningr veginn   pennyweight

ráð   direction; consent; (**pl.**) plot
sannr at ráðum   guilty of complicity
(1) ráða   chastise
(2) ráða   decide, determine, prevail, have one's way
ráða af, ór   disqualify
ráða fyrir   have (take) charge of, be responsible for
ráða sér á hendr   make oneself responsible for
reifa   sum up
reifing   summing up
rengja   reject
rétt(r)   common fold
rétta   frame (in words, the wording of)
rétta(r)farssök   case which requires personal compensation
(1) réttr   personal compensation
*(2) réttr (**adj.**)*   right(ful), lawful; qualified, not disqualified
réttr at e-u   (not dis)qualified in terms of something
réttr í (búa)kvið   qualified to serve on a panel (of neighbors)

réttr í kvöð qualified to be called (for the calling)
reyna test, confirm
rof breaking
til rofs to be revoked
rofna revoke
(h)ruðning challenge
rúmheilagr dagr ordinary day
ryðja challenge; clear
ryðja at e-u challenge on grounds of something
ryðja lögréttu clear the Law Council for a meeting
ryðja ór, upp remove
ryðja við e-n challenge on grounds of connection with someone

e-t verðr e-m at sakarspelli someone's case is spoilt by something
sakarvörn defense in a case
sakbœtr atonement
samkváma meeting
vera samvistum share living quarters
samþingsgoðar chieftains of the same assembly
sanna vouch (for)
sannaðarmaðr man to vouch (for something)
sannr at sök guilty of the charge
sannr ok óspiltr true and unspoilt
sátt, sætt (private) settlement
sáttargerð terms of settlement
sáttargerðarváttr witness of settlement terms
sáttarmaðr arbitrator
sáttarvætti testimony of settlement
segja e-n á brott say someone no longer belongs to an assembly group
segja fram present
segja sik í þing say one is joining an assembly group
segja sik ór þingi say one is leaving an assembly group
segjask ór resign, excuse oneself
sekja get condemned
sekjask be under penalty
sekr under penalty, condemned; outlawed
sekr at sátt outlawed as the result of a private settlement
sekt penalty; outlawry

full sekt fullest penalty
gera sekt impose outlawry
sektarfé property under penalty
sektargerð imposition of outlawry
selja (vb) transfer
setja kvið saman assemble a panel
setja niðr dómanda seat a judge
sitja sökum sínum invalidate one's case
sjálfkvaddr automatically called
skaðabœtr compensation for damage, damages
skaði harm (to person), damage (to property)
skaparfi natural heir
skapbœtandi proper payer
skapþiggjandi proper receiver
skapþing established assembly
skapörfuni natural heir
skil duties
skilja separate
skilja um e-t decide on something
skipta máli affect (a case)
skírborinn legitimate
skóggangr (full) outlawry
skógar-, skóggangsmaðr (full) outlaw
skuld debt
tekinn í skuld taken into service because of debt
skuldadómr debt court
skuldahjón household members who are a charge on the householder
skuldarmaðr bounden debtor
skuldaþing debt assembly
skuldfastr bound by debt
skuldfesti debt bondage
skuldleikar relationship
skyldr required
sókn prosecution, right to prosecute
sóknarkviðr prosecution panel (verdict)
sóknarþing prosecution assembly
spellvirki wilful damage
spilla (vb) spoil
standa fyrir (kviðburð, dómi) be an obstruction (to verdict-giving, judgment-giving)
standa fyrir e-m shield someone
(1) stefna summons
(2) stefna (vb) summon
stefna í gegn, at móti make a counter-summons

stefna e-m af sökum summon someone to lose the right to proceed at law
stefnudagr summoning day
fara stefnuför go to make a summons
stefnustaðr place for summoning
stefnusök summoning case
stefnuváttr summons witness
stefnuvætti testimony of summoning
stýrimaðr ship's master
sýkn not under legal penalty
sýkna (terms of) mitigation; reprieve
sætt (private) settlement
sættarmaðr arbitrator
sættask (á) settle
sækja prosecute
sök suit, case; charge; offense; cause; affair
at sökum in terms of legal involvement

taliðr enumerated; on the list of
telja tell; enumerate; claim
telja fram utter
teljandi enumerator
tengðir connection
tína rehearse
tólftarkviðr panel of twelve; panel-of-twelve verdict
trúnaðarváttr reliance witness
trygðir peace guarantee, peace

unna e-m e-s be content that someone has something
uppsaga announcement(s); law recital
útanþingsmaðr man of a different assembly
dómar eru úti courts are sitting
útlagr fined
útlagr við e-n fined (pay a fine) at the suit of someone

váðaverk accident
vaðmál homespun
vanda (vb) (especially) select
vanda at e-u have regard to something in selecting
vápnatak close of assembly
vara trade goods
vararfeldr trade cloak
láta varða make the penalty
varðar the penalty is; incurs, carries, is under, penalty

varðar eigi við lög is under no legal penalty
varnareiðr defense oath
varnargögn formal means of proof for the defense
varnarkviðr defense panel (verdict)
varningr trade goods
várþing spring assembly
váttorð testimony
váttr witness
veðmál pledge
véfang divided judgment
ganga til véfangs join in giving a divided judgment
vera (saman) at (í) véfangi með e-m be with someone, join, in giving a divided judgment
véfangseiðr divided judgment oath
véfangsmál matter concerning a divided judgment
véfengja give divided judgments
véllauss without guile
verjask máli have a defense in the case
vetr winter
vettvangr place of action
vígsbœtr compensation for killing, killing compensation
vígsvettvangr killing place
vígsök killing case
eiga vígt (í gegn) have the right to kill (in retaliation)
vígvölr whatever does duty for a weapon
vinna inflict; commit
vist lodging, board and lodging
vera á (í) vist be (in) lodging
vistfastr in settled lodging
vitni testimony
vitnisburðr testifying
vætti testimony; witness; witnesses
nefna í þat vætti name (witnesses, men) to witness
vættisburðr testifying
vættisvætti testimony of testimony, men to witness testimony produced
vörn defense, grounds of defense

þegn good man and true
leggja undir þegnskap sinn give one's word of honor
þing assembly

(prests) þing (**pl.**) (priest's) district
vera í þingi með e-m be in someone's assembly group
þingbrekka assembly slope
þingfararkaup assembly attendance dues
þingfastr attached to an assembly
þingfesti assembly attachment
þinghelgi formal inauguration of an assembly
þingheyjandi, -hámaðr assembly participant
þingmaðr man of an assembly group; assembly man
þingmark assembly boundary
eiga þingreitt have the right to attend an assembly
þingsafglöpun assembly balking
þingsköp assembly procedure(s)
þingunautr man of the same assembly (group)
þingvist assembly membership

eiga þingvært have the right to be present at an assembly
þingvöllr assembly ground
þjófskapr theft
þjófstolinn stolen
þjófsök thieving case
þriðjungr assembly third
þriðjungsmaðr man of an assembly third
þveiti bit
þýfð, þýfi stolen property

œll (til dóms) who may be sustained (pending judgment)
öln ell
önnungsverk laboring work
ördrag bowshot
örkuml lasting injury
örskot bowshot
örskotshelgi bowshot (cordon)

ADDENDA

English — Icelandic

assembly-fit þingfœrr
bride-price mundr
dowry heimanfylgja
mid-evening miðaptann
eykt eykt
night-time náttmál
outlawry; penalty sekt
partner félagi
court of priests prestadómr
40 pounds (weight) hálf vætt
Winter Nights vetrnætr
(major, minor) wound (meira, minna) sár

Icelandic — English

eykt eykt
félagi partner
heimanfylgja dowry
Lögberg Lögberg
miðaptann mid-evening
mundr bride-price
náttmál night-time
prestadómr court of priests
(meira, minna) sár (major, minor) wound
vetrnætr Winter Nights
hálf vætt 40 pounds (weight)
þingfœrr assembly-fit

Sources, Editions, Translations, Work in Progress

I Manuscripts from which Translated Matter is Derived

Grágás texts
  Gl. kgl. Sml. 1157 fol. (Codex Regius, Konungsbók; *c.* 1260) = K.
  AM 334 fol. (Staðarhólsbók; *c.* 1280) = St.
  Uppsala Universitets Bibliotek R: 713 (Troilsbók; 1600-1650).

Christian Laws Section only
  AM 346 fol. (Staðarfellsbók; 1300-1350).
  AM 347 fol. (Belgdalsbók; 1300-1350).
  AM 351 fol. (Skálholtsbók; 1350-1400).
  AM 135 4to (Arnarbælisbók; 1350-1400).
  AM 173 c 4to (1400-1500).
  AM 181 4to (1650-1700).

II Editions and Facsimiles

Hin forna lögbók Íslendinga sem nefnist Grágás. Codex juris Islandorum antiqvissimus, qvi nominatur Grágás . . . I-II (1829) [with Latin translation].

Grágás . . . udgivet efter det kongelige Bibliotheks Haandskrift . . . af Vilhjálmur Finsen for det nordiske Literatur-Samfund (1852; ljósprentað í Lithoprent, Reykjavík 1945; genoptrykt 1974 Odense Universitetsforlag) = [*Grágás*] I.

Grágás efter det Arnamagnæanske Haandskrift Nr. 334 fol. . . . udgivet af Kommissionen for det Arnamagnæanske Legat [by Vilhjálmur Finsen] (1879; genoptrykt 1974 Odense Universitetsforlag) = [*Grágás*] II.

Grágás. Stykker, som findes i det Arnamagnæanske Haandskrift Nr. 351 fol. . . . og en Række andre Haandskrifter . . . udgivet af Kommissionen for det Arnamagnæanske Legat [by Vilhjálmur Finsen] (1883; genoptrykt 1974 Odense Universitetsforlag) = [*Grágás*] III.

The Codex Regius of Grágás . . . With an introduction by Páll Eggert Ólason (Corpus codicum Islandicorum medii aevi III, 1932).

Staðarhólsbók. The Ancient Lawbooks Grágás and Járnsíða . . . With an introduction by Olafur Lárusson (Corpus codicum Islandicorum medii aevi IX, 1936).

III Translations

Grágás, Islændernes Lovbog i Fristatens Tid . . . oversat af Vilhjálmur Finsen for det nordiske Literatur-Samfund (1870).

Isländisches Recht. Die Graugans. Übersetzt von Andreas Heusler (Germanenrechte IX, 1937).

IV Work in Progress

H. Beck et al. "Projekt eines Grágás-Wörterbuches," *Skandinavistik* 4 (1974), 67-68.

Hans Fix. *Teilprojekt F Nordistik. Grágás 1852. Konungsbók. Datenaufnahme und KWIC-Index. Bericht* 1. Universität des Saarlandes, Saarbrücken, 1976.

Hans Fix et al. *Linguistische Arbeiten — Nordistik. Zur maschinellen Verarbeitung altisländischer Rechtstexte.* LA/N 2. Universität des Saarlandes, Saarbrücken, 1978.

Maria Bonner and Hans Fix. "Projekt 'Untersuchungen zu altisländischen Rechtstexten'," *Computers and the Humanities* 12 (1978), 177-82.

Hans Fix. "Grágás Konungsbók (GkS 1157 fol.) und Finsens Edition," *Arkiv för nordisk filologi* 93 (1978), 82-115.

Abbreviated Titles

Arnarbælisbók	AM 135 4to.
[*Grágás*] I (Ia, Ib)	*Grágás* . . . udgivet . . . af Vilhjálmur Finsen . . . 1852 (Förste Del, Anden Del).
II	*Grágás efter det Arnamagnæanske Haandskrift Nr. 334 fol.* . . . [ed. Vilhjálmur Finsen] . . . 1879.
III	*Grágás. Stykker . . . i det Arnamagnæanske Haandskrift Nr. 351 fol.* . . . [ed. Vilhjálmur Finsen] . . . 1883.
ÍF	Íslenzk Fornrit.
ÍF I	*Íslendingabók. Landnámabók.* Jakob Benediktsson gaf út (Íslenzk Fornrit I, 1968).
ÍS	*A History of the Old Icelandic Commonwealth: Íslendinga saga* by Jón Jóhannesson. Translated by Haraldur Bessason. University of Manitoba Icelandic Studies II, 1974.
K	Gl. kgl. Sml. 1157 fol. (Codex Regius, Konungsbók).
Skálholtsbók	AM 351 fol.
St	AM 334 fol. (Staðarhólsbók).
Staðarfellsbók	AM 346 fol.
Troilsbók	Uppsala Universitets Bibliotek R:713.

(NOTE. Line references given in this volume to [*Grágás*] I-III ignore in their counting those lines that contain only chapter numbers.)

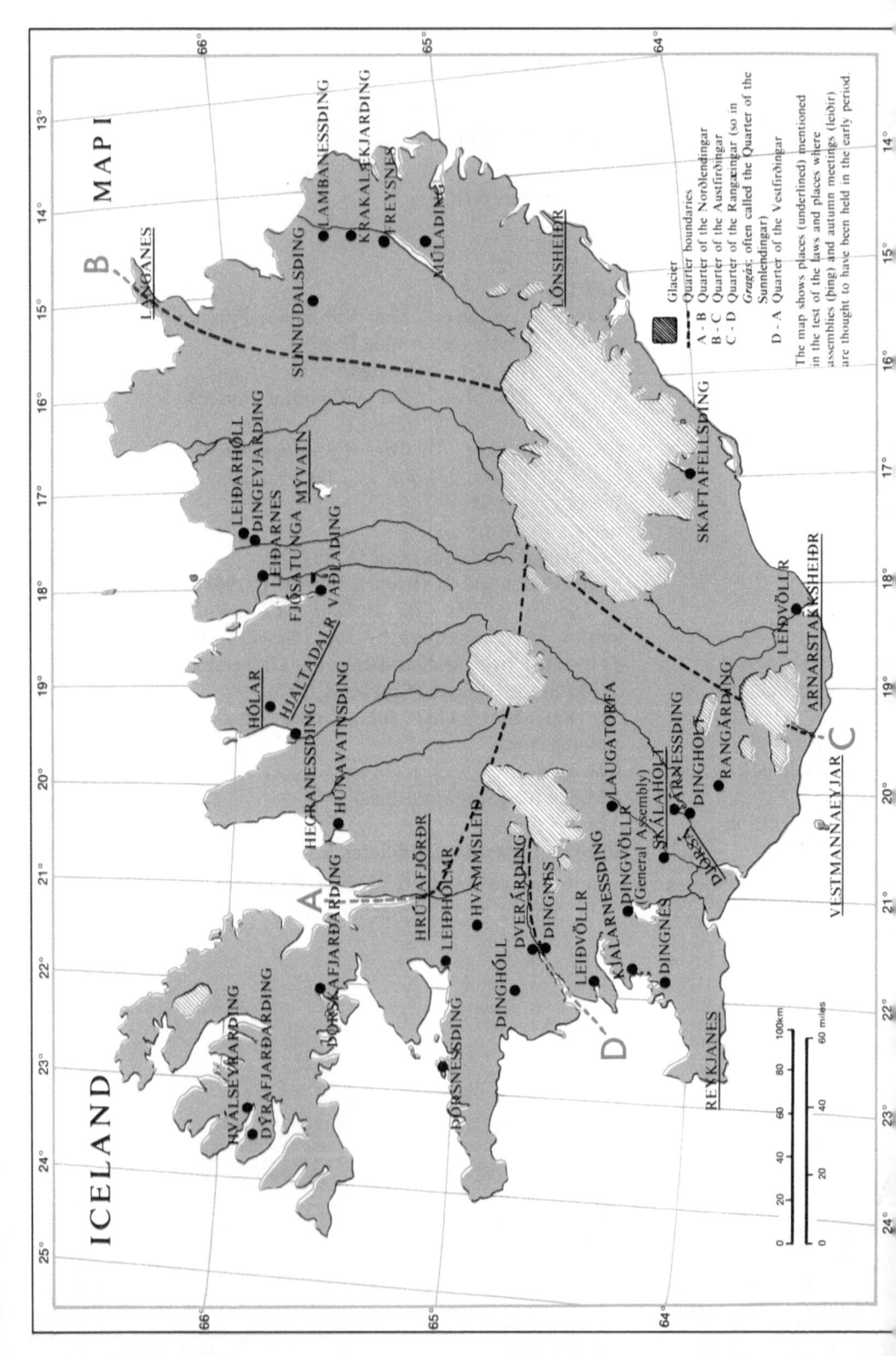

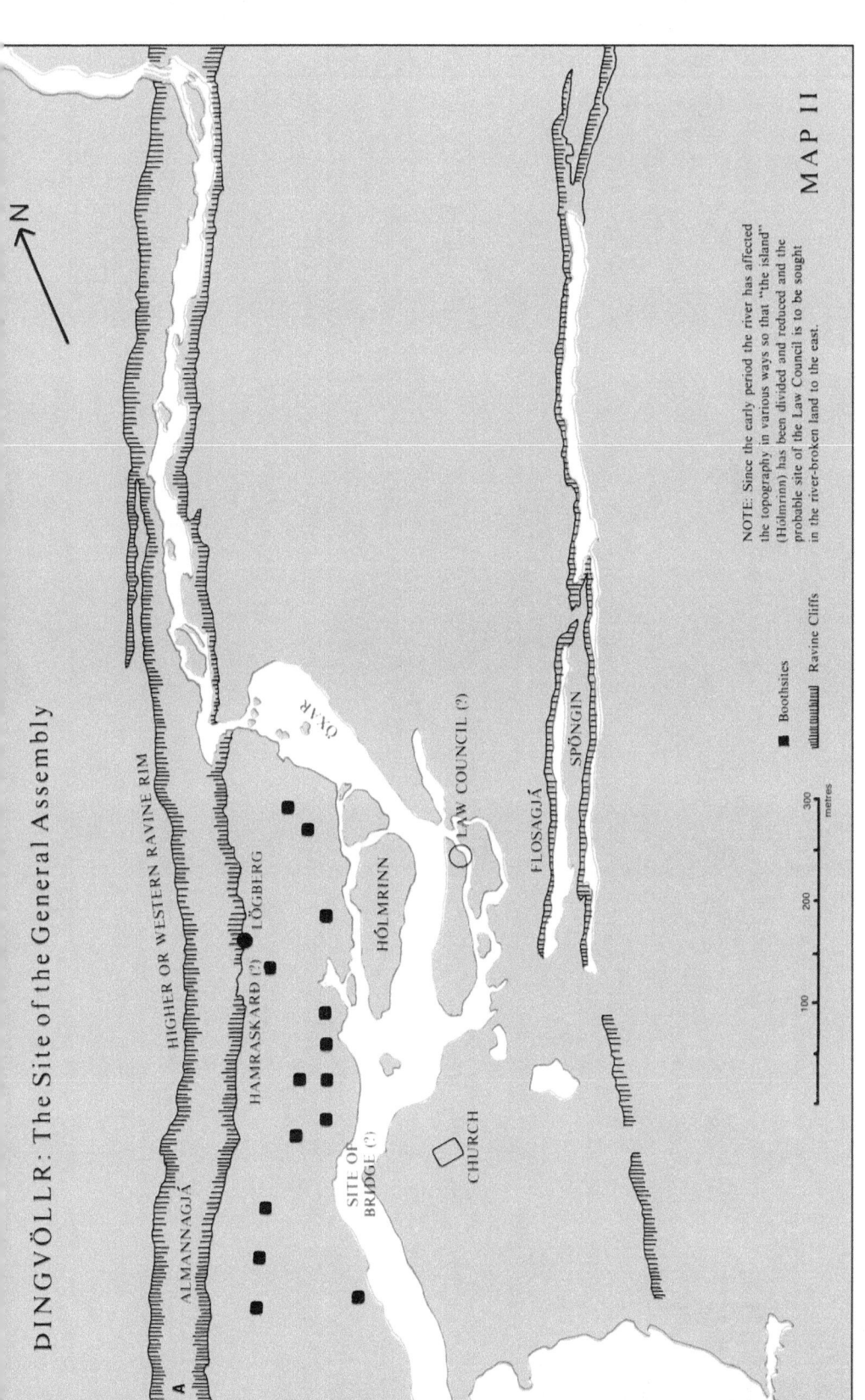

www.ingramcontent.com/pod-product-compliance
Lightning Source LLC
Chambersburg PA
CBHW021938290426
44108CB00012B/882